Abstracts of South Central Pennsyvlania Newspapers

Volume 3
1796-1800

F. Edward Wright

HERITAGE BOOKS
2007

HERITAGE BOOKS
AN IMPRINT OF HERITAGE BOOKS, INC.

Books, CDs, and more—Worldwide

For our listing of thousands of titles see our website
at
www.HeritageBooks.com

Published 1988 by
HERITAGE BOOKS, INC.
Publishing Division
65 East Main Street
Westminster, Maryland 21157-5026

Copyright © 1988 F. Edward Wright

All rights reserved. No part of this book may be reproduced or transmitted in any form or by any means, electronic or mechanical, including photocopying, recording or by any information storage and retrieval system without written permission from the author, except for the inclusion of brief quotations in a review.

International Standard Book Number: 978-1-58549-122-3

CONTENTS

Introduction v

Kline's Carlisle Week Gazette 1

The Pennsylvania Herald & York General Advertiser 67

York Recorder 117

The Adams Centinel 134

The Shippensburgh Messenger 134

The Franklin Repository 135

Appendix A: Letters remaining at the Post Office (Carlisle Gazette).. 141

Appendix B: Letters remaining at the Post Office (York advertiser) .. 146

Appendix C: Letters remaining at the Post Office (York Recorder) 153

Index 157

INTRODUCTION

This book is the third in a series of volumes of abstracts of South Central Pennsylvania newspapers in the interests of aiding genealogical research.

The Carlisle Gazette and Western Repository of Knowledge, generally known as the Carlisle Gazette, was founded on August 10, 1785 by George Kline and George Reynolds; Kline became the sole publisher with the August 3, 1791 issues.

The Pennsylvania Herald, and York General Advertiser was established by Jems Edie, John Edie and Henry Willcocks January 7, 1789. Willcocks turned over his interest to the Edie's in 1792. On July 31, 1793 John Edie became sole publisher and continued the paper until January, 1800, when it was succeeded by The York Recorder.

The York Recorder was founded by John Edie and Robert M'Clellan on January 29, 1800. In 1802 Robert M'Clellan became sole publisher, later joining with Adam King in partnership sometime in 1805.

The Adams Centinel was established in November 1800 and became the Gettysburg Star.

The Shippensburgh Messenger was establshed in 1797 by Henry and Benjamin Grimler.

The Franklin Repository was established April 21, 1796 by Andrew Dover and Robert Harper as successor to the Chambersburg Gazette (founded in 1793)

These abstracts were taken from microfilm copies (at the Library of Congress) of those issues of the Carlisle Gazette held by the Cumberland County Historical Society, Carlisle. Copies of the York Advertiser are held by the York County Historical Society. Issues of The York Recorder from which these abstracts were held by the York County Historical Society. Abstracts of the issues of the Adams Centinel and The Shippensburgh Messenger were taken from microfilms held by the Pennsylvania State Library. The single issue of The Franklin is held by the Library of Congress.

Abbreviations used in this volume:

a. - acres
adj - adjoining
admr - administrator or administratrix
co - county
dau - daughter
decd - deceased
exr - executor or executrix
Fri - Friday

Mon - Monday
Sat - Saturday
Sun - Sunday
Thurs - Thursday
twp - township
Tues - Tuesday
Wed - Wednesday
yr(s) - year(s)

F. Edward Wright
Silver Spring, Maryland

Kline's Carlisle Weekly Gazette

1. Wed Jan 6 1796
Whereas Robert ARMSTRONG sold to the subscriber, D. L. MOREL, a certain plantation, on the Susquehannah, and Little Juniata creek, he does declare not to be willing to pay the 3 bonds of 100 pounds each, before the contract shall be performed.
For sale - house and lot at upper end of High St.known by the sign of the Bulls Head; also tract in Shermans Valley - David LINSEY, Carlisle.
James NEELY, Reading twp, offers reward for horse stolen from the door of David MYERS, Berlin, York co.
The Collectors of Cumberland co are requested to exert themselves - Robert MILLER, Treasurer.
George COUCHER, Dickinson twp, Cumberland Co, has taken up a stray mare.
Persongs indebted to David BRIGH, late of Middleton twp, are hereby notified that their notes and bonds will be put in suit. George LOGUE, Carlisle.
Persons indebted to James M'CALLAY, late of Middletown, Dauphin co, shop-keeper and trader, are requested to make immediate payment to Cadwalader EVANS, Alexander HENRY, assignees of J. M'Callay.

2. Jan 13 1796
On evening of 31st ult, died in her 60th yr, after a lingering illness, Mrs. Mary GORDON, relcit of Alexander GORDON, inhabitants of this borough.
Stone house to be let in High St, opp Rev. Doctor DAVIDSONs - George KLINE, Carlisle.
To be sold in town of Shippensburgh, two houses and lots; apply to subscriber, Benjamin COPPANHAFFER, living on the premises.
William TURNER, living on the plantation of James CATO, offers reward for missing horse.

3. Jan 20 1796
In pursuance of an order of Orphan's Court of the county of Cumberland, will be sold by Daniel COLLINS and Ann Eve, his wife, late Ann Eve WOOMELSDORFF, admr of the estate of Daniel WOOMELSDORFF, decd, 22 acres in East Pennsborough twp - William LYON, Clerk.
Commissioners for the district composed of the counties of Cumberland, Mifflin and Franklin, John ARTHURS and Joseph McCLELLAND, will meet.

4. Jan 27 1796
Alexander LAUGHLIN, Newton twp, Cumberland co, has taken up a stray cow.
Jacob CREVER, Carlisle, requests those indebted to him to make payment.

5. Feb 3 1796
Morta HEIFGEN, Middleton twp, 3 miles from Carlisle, has taken up 2 stray heiffers.
Whereas Gabriel POPENMIRE, passed some bonds to a certain William BRISBIN, of Mifflin co, whereof there are two paid, and as I find a mortage in Mr. LYON's office of Carlisle for a certain sum of money, this is to forwarn persons not to take an assignment on any of said bonds.
Richard ROBINSON offers reward for mare stolen out of his stable in Chester co.

Kline's Carlisle Weekly Gazette

6. Feb 20 1796
A lot to be sold in Fannetsburg, Franklin co, where is erected a large two-story log house - John HUSTON, living on the premises.
John KAIRNS, having passed notes to William GALBREATH and John SKIPTON, in consideration of a tract of land, and being informed that said Galbreath and Skipton have assigned the notes to William KAIRNS, Kairns hereby requests such persons to come forward and make the title good.
Whereas my wife Elizabeth, hath absconded my bed and board, these are to caution the public against trusting her on my account. Frederick SANDERS, Cumberland co, Newton twp.
David GEORGE, living about 8 miles from Carlisle, offers reward for apprentice boy named Barny DUFF, alias Barny GEORGE, 17 yrs of age, 5 ft 7-8 inches.
Samuel FINLEY, & Co., Newville, request payment of accounts.

7. Feb 27 1796
Died after a long and tedious sickness, at an advanced age, Ralph STERRETT, citizen of this co. On Wed following his remains were deposited into the burying ground adjoining this town.
To be let - house in the Alley, lately occ by Mr. MORRISON, Tobacconists - John HUGHES, Carlisle.
To be sold at public vendue, agreeably to the last will of James CROCKET, late of Allen twp, tract of Limestone Land, 236 a. on Yellow breeches Creek, 1/2 mile from Major EGE's Iron Works, on great road leading from Carlisle to Rankin's ferry - Margaret CROCKET, John CROCKET, admrs.
To be sold - at the plantation of the subscriber in Newtown twp, Cumberland co, horses, mares, wagon and geers, milch cows, cattle, sheep, hogs, farming utensils and other articles - James NICHOLSON.
Whereas the partnership of John PEEBLES and Henry CONNELLY, cabinet makers, is this day, dissolved.
Sale of tract of 219 a. in Woodcock valley, about 9 miles from town of Huntingdon, and 53 a. adj, part of real estate of David ESSLEMAN, decd, to be sold by David M'MURTRIE, Esq., acting admr - Andrew HENDERSON, Clerk of the Orphans Court.

8. Mar 2 1796
Samuel DAVIDSON, on the premises, to sell tract adj town of Bedford, 400 a..
Sale of estate of Robert GALBRAITH, decd, at Lilburn, Allan twp, Cumberland co, a negro man - Mary GALBRAITH, James GALBRAITH, Andrew GALBRAITH, admrs.
Daniel WUNDERLICH, 1 1/2 miles from Carlisle, has taken up a stray heifer.

9. Mar 9 1796
For sale - tract of limestone land, 200 a., on banks of the Big-Spring, Westpennsborough twp, Cumberland co - David RALSTON, living on said premises.
In pursuance of an order of Orphan's Court, Cumberland co, will be sold, a tract in Frankford twp, Cumberland co, 8 miles from Carlisle, adj lands of Mathew WILSON, William GALBREATH, Widow ESPY, and Conedoguinet creek, 113 a., being the real estate of Ludwig EPRIGHT, decd. Title will be given by John ERNEST and Catharine his wife, late Catharine EPRIGHT, and Jacob ALTER, admrs of the estate of said Ludwig Epright.

Kline's Carlisle Weekly Gazette

John STEPHENS, Carlisle, having removed from the Fulling Mill, of Ephraim BLAINE, Esq., to a new and most commodious one of Capt. Gilson CRAIGHHEAD, on Yellow Breeches Creek, 4 miles from Carlisle, proposes carrying on the business of fulling and dying. Clothes may be taken in at: John HUNTER, Jacob CRAVER, Jacob WISER and William WALLACE, in Carlisle; John FRITZ, Stephen RHINE and George HACKET in Shermans Vally; Daniel LENHART between Waggoners gap and Carlisle, Adam LONGSTAFF(?) in the barrens, and John CAROTHERS (late Mr. WALKER's), Harrisburgh road.
Good encouragement will given to a miller and sawyer - Oliver POLLOCK, at Silver Springs.

10. Mar 16 1796
Whereas John DELANCEY of the borough of Carlisle, Coppersmith, did obtain from the subscriber a bond for sum of 50 pounds, and as the bond was obtained in a fraudulent manner, I caution persons from taking assignment thereof - Christopher BOWER, Sherman Valley
Sheriff's sale of tract in Rye twp, 100 a., property of John GRAHAM, 200 a. in Wayne twp, now Mifflin co, property of James ARMSTRONG, 200 a. in Fermanaugh twp, now Mifflin co, adj lands of Hamilton and others, property of James DAVIS; 210 a. in Rye twp, 8-9 miles from Borough of Carlisle, 40 a. clear, 2 house and barn, property of Samuel WHITTAKER, decd; 150 a. near Carmichael's Run, on Juniata, property of John MOOR; 150 a. on Ferguson's Run, 200 a. adj and 500 a. 1 mile from Old Town, property of James BURNS; 67 1/2 a. in Newton twp, property of William WILLSON - Jacob CREVER, Sheriff, Carlisle.
Sheriff's sale of house and lot in Main st, Carlisle, late the property of John AGNEW, Esq., taken as the property of John AGNEW, Junior.
Sheriff's sale of house in Carlisle, East side of Hanover St, number 182, proeperty of David ENGLISH and Elenor his wife.
Courts of enquiry of Damages and Extending of Lands for county of Cumberland will be held at the dwelling house of James POLLOCK, in the Borough of Carlisle.

11. Mar 23 1796
Susannah THOMSON, opposite Mr. POLLOCK's Tavern returns thanks to her friends and the public; her assortment of goods will be found of the best quality: groceries, teas, wines, widow glass, candles, and other.
The highest wages given for wood-cutters, colliers, forgemen and other labourers; apply to Daniel TURNER, Spring creek forge, Mifflin co.
To be let - a frame workshop in High st, adj house in which William DENNY now lives - William THOMSON, Carlisle.
Plantation for sale on great road, from Bedford to Fort Pitt, 8 miles west of Bedford Town, 278 a. - Henry SWAGER, on the premises.
Plantation in Rye twp, Cumberland co, to be sold, 207 a., half way between Clark's ferry on the Susquehannah, and Miller's ferry, on the Juniata - John THOMPSON, on the premises.
Wanted - gunsmiths, lock, stock, and barrel makers, by Samuel CRISWELL, in Carlisle.
The young horse Juniper will stand for mares this season at the stable of the subscriber, Matthew DAVIDSON, West Pennsborough twp.

Kline's Carlisle Weekly Gazette

12. Mar 30 1796
Lot for sale in borough of Carlisle occupied by the subscriber, John ARTHUR, as a store, the 3rd lot from the public square, fronting on Market St - John Arthur, Carlisle.
$50 reward for idle and evil disposed persons who make a practice of firing the woods at this season of the year. Michael EGE, Thomas THORNBURGH, John ARTHUR, James BOYD, Carlisle.
Thomas FOSTER has moved to the large house, lately occupied by Doctor George STEVENSON, where he keeps an House of Entertainment.
The horse, Sportsman, property of George CLARKE, in Greencastle, wil stand to cover mares at the sable of Samuel CROWEL, tavern keeper, town of Newville.

13. Apr 6 1796
Archibald LOUDON, bookbinder and stationer, in Carlisle, to sell copies of the New-England Primer.
Jeannet WOODS, widow, Dickenson twp, Cumberland co, has taken up a stray colt.
Robert ARMSTRONG has lost a silver watch on the road between Carlisle and the mouth of Little Juniata.
Cabinet Making Business - Henry CONNELLY, late a partner of John PEEBLES, has entered into partnership with John BRATTON of Newville.
Whereas a certain William M'CONNELL (foot Chapman or Pedlar) late of Lancaster co, Donegal twp, died at my house in Montgomery twp, Franklin co, on 20th inst, theses are to notify his heirs. Those with accounts of money of the decd deposited with them are to give their names to John SCOTT, esq. in Chambersborough or the subscriber, James SCOTT.
Sale of 2261 a. in Northumberland Co; apply to John STINMETZ or William BELL, Market St, Phila.

14. Apr 13 1796
Whereas the subscriber, Peter GOOT, West Pennsborough twp, passed a note to Jacob HAREHOEF, this is caution persons from taking assignment thereon.
The trustees of Dickinson College are to meet - John MONTGOMERY, President, pro tem.
Brown's Small Catechism, being now fully ready for the public, may be had at the Printer's Book blades and at principal stores in Carlisle, Shippensburgh and Newville. Abram CRAIG.
Limestone land for sale, Big Spring, West-Pensborough twp, Cumberland co - James IRWIN.
James SCOBEY, has removed from the house of Ephraim STEEL, to that of John HUGHES, in the Alley Southwest of the Court House, where he carries on boot and shoemaking.
Meeting of the Cumberland Troop of Light Horse, to elect a 1st Lieutenant, in the room of Lieut. John M'CURDY, resigned - John ALEXANDER, Insepecter.

15. Apr 20 1796
To be sold - at the dwelling house of the subscriber, William CHAMBERS, admr, in Middletown twp, milch cows, dining tables and other furniture.

Kline's Carlisle Weekly Gazette

16. Apr 27 1796
Married Tues 12th inst, by Rev Doctor NESBIT, William NOLAND, of Virginia, to Miss Catharine CALLENDER, of this town.
On Thurs 14th inst by Rev Doctor DAVIDSON, William DUNBAR, to Miss Betsey FORBES, both of this co.
At Harrisburgh, Fri last by Rev SNOWDEN, Samuel LAIRD, Esq., Attorney at Law, to Miss Betsey MONTGOMERY, both of Harrisburgh.
Sheriff's sale of house and lot in borough of Carlisle, property of Thomas and William M'MURRAY.
John CLARK, Allen twp, Cumberland Co, offers reward for indented servant girl, named Hannah MILLS, about 18 yrs of age, fair hair, she is thick and stout made, had on a stript linsey peticoat and short gown, cotton check apron, wool hat and sundry other cloths with her.
For sale - lot in the borough of Carlisle occupied by subscriber, John ARTHUR as a store.
Sale of plantation in Rey twp, Cumberland Co, 282 a., pursuant to last will of Benjamin ABRAHAM, decd; land adj DUGAN's old place and Richard COULTER's, Isaac JONES and others - William JAMES, James DUNWODIES, exrs.

17. May 4 1796
John MONTGOMERY, Carlisle, requests return of borrowed copy of the first volume of sermons preached at Berry Street, London.
Labourers are wanted at the Conewago Canal, Susquehanna River, Rankins Ferry, in York co - James THOMPSON.
To be sold - at the dwelling house of the late Richard LEE, waggon maker, decd, furniture and compleat set of waggon-makers tools - John OFFICER, and Jeremiah MILLER, Exrs.
Sale of 450 a. of patented land on Juniata River, within 8 miles of town of Huntingdon, Huntingdon co, formerly possessed by Jacob HARE; enquire of Frances REID, persent owner in Carlisle, or Andrew HENDERSON, Esq., Prothonatary of Huntingdon Co, in Hungtingdon.

18. May 11 1796
Masons and quarriers to undertake buildings at the Silver Springs; to whom generous wagers in cash. - David BRIGGS, living at Silver Springs
Michael ROSS, has laid out a town called Williams-Port on east bank of the West branch of the river Susquehanna.
Robert CHAMBERS has a yoke of large draft oxen for sale.

19. May 18 1796
Married Thurs last at the farm of John DUNBAR, by Rev. Doctor DAVIDSON, Doctor John CREIGH, of Lewistown, Mifflin co, to Miss Nelly DUNBAR, dau of John DUNBAR.
Died Sat 14th inst at Shippensburgh, Mrs. Margaret HEAP, wife of John HEAP, Esq., of that place, during a lingering illness.
Robert M'KIBBON, living within 3 miles of Shippenstown, has taken up a stray mare.
John HUGHES gives notice to owners of stills in the county of Cumberland, that they must enter their stills and give their election of choice how they intend working the following year.

Kline's Carlisle Weekly Gazette

20. May 25 1796
Wanted at the head of Bigspring, a journeyman tanner, or courier - Robert PEEBLES.
Tract on Big Spring, 12 miles above Carlisle - James IRWIN.
House and lot to be sold, in town of Newville, Cumberland co - Daniel BOYLE, Newville, Newton twp.
Whereas the subscriber, William THOMPSON, Hopewell twp, Cumberland co, hath passed 3 bonds, to John MORGAN, living now in Phila, this is to forewarn persons not to take assignment, as the title is disputed.

21. Jun 1 1796
GIRLLING & KIMPTON, from Phila, have opened a new store in York st, next door below the Spread Eagle, borough of Carlisle, where they have laid in a large and fashionable assortment of spring goods and groceries.
Partner wanted by the printer of this paper, John WINTER, Rights of Man Printing Office (Frederick-town)

22. Jun 8 1796
Married 31st of May by Rev Doctor DAVIDSON, John OFFICER, of this town, to Mrs. OFFICER, of this co.
31st May by Rev Doctor DAVIDSON, Nathan WOODS, to Miss Jean WEAKLEY, dau of James WEAKLEY, both of this co.
2d inst at York-town, by Rev CATHCART, John MONTGOMERY, junior, Esq., Attorney at Law, at the state of Maryland to Miss Polly HARRIS, dau of William HARRIS, Esq., of York town.
Jacob BYERS, 4 miles within of Carlsle, Middleton twp, has taken up a stray horse.
David steel offers reward for horse which strayed from M'CORMICK's farm near Carlisle; for reward deliver to Hugh McCORMICK, within one miles of Carlisle or subscriber in Lebanon twp - David STEEL.
James BEATTY, 5 miles of Shippensburgh, offers reward for light bay horse.

23. Jun 15 1796
Jane WALLACE, next door to Dr. GUSTINE, will take 6-8 young ladies, to instruct them in plain work, working Muslin, tambour, embroidery, &c.
Mr. PETICOLES, miniature painter, from France, has arrived in this town; he resides at Doctor STINNECKLE's, corner of York and Pomfret sts.
Whereas my wife Sarah having absconded, from my bed and board, without any reason or just cause, I hereby forwarn persons from giving her any credit on my account - George HABLE.

24. Jun 22 1796
Henry SHAEFFER, Washington co, Md., 2 miles from Hagerstown, offers reward for stolen gelding.
William G. HOLMES, 1 miles from Carlisle, offers reward for missing mare.
Joseph C. CHARLES, Bedford, is setting up a house at the west end of the town of Bedford, where he has opened a tavern.

25. Jun 29 1796
Inhabitants of the borough of Carlisle are required to attend a town meeting - by order of the Burgesses - David M'KEEHAN, Clerk of Corporation.

Kline's Carlisle Weekly Gazette

Robert GRAYSON, goaler, Carlisle, gives notice that a negro Isaac GINE alias ELLIS has been committed to the goal; says his is a slave for life, property of William PINKERTON, living near Fogs(?) manor Meeting house, Chester Co.

26. Jul 6 1796
Died Sat 25th ult, in an advanced age, the celebrated philospher, David RITTENHOUSE, Esq.
William DAWSON, Carlisle, follows the double Coverlet and Diaper weaving at the house of Robert BARCLAY, in the alley back of the German Church.
For sale and settlement - a number of tracts in Allegheny co - William POWER, Agent.
Sheriff's sales: plantation now in the possession of Jacob ALTER and others in Westpennsborough twp, Cumberland co, property of Richard WOODS; 100 a., in Greenwood twp, Cumberland co, adj lands of John SHUMAN and lands in possession of Barnabas RUDY, taken as property of William MAIZE and David MILLER; 67 1/2 a. in Newton twp, property of William WILLSON; 100 a. in Greenwood twp, Cumberland co, bounded on the east by lands of John CARPENTER, on the south by lands of Peter KAFFMAN, property of John PFOUTZ, sen.; house in the borough of Carlisle, opposite Doctor STEVENSON, in possession of James GIVIN, merchant.

27. Jul 13 1796
Sheriff's sales: tract in Tyrone twp, Shermans Valley, 200 a., property of Peter MOSES; tract in Hopewell twp, 194 a., property of Martin HEFFEINGER; 150 a. near Carmichaels Run, on Juniata, property of John MOORE; tract in Rye twp, 50 a., property of John GRAHAM; lot in borough of Carlisle on south side of plan No. (blank), property of Joseph POSTLETHWAIT.
A pair of saddle bags found; apply to William WALLACE, innkeeper, Carlisle.

28. Jul 20 1796
Whereas the house and lot in town of Lisburn, which was taken in execution last spring by Jacob CREVER, Sheriff, as the property of John LONG, who is only a tenant, which absolutely belongs to the estate of Thomas STARR, decd, now ye that I William STARR, admr, of said estate, forwarn persons from purchasing lot, for the property was entirely invested in Thomas Starr, decd.
Andrew HOLMES has taken up some stray sheep, at his plantion at the head of Bonny Brook, 1 1/2 miles from Carlisle.

29. Jul 27 1796
Died 5th inst, after a long and lingering illness, Ezekiel DUNNING, Esq., one of the first settlers in this county.
The subscribers having entered into contract to carry the mail from Phila to Fort Pitt, and for that purpose have determined to run a stage to carry the same, request that the roads be put in satisfactory repair - Matthias SLOUGH, John DUNWOODY, Hunt DOWNING, William GEER.

30. Aug 3 1796
York - Died at 2 o'clock on morning of Sabbath last at the age of 27 yrs, Miss Anna KENNEDY, dau of Robert KENNEDY; funeral at Presby Church.
Sale of several town lots at the house of Robert SMITH.

Kline's Carlisle Weekly Gazette

Tract for sale, 581 a., in Hamilton twp, Franklin co, adj lands of James
CAMPBELL, William DIXON and otthers, 1/4 mile from the old Louden road,
now in the tenure of Thomas, James and Alexander DUNCAN; apply to Judge
RIDDLE, Chambersburgh, Col. Joseph ARMSTRONG, near the premises, or the
subscriber at Thomas FOSTER's Inn, Carlisle during the weeks of the August
and October Courts of Commnon Pleas for Cumberland Co - John SHIPPEN
Charles LAPOLE, living near Potts-grove, Berks co, offers reward for stolen
horse.
Sundry lots for sale in town of Petersburgh, Cumberland co - D. L. MOREL, on
the premises.
Those indebted for service of the covering horse, Sportsman, property of
George CLARKE, are requested to make payment to John DUNBARR, Newville.

31. Aug 10 1796
The Blue-Ball tavern to be sold by John SKINNER, in Newton twp, Cumberland
co, on Walnut bottom road.
Whereas a note of a certain Alexander WEIR, upon me, I take this opportunity
to forwarn persons from taking assignment on said note - John DICKEY
Whereas my wife Elizabeth has absented hefrself from my bed and board,
without any just cause, and took with her several bonds, payable by Philip
OURICH, to me, this is therefore to forbid all persons from taking the
said bonds from her - Godfrey SANDERS.

32. Aug 17 1796
Sale of tract in Cumberland co, Allan twp on waters of Yellow Breeches
creek, 132 a. - Joseph ELLIOT, living on the prremises.
Agreeably to the last will of Roger DEVLIN, late of the borough of Carlisle,
decd, two houses and 2/3 of a lot will be sold, situate on south side of
Louther St, Carisle. - Margaret DEVLIN and George LOGUE, exrs.
Joseph M'KINNEY, living in Hopewell twp, Cumberland co, has taken up stray
steers.

33. Aug 24 1796
John DEWALD, living in Manheim twp, Berks co, offers reward for stolen mare.
School House on the road from Carlisle in Chambers' Ferry, near Williamson's
Tavern, was broke open and the school master chest, though locked by a
double lock, was broke too, and rummaged. Missing is a penknife with four
blades - James FLEMING, S.M.

34. Aug 31 1796
Jacob HENDEL, clock and watch maker, carried on his business in High st,
opposite to John CREIGH, Esq., Carlisle.
Jacob MILLER, blue dyer, carried on blue dying business in York st, in the
house of Marks ZIEGLER, next door to Doctor STINNECKIE, Carlisle.
John DELANCEY, coppersmith and tin plate worker, opposite John CREIGH,
merchant, Carlisle.
Wanted - a single man who understands the fulling business - John CAVIT,
Westmoreland co, Franklin twp.

35. Sep 7 1796
Farm for sale, 180 a. in Middleton twp, about 4 miles from borough of
Carlisle - James DOUGLASS

Kline's Carlisle Weekly Gazette

Tract to be sold, 150 a., late the property of George ESPY, decd, in Frankford twp, on Conedoguinet creek, bounded by lands the property of the heirs of Andrew M'FARLANE, decd, Samuel M'DOWEL - Thomas KENNEDY, John BROWN, exrs.
Negro man, Ned CATON, committed to jail of Dauphin Co, on his confession of having robbbed the wagon of John GRACE, coppersmith and tinman, of Philadelphia - Alex. BERRYHILL, Harrisburg.
William M'CRACKEN, living in Newton twp, Cumberland co, offers reward for negro wench named SALL, about 24 yrs of age, 5 ft 4 inches.
Meeting of the trustees of Dickinson College - James DUNCAN, Sec'y

36. Sep 14 1796
Married last week, Joseph STEEL, clock maker, to Miss JOHNSTON.
Two stone dwelling houses for sale in Millerstown, Cumberland co, on banks of river Juniata - William DITTERLINE
Log dwelling for sale in Thomsons-town, Mifflin co - S. DAVIS.
Alexander HOPPER, living in Path Valley, Franklin co, to sell tract of 153 a., 1 1/2 miles from Pott's Mill and same distance from Elliot's Mill, 4 miles from Fannetsburgh.
Robert PATTEN, Middleton twp, near to Waggoner's Gap, has taken up a stray cow.

37. Sep 21 1796
Married at York Town, on Wed last by Rev CAMBELL, David WATTS, Esq., of this town to Miss Juliana MILLER, dau of General Henry MILLER, of York Town.
House and lot to be sold by James M'CLINTOCK, in Shippensburgh

38. Sep 28 1796
Justus RELING, Newton twp, Cumberland co, 4 miles from Newville, has taken up a stray cow.

39. Oct 5 1796
George STEVENSON, Carlisle, to sell tract 1 mile west of Carlisle on road to Shippensburgh; also a house in Hanover st.
William M'CRACKEN, Newton twp, offers reward for negro man, named JONATHAN, about 25 yrs of age, 5 ft 7-8 inches.
English and German Almanacs available at bookstore of Archibald Loudon, Carlisle.
William M'MULLIN now carries on the fulling business at Captain Gilson CREIGHEAD's new fulling mill on Yellow Breeches. Cloth is taken in at Philip LAUFMAN, John KINCAID, George FRESHER, in Carlisle; James MOORE on Walnut bottom road; Thomas WILLIAMSON in the Barrens, John DILLs and William ROSS's in York co.
Tract for sale in Frankford twp, Cumberland co - Thomas KENNEDY.
Farm for sale in Tyrone twp, Cumberland co, 370 a. - William ROGERS, on the premises.
Committed to the goal of this co, a negro man who calls himself GEORGE, says he is a slave of Mr. RYALL, of New England, aged about 40 or upwards, 5 ft 6 inches - Robert GRAYSON, goaler, Cumberland co.

Kline's Carlisle Weekly Gazette

40. Oct 12 1796
Sheriff's sales: Tract in Newton twp, property of William WILSON; 71 a. in Newton twp, property of Joseph WILLSON; two-story stone house and kitchen in town of Shippensburgh, property of James M'CALL; 151 a. in Dickinson twp, property of John M'DONALD; 210 a. in Rye twp, property of Samuel WHITTAKER, senior, decd; unidivded half part of tract, 330 a., in Rye twp, bounded by lands of Joseph ELLIOTT, Robert JOHNSTON and John M'COY, property of Gilbert M'COY.
George KLINE offers reward for cows which strayed from the town.
William M'GEE offers reward for cow which strayed from the commons of Carlisle.
William SEABRIGHT has commenced the fulling business, at the new mill of William PARKER, on Conodoguinet creek, in Frankfort twp, 4 miles from Carlisle.
Thomas GRAHAM has lost a bundle of papers including receipts in favour of James GRAHAM.
Elijah LOWER, on the farm late of William REED's, 4 miles from Carlisle, has taken up 2 stray colts.
Payment is requested on subscriptions towards the building of a bridge across the Conodoguinet creek.
House and half lot of ground in Louther st to be sold, adj the alley back of the Presby Meeting House - John BROWN, tobacconist, now residing on the premises.

41. Oct 19 1796
John STEPHENS has returned to the fulling mill of Ephraim BLAINE, Esq., near Carlisle.
The Cumberland County Troop of Horse are to parade on Fri next - Samuel A. M'COSKRY, Captain. The Carlisle Infantry Company to parade tomorrow.
Whereas a bond which was passed by Abraham LUKENBILL and Jacob WAGGONER, payable to John DAVIS, decd. The bond was lodged with a certain Jacob GROVE of Shearmans Valley. The subscribers, admrs, of the estate of Abraham Lukenbill, forwarn persons from taking assignment of said bond. Francis KIEHL, Simon MINNICK, admrs, Middleton twp.
Store to be let immediately, at the corner of Pomfret, in York st, opposite John HUNTER's tavern, property of Abraham LOUGHRIDGE - William HUNTER, Abraham LOUGHRIDGE, Henry BURCHSTEAD.

42. Oct 26 1796
Married Tues 18th inst by Rev Doctor DAVIDSON, Robert EVANS, Esq., of Maryland, to Mrs. Isabella ALEXANDER, of this town.

43. Nov 2 1796
Died last week, Charles GREGG.
William HUSTON, 1/2 mile from Mount rock, has taken up a stray cow.
To be sold, 450 a., formerly property of Samuel CULBERTSON, decd, in Franklin co, Green twp, adj lands of Samuel Culbertson and John MIRES. - Samuel CULBERTSON, Joseph CULBERTSON, Joseph CULBERTSON, exrs.
Sale of household and kitchen furniture - Samuel FINLEY and co., Newville.
Fulling and dying at the mill of William GRAYSON, in East Pennsborough twp - William GRAYSON, jun. Cloth will be taken in at the following places: Carlisle - Robert GRAYSON, William EAKIN, Phillip LOUGHMAN, Meremiah MILLER,

Kline's Carlisle Weekly Gazette

Hugh BODEN and at the store of Jacob DREVER. In York co - at the store of John DILL and Robert LEECH. In the Barrens by Martin LONGSTAFF, Adam LONGSTAFF and Samuel WILLIAMSON. At Mount Rock by John MILLER. Near Lisbon by Samuel MATEER. In Shearmans valley by John LAW--?
Tracts of land in Huntingdon co for sale: 200 a. in Clark's valley, Sherley twp, 3 miles from Bedford company Furnace, 190 a. in Burnt Cabbin valley, adj James MORTON, in Dublin twp; 150 a. adj land lately belonging to Alexander M'DOWEL, in Dublin twp, about 2 miles from James JAMESON, Burnt Cabbins and other tracts. Benjamin ELLIOT.

44. Nov 9 1796
William M'CALL, near Shippensburgh, to sell house and kitchen in Shippensburgh. A Journeyman fuller is wanted.
Persons indebted to estate of William REED, late of Middleton twp, decd, are requested to make speedy payment - Hugh BODEN, George LOGUE, Carlisle, exrs.
Sale at the dwelling house of subscriber, Jeremiah M'KIBBIN, Newton twp, of horses, cows, cattle and other.
Geo. STURM & William DREVISH, having purchased the store of Jacob WISER, intend selling dry goods and groceries.
Thomas MICHAN offers reward for horse which strayed from the pasture of Daniel SEARFASS, living 3 miles from Carlisle.
Robert LEYBURN offers reward for cow lost out of a drove from Carlisle to Ephraim BLAINE's lower mill.
Martin SHAFFNER, 7 miles below Harrisburgh, Paxton twp, Dauphin co, offers reward for horse stolen out of his stable.
Alexander MACBETH, 5 miles from Carlisle, offers reward for Bob THATCH, about 25 yrs old, 5 ft 10-11 inches.
On Thurs night last, the Silver Spring tavern, property of Oliver POLLOCK, Esq., which was kept by Mr. BRIGGS, took fire and was consumed. Charles SMITH, one of the lodgers was awakened by the crackling of fire and gave warning to the others. A young man of the name of PARKS was killed by jumping out of a garret window. A daughter of Mr. BRIGGS about 10 yrs old was burnt to such a degree that she died. Mrs. BRIGGS and several others are very much injured.
Saturday night, the barn, with a quantity of grain, hay, &c., property of Col. Thomas CAMPBELL, of York co, was consumed.
Benjamin KIPPLER offers reward for mare stolen out of his pasture in Tuscarora valley, Mifflin co, Milford twp.
David LINDSEY offers reward for apprehenson of thief who stole 20 yards of linen off the commons of Carlisle, adj the subscriber's house, where it was bleaching.

45. Nov 16 1796
Died in this town, Thurs evening, Miss Jean THOMPSON, dau of late Rev. THOMPSON. Remains interred in the vault in the church.
Large new mill adj this town, property of Charles M'CLURE was consumed by fire.

46. Nov 23 1796
Married last week by Doctor Robert DAVIDSON, Robert KENNY to Miss Polly DAVIS.
Thomas CRAIGHEAD to Miss Rebecca WEAKLEY.

Kline's Carlisle Weekly Gazette

Archibald LOUDON to Mrs. Hannah HOLCHAM.
George SHULER, Allen twp, Cumberland co, has taken up a stray horse.
Sale at house of Casper DILLER, decd, horses, milch cows, cattle, sheep, hogs, wheat, rye, corn, buckwheat and oats, stills and vessels, road waggon, plantation waggon, plows and harrows and furniture. John CREVER, Philip BAKER, Middleton twp, exrs.

47. Nov 30 1796
Married by Doctor Robert DAVIDSON Thurs 24th inst, Paul RANDOLPH to Miss Susanna FLEMING, both of this co.
Patrick M'CARTHNEY, Carlisle, has taken up a stray heifer.
Whereas Jacob WISER of the borough of Carlisle, merchant, hath assigned to me for the use of his creditors in Baltimore, all his book debts, a list of which is left in the hands of David WATTS, esq., in Carlisle. - Thomas HICKSON
For sale - Dry Goods, China, Queens-ware, Pewter and Groceries, Wines and Spirits - Joseph HAYS. Joseph HAYS & Thomas PURDY at their store in Shearman's valley at George HACKER's tavern a neat and general assortment of dry goods and groceries.
Plantation for sale, 240 a., Frankfor d twp, 9 miles west of Carlisle, 1 mile from Alters' Mill, late the property of Robert M'CLURE, decd; apply to William M'CLURE, Shearman's valley, or James LAIRD, Esq., near the premises.
For sale - 100 a. of land in Newton twp, adj lands of Thomas DUNCAN, Esq.; also 100 a. adj lands of Charles M'CLURE; apply to John PEEBLES, near the premises or Robert PEEBLES, Springield.
Eight dollars, or 1000 feet of good pine boards will be given as a premium to person who will kill a wolf, within 10 miles of his plantation, in Rye twp, Cumberland co - Godfrey SIDLE, Rye twp.
Felty CORNMAN, Middleton twp, Cumberland co, 3 1/2 miles from Carlisle, has taken up a stray cow.
Thomas BUCHANAN offers reward for mare which strayed from his farm in Westpennsboro' twp, Cumberland co.
Francis GIBSON offers reward for horse which strayed from the barracks of Carlisle.

48. Dec 7 1796
RichArd HAUGHTON, Dancing-master, lately from Europe, intends to open a dancing school in Carlisle in the house of Mrs. DAVIS. He will teach a variety of Scotch reels, Fandangoes and Pasbys, being the present fashion in Europe.
Sheriff's sale of lot on which is erected stone house in which Alexander M'KEEHAN, late Treasurer of County now resides; lot on which is stone house occupied by Doctor Isaiah BLAIR; part of lot occupied by James LAMBERTON; lot whereon a brick house is erected now occupied by John NOBLE, property of Alexander M'KEEHAN; and other property of Alexander M'Keehan.
William HUSTON, 1/2 mile from Mount Rock, has taken up a stray cow.
Persons indebted to estate of William REED, late of Middleton twp, decd, are requested to make speedy payment - Hugh BODEN, George LOGUE, exrs, Carlisle.
To be sold at the Court house in Carlisle, houses and a lot on south side of Pomfret st, bounded by a house and lot of John ELLIOT on the west, a lot of Henry EBY on the east - as the property of John BURDOYNE, by virtue of Domestic attachment, issued out of the court of Common Pleas. Also the

Kline's Carlisle Weekly Gazette

creditors of the said John Burdoyne are notified to attend at the house of William WALLACE to make known their repsective demands. William LEVIS, John ANDERSON, William WALLACE, auditors.

49. Dec 14 1796
Died 29th Nov, Mrs. Tobitha M'BRIDE, consort of Alexander M'BRIDE, jun., of Dickinson twp.
Whereas Joseph M'DONALD of Newton twp, Cumberland co, got a note of me for 30 pounds I take this opportunity to forwarn persons from taking assignment on said note - John DAVOLT.
Lot to be sold with two story house and brick kitchen, late the property of John HEARY, decd, in East St, bounded by lots of Alexander BLAINE and Joseph SHROM, and the Letart Spring and now in the tenure of William MILLER - William ALEXANDER, Robert MILLER, exrs.

50. Dec 21 1796
Sheriff's sale of tract in Greenwood twp, 300 a., property of John CRANE; two story stone house and lot in borough of Carlisle, opposite Thomas FOSTER, property of John STEEL, esq.
Whereas the subscriber, Martin CLAUDY, Southampton twp, entered into an obligation with Samuel M'CLINTOCK, conditioned for the payment of 39 pounds unto Thomas MARTIN of Shippensburg, wagoner, which said obligation hath been fully paid.
Sale by order of Orphan Court of Cumberland co, of tract in Greenwood twp, 100 a., adj lands of William THOMPSON, Robert MOODY and lands late of Peter SHAW, as the estate of John SNYDER, decd. Terms of sale made known by Catharine SNYDER, admr.
Whereas Jacob CREVER, esq., High Sheriff of Cumberland co hath advertised the house and lot in which the subscriber lives, to be sold as the property of Alexander M'KEEHAN, Esq., late Treasurer of Cumberland co, these are therefore to warn that I have title to said house - John NOBLE.
Sale at the late dwelling house of William PATTON, of Westpennsborough twp, Cumberland co, decd, of real and persons property of said decd, 150 a., horses, &c. John PATTON, Robert LUSK, admrs.
Simon BOYD, Carlisle has taken up a stray cow and calf.
Henry BURCHSTEAD, Carlisle, to sell two story house in Pomfret st, Carlisle, between Dr. STINNECKE's and Jacob CARR's.
Alexander MAGEE offers reward for bull which strayed from a drove at the Stony Ridge.
Whereas the subscriber, James SCOBEY, Carlisle, passed a note of hand to John SPENDER for sum of $5.00, herby forwarns persons from taking said note.
Whereas James SCOBY left a mare at my house on Monday 12th inst, I do herby give him notice that if he doth not come and pay charges and take her away on or before Monday 2 Jan next, that she will be sold on that day for her keeping, at the house of Samuel CROUL, in the town of Neville, at 12 o'clock. John SPENCE, Newton twp.
The subscriber, Robert GIBSON, Allegheny co, having left the obligations and accounts for articles sold at his vendue in the hands of Mr. POSTLETHWAIT, in Carlisle, requests that they may be immediately paid.
Whereas Joseph M'DONNALD of Newton twp, Cuberland co, got a note of me for 30 pounds, I forwarn persons from taking assignment on the said note.

Kline's Carlisle Weekly Gazette

51. Dec 28 1796
Married Tues 20th inst, Thomas JONES to Miss Margery O"DONNELL, dau of
 Edward O'DONNELL, all of Juniata twp, Cumberland co
Those indebted to estate of Abraham LUKENBILL, of Middleton twp, decd, are
 desired to make payment - Francis KIEHL, Simon MINNICH, admrs.
Committed to jail of Cumberland co, a negro fellow who calls himself JAMES,
 and confessed before James M'CORMICK, Esq. of Carlisle, that he was last
 claimed by John QUIGLEY, of Somerset co, Pa, who purchased him of Robert
 ALLISON near Stoys Town; that he was on the road going over the river to
 see his brother and sister.
Frederick KLIPPINGER, Southampton twp, Cumberland co, has taken up stray
 cattle.
John BASZLER, living on Conodoguinet creek, near Mr. WALKER's mill, has
 taken up a stray cow.
Alexander SCROGGS, living on Big Spring, Cumberland co, has taken up a stray
 bull.

52. Jan 4 1797
Married Tues 20th of Dec last by Rev LINN, Joseph EATON, fuller, to Miss
 Jane MAXWELL, dau of James MAXWELL, all of Toboyne twp.
Mary DENN, near Carlisle, has taken up a stray red bull.
George FOSLER has taken up a stray heifer.

53. Jan 11 1797
Married in Phila on Thurs evening last, by Hilary BAKER, Esq.,
 Sickquoinneyouhee, alias John WALKER, one of the Chiefs of the Cherokee
 nation of Indians, to Miss Ann Jane DURANT of that city.
Persons indebted to subscriber, Jacob WISER, are requested to make payment
 to James M'CORMICK.
In pursuance of order of Orphan Court, Cumberland co, a tract of land will
 be sold in Tyrone twp, Cumberland co, 200 a., adj lands of Samuel
 BARNHIZEL, Jacob MILLER, David CARSON and George DOUGLAS, as property of
 Jacob BARNHIZEL, decd, fromerly property of Major William SANDERSON; terms
 of sale will be made known by John BARNHIZEL and Michael LAY, admrs of
 estate.
To be let - Farm & Tavern-seat, lately occupied by William M'CRACKEN; apply
 to John PEEBLES on the premises. Mount Hope.
James WEAKLEY, Dickinson twp, has taken up a stray steer.

54. Jan 18 1797
Married Thurs evening in this Town by Rev Dr. DAVIDSON, William BROWN, of
 Baltimore, to Miss Nancy LOUGHRIDGE, dau of Abraham LOUGHRIDGE.
Moses BULLOCK, Carlisle, lately from Ireland, carries on the wheel-wright
 business and the cane making, in Louther st, opp Mr. MATHEWS, the blue
 dyer.
Samuel HASLET, borough of Carlisle, has taken up a stray steer.
Samuel THOMAS, Washington Co, [Maryland] offers reward for negro man named
 WILL who ran away from Williamsport, about 30 yrs of age, short well made
 fellow; has tried to pass for a freeman by the name of GEORGE, and one of
 the BUTLER family.

55. Jan 25 1797
Partnership dissolved - of Matthias SLOUGH, Lancaster, and William GEER,
 late proprietors of the Lancaster, Harrisburg, Carlisle and Shippensburg

Kline's Carlisle Weekly Gazette

Line of stages. This line to be continued by Slough. William Geer has
joined the line of stages of which Messrs. REILEY, WEED and WITMER are the
proprietors.
Persons indebted to estate of Stephen DUNCAN & John DUNCAN, decd, to the
late partnership of Robert COLWELL & Co. of Shipensburgh, and to the
present on of James DUNCAN & Co., of the borough of Carlisle, whose
accounts are due, are requested to make immediate payment. James Duncan.
Two-story brick house and kitchen and half lot of ground to be sold - in
borough of Carlisle, adj Henry BURCHSTEAD, and opposite to Dr. ADAMS -
John ELLIOTT, Carlisle.
Joseph ANDERSON, Carlisle, offers reward for apprentice lad named James
JOHNSTON, about 18 yrs of age, about 5 ft, 6-7 inches, of dark
complection, taylor by trade, has a crooked ankle.

56. Feb 1 1797
John COMPTON, living in Frederick Co, Md, offers reward for negro man named
CAESAR, of yellowish complexion, about 28-30 yrs of age, stout, thick set,
5 ft 6-7 inches.
Sale of plantation, late of Casper DILLER, decd, Middleton twp, Cumberland
co, 3 1/2 miles from Carlisle, 460 a. - John CREVER, Philip BAKER, exrs.
Plantation to be let, 113 a., Tyrone twp, Shearman's valley, Cumberland co,
adj last of John DUNBAR, Martin BERNHIZLE, William M'CLURE, Robert CREE
and Samuel SIMISON. John SIMISON, living on the premises.
To be let - a good seat for a tavern and store, lately occupied by
JamesMOORE, on Walnut Bottom road, leading from Carlisle to Shippensburgh.
James Moore on the premises, Dickiknson twp.
John MONTGOMERY intends to decline keeping books - to sell present stock of
books [titles listed].
James CESSNA, Shippensburgh, to sell house in Shippensburgh, on south east
corner of High St and Earl St; has been occupied at a Tavern.
Died Wed last in Mifflintown, Mifflin co, in his 60th yr, James RAMSEY, for
a number of yrs an inhabitant of this borough.
Died on 22 Jan last, aged 68 yrs, Mrs. Jean DILL, wife of Col. Matthew DILL.
William FERGUSON, near Mount Rock, Cumberland co, offers reward for missing
horse.

57. Feb 8 1797
Married Thurs last by Rev HERBST, Henry REAM, of Baltimore, to Miss Polly
CREVER, dau of John CREVER of this Borough.
Married Sun night last, by Rev Dr. ADAMS, Thomas ARMOR, to Miss Serah HOGUE,
both of this place.
Alexander M'BRIDE, Dickinson twp, Cumberland co, has taken up 4 stray sheep.
Lot of ground to be sold, in twon of Newville, whereon subscriber, Samuel
FINLEY, lives.

58. Feb 15 1797
To be sold at house of Mr. M'CANDLESS, in Shippensburg, sundry merchandize,
broad-cloths, calicoes, lines, mislins, &c., by virtue of an attachment as
the propery of George SPRECHER. David M'KNIGHT, John HEAP, Shippensburgh,
auditors.

Kline's Carlisle Weekly Gazette

59. Feb 22 1797
To be sold in borough of Carlisle, lately occupied by subscriber as a store, and other property [listed] - John ARTHUR
Tract of limestone land for sale on Big-Spring, Cumberland co, 200 a. - David RALSTON.
Sale of plantation, 236 a., Frankford twp, Cumberland co, 10 miles west of Carlisle, 2 miles from Alter's Mill, adj lands of Col. BUTLER and Robert M'CLURE; apply to John SHARP on the premises or the owner, John WISLON, living in Geddes town.
Died in this town on Thurs last, William HASLET age 100 yrs and 9 months.
To be let - that noted Inn, lately kept by Col. Archibald STEEL, Borough of York - John CLARK, owner, York.
Tract for sale in Hopewell twp, Cumberland co, adj lands of David WILLS, David M'KINNEY, where Andrew THOMSON decd, lived, and now occupied by Gilbert KENNEDY, 260 a. - John M'KEE, William MONTGOMERY, guardians.
Negro man for sale, apply to John ARTHUR, at Spring Mills, near Carlisle, with whom the negro is left for sale by - James SMITH
For rent - Tavern and Ferry on Susquehanna, known as the Chamber's Ferry, 3 miles below Harrisburgh - William CHAMBERS, Benjamin JUNKIN, Joseph JUNKIN, guardians.
Sale of lot on main st in Shippensburgh, at the Branch, with 2-story stone house, and stone kitchen and hatter's shop, agreeable to last will and testament of David PORTER, decd. Alexander PEEBLES, Samuel PORTER, exrs.

60. Mar 1 1797
For membership in Carlisle Library Company apply to John CREIGH.
John RICHTER, Carlisle, having entered in to articles of agreement with John WRAY, of the Borough of Carlisle, who acted as Agent for Mathew ALLISON for a certain house and lot in Pomfret st and which agreement has not been met, persons are forwarned from taking assignment on any bonds there of.
240 a. to be sold, late the property of Robert M'CLURE, decd, in Frankfort twp, 9 miles west of Carlisle. William M'CLURE, James LAIRD, exrs.
Partnership of Finley MORROW and Archibald DUNN, to a wagon or team of horses, has expired.
George ANDERSON and John COCHRAN, late of Bedford co, not having fulfilled their agreement, this is to forwarn persons from takeing assignment on bonds - John KNISELY, Bedford co.
House for sale in Shippensburgh, adj public Spring; apply to James MEANS, adj the premises, or John M'CALLS, in Phila, No. 50, North Fourth st.
To sell plantation, 280 a., and other small tracts, Newton twp, Cumberland co; Paul MARTIN, Junior, livng near the premises will shew the property; also the subscriber, Thomas MARTIN, in Shippensburgh.
Dwelling house for sale in Fannersburgh; apply to Joseph BROWN, owner, or Robert NEWALL, merchant.

61. Mar 8 1797
Married in this town, Thurs evening last, George WISE, saddler, to Mrs. FISHER.
Young stud horse for sale - John STAYMAN, East Pennsborough twp, Cumberland co, 1 miles from Silver Spring.
James WHITE, Rye twp, Cumberland co, has taken up a stray horse.

Kline's Carlisle Weekly Gazette

Whereas my wife Elizabeth hath eloped from my bed and board, the 27th of Feb, 1797, this is to forwarn persons from crediting her on my account. - John SIMISON, Shearmans valley, Tyrone twp.
Sheriff's sales: (1) plantation, 167 a., east Pennsborough twp, 9 miles from borough of Carlilse, now in possession of Leonard FISHER, bounded by land of Simon CROUSE and others, property of Jasper READER, at suit of Jacob HINDS, adm of Joseph HINDS, decd.; (2) lot with log house, in town of Lisburn, Allen twp, property of John LONG, at the suit of Christian TIDWILER, adm of George PRATT, decd; (3) house and lot and Potash works in Shippensburgh, property of John COPELY at the suit of John DRINKER; (4) house and lot in borough of Carlisle, in possession of James Brown LEE, bounded west by a lot of William BLACK, as property of James ABERCRUMBIE, at the suit of David RALSTON. Jacob CREVER, Sheriff, Carlisle.
Sale by order of Orphan's Court, plantation , 160 a.in Middletown twp, 2 miles from Carlisle, bounded by Conodinguinet creek on the south, by land of Robert CHAMBERS on the west, on the North by land of John CULL, and on the east by lands of John TAYLOR and Francis and Thomas KELLY. John STEEL, adm.
John GRIMES offers reward for horse missing from Daniel NEVINS' on Herron's Branch.

62. Mar 15 1797
Died Thurs 9th inst in 41st year of her age, Mrs. Mary HOLMES, after a long continued illness.
Married 9th inst. by Dr. Robert DAVIDSON, Charles M'CLURE to Mrs. Rebecca PARKER, dau of William BLAIR. (This correspondent notes that this is the third marriage by this gentleman, and each time the family name of each of his wives was Blair.)
The horse, Sportsman, will cover mares this season at the stable of the subscriber, Samuel CROWEL, Newville - formerly property of G. CLARKE of Greencastle.
To be sold - 179 1/2 a. in Dickinson twp, Cumberland co, on Walnut Bottom Road, 11 miles from Carlisle - Balser WITMER.

63. Mar 22 1797
Reward of twenty dollars for apprehension of person who vandalized property [mostly that of James HAMILTON] given by: John CREIGH, William LYON, John CREVER, James ARMSTRONG, Samuel LAIRD, William IRVINE, John MONTGOMERY, James HAMILTON, who will pay 1/2 of the sum).
Sale of undivided tract of land, 330 a., bounded by lands of Joseph ELLIOT, Robert JOHNSTON and John M'COY, in Rye twp, property of Gilbert M'COY.
Sale of furniture, wagon, some cows - James ARMSTRONG.
The horse, Dragon, will stand at stable of the subscriber, Nathaniel WILSON, Middleton twp, Cumberland co.
Sale of a farm with a tavern seat, between Carlisle and Shippensburgh, occupied by William M'CRACKEN and others as a tavern upwards of 50 years. John PEEBLES, Mount hope.
Jacob CREVER, Dry Goods and Groceries, has removed to High st formerly occupied by Joseph THORNBURGH, lately by John ARTHUR, next door to John CREIGH, merchant.
Sale at the plantation of Simon CLOUZER, decd, Middleton twp, Cumberland co, 5 miles from Borough of Carlisle, horses, cows, plough, plough irons, milch cows, horn cattle, sheep, grain in the ground, and nearly 1/3 part of thie

Kline's Carlisle Weekly Gazette

plantation, 321 a. in all, adj lands of Robert MORRISON, Frederick NOACKER. Wendel MICHAEL, Carlisle.
Reward for lost silver watch; deliver to James MITCHELL or Edward THOMPSON, in Carlisle.

64. Mar 29 1797
Public quarterly examination of the students of the first Class of Dickinson College, composed of 13 young gentlemen. On the next day the following student delivered orations: Edwin PUTNAM, William BREDEN, Robert KEENEDY, Thomas MACOMB, Henry RIDGLEY, James GRAHAM, Thomas GREER, James THOMSON, Thompson HOLMES and Moses MONTGOMERY.
The horse, Jolly, wil cover mares this season at the stable of the subscriber, Robert FAUCET, Carlisle.

65. Apr 5 1797
Lottery tickets available for lots in Newton twp, Cumberland co - Thomas BUCHANAN, Locust Grove, near Carlisle.
About 10 days ago a person of the name of John M'FARLANE, lately from Ireland, was killed in an Oak Bank, at the head of the Big Spring, in Newton twp, by the clay giving way from the top.
Nathaniel WEAKLEY has removed to the inn, Indian Queen, High st, Carlisle.
John SMITH, shoemaker, has removed into a house of Ephraim STEEL's adj his dwelling house and opposite the Court House, Carlisle, where he continues to carry on the shoemaking business.
Pump-making - Martin RAUSH, Carlisle, has removed into this town, and at present lives in Louther St, nearly opposite to David ROWAN.
Potting business - Peter POTTAW, potter, has erected a new Pott House in High st, Carlisle, having learned his business in city of Phila, where he followed it for several years.
Whereas Henry SHOUP has obtained a note of my wife Sarah DIBLER in my absence, of 18 pounds, I do hereby forewarn persons from taking an assignment on said note - Michael DIBLER, Greenwood, Cumberland co.
The horse Rochester will stand at the subscriber's stable, 6 miles from Carlisle, in East Pennsborough twp - Andrew PARKER.
Whereas the subscriber has passed bonds to Henry and Samuel KELLY, in consideration for a tract for which said Kellys were to make a good title, which has not been done, therefore I forewarn persons from taking assignment on bonds given by me - James WILSON.
Lots given to persons building thereon in new town of Petersburgh for a brief period - D.L. MOREL.
Samuel CROWELL, Newville, has removed to new house, directly opposite to the one he formerly occupied and next door to Dr. John GEDDES, and he has lately got a general assortment of good liquors,. and other accommodations.
W. P. MATHEWS, Baltimore, cautions against paying money to James FITZPATRICK, escaped indentured servant, who for 2 years has occasionally engaged in business for Mathews.
Wanted - apprentice to the blacksmith business - William MOORE, Carlisle.

66. Apr 12 1797
Married on Thurs last by Rev Dr. DAVIDSON, John LOGAN to Miss Peggy CHAMBERS, dau of Robert CHAMBERS, all of this co.

Kline's Carlisle Weekly Gazette

Agreeable to a public notice given in the Carlisle Gazette, a number of the
  subscribers for building a stone or brick wall in order to inclose the
  burying ground of the Presbyterian congregation of Carlisle on the Glebe
  of Connodoguinet creek, met at the house of Nathaniel WEAKLEY, in the
  borough of Carlisle, and appointed Messsrs. John DUNBAR, Ross MITCHELL,
  William CHAMBERS, Patrick DAVIDSON, Charles COOPER and William
  FLEMING,trustees to superintend the building of the same, and to draw
  orders on John HOLMES who is hereby appointed Treasurer - George LOGUE,
  Clerk.
Plantation for sale, 145 a., near Spring Mill, 9 miles westward of Carlisle
  - Robert COCHRAN, on the premises.
Notice is hereby given to the inhabitants of Middleton, who live between
  Carlisle and the North Mountain, that they be punctual in sending their
  road tax for the year 96 to the subscriber - James GIFFEN.
Sale of patented land, 300 a. in Lack twp, Mifflin co, adj lands late of
  Col. M'GAW, decd, Capt. FERRIER, --- M'CLURE, Daniel LOUCHRY and others.
  Apply to Ralph BOWIE.

67. Apr 19 1797
Samuel HAY has commenced the Clock and Watch making business at the house of
  Jonathan FOSTER, shoemaker, Louther st, opposite Robert LAYBURNs tavern,
  sign of General Wayne, borough of Carlisle.
Sale of tract, 582 a., in Hamilton twp, Franklin co, adj lands of James
  CAMPBELL, William DIXON, 1/4 mile from old Loudon road, now in the tenure
  of Thomas JAMES and Alexander DUNCAN. Apply to Judge RIDDLE,
  Chambersburgh, Col. Joseph ARMSTRONG, near the premises, or the
  subscriber, John SHIPPEN, at Thomas FOSTER's Inn, Carlisle, and at
  Jonathan HAGER's Inn, Chambersburgh, during the Court week, or at his
  residence in Shippensburgh.

68. Apr 26 1797
John BIGLER, has moved to the house lately occupied by Nathaniel WEAKLEY,
  the sign of the Lamb, in York st, borough of Carlisle, where he keeps a
  house of Entertainment.
Sheriff's sales: (1) undivided tract of land, 330 a. bounded by lands of
  Joseph ELLIOTT, Robert JOHNSTON and John M'COY in Rye twp, property of
  Gilbert M'COY; (2) tract in Rye twp, adj land of SMILEY and others, 200
  a., property of Henry HATELY(?); (3) tract in Greenwood twp, Cumberland
  co, adj lands of William THOMPSON, 200 a., property of David MATTHIAS; (4)
  tract, 100 a., Mifflin co, formerly in Cumberland co, property of Thomas
  WADE; (5) 5 tracts in Raystown branch, one 4 miles above Fatman's place,
  another 4 miles from Spark's place, and others, all the property of George
  CROGHAN; (6) tract of 50 a. in Greenwood twp, Cumberland co, property of
  Christian WYLAND.
Sale of negro woman, about 36 yrs of age - Thomas FOSTER, Carlisle.

69. May 10 1797
Whereas Hugh M'Allister on 9 June 1793 at Carlisle, received letters of
  administration on the estates of John BRIANT, Philip MAGUIRE, Thomas
  GILLIS, John O'BRIAN, Barney BURNS and Arthur M'CLOSKY, soldiers, and who
  died intestate and without heirs, as attested by said Hugh M'ALISTER, and
  whereas Hugh M'ALISTER has not mady any settlement, he is notified to
  appear at the Register's office - William LYON, Register, Carlisle.

Kline's Carlisle Weekly Gazette

Whereas the subscriber, John SWEEZY, having passsed bonds to James DONNELLY in consideration of a tract of land, persons are cautioned not to ake assignment on said bonds.
Lost within a mile of Mount Rock, 26 dollars and a French crown, in silver. George M'CULLOUGH.
Persons who bought horses or cows at the subscriber's vendue on 29 March, 1796 are reqeusted to make immediate payment - Robert GIBSON.

70. May 17 1797
The Carlisle Light Infantry company are to meet at the Court house.
Alexander M'BETH offers reward for negro named BOAB, about 6 ft.
Reward offers for horse missing between Mount Rock and Shippensburgh. Bring to Enoch ABRAM, 3 miles west of Carlisle, or to John RHINE, tavern keeper in Carlisle, or to the subscriber, Jacob SNIVELY, within 3 miles of Harrisburgh.
Mathew MILLER, Middleton twp, has taken up a stray horse.
Cancers cured by Dr. John MORRIS, borough of York: Baltzer LAWER, Dauphin co, Lebanon twp, attests to remove of cancer from lip. Catharine BAKER (her mark) says Dr. John MORRIS removed cancer from her nose after 20 years. John GRUP, Lutheran minister, York co, Dover twp, certifies that Dr. Morris removed cancer from head and hand. Adam SMITH says his wife had a painful cancer on her nose for number of years and Dr. Morris removed it. William STOBER (his mark), witnessed by Valentine YARMUTH, Baltimore co, had cancer on his arm for 8 years and curied by Dr. Morris. Also cured: John ROSBROCK, Jacob SITLER, Frederick HORN, John HALLER, Matthais DETTER, Peter KUHL.
Whereas the subscriber, Andrew LAUSH, passed bonds to Peter STUNTZ for tract of land, he hereby gives notice not to take assignment on said bonds, as said Peter Stuntz has not performed his contract.
Henry LECHLER, has commenced the gun and rifle making business, in the house of William BLAIR, main st, borough of Carlisle.

71. May 24 1797
Left in my store sometime ago, a Testament, a spelling book and old Psalm book, newly bound - John MONTGOMERY, Carlisle.

72. May 31 1797
To be sold at dwelling house of subscriber, Middleton twp, horses, cows, sheep, hoggs, wagon and geers, farming utenisls - Nathaniel WILSON.
Abraham LOUGHRIDGE, borough of Carlisle, offers reward for missing mare.

73. Jun 7 1797 with supplement
Lot of ground to be sold adj Samuel JACKSON's, property of late Col. Robert MAGAW, decd. James HAMILTON, Samuel LAIRD, Exrs.
Robert PEEBLES offers lot for sale in Springfield, where he lives.
Alexander SCOTT to sell acre of land in village of Strasburgh, Franklin co, on which is erected a tanyard, bark house, currying shop and a large square log dwelling house in unfinished state. Apply to Joseph KERR or George HEMMILE at said place, or to Jacob GRAEF, esq., or the subscriber at Lancaster.
Andrew GALBREATH, East Pennsborough, offers reward for draught ox.

Kline's Carlisle Weekly Gazette

74. Jun 14 1797 with supplement
John ELLIOT offers reward for horse missing out of a field near Carlisle.
Cumberland County Troop of Light Horse to meet at the Court House - Capt. A. M'COSKRY, Capt.
Plantation for sale in Fouts's Valley Cumberland co, 6 miles from the Susquehannah, 218 a.; enquire of James TERRY on the prremises or E. SHUEMAKER, merchant, No. 127 Market st, Phila.
Robert DALRUMPLE and Thomas SMILEY, Carlisle, offer reward for mare which broke out of the stable of Thomas Smiley, inn keeper of the borough of Carlisle.

75. Jun 21 1797 with supplement
Wed evening last, died after a few days illness, Mrs. Elizabeth PETERSON, widow of the late Doctor Henry PETERSON of the state of Delaware. This lady who was in the prime of life, resided since the death of her husband with her mother, Mrs. Susannah THOMPSON of this borough. In the four years since Mrs. Thompson settled here, she has been so unhappy as to attend the funeral of 3 of her daughters.
Died Mon 12th inst., Mrs. BUCHANAN, wife of General Thomas BUCHANAN.
Died Sat last, Mrs. M'FARLANE, wife of Major William M'FARLANE; remains interred in the Old Presby burying ground near this borough.
Information sought on Elizabeth SMITH, grand-dau to Peter SMITH of Cumberland co, decd, to make application to the subscribers, exrs of the esate of said Peter Smith - William BOOR, Jacob WITMER, exrs.
Archibald LOUDON has just received at his book store in Carlisle a large and general assortment of books.
To be sold - Two stocking weaver's looms and furniture - John CREVER, Jacob CREVER, exrs.
Jacob BYERS notifies not to give credit to his wife Ann BYERS, as her behaviour has been so unbecoming a wife, and he is apprehensive she may endeavour to run him in debt or otherwise embezzle his property.

76. Jun 28 1797
To be rented on the shares for a fall crop a large field, adj the borough, 40 a. - James HAMILTON.
William THOMSON offers reward for slaves, Tom and Hannah HALL.

77. Jul 5 1797
James SCOBEY, Carlisle, offers reward for apprentice boy, Edmund LUCUS, about 14 yrs of age, pale complexion, with a down look.
John STEELE, Lieut., 3d U.S. Regt, Commanding, offers reward for deserters from the Barracks at Carlisle: John TOOL, an Irishman, about 40 yrs of age, about 5 ft 10 inches, fair complexion, grey eyes, wears his hair tied, has a sore spot on one of his legs, and cut on his forehead near the hair not yet well. He took with him a round hat and all his uniform clothing. Also reward for deserted Edward LUDRIDGE, an Irishman, about 30 yrs of age, a barber.
Whereas the subscriber having passed bonds to Henry NAVE. for 20 pounds each, persons are cautioned from taking assignment on said bonds.

78. Jul 19 1797
Dissolution of partnership of Joseph and Robert CRAWFORD.

Kline's Carlisle Weekly Gazette

79. Jul 26 1797
Sheriff's sales: (1) 100 a. in Mifflin co, property of Thomas WADE, at suit of Abraham KENDRICK; (2) 330 a. in Rye twp, bounded by lands of Joseph ELLIOTT and Robert JOHNSTON and John M'COY, property of Gilbert M'COY at the suit of William WALLACE; (3) tract in Southampton twp, called the Three Spring(?) Tract, 600 a., with saw mill, property of James M'CALLEY, at suit of James CUMMINGS & Co.; (4) house and lot in borough of Carlisle, now in the possession of James BROWNLEE , bounded on west by lot of William BLACK, property of James ABERCROMBIE, at suit of David RALSTON; (5) frame house with one end stone, on south side of High st, borough of Carlisle bounded on east by lot of George PATTISON and west by lot of William ARMOR, property of Thomas BUCHANAN, esq., at suit of William BINGHAM and Mordecai LEWIS.
Sheriff's sale of tract called Brindlestown, in Allen twp, adj lands of Stephen MOREHOUSE, Sylvanus SEELY, William M'MEEN, Jonas SEELY, Josias M'MEEN, property of George BRINDLE, decd, at the suit of John WILCOCKS, Alexander WILCOCKS, George FOX and Samuel FOX, admrs of William B. HOCKLEY, decd, assignee of Jacob FREY.
Michael WILAND forwarns persons from buying land under the name of Christopher WILAND, as I have bought the improvements from said Wiland.
This is to forwarn persons that Mary CUSKADAN, wife of the subscriber has left him without any cause - James CUSKADAN.

80. Aug 2 1797
Sheriff's sale: (1) 1000 a. in Milford twp, with a forge, property of Thomas BEAL and William STERRETT; (2) also property of Alexander and Samuel JACKSON, undivided half of 4 tracts, 1400 a. on Loss Creek, adj William HENDERSON near river Juniata; (3) lot in Lewistown on south west corner of main and Dorcas streets, property of Jarmin JACOB. Andrew NELSON, sheriff.
John STEEL, Lieut., 3d U.S. Regt, Commanding, Carlisle, offers reward for deserters from Barracks at Carlisle: Daniel DONOVAN, Irishman, 30 yrs of age, a cooper, dark complexion, 5 ft 10 inches, dark hair tied; Daniel HENDERSON alias HENESSE, 25 yrs of age, 5 ft 7 1/2 inches, grey eyes, dark complexion, short hair.

81. Aug 9 17997
Robert PATTON, Middleton twp, Cumberland co, near Waggoner's gap, has taken up a stray horse.
Deserted from barracks at Carlisle: Francis BURNS, Irishman, 25 yrs of age, about 5 ft 7 inches, weaver; and Isaac SLOVER, born in Jersey, 32 yrs of age, about 5 ft 7 inches, short black hair, cut close to the skin on the forepart of the head, has woman with him which he calls his wife, named Betsey, also from Jersey, who speaks with a tune peculiar to that state.

82. Aug 16 1797
On Friday evening last a daring attempt was made on the life of Jacob CREVER, esq., High Sheriff of this co, whilst in the execution of his office, by Jonathan WALLACE, who discharged a pistol which was loaded with ball, at the said sheriff which missed. After the confinement of Jonathan Wallace, his brother James and a son of Jonathan's came to the house of Mr. John CREIGH and likewise threatened the life of the sheriff and they are now confined in jail.

Kline's Carlisle Weekly Gazette

The Carlisle Light Infantry Company to meet at the Court House - Robert MILLER, Captain.
John WOODS, Hopewell twp, certifies that Richard RODGERS has taken up a stray horse.
Tanyard for rent, Tyrone twp, York co, 1 mile from Balser Smith's mill, on Promagen creek - John LEAB.
Tract for sale in Harrrison co, Va, on Crooked Run, west branch of Monongehala river, 755 a.; apply to John AMBLER, Connols town, Fayette co, Rev. George TOWERS, Clarksburgh, or to William DUCKETT, paper maker, near Shippensburgh, Cumberland co, Pa.

83. Aug 23 1797
100 a. for sale on Shearman's Creek, adj Paul FRAZIER and John STUART; apply to General William IRVINE, Carlisle.
Deserted from Barracks at Carlisle, John STEEL, soldier belonging to the U.S. army, generally believed to be an Irishman, although he says he was born in this state, 5 ft 7 inches, very dark complexion, short black hair, has lost the middle finger of his left hand, fond of strong drink, stout, fond of lifting people on his hand at arms length.
Samuel MARTIN, Allen twp, Cumberland co, has taken up a stray steer.

84. Aug 30 1797
On Saturday evening a Mr. LEONARD who lived about 3 miles from this town, in attempting to cross the Conodogninet creek on horseback was drowned.
Sheriff's sale of half a lot with 2 houses, and stable, on south side of Louther st, bound by property of John CREVER, Phillip LAUFFMAN, and John BARBER, property of Robert MORRISON.
Persons indebted to estate of George ESPY, late of West-Pennsborough twp, decd, are requested to settle accounts. John BROWN, Thomas KENNEDY, exrs.
Persons indebted to Wendel MICHAEL are desired to make payment.
David GROVE, Taboyne twp, Cumberland co, offers reward for Dutch servant man, named Martin VANSKER, a plaisterer, about 26 yrs of age, 5 ft 9-10 inches, dark complexion, short black hair and small beard, speaks broken English; had on dark blue broadcloth coat, long waisted, with mohair buttons, black fartinet short jacket, hemp linen shirt and tow trousers, hat much torn in the crown; can play on the violin, a good German scholar.

85. Sep 6 1797
Sheriff's sale: (1) plantation formerly occupied by Ezekiel DUNNING, now in the possession of Andrew HEICKS, in West-pennsborough twp, 223 a., bounded by lands of James CAROTHERS, John LOVE, property of Thomas BUCHANAN at the suit of John KIDD; (2) log house in Shippensburgh bounded by lot of William BELL, property of James M'CLINTOCK, at suit of John PARKS; (3) tract, 35 a., in Hopewell twp, property of Hugh M'MULLEN, at the suit of Henry MOOR; (4) tract, 50 a. with small cabbin, in Rye twp, bounded by lands of David SEMPLE, James WILSON and Juniata river, property of Mitchell BASKINS, at the suit of David WATTS; (5) plantatino, 100 a. by great road from Blue BAll to North's ferry on Juniata, Juniata twp, property of Jeremiah BUCKLY, at the suit of Alexander DOUGHERTY.
Whereas the subscriber having passed sundry note to Thomas BUCHANAN, Esq. and William SANDERSNO, in consideration of a tract of land, this is to

Kline's Carlisle Weekly Gazette

caution persons not to take assignment on said notes - Henry SASSERMAN, Tyrone twp, Shearman's valley.
Plantation for sale, 300-400 a. in Pitt twp, Allegheny co - Abdiel M'LURE, on the premises.
Whereas the sheriff of Cumberland Co has advertised sale of a tract in Juniata twp, as property of Jeremiah BUCKLEY, the said Buckley has not title to said land; title is verified to me - John GROSS.

86. Sep 6 1797
Married Tues last by Rev WAUGH, in the Lower Settlement, Samuel CRISWELL, of this town, to Miss Margaret MORRISON.
- On Thurs last in this town by Rev DUBENDORFF, David ALTER, of Westpennsborough to Miss Betsey MELL.
Aaron JOSEPH has for sale all kinds of gold and silver watches, rings, etc.; apply at William HIEGEL's York st, in Carlisle.
Isaac MASON, Hopewell twp, Cumberland co, has taken up a stray cow.
Whereas my wife Ketty hath absconded from my bed and board without any just cause, I suppose she is gone with a certain Ludwick STICHLER, and hath likewise taken with her of my property to a considerable amount, I do therefore discharge any person from harbouring her or crediting her on my accounty. Daniel WOLF, Mifflin twp.

87. Sep 13 1797
Isaac LEVER, Newville, has taken up a stray horse.

88. Sep 20 1797
Married Thurs 17th Aug in Juniata twp, Shearmans valley by Rev John LINN, Rev John HOGG, aged 82, to Miss Rossana M'EWEN, aged 38, of the same place.
Whereas I gave bond to Lydia BUCKEY, this is to caution persons from taking assignment on said bonds as they were given for purchase of a tract which has since been sold by the sheriff. Philip Creek.
Samuel LAIRD offers reward for horse missing from Commnons of Carlisle.
Joseph STEELE carries on business of watch & clock making.
William HAYES, living in Peters twp, Franklin co, offers reward for negro man named Cast STEEL, about 5 ft 9-10 inches, straight and well made, about 23 yrs of age.

89. Sep 27 1797
Married Thurs evening last by Rev Robert DAVIDSON, Col. Ephraim BLAINE, to Mrs. Sarah DUNCAN, of this borough.
Charles BOVARD has fresh supply of fall and winter goods, nearly opposite the sign of the Black Bear, Carlisle.
A young man wants employment to teach sciences. Application to be made to Hugh SMITH, Storekeeper, Shippensburg, or Joseph BRADY, student, Carlisle College.
Meeting of the Fire company - John MONTGOMERY, President, Carlisle.

90. Oct 4 1797
Graduation at Dickinson College - Degree of Bachelor of Arts conferred on: William BREDEN of York co, Thomas GREER, James GRAHAM, and James THOMSON of Cumberland co; Moses MONTGOMERY and Robert KENNEDY of Lancaster co; Thomas I. MACOMB and Henry M. RIDGELY, of Delaware; Edwin PUTNAM of Marietta, in

Kline's Carlisle Weekly Gazette

the Western Territory. Degree of Master of Arts conferred on Rev. Isaac GREER and Dr. John CREIGH, practitioner of Physic, Mifflin co.
Jacob SHULER, Hatter, has just commenced the hatting business in main st in borough of Carlisle, nearly opposite Robert MILLER, Esq.

91. Oct 11 1797
Married on 26th Sep, in Harrisburgh, by Rev. Nathaniel SNOWDEN, John ROBERTSON, Teacher of youth, to Miss Jane M'CRACKEN, dau of William M'CRACKEN, weaver, both of East Pennsborough twp, Cumberland.
Sheriff's sale of plantation, formerly occupied by Ezekiel DUNNING, now in the possession of Andrew HEICKS, in Westpennsborough twp, 223 a., bounded by land of James CAROTHERS, John LOVE, taken at the suit of Alexander M'BETH, as the property of Thomas BUCHANAN; also frame house with one end stone on South side of High St in borough of Carlisle,bounded on East by lot of George PATTERSON, on the West now the property of William ARMOR, taken as the property of Thomas Buchanan, at the suit of William BINGHAM and Mordecai LEWIS.
George CONOWAY has taken up a stray horse which broke onto the plantation late of George ESPY, Frankfort twp, Cumberland co.
Sheriff's sales of: (1) tract called Lairn, in Middletown twp, Cumberland co, beginning at a post on the corner of Robert PATTERSON's land, also adj David GEORGE's land and Andrew HOLME's land, sold as the property of Mathew LAIRD; (2) tract called St. John's, in Newton twp, Cumberland co, adj land of Daniel DUNCAN, David M'CURDY, James DUNLAP and Charles RODDY, sold as the property of John JOHNSTON.

92. Oct 18 1797
Sheriff's sale of: (1) tract in Hopewell twp, property of Hugh M'MULLAN, at the suit of Henry MOORE; (2) house and lot in town of Shippensburgh, bounded by lot on the East of William BELL, property of James M'CLINTOCK, at the suit of John PARKS; (3) half lot with two houses, bounded on the East by lot of John CREVER, on the South by lot of Philip LAUFFMAN, on the West by lot of John BARBER, property of Robert MORRISON, at the suit of Robert TAYLOR; (4) tract, 57 a., in Greenwood twp, Cumberland co, property of Christian WILAND, at the suit of Samuel and Obed FAHNESTOCK.
Sale by decree of Orphan's Court of Cumberland co of lot on East side of Hanover st, borough of Carlisle, property of George HOOVER, decd. - John CREVER, Jacob CREVER, exrs.
John STEPHENS continues to carry on the business of fulling and dying at the mill of Ephraim BLAINE, Esq.
Drugs & medicines of the best quality, 2 doors east of the Indian Queen, Carlisle - Isiah BLAIR.
Sale of lot (by order of Orphan's Court) in main st in town of Newville with house formerly occupied as a tavern by George KYFER, decd. Attendance will be given by Barbara KYFER, adm of estate.
Sale of tract (by order of Orphan's Court) in Middleton twp, 166 a., property of Henry M'KINLEY, decd; also lot on east side of Hanover st, Carlisle, property of Henry M'KINLEY, decd; terms made known by John STEEL adm of estate.
Sale of tract, 580 a. in Letter-kenny twp, Franklin co, adj lands of the town of Roxburg, 200 a.; apply to Samuel POSTLETHWAIT in Carlisle. Thomas WISLON, Franklin co.

Kline's Carlisle Weekly Gazette

Sale by order of Orphan's Court of tract in Middletown twp, on North side of
  Connodoguinet creek, bounded by lands of Robert CHAMBERS, John TAYLOR, and
  Francis and Thomas KELLY, 166 a. - John STEEL, admr.
Thomas MURRAY, living at Barn's Gap (or Dublin) has taken up a stray cow.

93. Oct 25 1797
Sheriff's sale of 1000 a. in Milford twp, with a forge thereon, almost new,
  property of Thomas BEALE and William STERRET; also property of Alexander
  and Samuel JACKSON: one moiety and undivided half of four tracts, 1400 a.
  on Loss creek, 400 a. on Caculamus creek, 146 a. adj David MILLER with
  dwelling house, 288 a. adj James HENDERSON, 12 a. in Milford twp adj
  William HENDERSON, near the river Juniata, and other - Andrew NELSON,
  Sheriff.
We are happy to announce that the Fever in the city of Phila has
  considerably abated. Friday's paper of that city, mentions that only five
  have died for the last 24 hours, and that the citizens are returning to
  the city.
On Saturday arrived at the Barracks, Lieutenant SHOEMAKER, with 25 men, from
  Baltimore.
Robert WRIGHT has removed to the Brick House, formerly occupied by Thomas
  TRIMBLE, corner of North and Water sts, where he continues carrying on the
  Skin-dressing, breeches making and glove making. Carlisle.
Whereas the subscriber by an unexpected and unforeseen attack of the Famous
  Jacob WISER and his agents, has been obliged to quit his store business in
  this town, he humbly requests all indebted to discharge their accounts.
  Those that neglect this notice will not blame him when they fall into the
  same cruel hands, wherein he had the misfortune to fall. Henry D.
  DAELHOUSEN, Carlisle.
Furniture to be sold at the dwelling house of Miss GORDON's, next door to
  Thomas FOSTER.
William GREASON continues his fulling mill; he will receive cloth at Messrs.
  William WALLACE's tavern and Charles BOVARD's tavern in Carlisle, at Hugh
  SMITH's tavern on the great road from Carlisle to Croban's gap, at John
  LAWSHE's tavern, Shearman's valley, at Honicle KRITZER's on the Harrisburg
  road, at the house of Adam LONGSTAFF in the Barrens, at Thomas
  WILLIAMSON's tavern, on Trindle's road, and at Robert LEECH's tavern, York
  co.
Robert BLAINE offers reward for horse missing out of his meadow, adj his
  mill on the Conodoguinet creek, 1 mile from Carlisle.

94. Nov 1 1797
Deserted from the Barracks at Carlisle on the night of 25th inst: William
  GRIFFEN, an Irishman, 38 yrs of age, 5 ft 7 inches, dark complexion, brown
  hair, much marked with the small pox, by trade a saddler; William JOLLY,
  an Irishman, 29 yrs of age, 5 ft 8 inches, fair complexion, short sandy
  hair, by trade a plaisterer, blind of the right eye; and on the 27th: John
  SMITH, born in Pa, 22 yrs of age, 5 ft & 1/4 inches high, short black
  hair, by trade a taylor. John STEELE, Lieut, 3d U.S. Reg.
Patrick DAVIDSON, Middleton twp, Cumberland co, has taken up 4 stray milk
  cows.
Sale at the late dwelling house of John WILLS, decd, now John LAUGHLIN,
  Hopewell twp, Cumberland co, horses, cows, hogs, farming utensils, wheat
  and rye by the bushel, furniture, and other. John M'KEE, John CAUGHLIN,
  admrs.

Kline's Carlisle Weekly Gazette

95. Nov 8 1797
Married 31st ult in Lisburn by Rev Samuel WAUGH, James LIGGET, of Newbury twp, York co, to Miss Isabella HANNAH, of Lisburn, Allen twp.
--- at Pittsburgh, Jacob KELLER, saddler, to Mrs. M'COUMB.
Partnership of James DUNCAN, and Co. dissolved.
Henry WUIGLEY, Allen twp, Cumberland co, offers reward for misssing mare.
William M'MULLIN continues his fulling business at Gilson CRAIGHEAD's mill.

96. Nov 15 1797
Died 12th inst in her 75th yr, Jannet M'KEEHAN, wife of Alexander M'KEEHAN, of this Borough, after a painful and lingering illness; remains interred at the old burying ground.
Married at Lancaster, Sat evedning 4th inst, William HAMILTON, printer, to Miss Juliana HUBLEY, dau of John HUBLEY, Esq. all of Lancaster.
Sale of corner house in Shippensburgh; has been occupied as a tavern; enquire of James CESSNA in said town, subscriber.
William WALKER, Newton twp, Cumberland co, has taken up a stray steer.

97. Nov 22 1797
On the 14th inst, arrived at the Barracks, at this place, a company of artillery under the command of Lieut. MARSEHALD(?) - on Thurs the whole of the troops about 100 in number marched from the barracks under the command of Lieut. John STEELE for Pittsburgh, from whence it is expected they will descende the Ohio, for Natchez.
Died 16th inst, in her 78th yr, Mrs. Rebecca ARMSTRONG, relict of the late General John ARMSTRONG, of this borough, having received several paralytic shocks by which her faculty of speech and powers of mind were muchaffected.
Died 15th inst in her 36th yr, Mrs. Eleanor M'CURDY, wife of John M'CURDY of this Borough, labouring for 3 yrs under a lingering disease and for 3 weeks previous to her death, her sufferings were great.
Died 15th inst, Philip PENDERGRASS, in his 72d yr, of this Borough.
Sale of plantation whereon he now lives, 116 a. William CULBERTSON.
A mare was left at the house of Valentine GAMBER, Tyrone twp, Cumberland co, 10 miles from Sterrett's Gap, supposedly the property of John GRAFF of Lancaster co.
Isaac WILLIAMS, lately from Phila, carries on the boot and shoe-making business next door to Jeremiah MILLER's in this town.

98. Nov 29 1797
Plantation to be sold, 260 a., in Middleton twp, 4 miles from Carlisle - Daniel WONDERLICH, Benjamin CRAIN, Martin KITCH, guardians.

99. Dec 6 1797
George KLINE, Editor, requests payment of all debts by 1 Jan next, having been unfortunate by becoming one of the bail for James WALLACE, when he was elected sheriff for this co and now obliged to pay sums of money, owing to said Wallace's neglect in doing his duty; also disappointed in receiving a sum of money from Wendel MICHAEL on account of a house and lot he purchased.
Committed to jail, negro fellow who calls himself JOE, alias Richard MARSHALL, charged with being the property of Mr. BUCKWORTH of Hobbs Hole, Va.

Kline's Carlisle Weekly Gazette

100. Dec 13 1797
Died at Yorktown, Pa, Mon 4th inst, James SHORT, merchant, aged 42 yrs.
John HUGHES, Office of Inspection, calls on all distillers in Cumberland co to pay their excise.

101. Dec 20 1797
A horse, unfit to travel, was left at the subscriber, Thomas MARTIN, Shippensburgh.
House to be sold, occupied by the subscriber in High St - Isaiah BLAIR.
Whereas the subscriber, being under duresse, did sign a note unto a certain Solomon LIGHTCAP, for 100 dollars, payable in 3 months, without receiving any valuable consideration therefor, she doth therefore forewarn persons not to take assignment thereof - Hannah GILBREATH, Hopewell twp.

102. Dec 27 1797
My wife Agness CAMPBELL, having for some time experienced the manifold evils of a married state, the some time past left me to mediate on the blessings of a single life, and as I am a sorrowful witness of her negligence in fulfilling her contracts, I am induced to caution all persons not to trust her on her own account; and actuated by a principle of safety to myself, I forbid any person to trust her on mine, as I will not pay and debt she may contract after this date. David CAMPBELL, Rye twp.

103. Jan 3 1798
Special meeting of the Fire Company of Carlisle - John MONTGOMERY, Pres.
John BRATTEN claims the house offered for sale previously by the sheriff as the property of Christian HOUSENOT is no long the property of Housenot but that of himself.
William GILLESPIE claims absolute legal title in the land formerly claimed by Peter SIPE, Frankford twp, Cumberland co.
Plnatation for sale, 300 a., in Cumberland co, Dickinson twp - John HARPER.

104. Jan 10 1798
James FLETCHER and Co. is commencing the wholesale and retail business of dry goods and groceries in the store lately occupied by Jacob CREVER, next door to Mr. LAUFFMAN's tavern. Any commands in the above business will be received by John RUSSELL at Roxbury, Robert LUSK, Newville, and James FLETCHER, No. 25. near Bowley's wharf, Baltimore. A young man of good conexion will be taken as a clerk, or an apprentice, in the store at Baltimore.
Edward BRATTEN who recently resided in Myer's town, Dauphin co, is hereby informed that his brother James BRATTEN, has lately arrived from Ireland, having letters and other matters of importance to communicate to him. Edward Bratten can see his brother by applying to John REILY, esq. Atty at Law in Myer's town, or William WRAY, esq. in Harrisburgh.
The partnership of George STURM and William DREWISH will dissolve. The store will be removed to the house now occupied by Wendel MICHAEL next door but one to Mr. FOSTER's tavern, where said George Sturm will carry on the baking business.
Stophel RICHWINE, 1 mile from Carlisle, has taken up a stray mare which came to his plantation in Middleton twp, Cumberland co.
Three negroes to be sold - William KILGORE, Newton twp, at Greensprings.

Kline's Carlisle Weekly Gazette

John BLACK, Racoon valley, Juniata twp, has taken up a stray bull.

105. Jan 17 1798
Has removed from the house of James DAVIS, to the house lately occupied by Jonathan WALLACE, and next door to Edward MAGAURAN in York st, where she has for sale bonnets, silks, hats, cloaks, caps, turbans, muslin shauls, &c. ["Her" name is not given.]
House and lot for sale, now occupied by the subsriber, Samuel CROWEL, Newville.
Whereas Samuel NICHOLSON of Green twp, Mifflin co, obtained 5 bonds of the subscriber, as consideration for a tract in Milford twp, Mifflin co, and said Nicholson not having complied with his contract, and a claim of title is made to said land by a certain Benjamin DAVIS, persons are cautioned not to take assignment on said bonds. Andrew KUHN, Milford twp.
Persons indebted to firm of LONGWELL & WHITLEY, are desired to settle their accounts.
John RINEHART, Tyrone twp, Cumberland co, has taken up a stray ewe and a wether.
House to be let on the alley, now occupied by Mrs. PATTEN - John HUGHES.
Silver watch found on road from Carlisle to William MOORE's Mill. Charles WILLIAMS

106. Jan 24 1798
Died 5th Jan 1798, in her 25th yr, Miss Jane CHAMBERS, dau of Robert CHAMBERS; interred in the burying ground, at Carlisle.
Earthquake felt in Lancaster on Thurs 11th inst.
Tanyard sold on north end of Bedford st, Carlisle - Apply to Joseph WALLACE in Shearman's Valley, George KLINE, or John CREIGH, the latter in Carlisle.
House and lot for sale, occuped by subscriber, in Carlisle, High St. - Lemuel GUSTINE.
300 a. for sale 1 1/2 miles from Carlisle. James BLAINE, Carlisle.
House of rent opp Mr. FOSTER's and in possession of John ISETT; also house in possession of John UNDERWOOD, merchant; apply to James GIVIN, or subscriber, William MOORE.
Sale of house on corner of public square in York st, now occupied by David WATTS, this being the house in which the late colonel MAGAW resided, to be sold as part of his estate - Samuel LAIRD, and James HAMILTON, Carlisle, exrs of Robert MAGAW.
House to be leased in Hanover St, next door to John WRAY; apply to William BARTON, Esq. in Phila or the subscriber, George LOGUE.

107. Jan 31 1798
James MOORE [scratched through to read John MOORE] to rent large and covenient house and tenement, now occupied by William ROBINS [?] and Benjamin SMITH, for a store and tavern, 7 1/2 miles from Carlisle.
Dwelling house to be sold in Springfield, opp McCRACKEN's mill, at the head of Bigspring - John WALKER, Springfield.
Brick house in the borough of Carlisle for sale, between Dr. STINNECK's and Dr. FRANK's and opposite Dr. ADAMS - John ELLIOTT.

Kline's Carlisle Weekly Gazette

108. Feb 7 1798
To be sold at the dwelling house of the subscriber in Middleton twp, grain in the ground, horses, waggon geers, ploughs, cows, hogs, farming utensils. James CRAIGHEAD.
For sale - new road wagon and 4 horses, with geers, blankets, handscrew, plow irons, cows, sheep, feather beds, &c. Archibald RAMSEY.
Philip SNYDER wishes to contract for the building of a bridge over the Conodoguinet Creek.

109. Feb 14 1798
Died Sun 4th inst, in his 62d(?) yr, William DENNY, of this borough, after a few weeks extreme illness, which had been preceded by great infirmity for many yrs.
Samuel A. M'GOSKRY requests payment of debts. Carlisle.
Courts of Enquire of Damages and Extending of Lands will meet at the dwelling house of William HEIGLE, Carlisle.
George M'KEEHAN, Westpennsborough twp, Cumberland co, has taken up a stray heifer.
Hugh MOFFIT, Mifflin twp, Cumberland co, has taken up a stray horse.

110. Feb 28 1798
Members of the Carlisle Library Company to meet - William THOMSON, Librarian.
Mr. BACONAIS informs the ladies and gentlemen of Carlisle, that his second practising night will be on Fri at Mr. WALLACE's. Tickets may be had at Thomas FOSTER's.
Dwelling house of one of the subscriber's in Newville to be sold - John BRATTEN, Isaac LEFEVER.
Several larg tracts for sale - apply to James DAVIS, Carlisle.

111. Mar 7 1798
Died Mon morning 26th Feb, in his 59th yr, on his plantation in Eastpennsbro' twp, John CAROTHERS, esq., one of the justices of the peace of this co; his remains interred in the buryihng place at Silver Spring Meeting house.
Meeting held at Andrew CULBERTSON's to consider building an English Schoolhouse: David MAHON, Esq., Chairman, Capt. Matthew SCOTT, sec'y.
Commissioners elected: William BARR, William BROOKENS, Samuel M'CLURE and Francis CAMPBELL.
Reward offered of two eleven penny bits for apprentice lad named John DUNLAP, to the tanning business, having almost one whole week to stay.
Persons indebted to estate of Gabriel GLENN, decd, are requests to pay their debts. Benjamin M'KEEHAN, Jane GLEN, Big Spring, exrs.
Lot of ground to be sold at the east end of High st, boroughof Carlisle. Alexander BLAINE.
Plantation for rent, 110 a., adj James LAIRD in Frankford twp, Cumberland co. Wendel MICHAEL, Carlisle.
Whereas my wife Jean hath absconded from my bed and board, without any just reaon I do therefore discharge all persons from crediting her on my account. Daniel WELCH.

Kline's Carlisle Weekly Gazette

112. Mar 14 1798
Sheriff's sales: (1) tract, 203 a., Westpennsborough twp, Cumberland co, bounded on the south by lands of David RASTON, property of Joseph CRAWFORD; (2) two lots with two small houses, on south side of Louther st, Carlisle, of James STEWART, decd.
Mrs. THOMSON intending to give up business will sell stock of goods, Carlisle.
As I propose leaving this place in a short time, person indebted to me are requested to make payment. William BELL, Shippensburg.
Thomas BURCHFEILD, Carlisle, offers reward for apprentice boy named Hugh M'NEAL, about 18 yrs of age, red complexion with a down look.
James BROWN, living in Newton twp, offers reward for boy of 16 yrs, 5 ft 4 inches, of a slim make, dark complexion, has hair cued [name not given].
Partnership of George KLINE and William DUCKET, in the manufacture of paper, is dissolved; paper manufactory will be carried on in Southampton twp, Cumberland co, 16 miles from Carlisle by George KLINE.
Died Fri last in this town, John WALLACE; remains interred into the burying ground adj this town.

113. Mar 21 1798
Sheriff's sales: (1) tract, 218 a., bounded by land of David BOAL, taken at the suit of Edward SHOEMAKER, surviving, Josiah TWAMLY, as the property of James TERREY; (2) tract, 200 a. with house and stone chimney erected in Rye twp, bounded by lands of Matthew HENDERSON, widow HOGE and Joseph KIRKPATRICK, taken at the suit of William WALLACE, assignee of James M'CALLY, property of John LAWSHE; (3)
Married in city of Phila, 15th inst, by Rev Dr. ROGERS, George WILSON, Esq. of Mifflin co, member of the senate of Pa, to Miss Isabella WHITE, of that city.
Whereas the subscriber went in a judgment bond for the use of John WRAY to James WALLACE, Sheriff, to keep him and his securities from sustaining any loss then entered on the docket against said John Wray, I request said bond to be brought forward - Robert HUSTON.

114. Mar 28 1798
A concert for the benefit of Mr. SHULTZ.
Samuel CRISWELL, Carlisle, offers reward for apprentice Philip SMITH, 16 yrs old, fair complexion, stout made, left-handed, looks across his nose with his left eye, very apt to swear; took with him an old coating coat, old blue overalls trimmed with red, old hat he stole.
The horse figure will cover mares this season at the stable of William EAKINS, Walnut bottom road - Michael BEYERLY.
Sale of plantation, 400 a. 1 mile from Lewistown, Derry twp, Mifflin co, in the tenure of Henry LAUGHBAUGH; one of 657 a. in Lack twp, said co, in tenure of Matthew HUNTER; one of 176 a. in Shirley twp, Huntingdon co, in tenure of Henry HOUGHINBERGER, and others - John GLEN, Carlisle.

115. Apr 11 1798
Died Sun last, George MORROW, student in the Dickinson College, from state of North Carolina. About two weeks ago he was seized with the small pox, which proved his death.

Kline's Carlisle Weekly Gazette

Married Tues 3d inst by Dr. DAVIDSON, James NEELY, of York co, to Miss Peggy M'BETH of Cumberland.
Gunsmith business - Henry LECHLER, has removed his shop from Lancaster into this house in York st, formerly occupied by George HOOVER and opposite John HUNTER's tavern; continues to make rifles and shot guns.
Plantation to be sold on which the subscriber now resides, 232 a., Frankford twp, Cumberland co, on Conodoguninet Creek, about 1 mile from Snyder's merchant mill and about same from merchant mill of Jacob ALTER. William GALBREATH.
George STURM has moved his store to Hanover st, next door to Wendel MICHAEL's store where he has for sale a general assortment of groceries, dry goods and hard ware.
Moses BULLOCK, wheelwright and windsor chairmaker continues his busines in all its various branches in Louther st, Carlisle. Chairs of his making may be had of Robert M'CAN in Newville.
Whereas the subscriber having passed a bond to George FRIDLEY bo the payment of 155 pounds, which said bond I forewarn persons from taking assignment. Baltzar DITLER, Allen twp, Cumberland co.
James BROWN, Bigspring, offers reward for apprentice boy, William MEEK, 16 yrs of age, 5 ft 6 inches, dark complexion, fond of company; had on and took with him a new fur hat of a cinnamon or brown colour, a sailor's jacket and overalls of plain nankeen partly new, a muff coloured coat of broadcloath, one shirt, one pair of homespun cotton trowsers stripped blue and white, one pair of grey yarn stockings, one pair of coarse leather shoes, new bandana handkerchief.
Hamilton HAZLETON, Whitesmith, makes all kinds of trepanning instruments, tooth drawers, Doctor's instruments, lock making, spindles and handles for spinning wheels, in town of Milford, on the Walnut Bottom road, 6 miles from Shippensburgh.
If Agness ROBINSON who serves part of her time to big John GLEN, on Yellow breeches, be living, and will send an account of her residence to John M'DANNELL, on Connedoguinnet creek, near Carlisle, it will very much oblige her disconsolate mother, who lives there, and cannot hear any thing of her. She wishes to know whether William ROBINSON who liv'd with Elizabeth WILEY, or her son Samuel in Paxton, near Harrisburgh, be living. Agness ROBINSON.
All persons indebted to the subscribers are requested to make payment. James MOOR, Benmamin SMITH.

116. Apr 18 1798
John WRAY candidate for sheriff.
To be sold at the house of Jacob CART, decd, 5 horses, 1 road wagon, a light wagon, with variety of geers, plows, harrows and other. Jacob CART, Jacob CREVER, exrs.

117. Apr 25 1798
Died Sun last after a short illness, Philip BAKER, of Middleton twp; his remains were buried in the German burying ground in this town.
Samuel MARTIN, 14 miles from Hagers town, offers reward for apprentice boy to the blacksmith business, John STORY, about 5 ft 6 inches, fair smooth faced, about 18 yrs of age, has mark on the fore part of his head under his hair.

Kline's Carlisle Weekly Gazette

118. May 2 1798
John CAMPBELL has opened a tavern in Greencastle, Pa, in the house lately occupied by Robert M'CULLAGH, at the sign of The Franklin Head.
The horse, Sporter, will be kept for mares this season, at the stable of Robert PEEBLES, at the head of Big-spring. Thomas KENNEDY, Jun.
Died Sun evening last, Robert GIBSON, old inhabitant of this co.
Samuel QUIGLEY, Shippensburgh, has taken up a stray mare.
To be sold at the late dwelling house of Philip BAKER, decd, 3 miles from Carlisle, horses, colts, milch cows, a wind mill and other - John BAKER, and Peter FISHBURN, admrs. Plantation of decd to be rented, 300 a..
To be sold - on the premises late of Robert GIBSON, decd, old waggon, cart, horses, cows, hogs, furniture, farming utensils - Ross MITCHELL, William ALEXANDER, Robert MILLER, exrs.

119. May 9 1798
Robert GRAYSON, John CAROTHERS and Jonathan WALLACE, candidates for sheriff.
Alexander M'BETH has erected a machine for the purpose of making hoisting screws for raising millstones and a wheel for turning mill spindles and can make all kinds of mill irons, at his farm on Big-spring, Cumberland co.
Samuel CRISWELL continues to make gun locks, gun barrels and stocks.

120. May 16 1798
Sale by order of Orphan's Court of tract of land in Middleton twp, Cumberland co, 166 a., late the property of Henry M'KINLEY, decd; attendance will be given by John STEEL, admr of decd.

121. May 23 1798
Died at his seat in Shippensburgh, Sun last, about half after ten in the morning, Capt. Mathew SCOTT, parent and husband, long a res of this little town; served in the rev, taken prisoner in the battle of Long Island, where he endured unparalleled hardhips, but when exchanged, he continued a onsiderable time in the service until sickness and other hardships obliged him to resign. His remains were interred in the public burying ground.
Public sale at the late dwelling house of William CULBERTSON, decd, Eastpennsborough twp, horses, milch cows, wheat, rye, 8-day clock, furniture - Thomas URIE, Andrew PARKER, exrs.
Whereas the subscriber having passed bonds unto James LAMB for a certain tract in Tyrone twp, I do hereby forwarn persons from taking assignment of said bonds. Maximilian HAINES, Tyrone.
Lot for sale in Allen twp, Cumberland co, 1 a. - Joseph ELLIOT.

122. Jun 6 1798
Died Sat 2d inst, Mrs. FLEMMING, wife of James FLEMMING, in the vicinity of this Borough.
Died last Sunday evening in her 58th yr, after an illness of some months, Mrs. Mary CAROTHERS, widow of John CAROTHERFS Esq., late of Eastpennsborough twp; her remains interred in the Silver Spring burying ground.

123. Jun 13 1798
Committed to the jail of this co on Mon last, Sarah CLARK, on suspicion of being the person who has poisoned the family of John CAROTHERS, Esq. in the

Kline's Carlisle Weekly Gazette

lower settlement of which Mr. Carothers and his wife, have died, and several of the family are now very ill.
Patrick M'FARLIN, sign of the Swan, now occupies the tavern lately kept by Mr. GEYER, in Dover, at the great road leading from York to Carlisle, 7 miles from York, where he has a general assortment of the best liquors, good beds, stables, an attentive hostler, &c.
Catharine FISHBACH, Borough of Carlisle, offers reward for missing cow.
Notice to --- M'CLACKEN, son to Patrick M'CLACKEN, a peddlar who traded on the Eastern of Maryland and Virginia, which said Patrick M'Clacken died in the Dec last, and being possessed of something which may prove an advantage to his son, he is requested to make application to William DUFFEY, Drawbridge, Phila.
Whereas my son Philip ASPEN of York co, aged 24 yrs, had the epilepsy or falling sickness, applied to Dr. John ADAMS in Carlisle who cured him. witnesses: James BAIRD, Jacob KEIGLEY.
Whereas I, John USHEA, Carlisle, 27 yrs old, had the falling sickness daily, disturbed with the disease for upwards of 23 yrs, Dr. John ADAMS, in Carlisle, [cured him].
Andrew HOLMES, Middleton twp, has taken up a stray horse.
Peter JONES, Newbury twp, York co, has taken up a stray mare.

124. Jun 20 1798
Robert WRIGHT carries on skin dressing, in oil, brains and allum and can supply breeches, panteloons, slips, sword belts, gloves, parchment for writing, carpenter and masons aprons, &c.
The Carlisle, York and Baltimore Line of Stages. A stage starts from the house of Thomas FOSTER, every Tues at 10 o'clock, under the direction of Matthias SLOUGH, and arrives in York, at the house of Philip GOSSLER, at 7 o'clock, Wed morning; another stage starts from there, at 8 o'clock, the same morning under the direction of James LONG, taking its route through hanover, Reisterstown and arrives in Baltimore, on Thurs at 12 o'clock, at the house of John SEARS; starts Fri at 9 o'clock and arrives in York Sat at 2 o'clock. To that passengers can proceed to Carlisle on Sunday. Matthias Slough and James Long, York.
Hugh M'ALISTER, Shearman's Valley, candidate for sheriff.

125. Jun 27 1798
At a Court of Oyer and Terminer which commenced at Harrisburgh for the county of Dauphin on 11th inst, Charles M'MANUS, John HAUER, Patrick DONAGAN and Francis COX, were brought to trial for the murder of Francis SHITZ, at Heidleberg twp, in said co on night of 28 Dec last, M'Manus a principal, the res as accessaries before the fact. M'Manus and Hauer sentenced to death, the others were acquitted. [Shitz was the brother-in-law to Hauer - see July 18 issue]
Robert KENNY, Middleton twp, has taken up a stray mare and colt.
John GIVEN, determined to return to his native country in a short time, requests persons to settle their accounts.
John BROWN, West Pennsborough twp, Cumberland co, had taken up a stray mare.

Kline's Carlisle Weekly Gazette

126. Jul 4 1798
Yesterday was apprehended on a warrant and brought before William LEVIS and James M'CORMICK, Esqrs., James BELL, of Stoney Ridge for Treasonable Expressions.
Now in the Press: "A correct Account of the Trials of Charles M'MANUS, John HAUER, Elizabeth HAUER, Patrick DONAGAN, Francis COX, and others, at Harrrisburgh..."
William SANDERSON, Carlisle, gives notice to his creditors that he has petitioned for relief from debts.
Sale of plantation in Westmoreland co, Fairfield twp, 400 a.; apply to Major Henry HICE, in Ligonier valley. Alexander BARR.

127. Jul 11 1798
New Store - William DREWISH, late a partner of George STURM, has commenced business in the house of John HOLMES, opposite to James DUNCAN, in High St, where he has laid in a fresh and general assortment of Dry Goods and Groceries.
Andrew STONES, Carlisle to petition for relief from debts.
John STOUFFER, Paradise twp, 6 miles from borough of York, offers reward for stolen horse.
4 OF JULY CELEBRATIONS -
Carlisle - Companies of infantry and cavalry paraded to the public square, marched to the Presby Church, then to farm of Andrew HOLMES for dinner and drink.
Shippensburg - Dr M'KNIGHT, Esq. Pres. of the day, Dr. John SIMPSON, Vice Pres., John SHIPPEN, Esq., sec'y; Managers: Joseph KNOX, Dr. John RIPPEY, Hugh SMYTH, Wm. BARR.
Robert GRAYSON, goaler, Carlisle, offers reward for Ludwick STRICKLER who escaped over the Prison Yard wall, committed on suspicion for horse stealing, of German extraction, 5 ft 10 inches, dark complexion, speak broken English.
William N. GALBREATH, Carlisle, has petitioned for relief from debt.
William SANDERSON has petition for relief from debt.

128. Jul 18 1798
To be sold at the dwelling of the subscriber, Carlisle, a two-story house, also drugs and medicines - Charles F. STINNECKE, who intends to remove to Baltimore.
John BIEGLEY (his mark) to petition for relief from debts.
Charles DOWNEY has applied for relief from debts.
William BROWN gives notice that his wife, Nancy BROWN, has left his bed and board, and hereby forwarns persons from giving her credit on his account.
James NOBLE has petitioned for relief from debts.

129. Jul 25 1798
Whereas a man who calls himself George Washington CUSTIS, became indebted to the subscriber and left certain books as a pledge, these books will now be sold - Nathaniel WEAKLEY.
The Cumberland County Troop of Light Horse to parade at the Court House, Carlisle - Sam. A. M'COSKRY, Captain.
Sheriff's sales: (1) tract in Allen twp, Cumberland co, 150 a., fulling mill and saw mill thereon, bounded on the North by lands of John BRENIZER,

Kline's Carlisle Weekly Gazette

property of John ANDERSON; (2) tract in Middleton twp, 1 mile from Carlisle, 150 a., bounded by land of William LYON, Esq., James HAMILTON, property of John GLENN; (3) tract in Dickinson twp, Cumberland co, 200 a., bounded by land of James PATTERSON, Thomas BUCHANAN, Joseph DUNCAN, property of Joseph BROWN; (4) tract, 100 a. with square long house, bounded by land of James ARMSTRONG, property of Peter SIPES; tract, 150 a., in Middleton twp, 2 miles from Carlisle, bounded on south by land of Robert BLAINE, north by lands of Mrs. KELLEY, property of John KINKEAD; (5) tract in Rye twp, 100 a., of John SMILEY, property of Thomas SMILEY; (6) two plantations in Dickinson twp, Cumberland co, one of 103 a. bounded south by lands of Michael EGE, on west by John EWING, on east by William EWING; also tract 25 a., bounded on east by land of John HARPER, south by Michael EGE, west by William EWING, property of William M'FARLAND; (7) tract of 224 a. adj Joseph MITCHELL in Hamilton twp, formerly Cumberland, now Franklikn co, with two improvements, one about 25-30 a. clear with small cabbin, now in possession of John BUITZFIELD, the other of 25 a. with weaver's shop and small cabbin, now in the possession of --- LITTLE, property of Charles M'CORMICK; (8) two houses, Carlisle, adj lot of Teeterech UHLER, and on the south a lot of Wendel MICHAEL, now in the possession of George WISE, proerty of George FRESHER; (9) lot with two house on east side of Hanover st, bounded by lot of Joseph YOUNG, property of Samuel GREER.
Thomas CRAIGHEAD, sen., Middleton twp, Cumberland co, has taken up a stray horse.
John ATCHISON offers reward for horse missing from plantation of John MOORE.
Circus at goal yard, Carlisle. Mr. SULLY and co.

130. Aug 1 1798
Sale of riding charir, and harness, pair of roan horses, well broke to a carriage, billiard table, at John HUNTER's Tavern - George PATTISON, Auctioneer, Carlisle.
William BELL has received and is opening for sale at his store in Shippensburgh, a neat assortment of Goods.

131. Aug 8 1798
Chambersburgh - Died Sat last, Mrs. RIDDLE, consort of John RIDDLE, esq. of this place.
Henry M'CONNEL, Greenwood twp, Mifflin co, offers reward for servant boy, named Thomas BURNS, 16 yrs of age, 5 ft 3-4 inches, of a sandy complexion.
Martin GEORGE, Franfort twp, Cumberland oc, has taken up a stray steer.
Will be sold - possessary right of an out lot of the state of Robert GIBSON, late of Middleton twp, decd, adj lots of Dr. M'COSKRY and Adam JOHNSON, 13 a. - Ross MITCHELL, William ALEXANDER, Robert MILLER, exrs.

132. Aug 15 1798
Died Fri night last, Samuel GRAY, merchant of this town; remains were interred in the burying ground adj this town.
Robert SEMPLE, Dickinson twp, has taken up a stray horse.
Stolen from the house of James CRAIGHEAD, Carlisle, a half worn saddle, a great coat of double milled Drab, triangular muslin neckcloth, pair of cotton stockings, white pocket handerchief with red edging, marked B.A. and bead plane 1/2 inch wide, stamped B.A. - Benjamin ANDERSON, Lisburn.

Kline's Carlisle Weekly Gazette

133. Aug 22 1798
Died 18th inst, in his 72d yr, William FLEMMING.
Meeting of the Shippensburg & Newville Troop of Horse at Samuel CROWELL's tavern, Jeremiah M'KIBBEN, Esq in the Chair, Dr. David JAMESON, Jun. Sec'y. Resolutions adopted: Committee appointed to receive applications at Newville and vicinity: John BRATTEN, P. BECK, John FOX, W. BELL, J. WOODBURN, D. OVER, J. ROBERTS, and J. SHOWALTER. That coat, the cap and equipments of John SHIPPEN, Esq, be adopted as the uniform and equipments of the Troop. - [and other resolutions]
Chambersburg - Died Fri evening last, after a long and severe indisposition, Mrs. Elizabeth RIDDLE, consort of Hon. James RIDDLE, Esq.
Carlisle Blues - Enrollment is open to join the Light Infantry Company attached to the Second Battalion in the Fourth Regiment, Cumberland Co Militia.
Jacob WAGGONER, Jun. candidate for sheriff.
Anthony ASHER, Carlisle Jail, to petition for relief from debts.
Peter NUGENT has petitioned for relief from debts.
Jacob HOOVER, 8 miles from Lancaster, Maddick twp, Lancaster co, offers reward for apprentice boy, named Jacob KESSLOR, 14-15 yrs old, short red hair, had on a low crowned wool hat partly new, pair of white linen trousers, red jacket, new shoes.
Two-story stone house for sale on Hanover st, Carlisle; apply to George PATTISON, or Henry M'KINLEY.

134. Aug 29 1798
Charles M'MANUS carries on the distilling business in borough of Carlisle.
The volunteers composing the Shippensburgh Light Infantry Company to parade at the Upper Market House - Thomas MARTIN, Captain, Shippensburgh.
3d Company of militia of the first Regiment of Cumberland Brigade, to meet at the Upper Market House in Shippensburg - Andrew CULBERTSON, Capt.
Members of the 5th Company, 1st Regt, Cumberland Brigage to meet - Nicholas KREHL, Capt.
John DAVIDSON, Jun., Newville, offers reward for John SHAW, apprentice to the tanning business, John Shaw, about 19 yrs of age, 5 ft 10 inches, stout made, down look.
Thomas SMILEY, Carlisle, has petitioned for relief from debts.

135. Sep 5 1798
The co-partnership of James SMITH, and Co. is dissolved. Persons indebted to make payments to James W. SLOAN - John SMITH, James SMITH, Aaron SMITH, James W. SLOAN, Baltimore.
Daniel CAMRON offers reward for horse missing from pasture of James CALWELL, near Shippensburgh; deliver to Daniel CAMRON or to Thomas SMILEY, Tavern keeper in Carlisle.
Whereas I have two notes to Joseph DIERMENT(?), let no person take an assignment thereon, as I am determined not to pay the same, having not yet received valuable consideration for them. Patrick DILLON (his mark)

136. Sep 12 1798
Sale of 18 draught horses, with their geers, and other of James HAMILTON, decd - Abraham HERR, Melcher MILLER, Jeremiah MILLER, Carlisle, admrs.
Alexander BLAINE has taken up 8 stray sheep.

Kline's Carlisle Weekly Gazette

137. Sep 19 1798
Fire consumed two barns and a large quantity of grain of Richard WOOD, on Yellow Breeches creek, lost estimated at 1400 pounds. This accident we hear was owing to a young man who fired at a pidgeon on the roof of one of the barns.
Wendel MICHAEL who intends to remove from this place to Baltimore to sell three houses and lots in Carlisle, one occupied by George STURM.
John JOHNSTON, offers reward for horse missing from pasture of Mr. BRIGGS, tavern keeper, at the Silver Springs; deliver to John GLEN, Carlisle, or the subscriber in Lack twp, Tuskarora valley.

138. Sep 26 1798
Sherriff's sales: (1) 300 a. in Juniata twp, Cumberland co, bound by lands of John KEAN, property of Griffith JONES; (2) plantation in Rye twp, 100 a., bounded by lands of John SMILEY, property of Thomas SMILEY; (3) house on north side of Pomret st, bounded by lots of Peter BARTHOLOMAY and Thomas DUNCAN, property of John PAULY.
Sale of tract, 240 a. on Yellow Breeches creek, Allen twp, Cumberland co, adj lands with William PARK, John --- - Graham ANDERSON.
Whereas the subscribers passed three notes to James M'CLINTOCK, and whereas the said M'Clintock hath not complied with his contract, we herby forwarn persons from taking assignment - George YEATS, Thomas YEATS, Shippensburgh.

139. Oct 3 1798
Married on Thurs at Chambersburgh by Rev James LANG, Robert HARPER, Printer of the Franklin Repository, to Miss Priscilla DOUGHERTY, both of that place.
Degrees of Bachelor of Arts conferred on the following at Dickinson College: James ADAIR, Samuel AGNEW, George HAYS, Amos A. M'GINLEY, Alexander MENTEITH, Robert PROUDFIT, Henry WILSON and John WAUGH of York County - William MITCHELL, Andrew BVCHANAN and Levi BULL, of Chester co; James GUTHRIE, William RAINEY and John WRIGHT of Westmoreland co; John B. ALEXANDER, Joseph BREADY, John COOPER, James GREASON, James GUSTINE, Thomson HOLMES and Robert HUSTON of Cumberland Co, all of this state; Joshua KNIGHT of Connecticut; Thomas STOCKTON, of Delaware and William DOWNEY of Maryland. The Degree of Master of Arts was conferred on David HAYS and James BROTHERTON of Franklin Co; Isaac WAYNE of Chester co, Pa; and George REID of South Carolina.
William M'FARLAND to petition for relief from debts.
Matthew ADAMS, Shippensburgh, offers reward for mare missing from commons of Shippensburgh.

140. Oct 10 1798
To be sold at the dwelling house of the subscriber in Frankfort twp, 3 miles from Carlisle, horses, milch cows, beef and young cattle, oxen, and other - John M'DANNELL.
Robert BARR, Harrisburgh, offers reward for mare missing from pasture of Edward MORTON, on the Carlisle road 3 miles from Harris's ferry.
Roger MULHOLLAN has petitioned for relief from debts.
Andrew HERWICK, Carlisle Jail, has petitioned for relief from debts.
Sale of lands for which taxes due - John JORDAN, Joseph SHROM, Commisssioners.

Kline's Carlisle Weekly Gazette

Samuel DUNCAN offers reward for cows missing from commons of Borough of Carlisle.
A young mare was left with me by a man who calls himself Jacob BECKSON. The mare is said to belong to a certain Philip GLONINGER, 5 miles from Chambersburgh. The owner is requested to prove and take his property. John CAPP, Harrisburgh.
William MAXWELL, Cumberland co, Hopewell twp, on the Walnut Bottom road, has taken up a stray horse.
John WONDERLICH, 1 miles from carlisle, offers reward for stolen mare.

141. Oct 17 1798
Henry GOEBEL has opened a general assortment of groceries in the house formerly owned by John STEELE, Esq., opposite Mr. FOSTER's tavern.
James LOGAN, Miller, living with Philip STRUMBAUCH, Southampton twp, Franklin co, offers reward for Henry FAUGHT, by trade, a miller and cooper, who absconded from the service of Philip Strumbauch and stole several articles of the subscriber [clothing, silver watch, all listed]
James CAROTHERFS West Pennsburgh twp, has taken up 2 stray colts.
Died at Yorktown Tues 2d inst, after a long and painful illness, Mrs. Catharine HARTLEY, consort of the Hon. Thomas HARTLEY, Esq., member of Congress.

142. Oct 24 1798
Married 18th inst by Rev Dr. DAVIDSON, Rev Thomas HOGE, of Northumberland, to Miss Betsey HOLMES, of this town.
Caution - whereas by a decree of the Orphan's Court held at Chambersburgh, for the county of Franklin, the letters of administration of the estate of William CONNEL, decd, granted to Mary CONNEL, stand repealed, and thereof is committed to the subscriber, innkeeper of Shippensburg and whereas said Mary withholds sundry notes of said estate, persons are hereby cautioned to guard against fraud or impoistion by taking any assignment of said notes. Robert PORTER, admr.

143. Nov 14 1798
Married Tues last (13th inst) by Rev Dr. DAVIDSON, David HARRIS, merchant of the town of York, to Miss Sally MONTGOMERY, dau of John MONTGOMERY Esq. of this Borough.
Last week a barn with a quantity of grain was burnt, property of James FLEMING, 2 miles from this town.
Dr. John CREIGH lives next door to Charles COOPER in Carlisle, where he has medicine for sale, and offers his services as a physician.
To be rented, plantation in Middleton twp, 4 miles from Carlisle, 230 a. - Hugh BODEN, George LOGUE, exrs of Wm. REED.
Sheriff's sale of tract in Greenwood twp, Cumberland co, on Susquehana river, adj claim of Marcus HULINGS, property of Benjamin DUNCAN. John CAROTHERS, sheriff.
James HALL has petitioned for relief from debts.
David KESLER, Yellow Breeches, offers reward for missing mare.
James GEDDES, Frankford twp, Cumberland co, has taken up a stray bull.
The partnership of HANNA and MARTIN, Boot and Shoe maker, of the borough of Carlisle, is dissolved - James MARTIN.
Samuel BRYSON, Mifflin twp, Cumberland co, offers reward for stolen horse.

Kline's Carlisle Weekly Gazette

Peter PATTAW, potter, Carlisle, offers reward for boy named Matthew YOUNG (to learn the potting business), about 17 yrs old, 5 ft 4-5 inches high.

144. Nov 21 1798
John DORON, Carlisle, has petition for relief from debt.
Married on 20th inst by Dr. R. DAVIDSON, Robert WRIGHT of this Borough to Miss Nancy HOLMES, dau of Thomas HOLMES of York co.
Persons having claims against Thomas BUCHANAN, late Sheriff of this co, and of the land of William M'FARLAND, should make them to Samuel POSTLETHWAITE, William LYON and James DUNCAN.
Deserted 18th Nov 1798 from the Barracks, Carlisle: James WILSON, private in the 2d Regiment of Artillery and Engineers, native of Ireland, about 5 ft 7 inches, 38(?) yrs of age, blue eyes, brown hair, light complexion. Callender IRVINE, Captain.

145. Nov 28 1798
Whereas there is some property in my custody to be contributed to the use of Gasper RHOADES, late of Cumberland co, persons making due application may have their accounts remitted as far as the aforesaid Rhodes property will admit of. Enoch LEWIS.
Town meeting of the borough of Carlisle - James M'CORMICK, C.B.
Appointed for the co of Cumberland: Principal Assessor: John ARTHUR; Asssistant Assessors: James M'CORMICK, David M'KNIGHT, Joseph M'KINNEY, James BROWN, John SHANNON, Joseph PIERCE, James LAIRD, Samuel WEAKLY, John MILLER, John M'DONALD, Andrew GALBRAITH, Patrick M'NAUGHTON, Frederick REINHART, Edward WEST and John MORRISON - Michael SMYSER, Commissioner of the 6th Division, in the District of Pa.
Andrew MOORE, Eastpennsborough twp, Cumberland co, offers reward for missing cow.
For sale - farm known as Mount Rock, on main road from Carlisle to Pittsburgh, 7 miles from Carlisle, 400-500 a. John MILLER.
For sale - farm, late the property of James OLIVER, Esq., decd, on Conodiguinet Creek, in Eastpennsborough twp; apply to John WALKER, esq. adj the premises, or the subscriber, John OLIVER, in Carlisle.
Isaac ANGNEY, now living on the Rough Spring, 3(?) miles from Carlisle, opposite to Col. CHAMBERS' on the Harrisburgh road, requests payment of debts.

146. Dec 5 1798
Married Thurs last by Rev. WAUGH in East Pennsbro., Jonathan HOGE, jun. to Miss Eleanor BRIGGS, both of East Pennsborough.
Metting of Lodge No. 56 held in Carlisle. John UNDERWOOD, Sec'y.
James BAIRD, CArlisle, has moved to High st, whre he will carry on house, sign and ornamental painting and gilding in general.
Charles DOWNEY has petitioned for relief from debt.

147. Dec 12 1798
At a meeting of Captain SHIPPEN's New Troop of Calvary, Joseph SHOWALTER was elected Cornet of said Troop.
Joseph SHOWALTER, Big-Spring, has taken up a stray horse.
John ELFRY has petition for relief from debts.

Kline's Carlisle Weekly Gazette

148. Dec 19 1798
Married 13th inst by Dr. R. DAVIDSON, Robert ELLIOT, to Miss Rebecca
  FLEMING.
Also John LYTLE to Miss Barbara LEFEVRE.
Agreeably to late will and testament of Andrew CROCKET, late of Allen twp,
  Cumberland co, decd, will te sold, a tract of patented limestone land, on
  Yellow Breeches Creek, 5 miles of Carlisle, adj Michael EGE's Iron Works -
  Elizabeth CROCKET, George LOGUE and Thomas CLARK, exrs.
William CONDRY, offers reward for horse missing from stable of James DAVIS,
  Carlisle.
Sheriff's sales: (1) 190 a. adj lands of Samuel DAVIDSON, heirs of John
  HARRIS and lands of James HARRIS, in Fermanagh twp, Mifflin co, property
  of William M'COY; (2) house and lot on corner of Louther and Bedford sts,
  Carlisle, property of Thomas M'MURRAY and William M'MURRAY; (3) house and
  lot on south side of Main st in town of Newville, bounded by lots of John
  DUNBAR, George M'KEEHAN, adj Meeting house ground, property of Ludwick
  ANDREW.

149. Dec 26 1798
Sheriff's sales of:
(1) certain property of John NICHOLSON in Rye twp, adj land of Humphrey
  WILLIAMS, James STARR, James M'FARLANE, John WILEY, 307 a.
(2) land of James RASTER in Greenwood twp, adj land of widow WALLACE and
  Matthias BLOUCHER, 150 a.
(3) land of Robert COCHRAN, in Dickinson twp, 164 a., adj lands of J.
  ARTHUR, Michael EGE.
(4) tract of James R. HOGE, 4 miles from Carlisle, 80 a.
George WEISE, Carlisle, has apprehended --- BROWN, alias Peter STEVENS, in
  whose custody was found a light bay horse, supposedly stolen and to be the
  property of either Jacob MIXSELL or Ludwick MORTER, living in Emmitsburgh,
  Md.

150. Jan 2 1799
Sheriff's sale of possessory right to out lot on southside of York road, 1/2
  mile from borough of Carlisle, bounded by property of Charles M'CLURE and
  Jacob CREVER, 37 a., taken as the property of James DAVIS at the suit of
  William TURNBULL.

151. Jan 9 1799
to be sold - tract of limestone land, 208 a., adj lands of John and William
  MILLER, Peter BLACK - Runnel BLAIR, Mount Rock.
Tavern seat to be rented, at the Sign of the Bull's Head, at the south west
  corner of Market st, in the borough of Carlisle; apply to David LINDSAY on
  the premises. John BOYLE petitions for relief from debt.
Sale of farm of James ARMSTRONG, decd, Frankford twp, Cumberland co, 10-11
  miles from Carlisle, 200 a. - Adam BRITTAIN, John BROWN, exrs, living on
  the premises.
House and lot for rent at the corner of Pitt st, Carlisle - David ROWAN.
In pursuance of an act of General Assembly, an attachment hath been granted
  against Jotham W. CURTIS, late of this co, to the value of 6 pounds.
  Frederick HARTER.

Kline's Carlisle Weekly Gazette

152. Jan 16 1799
Abraham LOOS petitions Court of Common Pleas, Pittsburgh, for relief from debts.
House and lot for rent, in possession of Robert GRAYSON; also house in posssession of John GLENN, both being well suitted off for a store; also on shares, a plantation on Mount Rock in the possession of Thomas CROCKET; also adj the above in possession of Alexander JOHNSTON. Apply to James GIVEN, merchant in Carlisle, or to the subscriber, William MOORE, Middleton twp.
Persons indebted to the estate of Samuel GRAY, late of Carlisle, decd, are notified that the books will be lodged in the hands of James M'CORMICK, Esq. The books of the Shippensburgh store will be left with James LOWRY, Esq. of Shippensburgh for settlement. Persons with demands against the estate will please forward them to Thomas DUNCAN, Esq. of Carlisle, or to the subscriber, James C. WILLIAMSON, admr, Phila.
Persons indebted to estate of George HITTER, of Westpennsboro' now Frankfort twp, decd, are requested to make payment. David SNYDER, Exr.
James STERRETT, Newton twp, Cumberland co, has taken up a stray steer.
John BLACK, Juniata twp, Cumberland co, offers reward for stolen mare and colt.
Isaac MEASON, James BONNER, John BELL, all from Carlisle, have petitioned for relief from debts.

153. Jan 23 1799
Died 17th inst, in his 76th yr, William WOODS, after a tedious affliction.
On 13th inst, James ANDERSON, proprietor of the Ferry on Susquehanna, of that name, after a short illness, in his 59th yr.
On 10th inst, Mrs. Margaret POLLOCK, of distinguished birth and family, wife of Oliver POLLOCK, Esq, aged 52 yrs; her remains were deposited near the present res of the family, at Silver's Springs. She left a husband and 7 children. She was born in Ireland, and descended from a noble family by both her parents - O'BRIEN, of the house of Clare; and KENNEDY, of Ormond, whose sons were distinguished in foreigh services.
The Phila, Reading and Harrisburgh Mail Stage will arrive at Mr. FOSTERs, Carlisle, every Sat evening, and leave it for Phila every Sun at nine in the morning. William COLEMAN, Reading.
House to be let, leading west from the center square in the borough of Carlisle, now in the occupancy of Mrs. ELLIOT; apply to John HUGHES.
Sale of farm, late the property of John CAROTHERS, Esq., on the Connedoguinet Creek, East Pennsborough twp, county of Cumberland, 7 miles from Carlisle, 283 a.; apply to John Carothers, Esq., Carlisle, or Thomas CAROTHERS near to the premises.
Whereas Katherine NELSON my wife has eloped form my bed and board without any just cause, this is to warn the public not to give credit to her on my account. (absent since last spring) William NELSON.

154. Jan 30 1799
Sheriff's sale of house and half lot in Carlisle, property of John C. ADAMS; also house on south side of High st, Shippensburgh, property of John STUART. John CAROTHERS, Sheriff.

Kline's Carlisle Weekly Gazette

155. Feb 6 1799
Tax assessments may be inspected at: (1) House of Samuel CROWELL, Newville; House of David BRIGGS; House of George THOMAS in Juniata twp; House of Thomas M'CLURE in Tyrone twp. John ARTHUR, Principal Assessor, Third Assessment Dist, Cumberland.
Sheriff's sale of tract of 200 a., bounded by land formerly the property of James SAMPLE and others, to be sold as the property of David SAMPLE, Esq., decd.

156. Feb 13 1799
Farm for rent, late the property of Rodger CAROTHERS, decd, 90 a. James CAROTHERS.
Agreeable to last will of Jacob CART, late of Carlisle, wil be sold, half lot with log house and kitchen and stable, south side of Pomfret st, opposite John RHINE's Tavern, being part of lot adj Jacob CARR, on the east and Dr. FRANK on the west. Jacob CREVER, Jacob CART, exrs.

157. Feb 20 1799
150 a., with 2-story house, 5 miles from Shippensburg - Robert STARRITT on the premises.
Deserted on 16th Feb, from Barracks of Carlisle, Edward BOYLE, private, in the 2d Regiment of Artillerists and Engineers, native of Ireland, 19 yrs of age, 5 ft 9 inches, spare made, gray eyes, brown hair, dark complexion, down look. Callender IRVINE, Capt. 2d R.A.E. Commanding
Apply to David WATTS, Esq in Carlisle who is empowered to sell land which is sufficiently large enough for three farms - near Waynesburgh.
Nicholas SHULTZ, Carlisle, has petitioned for relief from debts.

158. Feb 27 1799
A dark bay horse has been left with the subscriber, John HUNTER, Carlisle, who suspects it was stolen; the person said his father kept the Indian Queen tavern in Baltimore; appeared to be about 18 yrs of age.
Tavern seat for rent, property of Andrew BYERLY on Shippensburgh road.
Store for rent - James DUNCAN, Carlisle.
Two tenements on south west side of the square of Carisle, now in the tenure of Mrs. GIBSON and John SMITH; apply to Ephraim STEEL.
Partnership between John FOX and Archibald CAMBRIDGE, Newville, cabinetmakers, in Newville, is dissolved.
Agreeable to will of William BLAINE, Esq., farm in Toboyne twp, Cumberland co, is to be sold, 226 a. - Samuel LYON, John ARMSTRONG, exrs.
Tract for sale, 150 a., south east of Carlisle, adj lands of James FLEMING, Charles M'CLURE, James HAMILTON and William LYON, Esqrs. - John GLENN.

159. Mar 6 1799
Two apprentices are needed at the paper-making busniess; apply at Pine-Hill Papermill, Southampton twp. John & Wm. BUCHANAN.
Sale of 100 a., Walnut Bottom road, 3 miles from Carlisle; also house and lot of subscriber in Carlisle, opposite the German church, as the subscriber wants to leave this part. Joseph YOUNG, Copper Smith.
Negro man was committed to jail, apprehended as a runaway; says his name is CHARLES and is property of Thomas M'KEE of Tawnytown, about 40 yrs of age,

Kline's Carlisle Weekly Gazette

5 ft 7-8 inches high; appears to be troubled with rhumatic pains. Christian SHADE, jailor, Carlisle.
Tract of land in Newville for sale, 100 a., in Southampton twp, estate of Peter NUGENT, insolvent debtor. Joseph CRAWFORD, Alexander GLEN, trustees.
Persons indebted to estate of Robert GIBSON, late of Middleton twp, decd, are requested to pay same. Ross MITCHELL, Wm. ALEXANDER, Robert MILLER, exrs, Carlisle.
F. I. HALLER, Atty at Law, has removed his office into Loughbridge's corner, the 5th door south of Dr. NESBIT.
Thomas SMILEY has petitioned for relief from debts.

160. Mar 13 1799
Died last week at Newville, Rev WILSON.
To be rented - house wherein Joseph ANDERSON now lives; apply to Edward MAGAURAN.
To be let - in town of Newville, house well adapted for storekeeping, formerly occpuied by Major FINLEY; apply to Jeremiah M'KIBBON, Newville.
John LAWSHE, Lewisburg, Northumberland Co, has petitioned for relief from debts.

161. Mar 20 1799
I require the Cumberland county Troop of Cavalry to hold themselves in Readiness to march at a moments warning. It is expected that every member will be completely equipped, and furnish himself with a valeese as soon as possible. Samuel A. M'COSKRY, Capt., Carlisle.
The roll of the Carlisle Blues is open [to fill its ranks]. George KLINE, Capt.
William KIRKPATRICK, Lancaster, offers reward for indented servant girl, Nancy CARLAND, about 12 yrs of age, of a small size, sandy couloured hair, has a mark on one of her cheeks, under the ear, one yellow ground gown, one red striped ditto, one light India calico ditto, one blue moreen petticoat, old red coating cloak, and sundry other articles. There is good reason to believe she was stolen away by her father, Daniel CARLAND, by trade a mason, a man of small size, 30-38 yrs of age, resided some time ago at Codorus Forge, and has lived lately in the neighbourhood of Carlisle.

162. Mar 27 1799
Died Sun 24th inst, after a short illness, Mrs. Mary BLAINE, wife of Alexander BLAINE.
Capt C. IRVINE's company marched from here on Wed last for Reading.
Meeting of the inhabitants of the Borough of Carlise - James M'CORMICK, George LOGUE, Burgesses.
Henry GOEBEL, has just received a general assortment of groceries and liquor.
Tract for sale, 250 a., adj the Silver Springs, in East-pennsborough twp, Cumberland co. Oliver POLLOCK.
Agreeably to the last will of Elizabeth ROSS, decd, will be sold a stone house in Carlisle, now in the tenure of John OLIVER, storekeeper - William LYON & Samuel LAIRD, exrs.
The horse, White Nose will cover mares this season at the stable of Nicholas SPONSLER at Robert BLAINE's mill, near Carlisle.

Kline's Carlisle Weekly Gazette

To be sold by auction, at the dwelling house lately occupied by Mrs. Frances REID, Carlisle, household and kitchen furniture - George PATTISON, auctioneer.
To be let, house at present occupied by Jonathan FOSTER, in Louther St - James DUNCAN, Carlisle.

163. Apr 3 1799
Jacob HENDEL, clock and watch maker, has moved into the house next door to Thomas FOSTER's tavern, Hanover st, lately occupied by John CAROTHERS, Esq. in the borough of Carlisle, where he makes eight day and 30 hours clocks.
The accounts respecting the Northampton insurrection are very contradictory. We understand that the Federal troops from several states have marched for the seat of insurrection, some companies have arrived at Newton in Bucks co.
Married on 25th ult in the city of Phila, by Rev Dr. ROGERS, Robert HAMILTON, of that city, to Miss Jesse M'NAUGHTON, dau of Patrick M'NAUGHTON, Esq. of this co.
Grayson's Hotel - Robert GRAYSON, having removed to the house lately occupied by John HUNTER, sign of General Washington, Hanover st, Carlisle, and having provided himself with necessary accommodation, he hopes to give general satisfaction.
The horse, Delaware Brown will cover mares this season - George WEISE.

164. Apr 10 1799
Jacob WALTENBERGER has petitioned for relief from debts.
John DILLER, requests immediate payment. He has removed from this place and has left his bonds and notes with Thomas URIE.

165. Apr 17 1799
Married in this borough on Thurs last, by Rev Dr. DAVIDSON, Dr. James POSTLETHWAIT, to Miss Betsy SMITH, dau of late Major James SMITH of this co.
In East Pennsborough, on same day, David BELL to Miss Isabella HOGE, dau of Jonathan HOGE, Esq.
In this borough, Sat last, John HANNA, to Miss Hannah SMITH, dau of John SMITH, black smith of this town.
Partnership of Joseph SHANNON and Hugh BRYSON is dissolved.
Thomas URIE offers one cent reward for indented boy named John MORRISON, 17 yrs of age, had on drab coloured cloth coat, waistcoat and overalls, fair complexion, squints very much.
Samuel CULBERTSON, living 5 miles of Carlisle, offers reward for mulatto boy, named RICHARD, about 17 yrs of age.
The horse Patroclus will stand at Mr. BRIGGS, Silver Springs, and at the Happy Retreat, 1 mile from Carlisle - Peter LATSHAW.

166. Apr 24 1799
Married last week by Rev WAUGH, in East Pennsborough twp, Matthew MILLER, of Middleton twp, to Miss Jane GALBREATH, dau of Andrew GALBREATH, Esq. of East Pennsborough.
Such masons, bricklayers and carpenters as are inclined to undertake building a house for Dickinson College at Carlisle will please make proposals to John CREIGH. Contributors are requested to pay at least a part of their subscription to Mr. MONTGOMERY, Treasurer, as ready money is needed to pay several labourers already at work.

Kline's Carlisle Weekly Gazette

Subscribers to Halyburton's Enquiry into the Principles of the Modern
Deist's are desired to call for their books - Archibald LOUDON, Carlisle.
The gentlemen of the 2nd Troop of Light Dragoons, Cumberland co, are
requested to meet at the Tavern lately occupied by Andrew BYERLY, Walnut
Bottom road, in complete uniform. John SHIPPEN, Captain, Shippensburg.

167. May 1 1799
Died in this town last week, Miss Sally CALHOON, dau of Andrew CALHOON, decd
Thomas KENNEDY answers charges regarding the removal of the state seat of
government.
John WRAY, in want of money, requests immediate payment of debts, and
threatens to publish list of those who neglect compliance.
Henry SHEPLER has established a line of stages beteen Lancaster, Harris-
burgh, Carlisle and Shippensburg.
John WILHELM has petitioned for relief from debts.
Joseph Z. JONES has petitioned for relief from debts.

168. May 8 1799
Cheap Grocery store - George DAWSON, Loughridge's Corner, opposite to Mr.
GRAYSON's Hotel, Carlisle.
Sale of 10 horses with their gears, two waggons with waggon cloths, hand
screws and buckets. George GIBSON.

169. May 15 1799
Died on Tues 7th inst, in Lewistown, after a very short illness, Jerman
JACOBS.
To sell tract of land in Mifflin twp, adj with William MAFFET, 56 a., late
the property of Godfrey SANDERS, insolvent debtor - Jacob FETTER, Isaiah
GRAHAM, assignees.
At a meeting of the Board of Property, Daniel BRODHEAD (Sur. Gen.), Francis
JOHNSTON (Rec. Gen.), and John HALL (Sec'y), present of the Land Office.
H. HURST, atty for Simon GROUSE claims tract of 245 a. in Eastpennsborough
twp, surveyed in virtue of a warrant dated Jun 1762, granted to
Christopher SEELY - that in the draft of the said tract the Deputy
Surveyor made the note, "N.B. This survey caveated in consequence of an
early warrant granted to George CROGHAN and assigned to George ARMSTRONG."
The petitioner was unable to find either George Armstrong or any of his
representatives. - For John HALL, Esq., Secretary of the Land Office.
An. LUFBOROUGH.
Deserted from the Rendesvous at Carlisle, John MONTGOMERY, otherwise John
HIGGINS, enlisted soldier, born in Ireland, aged about 30 yrs, 5 ft 8
inches, ruddy complexion, gray eyes, brown hair; had his eyes very much
blackened and bruised by boxing. A. D. DAVIS, 2d Lieut. 10th Regiment.
Sheriff's sale: (1) tract of 100 a. bounded by Shearman's Creek and lands of
John SMILEY; (2) 250 a. bounded by aforesaid tract and lands of John
Smiley and Benjamin CUNNINGHAM; (3) 200 a. of land bounded by lands of
James LOUTHER; (4) 300 a. bounded by the above lands, this last tract in
dispute with James SCOBEY, the whole seized as the property of Thomas
SMILEY, Delinquent Collector of Taxes for 1783.
Sheriff's sale: (1) tract in Rye twp bounded by James M'LAUGHLIN's claim,
Frederick WATTS claim, John M'COY's land, claim of William BASKINS, John
CRAIG's claim.

Kline's Carlisle Weekly Gazette

170. May 22 1799
Deserted from the rendezvous at York town, Pa, John M'CLEAN, born in
Glasgow, Scotland, says he is 35 yrs of age, but appears older, and that
he was waiter and barber to Gen. ST. CLAIR, 5 ft 5 1/2 inches, black hair;
had on grey drab coat, pair of half boots, tied up behind with garters,
new shoes, and of my property: 5 razors, in three cases, one of them green
handled, and four new of the best kind. Andrew JOHNSTON, Capt. 10th regt.
Andrew PATTERSON, Mifflin twp, Cumberland Co, offers reward for missing
horse.

171. May 29 1799
Died last week after a long and painful illness, Mrs. WEISS, wife of Jacob
WEISS, of Middleton twp.
Joseph WOOD has opened an house of Entertainment in the house formerly
occupied by Isaac ANGNEY, at the Sign of the Cross Keys, in Hanover St,
Carlisle.
Meeting of Orphan Court - William LYON, Clk.

172. Jun 5 1799
Daniel M'CLINTOCK has petitioned for relief from debts.

173. Jun 12 1799
For sale - 3 lots in town of Newville with log dwelling house on each -
William M'MONIGLE.
Adam HATHORN petitioned for relief from debts.
Ready money for good oak shingles, clear of sap. Richard PARKER.

174. Jun 19 1799
Jacob HENDEL appointed Justice of the Peace of this Borough, making the
fourth Justice in the borough of Carlisle.
St. John's Day - Members of Lodge No. 76 are desired to attend at the Lodge
Room, house of Thomas CLARK, town of Newville - By order of the W. Master
- Robert LUSK, seceretary.
Patrick LYNCH has applied for relief from debts.
Merchant mill to leased on Chew's Farm, Washington co, Md. Benjamin
GALLOWAY, Chews-Farm.

175. Jun 26 1799
The Corner stone of the New Edifice for Dickinson College was laid.
Robert MILLER has been elected Treasure of the County: John JORDAN, Joseph
SHROM and David ROSS, Commissioners.
Ellis WOODWARD and John GRISE have petitoned for relief from debts.
Isaac HOFFER, barber, continues to reside in Louther st, near the sign of
the Black Bear, Carlisle, where he grinds and sets razors, grinds
scissors, keeps cues and braids for sale.
This is to forwarn persons not to give credit on my account to Elizabeth
SIMISON, as I am determined not to pay any debts of her contracting from
this date. John SIMISON.
John BARR, Carlisle, has petitioned for relief from debts.

Kline's Carlisle Weekly Gazette

176. Jul 3 1799
Sheriff's sales: (1) tract in Toboyne twp, 200 a., bounded by lands of William BROWN, property of John JORDAN; (2) tract in Armagh twp, now Mifflin co, 200 a., property of James SCOTT; (3) tract in Tyrone twp, 87 a. bounded by lands of David LINDSEY and William ADAMS; (4) tract of 100 a. in Tyrone twp, property of David and William ADAMS; (5) tract in Horse Valley, Franklin co, near the head of Conodoguinet Creek, 223 a., bounded by lands now in the tenure of Robert CAMPBELL, tract in said valley, 199 a., in the tenure of William FOWLER and ROSBERRY, another tract in said valley, 60 a., tract in Amberson's Valley, 135a., adj lands now or late of Barnabas CLARK, and tract in Westpennsborough twp, 197 a. bounded by lands now or late of Thomas BUTLER, --- Cookson and William WEST, property of Samuel PERRY.
Creditors of Josiah FOSTER to petition for relief from debts.
Farm for sale in Greenwood twp, on Cockalamus creek, Cumberland co, formerly the property of Nicholas BOARS, and at present occupied by James TERRY, 218 a.; apply to Thomas DUNCAN, Esq., Carlisle, or the subscriber, No. 127 Market St., Phila, Edward SHOEMAKER.

177. Jul 10 1799
Sheriff's sale of tract of 280 a., in Juniata twp, property of David ENGLISH.
Joseph HEWITT, Menalen twp, York co, 3 miles of Pine Grove Furnace, offers reward for Thomas HEWITT, runaway - is always talking to himself, fair complexion. Notify Joseph Hewitt or Benjamin BLACKFORD, or Michael EGE.
George GREEN has petitioned for relief from debts.

178. Jul 17 1799
Married 9th inst, by Rev SNOWDEN, at Silver's Springs, Dr. Samuel ROBINSON, to Miss Polly POLLOCK, eldest dau of Oliver POLLOCK, Esq.
Carlisle Light Infantry will parade at Court House. Robert MILLER, Capt.
John NOBLE offers reward for missing sheep.
Thomas RUSSEL, Southampton twp, Cumberland co, has taken up stray horse.
Cunningham SCOTT has petitioned for relief from debts.

179. Jul 24 1799
About 160 of the U.S. troops lately raised in the Western parts of this state left Carlisle Barracks Mon last under the Command of Capt. M'KINNEY.
Sheriff's sale: (1) paper mill and tract in Southampton twp, 164 a., property of William DUCKET; (2) two stone tenements on Letart spring, Carlisle, property which formerly belonged to John POLLOCK, taken in execution at the suit of John CARSON; (3) house in south side of High st, Town of Shippensburgh, of John STUART.
Robert WRIGHT offers reward for cow which strayed away.
Jacob CART, Carlisle, offers reward for missing cattle.
This is to give notice to persons not to give credit to my wife Jean ABERNATHY - John ABERNATHY, Tyrone twp.

180. Jul 31 1799
Jacob CART offers reward for apprentice lad, James CUNEY, by trade a butcher, age about 19 yrs, 5 ft 6 inches, blackish hair, down look. He went away in company with John DUM, John M'COY and William PEDAN.

Kline's Carlisle Weekly Gazette

Farm for sale opposite Mifflintown, Mifflin co, 150 a. Joseph M'CLELAND, Milford.
George DOUGHERTY, 1 miles above Carlisle, offers reward for heifer calves which strayed; give information to James RONEY or Simon BOYD, in Carlisle.
Quarterly meeting of the Union Fire Company - Joseph HAYS, clerk.

181. Aug 7 1799
Died Mon, 29th Jul last, Margaret LOGAN, wife of John LOGAN, and dau of Robert CHAMBERS, in her 24th yr, of a lingering disorder.
Sarah CLARK, who was tried last Court for the Murder of John CAROTHERS, Esq., was yesterday brought to the Bar, and received the sentence of Death.
James CLENDENNEN has commenced business next door to William WALLACE, Tavern keeper, sign of the Black Bear - Dry goods and Groceries.
I, James ELLIOTT, mason, of the Borough of Carlisle, having circulated sundry reports respecting Nancy BUCHANAN, wife of Arthur BUCHANAN, injurious to her reputation, part of said reports I have since discovered to be false and other part with insufficient foundation; and to the best of my knowledge she is innocent. In the presence of: William LEVIS, John SMITH.
George BECK and John BECK, Carlisle, have petitioned for relief from debts.
Andrew DICKSON offers reward for apprentice lad named William WELSH, by trade a blacksmith.
George BACHMAN and William MILLER have petitioned for relief from debts.
John KINKEAD has removed to his house, corner of York and Louther st, opposite to William WALLACE's tavern, where he has opened an House of Entertainment.
John PATTON, Centre-Furnace, Mifflin co, offers reward for negro man, named JOHN, about 22 yrs of age, 5 ft 5-6 inches, round faced with short turned up nose, speaks good English; also negro girl named FLORA, about 18 yrs old, slender made, speaks bad English and a little French, has a scar on her upper lip.
325 a. for sale, 1 1/2 miles from Carlisle - James BLAINE, in Carlisle.

182. Aug 14 1799
Andrew DICKSON offers reward for apprentice lad named William WELSH, by trade a blacksmith.
We the subscribers, composing the Grand Jury of the County of Cumberland, with one member dissenting, do resolve that we will support with our best exertions, James ROSS, of Pittsburgh, at the ensuing General Election as Governor: Samuel POSTLETHWAITE, William ALEXANDER, Samuel A. M'COSKRY, Jacob RAUM, John WALKER, Matthew MILLER, James POWER, Jacob HENDEL, Teedrick UHLER, Michael EGE, Jacob MILLER, Andrew EMMINGER, George COVER, Alexander LECKEY, Andrew MATEET, John M'MEEN, John MORRISON. Jacob ALTER, dissenting.
For sale - a team complete of five horses with gears, a wagon - William GIRLLING, Carlisle.
Stone dwelling house for sale in Carlisle - James ARMSTRONG.
Hugh HAZLETON, living in Baltimore, offers reward for apprentice lad named Neal BROWN by trade a White Smith, about 5 ft 5 inches, a little marked with small pox; he worked some time near Newville at Wheel Spindles and Hindles.
In pursuance of order of Orphan Court a tract, of Thomas WILEY, decd, will be sold, 597 a., in Tyrone twp, Cumberland co, adj lands of William POWER, John HU..., William DUFFEY. Alexander POWER, admr.

Kline's Carlisle Weekly Gazette

Nathaniel ECCLES, Christian HOUBBLE, Frederick SPECK and Margaret DILLER, Carlisle, have petitioned for relief from debts.

183. Aug 21 1799
Died yesterday morning, Adam LOGUE of this town.
Jacob CREVER, Esq., appointed Justice of the peace in the Borough of Carlisle; we have five justices in Carlisle, 2 of whom are Germans.
D. SEARLE, A. B., continues to instruct young Ladies and Gentlemen at his Grammar school near David WALKER's, in East Pennsborough twp.

184. Aug 28 1799
Died Sat morning 24th inst at half past 7 o'clock at Shippensburgh, Pa, in her 20th yr, after a three weeks painful disease, Miss Elizabeth SHIPPEN, dau of Joseph SHIPPEN, Esq. of Plumley farm Chester co.
Died on 25th inst, Col. William LUSK, and on the day following his remains were interred at Newville.
Married in Phila on Thurs 15th inst, John HOFF of Lancaster to Miss Mary BOYER, dau of Frederick BOYER of this town.
Dry Goods - George STURM
William DREVISH wants to purchase a quantity of clean flaxseed, Carlisle.

185. Sep 4 1799
A child of Mr. BRADLEYs of this town, of two yrs old was killed on Sat last near the Square, by a wagon running over its body.
Arrived on Sat last in this town commanded by Lieut. B. WALLACE, 55 U.S. troops, parts of four companies recruited in the western counties, belonging to the 10th Regiment.
Deserted from the Encampment at this place, William M'CORD, by trade a carpenter, born in Pennsylvania, fair hair, fair complexion, 5 ft 10 1/.4 inches high. Ben. WALLACE, Jun., 1st Lieutenant, 10th Regt, Infantry., Shippensburgh.
Having bought a house to move in a short time, every person indebted to the undersigned is desired to settle off their accounts - John FORSYTH, Grocer, Carlisle.
Goerge DININGER, Carlisle, requests persons indebted to make payment to John BIEGEL, tavern keeper, in Carlisle.
John MILLER, living 4 1/2 miles from Green Castle, offers reward for horse stolen out of his pasture.
By order of Orphan court a lot with two log dwelling houses will be sold, in Shippensburgh, late the property of Stophel POISTLE, decd; attendance given by Andrew POISTLE, adm; also two lots with log dwelling house in Carlisle, late the property of Richard LEE, decd; terms made known by John OFFICER and Jeremiah MILLER, exrs of last will of decd.
Whereas my wife Barbara has absconded from my bed and board without any just cause or reason, I hereby forwarn persons from giving her credit on my account. Ephraim STRAUSS.
Joseph YOUNG, Coopersmith in Carlisle, offers reward for apprentice lad, named William PEADEN, coppersmith by trade, 19-20 yrs of age, 5 ft 5-6 inches, dark complexion; his hair hangs loose, round shouldered, fond of gambling.

Kline's Carlisle Weekly Gazette

186. Sep 11 1799
For sale in Silver Springs, 700 a. on road between Harrisburgh and Carlisle, leading to Fort Pitt. Apply to William Lewis, esq. Phila, James Hamilton, Esq Carlisle, William Riddle, Esq. Reading, William Montgomery, Esq. lancaster, or the subscriber, on the premises, Oliver Pollock.
William Dunbar has petitioned for relief from debts.
George Schneider, Carlisle, offers reward for apprentice lad, named Martin Livenger, about 18 yrs of age, 5 ft 5-6 inches, black eyes, somewhat of a down look, short black hair, fair complexion, apprentice to the shoemakeing business, and has went for Baltimore.

187. Sep 18 1799
Died Thurs, 12th inst, aged about 70 yrs, Mrs. Elizabeth MILLER.
Duel fought at Bristol between Captain JOHNSTON and Lieutenant SHARP, both officers in the 10th regiment, in which the latter was killed.
Married Thurs last by Rev HAUTZ [?], Samuel KROP, to Miss Catharine SPOTSWOOD, both of this place.
Died at Fort Fayette, on 1st inst, Lieut, David THOMPSON, of the 2d U.S. Regiment of Infantry, after a painful and tedious illness.
Sheriff's sale of paper mill and tract in Southampton twp, 164 a., formerly the property of James LEEPER, also grist mill and saw mill, bounded by lands of John M'CULLOUGH, Christopher WALTERS, William CULBERTSON, property of William DUCKET.
Isaac KUNTZ, Carlisle, has petitioned for relief from debts.
The companies of the First and Second Battalions of the 4th Regiment of Cumberland Militia, will assemble for exercise - William ALEXANDER, Lieut. Col. Com'dt.

188. Sep 25 1799
More details on the duel fought by Capt. JOHNSTON and John SHARP paymaster in Bristol twp, Bucks co. Inquisition taken before Joseph CLUNN, J.P. Oaths taken from: Dr. Amos GREGG, Dr. Joseph P. MINNICK, Benjamin LAZELEAN, Jonathan PERSELL, Benjamin WALTON, William M'ELHENEY, James SORRIL, Richard LLOYD, Jacob COSTINE, John JOHNSON, Joseph STACKHOUSE, Charles BOFFONETT. It was determined that John Sharp was on 12 Sep inst shot with a pistol ball fired from a pistol of Capt. Johnson.
Joseph HAYS has at his store in Carlilse, bar iron, assorted, steel, ten-plate stoves, large kettles, &c.
To be sold at late dwelling house of Samuel PAXTON, of East Pennsborough twp, Cumberland co, decd, horses, cows, sheep, hogs, wagon, plough, harrow, hay, wheat, rye, ten plate stove, beds and bedding, furniture - Agness PAXTON and Richard GREGARY, admrs.
George BALSBAUGH offers reward for horse stolen out of the pasture, 2 miles from Humelstown, Dauphin co, Derry twp.
Daniel M'MURPHY, still continues to carry on the fulling and clothing business at Col. Wm. M'FARLANE's fulling mill, on Big Spring.
Sale of 307 a. in Mifflin twp, Cumberland co; apply to James NICHOLSON, on the premises.
Vincent GRIBBEL has commenced the fulling and dying business at Capt. Gilson CRAIGHEAD's fulling mill, on Yellow Breeches Creek. Cloth will be taken in and delivered when dressed, at William GODFREY's, York co; Robert

Kline's Carlisle Weekly Gazette

LEECHes, near Dill's Tavern; and at Robert GRAYSON's, Carlisle and at the mill of the subscriber.

189. Oct 9 1799
The companies composing the 5th Regiment of Cumberland co Militia, will assemble for exercise on William MILLER's place, Mount Rock. Major Jared GRAHAM, Com'dt. West Pennsbro' twp.
James HAMILTON offers reward for information on the malicious person or persons whilst the subscriber was abroad, destroyed a milch cow, by cutting the sinews of her leg with a knife.
Henry REEHM, on Letert Spring, Carlisle, seeks an apprentice to the tanning and currying business.

190. Oct 16 1799 - Samuel WOODS vs. the heirs and representatives of Wm. WOODS, decd, in the Common Pleas of Bedford co.

191. Oct 23 1799 - For sale - house and lot in Hanover st, Carlisle, known as the Seven Stars, stone house and kitchen - John TEMPLETON, on the premises.

192. Oct 30 1799
Married Thurs last by Rev WAUGH, John CHAIN to John Sidney MOFFATT, both of East Pennsborough twp.
"Whereas I was charged by John WALKER, Esq. in a public manner, on the 4th day of Oct last, with being concerned in a treasonable conspiracy, consisting of 500 persons in Cumberland co ... I call upon the gentleman ... to step forward ... " Joseph JUNKIN.
Negro man to be sold, shoe maker - William BLAIR, Carlisle.
John STEPHENS, fuller and dyer; cloth will be taken at Messrs William WALLACE, Jeremiah MILLER, George WEISS, William HEIGLE, John RHINE, Charles BOVARD and John POPE's in Carlisle - John STERREM on the mountain, WINGARTs store Landisburgh - George HACKET - Thos. M'CLURE - John FRITZ, at the Bark(?) tavern and George THOMAS at the Blue Ball, in Shearman's valley - Nicholas KRITZ.., down the big roar - Adam LONGSTAFF in the barrens - Abraham HERR on the Lisburn road - and Mr. DILL's tavern in York co.
John EVERS has taken up a stray mare.

193. Nov 6 1799
Died Sun last, after a tedious illness, Miss Margaret DAVIS, dau of Col. John DAVIS, decd. Her remains were interred in the old Presby burying ground.
On Wed last was executed on the commons east of this town, Sarah CLARK, who was convicted for poisoning the family of John CAROTHERS, Esq. of Eastpennsborough twp, Cumberland co.
James GIVIN, Carlisle, in addition to his general assortment of dry goods, Hardware, ironmongery, cutlery, queensware and groceries, has just received by the ship George, from Londonderry, a compleat assortment of linens.
John MILLER, living about 4 1/2 miles from Green Castle, offers reward for missing horse.

194. Nov 13 1799 - John FRY, ladies shoemaker, has commenced business next door to the sign of the White Bear, in York st, Carlisle.

Kline's Carlisle Weekly Gazette

195. Nov 20 1799
400-500 men of the 10th U.S. regiment of Infantry commanded by Col. Thos. L. MOORE, arrived at the Barracks adj this borough Fri last, and we understand are to remain here during the winter.
John ELLIOT, Carlisle, offers reward for missing bull.
Two story house for sale on south side of the Main st, Newville, for store or tavern - James ANDERSON, Newville.

196. Nov 27 1799
Died at Fort Wayne, on 21st ult, Capt. Daniel BRITT of the 1st Regiment of Infantry.
Died Sat night last Mrs. Rebeckah PARKER, relict of James PARKER of East Pennsborough; remains interred in old Presby burying ground.
Married Thurs last, Joseph LATSHAW, to Miss Polly RIDDLE, both of this place.
Half lot and buildings to be sold - William BLAIR
George KERR, Mouth of Bald Eagle creek, Lycoming co, offers reward for Thomas PAINE, 5 ft 5-6 inches, dark complexion, shakes with the palsey, charged with feloniously taking from the subscriber a pinch back watch, which since has been found about 43 miles from my house, where he disposed of in exchange for a common silver one.
James CAROTHERS, West-pennsborough twp, Cumberland co, offers reward for missing draught ox.
John ERWIN has petitioned for relief from debts.

197. Dec 4 1799
Yesterday passsed through this town on their way for Pittsburg, Capt. SHOEMAKER's copmpany of U.S. troops - it consisted of about 90 men, appeared healthy, neat and clean.
Persons indebted to the estate of John NORTH, late of Greenwood twp, Cumberland co, decd, are requested to make immediate payment. Katherine NORTH, William NORTH, John JORDAN, admrs.

198. Dec 11 1799
Died - John JORDAN, Esq. one of the Assoc Judges of the Court of Common Pleas in this co; his remains were interred in the burying ground adj this town. He has during life been an uniform Whig; served in the militia during the Rev war, as a Lieutenant, Captain and a Major. In 1783 he was elected a Justice of the Peace.
Alexander POWER, offers reward for horse missing from the pasture of the Rising Sun, 1 1/2 miles below Carlisle.
Daniel CERFASS, Dickinson twp, Sign of the Cumberland Wagon, has taken up a stray horse.
Jan 1 1800
Arrived on Sun last in town about 60 troops from Pittsburgh, commanded by Capt. David DUNCAN, belonging to the 10th U.S. Regimsnt, which are stationed at this place.
Died at his seat in Fermanagh twp, Mifflin co, Thurs 19th inst, Samuel BRYSON, Esq., one of the assoc judges for said co.

Kline's Carlisle Weekly Gazette

199. Jan 8 1800
Died Wed last in his 75(?) yr, John M'DANNEL; remains interred in the Presby Burying Ground at Newville.
Married Sat last at York Town, Lieut. Anthony GALE, of the Marine Corps, Phila, to Miss Kitty SWOPE of this town.

200. Jan 15 1800
The co-partnership of QUIGLEY & BROWN being dissolved. Samuel BROWN, Springfield.

201. Jan 22 1800 - Died Mon last, Mrs. James LEYBURN of this borough, after a short illness.

202. Jan 29 1800
Died Mon morning last, after a lingering sickness, Miss Gitty(?) THOMPSON, dau of the late Rev THOMPSON; her remains were interred in the burying ground adj this town.
Political squabble - John WALKER, Eastpennsborough twp, Cumberland co defends himself from charge by Mr. JUNKIN. Persons named or witnesses: Alexander M'BETH, William ALEXANDER, Jonathan HOGE, Nathaniel WILSON.

203. Feb 5 1800
The subscriber intending a voyage to Europe, all persons having accounts open with hime are desired to settle them. Robert HUSTON, Carlisle.
Limestone land for sale, 100 a., on the Walnut Bottom road, 2 1/2 miles from Carlisle. Also house and lot which the subscriber now lives in, on Hanover St, Carlisle, opposite the German Church. Joseph YOUNG, coppersmith.
House for sale which the subscriber now lives, in Carlisle, fit for business or to accommodate a numerous family, with excellent well of water in the yard, stabling, carriage house, &c. William IRVINE.
House to be let in Carlisle, opposite the jail, lately occupied by John GLEN; also house in Pomfret st, in the tenure of Daniel DUNLAP; also plantation in Dickinson twp, latly occupied by Alexander SHAW; also 2 negro boys well used to drive a team and all kinds of farming work. William MOORE, Middleton twp.
Dr. M'COSKRY requests payment of debts.
James CAROTHERS to let plantation.
Persons indebted to estate of Abraham HIDE, decd, are requested to pay. Elizabeth HIDE, John GREEGER, exrs.
Tavern house at Mount Rock for rent. John MILLER.
Two story stone house for sale, Hanover st, Carlisle. Jacob MATTER, 2 miles from Carlisle.
300 a. for sale in Rye twp with dwelling house, 12 miles from Carlisle. James SCOBY, Carlisle.
Reward for person who finds 50 dollars in bank notes that was lost by Samuel SIMISON.
John M'CURDY, Carlisle, has taken up a stray horse.
Two story house for sale in Shippensburgh. William BELL.
William CRALL, offers reward for horse stolen out of the stable of Matthew HENDERSON, 1 mile from Carlisle.

Kline's Carlisle Weekly Gazette

204. Feb 12 1800
Died Jan 30th 1800, in his 52d yr, John RIPPETH of Westpennsborough; his remains were interred in burying Ground at the Big Spring. He left 6 children.
Houses to be let in the south part of Carlisle - Robert BARKLEY.

205. Feb 19 1800
Died at Pittsburgh on Wed 5th inst, David HOGE, of that town.
Agreeable to last will of Andrew THOMPSON, decd, late of Hopewell twp, Cumberland co, the land and improvements of said Thompson will be sold, adj lands of John M'KEE, David M'KENEY and others. David WILLS, John SNODY, exrs.
Stone house in High St, Carlisle, to be sold, formerly occupied by the subscirber, now by Mrs. SWOPE, 4 rooms to a floor, stabling, carriage house, excellent well - L. GUSTINE.
John ROBINSON has petitioned Franklin Co court for relief of debts.
To be sold wherein the late John M'DANNEL dwelt, Carlisle, opposite Dr. DAVIDSON's; apply to John NOBLE near the premises.
Tract to be rented nearly adj Carlisle, 250 a. James HAMILTON.

206. Feb 26 1800
Married Thurs 13th inst by Rev Dr. DAVIDSON, Jereat POLLOCK to Miss Polly BRIGGS, both of this co.
Tract of 178 a., in Toboine twp, Cumberland co, late the property of Alexander M'NAIR, decd - Robert LAUGHLIN, John GARVIN, exrs.
Administration accounts taken on the following estates: Roger DEVLIN, Rachel WALKER, Robert HAWTHORN, William M'CORD, jun., David SOMERVILLE, George WENZEL and Henry ECCLEBERGER, decd - to be presented the Orphan's Court for confirmation. George KLINE, Register.
A statement of the Orders drawn by the Commissioners of Cumberland County on the Treasurer, 1 Feb 1799 - 1 Feb 1800.

Thomas ADAMS assessor of Toboyne
Joseph ANDERSON witness vs Col. FERGUSON
George ARMSTRONG witness vs M'NAMARA
Jacob BARRICKSTRESSER witness vs Jos. PATTON
James BOYD witness vs Michael FORTNEY
Adam BRITAIN assistant assessor [of Mifflin twp]
David BROOKINS assessor of Shippensburgh
David CAMPBELL defendants bill in case agnst CAMPBELL for forgery
David CAMPBELL serving supoeneas
John CAMPBELL assistant assessor [of Shippensburgh]
Mary CAMPBELL witness vs John KINKEAD
Armstrong CAROTHERS witness vs M'NAMARA
John CAROTHERS prosecutor agnst Sarah CLARK; execution of Sarah Clark
John CAROTHERS assistant assessor [Westpennsbro']
Sarah CLARK prosecuted and executed
Thomas CLARK white-washing prison
William CLARK taxes paid by mistake
John CLENDENING assistant assessor [of Eastpennsbro' twp]
John CONNELLY assistant assessor of Frankford twp
George COOVER assistant assessor [Allen twp]
Adam COPE assistant assessor [of Carlisle]
Jacob CREVER sheriff's fees
Meredith DARLINGTON assistant assessor [Juniata twp]
Patrick DAVIDSON assistant assessor of Middleton
James DIVEN assessor of Tyrone twp
Stephen DUNCAN sheriff's fees in case vs Stephen Duncan, late treasurer

55

Thomas DUNCAN council for the board
William EWING witness vs Jos. Patton
Col. FERGUSON prosecuted
Michael FORTNEY prosecuted
Samuel GALBREATH assessor of Rye twp
Alexander GALLY assistant assessor
John GARDNER assistant assessor of Toboyne
Robert GRAYSON ten plate stove (1)
Charles W. HARTLEY Atty general's fees
Thomas HARTLEY, esq. Atty general's fees
Abraham HERR witness vs M'Namara
Nicholas HICKES assistant assessor of Tyrone twp
Robert HUNTER assistant assessor of Toboyne
James HUTTON constables fes
David IRVINE clerk of the sessions, holding constables court
James IRVINE assessor of Eastpennsbro' twp
Samuel IRVINE Coroners fees
Samuel JACKSON taking care of Court-house, also candles and one load of wood
William JAMES - ordered to move him from Dauphin goal to Carlisle goal
William JAMES prosecuted
John JORDAN commissioner
Leonard KELLER assessor of Carlisle
Deborah KINKEAD vs John Kinkead
John KINKEAD prosecuted
George KLINE printing list of unseated lands; other printing
James LAIRD assistant assessor of Frankford twp
John LAMB assistant assessor [of Allen twp]
James LAMBERTON assessor of Middleton
Alexander LAUGHLIN, Esq. jusitce's and constable's fees.
Robert LINDSEY assessor of Frankford twp
George LOGUE clerk; coroners fees
Abraham LONGNECKER assistant assessor [of Eastpennsbro' twp]
Archibald LOUDON paper for commissioners
Alexander LYON transcript of the public records

John M'DANIEL assessor of Allen twp
John M'GLAUGHLIN witness vs William James
John M'KEE assessor of Hopewell twp
George M'KEEHAN assessor of Westpennsbro'
David M'KINNEY assistant assessor [of Hopewell twp]
Daniel M'NAIL witness vs M'Namara
John M'QUEAD witness vs Beatty and others
David MAHON assistant assessor [of Shippensburgh]
Catharine MAHONY witness vs John Kinkead
James MARTIN witness vs Beatty
William MILLER assistant assessor [of Carlisle]
George MITCHEL assessor of Greenwood twp
James MITCHELL assistant assessor [Greenwood twp]
Patrick MONEY prosecuted
George MONROE assistant assessor [Juniata twp]
John MONTGOMERY sinking public well on N. W. corner of the public square
William MONTGOMERY assessor of Mifflin twp
John MOORE assistant assessor of Dickinson
David L. MORREL witness vs Beatty and others
James MORRISON witness vs Jos. Patton
John MORRISON prosecutor vs Patrick Money
John NEAL Assessor of Dickinson
James NICHOLSON assistant assessor [Mifflin twp]
William NORTH assistant assessor [of Greenwood twp]
Henry ORTH removing William James from Dauphin goal to Carlisle
James PATTON, Esq. justices and constable's fees
Jos. PATTON prosecuted
Joseph PIERCE assistant assessor [Westpennsbor']
John RAMSEY prosecutor of Samuel Thompson & others
John RAMSEY assessor of Juniata twp
Thomas RIDGE witness vs John Winant

Kline's Carlisle Weekly Gazette

David ROBB commissioner
James ROWNEY fees as constable Sep 1791-Jun 21 1799
Gilbert SEARIGHT assistant assessor of Middleton
Christian SHADE Goaler
Leonard SHANNON witness vs Fortney
Joseph SHROM commissioner
Thomas SMILEY, insolvent for his fees
David SNIDER bridge over Conodogunet creek near Newville
Teterich UHLER glazing Court-house
Robert WALLACE assistant assessor
David WATT witness agnst D. Campbell
Edward WEAKLEY assistant assessor of Dickinson
Edward WEST assistant assessor of Tyrone twp
John WINANTS fees paid to witness in commonwealth vs John Winants
John WOODS assistant assessor [of Hopewell twp]
Englehart WORMLEY fees in his prosecution
John WORMLY witness vs William James
John YEALY clerk's fees in his prosecution

207. Mar 5 1800
Thomas RUSSELL offers reward for horse missing from stable of William WALLACE, Tavern keeper in Carlisle. Deliver to Wm. Wallace in Carlisle, or to John LEWIS at Andrew BYERLY's old tavern on the Walnut Bottom road.
John WRAY, Carlisle, has petition for relief from debts.
James RAMSEY has opened a store in the house of George STURM, next door to Mr. FOSTER's tavern, Hanover st, Carlisle.
Whereas two persons named Samuel REYNOLDS & Wm. WRIGHT about 4th July 1796 left 6 pieces of silk, I give notice that unless they call for said silk it will be sold for expences. Patrick COCHRAN, Shippensburgh.
Whereas Peggy BROWN, now the wife of the subscriber, has eloped from his bed and board, without just cause ... I warn persons that I will not pay any debts by her contracted. Joseph BENSON.
Merchant mill and saw mill to be let, with two water wheels and two pair of stones, one of them burrs, on west branch of Kishacoquilas, 12 miles from Lewistown; apply to Col. James POTTER, of Lewistown, or to John REED, near the premises, or the subscriber in Franklin co. James POE.

208. Mar 12 1800
John P. THOMSON, appointed Deputy postmaster for Carlisle in place of Billy LEVIS, a stauch, steady patriot.
Adam KOPE, appointed by the burgesses, as clerk of the Market for Carlisle, in place of John M'CURDY, an old and respectable officer.
Married 6th inst, by Rev Robert DAVIDSON, Samuel DUNCAN, Esq., Atty at Law, to Miss Elizabeth CREIGH, dau of John CREIGH, Esq.
Died at Pittsburgh on Thurs morning last, 6th inst, in her 27th yr, of a lingering and painful illness, Mrs. Catharine SEMPLE, consort of Steel SEMPLE, Esq. of that place.
Sale of commodious two story stone house in Millers Town, Cumberland co, and 80 a. of land, 1 miles from town. Apply to Samuel UTTER, Esq. near the premises. Mordecai DAVIS.
James RAMSAY has opened a store in the house of George STURM, 3rd door to Mr. FOSTER's tavern, Hanover St. Dry Goods and Groceries.

209. Mar 26 1800
Married Wed 12th inst by Rev M'CONNEL at the farm of Joseph JUNKIN, in East Pennsborough twp, John FINDLEY of Westmoreland Co, to Miss Elizabeth JUNKIN, dau of Joseph Junkin of this co.

Kline's Carlisle Weekly Gazette

Regimental Orders - The companies composing the 5th Regiment of Cumberland co Militia will assemble - Jared GRAHAM, Maj. Commandant. Westpennsborough twp
The horse, Tom Bolin, will stand to cover mares this season at the house of Mr. KROTZER, tavern keeper, 1 mile this side of Strasburgh. John SPENCER, Shippensburgh.
Whereas the subscriber, Archibald M'KOY, having passed 3 bonds to Thomas MARTIN of Shippensburgh, this is to warn persons that he will not pay them, as the contract has not been fulfilled by Martin.
Persons indebted to the estate of Jered PATTERSON, Newton twp, decd, are requested to make settlement. John BLACK, admr.

210. Apr 2 1800
The 4th Regiment will assemble in the respective companies. Appeals will be held at the house of Nathaniel WEAKLEY, Carlisle by the officers. William ALEXANDER, Lt. Col. Commanding the 4th Regt.
A Runaway - Whereas Robert M'COY, was on 28th Feb last, lawfully joined in the bands of wedlock, to the subscriber, and on Thurs last, without any just provocation or warning, left me, destitute of everything. This is therefore to caution all where this notice may come, from harbouring this bale, insinuating man, lest he may again occasion distress to afflicted parents and unoffending families. He is about 25 yrs of age, of a middling stature, and has long white hair; has followed school keeping for some years past. Mary M'COY, Derry twp, Dauphin co.

211. Apr 9 1800
Lancaster - Died in this borough on Fri, 28th ult, in his 59th yr, Mathew IRWIN, Esq., Master of the Rolls for the Commonwealth of Pennsylvania; remains interred in the burial ground of the English Presby Church.
Married Mon evening, 31st Mar, by Rev Dr. DAVIDSON, Lieut. OFFLEY, quarter master of the 10th regiment, to Miss Polly GREER.
A School for the tuition of youth in Reading, writing, arithmetic, bookkeeping and English grammar in the house lately occupied by John GLEN, Carlisle. John GIBBONS.
William DREVISH, has removed his store into the corner house of Dr. GUSTINE, opposite to Ephraim STEEL, facing the Market, Carlisle. A General assortment of dry goods and groceries - and best liquors.

212. Apr 16 1800
The horse, Bucephalus, property of Michael EGE, will stand at Carlisle Iron Works.

213. Apr 23 1800
Died Sat 19th inst in his 71st yr, after an illness of 2 days, which we are infomred was by a stroke of the palsey, Jonathan HOGE, Esq., one of the Assoc. Judges of this co. The Republicans may regret the loss of him from the Bench.
Line of stages will commence from Lancaster through this town to Shippens- burgh. [schedule given] - Henry SHEPLER.
James LAMBERTON, Carlisle, requests payment of debts.
Whereas the subscriber having passed seven bonds to Nicholas BOAR, of Bedford Co, this is to forwarn persons not to take assignment on said bonds.

Kline's Carlisle Weekly Gazette

214. Aor 30 1800 - Appointments: William MOORE, Esq. Assoc Judge, in the room of J. HOGE, Esq. decd, for this co. George LOGUE, Esq. Brigade Inspector for this co.

215. May 7 1800
Married on Thurs 24th Apr at New-Castle, by Rev Robert CLAY, Jh. L. D'HAPPART, to Miss Elizabeth THOMPSON, dau of the late General William THOMPSON.
Sale of tract in Mifflin twp, Cumberland co, 108 a.; also lot in town of Newville, and two lots in Newville. Archibald M'COY, Newville.
Testimonials regarding Hamilton's Worm Destroying Lozenges by: Michael DUFFY, No. 47 Wilkes st, Fell's Point, Baltimore city. He states on May last, his three children, boy of 7, girl of 5 and girl of 3, were taken ill with a common fever, troubled with convulsive fits, etc. - are now recovered. Aquila GOLDING, Hartford Road, 2 miles from Baltimore, had violent gnawing pain in his stomach ... and recovered with Hamilton's Lozenges; likewise his brother.
To be sold - agreeable to last will of Michael BOW, Carlisle, decd, house and two lots whereon the said Bow lived, now in the possession of John HERLEY, one of the legatees. John GAW, surviving exr.

216. May 14 1800
Appointments: David MITCHELL, Esq. Brigadier General of the 2d Brigade, 7th Division of the Militia, composed of Cumberland and Franklin. Solomon MAYER, Esq. Brigade Inspector for the county of York.
Andrew HUNTER, Carlisle, offers reward for horse missing from the Commons of Carlisle.
John HERBST offers reward for horse missing from the Commons of Carlisle.
Pat. CHEVENEY has commenced the stone cutting busniess, in the house formerly occupied by Matthew ALLISON, corner of Pomfret and Bedford Sts, Carlisle.
John LECHLER, Tin Plate Worker, has commenced the tinplate business in the house of Henry LECHLER, Gunsmith, York st, Carlisle.

217. May 21 1800
Died last week, Dr. James FORBES, son of John FORBES of this co.
Stone dwelling house for sale, with convenient out houses, Carlisle; apply to James DUNCAN, Esq., William BLAIR, of Carlisle, or the subscriber, Isaiah BLAIR, Washington, Pa.

218. May 28 1800
The duel which took place at Hagerstown was between Capt. GIBB and Lieut. FRANKLIN, in which the former was wounded. - both officers belonging to the 10th regiment.
John SPOTWOOD, living in Carlisle, offers reward for horse, missing from the Commons of Carlisle.
Joseph DODDS has taken up a horse near Mr. EGE's Forge, trespassing on the premises of the subscriber in Allen twp, Cumberland co.
French burr millstones for sale; apply at Alters Mill, 8 miles west of carlisle. Jacob ALTER, Junior.

Kline's Carlisle Weekly Gazette

219. Jun 4 1800
A duel took place yesterday, between Lieut. LAYBOURNE and Lieut. EVANS, of the 2d regiment of artillerists and Engineers, in consequence of a difference which had existed some time. They discharged a brace of pistols each. Lieut. Layburn's last shot entered Lieut. Evan's right side which wound although severe, was not mortal.
John TAYLOR, living in Middleton twp, Cumberland co, offers reward for apprentice boy named Samuel RANNALS, about 15-16 yrs of age, of a low size.

220. Jun 11 1800
Died Wed morning last in her 30th yr, after a long and painful sickness, Mrs. Margaret WEAKLEY, wife of Nat. WEAKLEY; remains interred in the burying ground adj this town.
Married last week by Rev Dr. NESBIT, William HOLLING, of Va, to Miss Jean SANDERSON, dau of Robert SANDERSON, of Middleton twp, in this co.
The Field Officers elect of the 1st Brigade, in the 7th Division, are to meet at the house of George WISE, Carlisle. George LOGUE, Brigade Inspector.
Whereas my wife Elizabeth hath eloped from my bed and board, without any just cause and hath otherwise behaved herself in an unbecoming manner, I do hereby forewarn persons from crediting her on my account. Godfrey SAUNDERS, Mifflin twp, Cumberland.

221. Jun 25 1800
Appointments: John M'KEE, of Hopewell twp, and Joseph DODDS, of Allan twp, in this co, Justices of the Peace. William RAMSAY of Carlisle, Deputy Surveyor for this co.
Adamantine Guard or Second Troop of Cumberland co Cavalry, Samuel CROWELL, Captain Elect, Newville, requests the troop assemble.
George FRESHER has petitioned for relief from debts.
Joseph LATSHAW, offers reward for milch cow which strayed from William MOORE's Mill on Yellow Breeches.
The following administration accounts have been filed: Susanna THOMPSON, exr of last will of Elizabeth PETERSON, Carlisle, decd; John CLARK, surviving exr of last will of Alexander M'NAIR, late of Toboine twp, decd; Sarah DEVLIN and George LOGUE, exrs of last will of Roger DEVLIN, Carlisle, decd; Samuel CROWELL, exr of last will of Rachel WALKER, decd, who was admr of estate of Joseph WALKER, late of Newton twp, decd; James HAMILTON and Saml. LAIRD, Esqrs, exrs of last will of Robert MAGAW, Esq. of Carlisle.
Marshal's sales of property of Oliver POLLOCK, in East Pennsborough twp, Cumberland co.
Persons indebted to estate of late Samuel PAXTON, decd, are requested to make immediate payment. Agness PAXTON, Richard GREGORY, admrs.

222. Jul 2 1800
Married Thurs last by Rev Dr. DAVIDSON, Lieut. POTTS, of 10th U.S. Regiment, to Miss Betsey HUGHES, dau of John HUGHES, Esq. of Carlisle.
Patrick LIGGET (his mark) offers reward for apprehending the thief of articles from his house. The thief is supposed to James ROBB, alias James ROBINSON, 5 ft 10 inches, swarthy complexion, black hair.
Samuel JOHNSTON offers reward for poney missing from commons of Carlisle.
Robert ARMSTRONG to sell house in town of Petersburgh.

Kline's Carlisle Weekly Gazette

223. Jul 9 1800
York - Died on Mon night last at the house of Capt. GOSSLER, in this borough, Lieut. John DOUGLAS, late of the 10th U.S. Regiment.
Died on Mon last, Alexander BLAINE, and interred in burying ground adj this borourgh.
Atcheson LAUGHLIN offers reward for two horses stolen out of his pasture at Newville, Cumberland co.
Henry REEHM, Tanner and currier, Letart Spring, Carlisle, seeks to get apprentice to the tanning and currying business.
James DUNCAN, Carlisle, havingh been lately appointed Treasurer of Cumberland Co, by the Board of Commissioners, requests all delinquent Collectors of state and co taxes to discharge their responsibilities without delay.
Henry GOEBEL, has received at his store, opposite Mr. FOSTER's tavern, a fresh supply of liquors.
300 a. of land for sale, situated on a large run, in Armstrong twp, Westmoreland co. Mary FILSON, living on the Walnut Bottom, 10 miles from Carlisle.

224. Jul 16 1800 - Henry PATTERSON offers his services as a teacher in the following branches: Reading, Writing and Arithmetic; English Grammar; Geometry; Euclid's Elements; Surveying and Navigation. Persons wishing to employ him, direct their inquiries to John M'KEE, Hopewell twp.

225. Jul 23 1800- William BOYD, Adams co, Menallen twp, has taken up a black horse.

226. Jul 30 1800
James CLENDENNEN, Carlisle, offers reward for horse which strayed from the plantation of John HUSTON, Eastpennsborough twp, Cumberland co.
The partnership of Jacob PEALE and Samuel REYNOLDS, hatters, of Shippensburgh, has been dissolved. The business will be carried on Samuel Reynolds, at the same place.

227. Aug 6 1800
Reward for horse missing from commons of Carlisle; deliver to Jacob FETTER, Carlisle.
Jacob SNAVELY, East Pennsbroough twp, offers reward for mare.

228. Aug 13 1800 - Chinese Doctor - Dr. John HOWARD, lately from Canton in China, now living in York st, at George WEISE's tavern, Carlisle, will undertake to cure any disease or complaint.

229. Aug 20 1800
Phila - Died last night at his country res near Frankford, Robert CAMPBELL, Bookseller and Stationer of this city.
Married Wed last, at the farm seat of William GODFREY in York co, by Rev CAMPBELL, John OLIVER, merchant of Carlisle, to Miss Hannah GODFREY, dau of William GODFREY.
Whereas Samuel QUIGLEY, of Shippensburg in Cumberland co, obtained from the subscriber several bonds, this is to forwarn persons from taking assignment on these bonds, as Quigley has not made good his contract. Henry LEAR.

Kline's Carlisle Weekly Gazette

230. Aug 27 1800
A Meeting of the Republicans of this co convened at the house of William HEIGLE, Runnel BLAIR, Esq. in the chair, and James MOORE, Esq. Secretary.
By order of the assignees of GAZZAM, TAYLOR and JONES, will be sold a variety of store goods and a lot in Louther st, opposite Alexander THOMPSON's - Edward MAGAURAN, agent, Carlisle.
To be sold at Public vendue - furniture [described] - John OFFICER.

231. Sep 3 1800
Died Mon last after a short illness, James POLLOCK, one of the earliest inhabitants of this co.
A new town called Griersburg, has lately been laid out in Beaver formerly Alleghenny co. Lots may be purchased from George GRIER, living on the Walnut Bottom road, or from William MARTIN and Thomas SPROAT, living at the place.
To be sold at the late dwelling house of Alexander BLAINE, decd, Middleton twp, Cumberland co, horses, cows, sheep and hogs, rey in the sheaf or bushel, waggon and geers, ploughs, sledge, harrow, furniture and other. James M'CORMICK and Jonathan HOGE, admrs.

232. Sep 10 1800
Last Monday commenced the Court of Oyer and Terminer and General Goal Delivery of Cumberland co with John Joseph HENRY, Esq. presiding as the new president. Robert PORTER of Shippensburgh was tried for the murder of Barnabas DUFFY, stabbing said Duffy at a Regimental Review on 21st Apr last - acquitted. John and William M'ALISTER were tried for the murder of CAESAR, a negro man, on 14th Apr last, property of John M'Alister. [Testimony of William YUN(?) is given in full in this article. He describes how the negro man was beaten and abused, accused of stealing money; mentions Jane OGDEN grand daughter to John M'Alister, Mary OGDEN dau of John M'Alister. Found guilty and sentenced to 5 yrs in the penitentiary of Phila. The youngest man was over 50 yrs. Other cases: a certain GRIFFITH for burning the foundary of Michael EGE, John HENRY and John HENRY, junior, his son, charged with death of negro woman; jury found death to be a misadventure.
George DAWSON defends the efficacy of his patent medicines.
Members of the Union Fire Company will attend with their buckets in the Centre Square for the purpose of exercising the Engine. James DUNCAN, Clk.
Samuel DUNCAN, appointed Surveyor of the Revenue, 3d Assessment District, 6th Division, consisting of Cumberland Co.

233. Sep 17 1800
Philip GROVE, waggon-maker, Carlisle, seeks apprentice to the waggon making business.
Whereas the subscriber having passed 12 bonds for 60 pounds each, payable to Peter GANDER, living in the state of Va, in consideration of a tract in Mifflin twp, Cumberland co, I forwarn persons from taking assignment on bonds as Gander has not made the land agreeable to contract. Abraham JUMPER.
Sale of plantation in Hopewell twp, 8 miles from Shippensburgh, 510 a., late the property of Abraham SMITH - Jacob SMITH and James SMITH, exrs.

Kline's Carlisle Weekly Gazette

Persons indebted to estate of John SHIMP, late of Middleton twp, Cumberland co, decd, are desired to make payment - Adam COOPER and Jacob WHITMORE, admrs, Middleton twp.
Hugh M'ALISTER, Mifflin co, Fermanagh twp, offers rewad for lost watch.
William MOORE, Middleton twp, offers reward for lost watch.

234. Sep 24 1800
Died at Landisburgh, Shearmans Valley, George CROOK, lately from Baltimore; it is believed he died from the Yellow Fever.
On Monday 15th at Baltimore, Dr. Charles STIMMECKIE, formerly of this town.
On Wed last, at the Mouth of Juniata, Daniel CLARK, oldest son of the late John CLARK, decd.
The subscriber, having practiced the teaching of the Latin and Greek languages for more than 30 yrs, in several established public institutions, under the direction of reputable professors, particularly Rev Dr. James DAVIDSON and Rev Dr. Charles NISBET, proposes to open an Academy in the borough of Lancaster.
Andrew MURRAY, taylor, Carlisle, offers reward for apprentice lad, named Anthony M'GAGHEY, by trade a taylor.
Married Tues 16th last, by Rev WAUGH, Charles PATTISON, of Carlisle, to Miss Polly MATEER, of Allan twp.
George CROCKET certifies the curative effects of Dawson's ague drops.
Reuben LEWIS certifies that his wife was cured of the ague and fever by Mr. DAWSON's ague drops; also testimonials from John SMITH and James HALL, Carlisle.
The following Administration Accounts have been filed: Supplementary administration account of Henry SNIVELY, surviving exr of last will of Henry Snively, decd; administration account of James WILSON and Levi WILSON, exrs of last will of William WILSON, decd, late of Tyrone twp; supplementary administration account of John SOMERVILLE and John REYNOLDS, admrs of estate of David SOMERVILLE, decd; account of John CLARK, surviving exr of last will of Alexander M'NAIR, decd, late of Toboyne twp; Supplementary account of Henry FURRER, surviving exr of last will of Robert PATTERSON, decd, late of East Pennsborough twp; admistration account of Christen LOUDON and Archibald LOUDON, admrs of the estate of James LOUDON, decd, late of Rye twp.
John STEEL has taken up two stray cows.
The Cumberland Co troop of horse to parade in Carlisle - Mathew MILLER, Capt.
James CLENDENNEN, Dry goods and groceries, request payment of accounts.
Charles CUMMINS, living in Franklin co, near Strasburg, offers reward for negro man, named BILL, about 5 ft 5-6 inches, abut 26 yrs of age, short thick built.

235. Oct 1 1800
Married in Adams co, on Thurs last by Rev Samuel WAUGH, James RAMSAY, merchant, of Carlisle, to Miss Elizabeth SMITH, dau of Captain John SMITH of Adams Co.
On same evening in Carlisle, by Rev Dr. NESBIT, Mr. KNIX, late a Lieutenant in the 10th Regiment, to Miss Hannah DOUGLAS, dau of John DOUGLASS, merchant of Carlisle.

Kline's Carlisle Weekly Gazette

Notice to persons who applied for Tavern Licences - Frederick J. HALLER, clerk of the Court of General Quarter Sessions of the Peace, of Cumberland co.
Persons indebted to the estate of Jonathan HOGE, Esq, decd, late of East Pennsborough twp, Cumberland co, are requested to make payment. James HOGE, John CAROTHERS, admrs.
Sheriff's sale of tract of land, 1000 a. in Rye twp, on the Susquehanna, at the mouth of Fishing Creek, a dwelling house, large orchard, distillery, fishery, property of John W. KITTERA, Esq. - John CAROTHERS, Sheriff.

236. Oct 8 1800
Married Thurs 25th Sep last by Robert LUSK, Esq., Henry HILL, of Hopewell twp, to Miss Grizzy CUPELS, of Mifflin twp.
Charles M'MANUS, Carlisle wants to purchase at his new distillery in Carlisle, a quantity of Rye and other grain, also hops and cord wood.
Will be sold agreeable to last will of John SANDERSON, decd, 344 a. in Tyrone twp, Cumberland co, 16 miles from Carlisle, on great road leading from Clark's ferry to head of Shearmans valley. William LINN and Wilson M'CLURE, exrs.

237. Oct 15 1800
Accident - As John CHAIN started with his waggon to go home, his horses took fright and ran off, and by his endeavours to catch the hind horse by the bridle he fell off, and the waggon ran over him, he expired in a very short time. He was a young man in the prime of life and has left a widow and distressed mother and relatives.
William BLAIR offers reward for mare missing from pasture of Samuel RAMSAY.
18 pence per pound will be given for clean combed hog's bristles - Samuel JACKSON, Mifflin Town.

238. Oct 22 1800
A fulling mill to let, Frankford twp, about 4 miles from Carlisle. William PARKER, living on the premises.
The 12th Regt of the Pa Militia will assemble - Captains of the 1st Battalion: John SANDERSON, James MORLAND and Jonathan HAWSON; Captain in the 2nd Battalion: John UNDERWOOD, George CART, and Philip LAUFFMAN. Charles BOVARD, Liuet. Col. Com. 12th Regt.

239. Oct 29 1800
Thirty dollars reward will be paid for the apprehending of a swindler, who went by the name of John HENDERSON, has in possession false notes on sundry persons by which he obtained various articles. He is about 5 ft 5-6 inches high, slender, smart made fellow, thin faced, brown bushy hair, fair complexion. - George PATTISON, John ANDERSON, John FRY, Jacob HENDEL, Carlisle.

Kline's Carlisle Weekly Gazette

240. Nov 12 1800
Died Sat 1st inst, after a very painful illness, Mrs. Nancy CRAIGHEAD, wife of Major Gilson CRAIGHEAD; remains interred into the burying ground adj this town.
- On Sat 8th inst, after a lingering and painful disease, Captain John STEEL, of the U.S. Army; remains interred with honours of war, attended by Captain Mathew MILLERs Troop of Horse and Captain Robert MILLERs Company of Infantry.
- On Sun last, Richard HEMMING.
John WEAVER, 3 1/2 miles below Carlisle, offers reward for horse stolen from his pasture.
Whereas a man calling himself Samuel JOLLY brought with him to the subscriber a grey horse [which on close examination was found to be stolen]. Owner may claim him. George M'CANDLISS, Shippensburgh.
45 a. of limestone land for sale on south side of Yellow Breeches Creek - James R. HOGE, on the premises.
The subscriber executed 3 notes in favour of James MOOR, of Shipensburgh, which notes the subscriber is now determined not to pay - Ebenezer CAMPBELL.

241. Nov 19 1800 - Adam LYDICK, Allen twp, Cumberland co, has taken up a stray steer.

242. Nov 26 1800
Earthquake shock in Carlisle on Thurs morning last, more severe towards Harrisburgh and Reading.
Died Thurs last at his farm adj this town, Stephen FOULK, Sen.; his remains interred at Huntingdon, York Co, in and advanced stage of life, a long time sick.
Richard DOUGHERTY to open an English School in Carlisle.
Persons indebted to estate of William CAMELON, decd, are requested to make payment. David WILLIAMSON, exr.
David GREER, Dickinson twp, Cumberland co, about 5 miles from Carlisle, has taken up a stray mare.

243. Dec 3 1800
Married on Tues 25th Nov ult, Rowland CURTAIN, merchant, of Bell Fount, to Miss Margary GREGG, dau of John GREGG of this co.
Died last week in the City of Phila, John NICHOLSON, Esq., late Comptroller General for the Sate of Pa.
To be sold at the dwelling house of Stephen FOULK, Sen, decd, Middleton twp: wheat, rye, hay, horses, cows, working oxen, cattle, sheep, wagons, ploughs, masons, carpenters and coopers tools, and other. Samuel BLACKBURN and Thomas FOSTER, exrs.

244. Dec 10 1800
These are to certify that William GILSON, on his way from Westmoreland Co, says he had his saddle bags opened and a quantity of money taken out and papers among which was bons of John MILLER, of Cumberland co. He says he is nearly certain that they were taken out at the house of Josiah SMITH, near Mercersburgh. James IRWIN, Josiah SMITH, Mercersburg, Franklin co.
For sale - plantation, 165 a., in Eastpennsborough twp, about 3 miles from Walker's mill - John CLENDINEN.

Kline's Carlisle Weekly Gazette

Just received and to be sold by A. LOUDON, the Beggar Girl and her
Benefactress, in 3 volumes. [other titles given]

245. Dec 17 1800
John OLIVER has received a neat and general assortment of Dry Goods,
Groceries, Hardware, & Cutlery, China & Queens Ware.
Persons in possession of Public Arms, property of the Commonwealth, are
hereby enjoined to deliver them to the subscriber - George LOGUE, Brig.
Insp., First Brigade, 7th Division, Pa, Militia.
Alexander THOMPSON, offers reward for filly missing from the commons of
Carlisle.
Daniel M'DANNEL, living on Conedoguinet Creek, has taken up a stray horse.

246. Dec 24 1800
Married Thurs last by Rev Francis HERRON, Abraham SMITH of this co, to Miss
Jane LINN, dau of William LINN, of Franklin Co.
Died Wed 17th inst, Mrs. Margaret WILSON, wife of James WILSON, merchant of
Landisburgh, in her 38th yr, long time affected with a painful disease;
remains buryed at the Centre Meeting house. She left a husband and 5
small children.
To be let on the shares, a plantation - James CAROTHERS, Sen., Cumberland
co, Westpennsbro' twp.

247. Dec 31 1800
Died on Sun morning, 31st inst, about 6 o'clcok, Major Gen. HARTLEY, in his
52d yr. He took an early and active part in the late Revolution,
commanded a Regiment. After quitting military life he returned to the
practice of the Law, member of the state convention which adopted the
Federal constitution; later represented the county of York in Congress.
His remains were interred in the burial ground of St. John's Church.
To be rented, a plantation in Middletown twp, 5 miles from Carlisle, 1 1/2
miles from Jacob WAGGONER's, 200 a., estate of Peter LANE, decd. Benjamin
CRANE, Martin KITE, Guardians.
To be sold - 157 a. in Southampton twp, Cumberland co, adj lands of Thomas
DUNCAN, Esq., Robert M'CUNE, Samuel CHESNER, and others; the Great Road
from Shippensburgh to Carlisle goes through said tract. Conrad VARNOR.
Persons who purchased articles at the vendue late the estate of Adam MELL,
decd, and whose notes are due, are requested to make payment. John MELL,
admr.
To be let - plantation and saw-mill in Greenwood twp, Cumberland co, late
the este of John NORTH, decd, 310 a., adj Joshua NORTH and the Juniata
river. Catharine NORTH, William NORTH, John JORDAN, Greenwood twp, admrs.
Plantation to be let, 115 a., in Allen twp, Cumberland co. William BORE, &
Andw. EMMENGER, Guardians.

The Pennsylvania Herald & York General Advertiser

248. Jan 6, 1796
Jacob KEYSER, of Codorus Twp, York Co, offers 6 cents reward for runaway German Servant Girl named Margaret WARTIN; she is marked with the small pox, wore a striped lindsey peticoat & red flannel short gound.
Whereas my wife Ruth HART eloped from my bed & board without any just cause, I caution persons not to give her any credit. Jacob HART.
John GREER has removed his store (in-part) from his old situation to the Corner House on the public square, north side of High St., formerly occupied by John EDIE, Esq. as a printing office, and next door to Mr. Baltzer SPANGLER's Tavern, sign of the Black Horse. Has a large & handsome assortment of goods for the approaching season.
Tract for sale in Mountjoy Twp., York Co, adj lands of Thomas & Samuel M'CUNE and Samuel HUTCHENSON; 150 a., late the property of Thomas ORBISON, decd, on which there is a dwelling house, barn & other buildings. Apply to William EGNEW, living on the premises or to William BAILEY at Mountpleasant Twp.
William EMMIT has for sale a Merchant Mill, Saw Mill & Distillery in Tom's Creek, within 1/2 mile of Emmitsburgh (Md); dwelling house at mill. On great road from Frederick Town (Md) to Carlisle. Apply to subscriber in Emmitsburgh.
To be sold by Public Vendue, plantation of 166 a. in Mountpleasant Twp, York Co, 1 mile from Oxford, adj lands of Andrew M'ILVAIN, William STURGEON, Martin SHUP & others, late the estate of Michael CLAPSADLE, decd. 2 dwelling houses, one stone the other log, barn with under story of stone. Apply to Daniel CLAPSADLE.
John MORRIS, Notary Public & Conveyancer, informs that he continues to transact business in his office, 2d door from the Bridge near the Sign of the Ship, Borough of York, where acknowledgements of Deeds, Letters of Attorney, &c. are drawn up.
Andrew JOHNSTON has just received at his shop, next door west of Col. Archibald STEEL's & opposite Capt. Philip GOSSLER's Tavern, in the Main St., York Town, wines, liquors & groceries.
Conrad LAUB, Collector of Revenues, informs owners of stills in York Co that licenses are due.
Samuel PORTER selling plantation in Hammiltonbann Twp., York Co, 269 a., 2 dwelling houses, double barn, stables & other out houses. There is a laid out road across the South Mountain by the Cold Spring which passes through this tract near the dwelling house to James MARSHALL's Merchant Mill, which is about 3 miles. Apply to subscriber living on premises.
For sale - in Manchester Twp, 1/4 mile from Borough of York, 12 a. under good fencing & divided into 5 parts by cross fences. Has thriving hop-yard, good barn & stable, stone still house & implements. Apply to William HARRIS, York Borough.
Persons indebted to James SHORT are requested to make payment. Also he is selling a fine assortment of goods & tract of land in Hammiltonbann Twp, 300 a. Apply to David DUNWOODY or William TAYLOR near the premises.
Persons indebted to the estate of Jacob ROMICH, late of York Co, decd, are required to settle up by 1 Feb next. Jacob FAUS & Rosina ROMICH, Adm'rs.
Robert DUNN has for sale 4000 a. of Genesee lands lying within 3 miles of the Conondaque Lake & 3 miles from Crooked Lake, within 12 miles of the County Town. Also 500 a. on the Honeoy Lake.
To be let by Alexander COBEAN, living on the premises, Complete Merchant Mill on Marsh Creek, Cumberland Twp, York Co, 3 1/2 miles from Gettysburgh. Has dwelling house, store house & still house, barn &

stables. He also offers for sale tract adj the above of 154 a., with new Saw Mill, Stone dwelling house 2-stories high & large double barn. Also all persons indebted to the subscriber are requested to pay up.
Robert WILSON occupies the Tavern kept by Robert DUNN, the sign of the Waggon, on the North side of High St, Borough of York, where travellers can be entertained.
To be let for 3 or 4 years - plantation adj Hunter's Town known by the name of "Greenplace," 314 a. Apply Alexander RUSSELL, Esq. near Gettysburg or to James RIIDLE in Chambersburg.
Whereas Frederick DIEHL purchased from Thomas Sim LEE, Esq., a piece of land, part of tract called "Franconia" in Mountjoy Twp, York Co, for payment of which the subscriber executed Bonds to said T. S. LEE. One remains unapid & will become due in April. This is to caution persons not to take an assignment of said bond.
Whereas a certain Peter HUBER of Lancaster Co, obtained a bond from Jacob ERB(?) of York Co, ERB warns all persons against taking said bond.
The Trustees of the Methodist Meeting House have determined that said Meeting House is found to have windows broken & destroyed by the Sons of credible Inhabitants of this Borough (York) & being duly informed who they are: Those who have been busily imployed in the said wicked purposes are desired to make and amend said Windows & repair them, or be dealt with according to law. Jacob SITLER, James WORLEY, Senr. & George NAILER, Trustees.

249. Next available issue Jan 20, 1796
Charles WILLIAMSON, Bath, Ontavio Co, NY, having a great extent of digging to be performed by early next summer in the Genesee Country, & hiring persons to do same. Work to be executed at 3 different places, viz. at a set of Merchant Mills near the Friend Settlement, a set of Merchant Mills north from Geneva, building at he forks of Canadurqui & Mud Creeks & at Williamsburgh on the Canaseraga (?) Creek. Also seeking Master Carpenter.
Public auction to let plantation, property of James BLACK; in the intersection of the 2 public roads from York to Chambersburgh & from Baltimore to Shippensburgh. There has been a public house of entertainment long kept on the premises. Samuel COBEAN, William GILLELAND & Alexander RUSSELL, Trustees.
Robert LUCAS, living near Shepherds Town, Berkley Co, Va, offers reward for runaway Negro man named Daniel, 27 years of age, 5 ft 8 in high, stout made, small scars on his left side, pretends to Religion in order to deceive & pass for a free man.
All persons indebted to estates of Richard M'ALISTER, Esq. & Abdiel M'ALLISTER, both late of Town of Hanover, York Co, decd, are requested to pay Jacob RUDISELL, Esq., an exec'r. living in Hanover. Archibald & Jesse M'ALISTER & Jacob RUDISELL, Ex'rs.
John PORTER selling farm in Carrolsburgh, 215 a., with 2-story stone house & other out buildings. (Hamiltonsbann Twp)
Was committed to custody a Negro Man who calls himself Jack, says he belongs to John SUMMERFIELD of St. Mary's Co.; can read German. 5 ft 8 in high, about 25 years of age. Also committed to myu custody a certain young Man who has the appearance of a Mutiee, calls himself William SPENCER, says he came frorm Gunpowder Falls; about 22 years, 5 ft 6 in high. Michael GRAYBELL, Gaoler, York.
For Sale - plantation & tract in Dover Twp, York Co, 203 (?) a. with 2-story stone house & spring house, barn & stable; subject to Dower's Right. Apply George WOGAN & William WELSH, Ex'rs. Borough of York

The Pennsylvania Herald & York General Advertiser

249. (Con't.)
Whereas an advertisement was published offering a reward for the apprehension of a certain Michael HEVICE & for restoration of Catharine SPENCE to her Friends, this is to notify that said HEVICE has been taken & Catharine is now with her Mother & Step-father. Michael & Mathias SCHMYSER, Guardians of Catharine SPENCE.

250. First page missing, from dates of ads assumed issue of Jan 27, 1796
Jacob HOOBER, Millwright, living in Strasburgh Village, 8 miles from Lancaster on the great road from Lancaster to Newport, selling as usual French Burr Millstones & Boulting Cloths, Rolling Skreens.
Jacob LEMMON selling plantation called Springfield, 600 a. whereon he now lives; has Merchant Mill & 2-story dwelling House, Kitchen, Spinning Room & barn with good stables. About 23 miles from Baltimore & 10 from Rauble's Tavern. Also another tract within one mile of above of 430 a. Apply to Joshua LEMMON in Baltimore or Jacob on premsies.
James SHORT offers for sale a large assortment of goods & tract of land in Hammiltonsbann Twp, 160 (?) a., log house, double barn &c. Apply to David DUNWOODY or Wm. TAYLOR, near the premises.
Jacob WELSH selling plantation within 5 miles of Carlisle in Cumberland Co. of 350 a. Large 2-story stone dwelling house, 50 ft in front with Kitchen & smoke house adj.; barn 76 ft in length; still house & tanyard of 26 vats with house, garden & stables. Apply to Jacob WELSH on the premesis or to Jacob WELSH living near Berlin.
Whereas I gave 2 notes to Joseph MARSHALL, this is to caution persons from taking said notes as I mean to dispute payment. John ECKENROTH.

251. Feb 3, 1796
Farm in Cumberland Twp, York Co of 600 a. to be sold by William VANCE. Has 2 dwelling houses, 2 barns, good orchard, spring house. Call upon George GONSE on the premises or William VANCE.
Frederick EICHELBERGER has taken in stray livestock.

252. Feb 10, 1796
Pa. Legislature passed a bill for the relief of Joshua WORSHAM & a bill to enable Oliver POLLOCK & Henry NEAFF to erect dams on Conedogwynet Creek. Also a petition from Dr. Samuel DUFFIELD, Physician of Port of Phila, stating the insufficiency of his compensation for his duties & praying relief.
Nancy BURGESS requests the merchants & tradesmen of Borough of York not to deal with or trust William BURGESS of said Borough, as he is so deranged as to render him incapable to transacting business.
Joseph UPDEGRAFF selling tract in Newberry & Dover Twps, 9 miles from York, 356 a., with Oyl & Saw Mills. Laurel Run runs through same for near 2 miles, then empties into great Conowago Creek. Apply to John FORSYTH, Deputy Surveyor.
All persons having demands against the estate of John LEAMOR, late of Warrington Twp, decd, are requested to present same. John BOWER & George HARMAN, Ex'rs.
Robert KERR has taken in a stray cow at his plantation in Nickolsons Gap, York Co.

Feb 17, 1796 (First two pages only, no new local information.)

The Pennsylvania Herald & York General Advertiser

253. Feb 24, 1796
Sheriff's Sales: (1) Estate of Adam BROWN, mesinage & 2 lots of ground, also a certain Store House & half lot in Town of Berlin, adj lots of Widow BORDENHEIMER & John NOGGLE. (2) Estate of George STEPHENSON, one undivided thrid part of 50 a. in Chanceford Twp, part of Burkholder's Ferry. Also 100 a. in Shrewsbury Twp, adj lands of Jacob SPEAKLY & others. Also 200 a. in Germany Twp, adj lands of the DIGG's & heirs of Peter LITTLE, decd. Seized & taken to be sold by William M'CLELLAN, Sh.
To be sold on the premises, tract in Mountpleasant twp, late the property of William COOPER, Senr., decd; 130 a., dwelling house, double barn &c. Also sold on same day horses, cows, sheep, hogs, oxen, grain in the ground & by the bushel, hay in stacks &c. William & James COOPER, Ex'rs.
To be let for one or more years - plantation in Newbury Twp., York Co, late the estate of Joseph TODD, decd., 100 a., 2-story house & double barn. Thomas OWEN & Eli KIRK, Guardians.
To be sold - plantation in Chanceford Twp, York Co, within 2 miles of Maj. TURNER's Mill, 156 a., dwelling house, double barn &c. Apply to James BROWN on the premises.
For Sale - 2-story brick house with 3/4 of a whole lot of ground on the North side of High St, Borough of York, adj lots of Gen. MILLER & John ROTHROCK. Has barn with stables. Apply to George WORLEY, living on the premises.
A bill for the relief of Valentine ECKHART was read & passed in the Pa. Legislature; & the bill for relief of John M'KINNEY was agreed to. Bill to authorize Brintnell ROBERTS to erect a mill dam over part of the Youghegeheney river was agreed to.
To be sold noted Plantation in Town of Hanover, York Co, late the property of Richard M'ALLISTER, Esq., decd, adj Town of Hanover, 18 miles from York & 45 from Baltimore; 240 a., brick House & Kitchen, each 2 stories high, on lot of ground on the center square in said Town, a new bank Barn 96 ft by 30 of Brick & Timber above. The ground rents of said Town of Hanover will also be sold with the premisses. Also the one undivided moiety of 539 a. on the waters of Gunpowder (Co of Baltimore) near Hoffman's Paper Mill. Also 35 a. timber land in Mountjoy Twp, York Co, 3 miles from Hanover, near the road from Little's Town to Gettysburgh. Archibald & Jesse M'ALLISTER & Jacob RUDISELL, Exr's.
William M'GREW selling plantation in Strabane Twp, lying along great Conewago Creek, 300 a. New double barn. Apply to M'GREW living thereon.
For sale a tract in Berkley Co., Va., 11 miles from Martinsburg the County Town, 14 from Bath & 6 from the river Potowmack; 400 a., dwelling House, Kitchen, Stables &c. The subscribers by consent, being determined to dissolve their partnership in said land & other property thereon. Apply to Samuel REED, who lives in Martinsburg or Wm. STEPHENSON on the premises.
The partnership between Lewis MICHAEL & Co., York Town & Hanover M'Allisters Town is dissolved by mutual consent. Nicholas SINGER has commenced store keeping at the store house of Lewis MICHAEL & Co. in Yrok Town.
All indebted to the estate of James ALLEN, late of Strabane Twp, decd., are desired to pay same to James ALLEN, Adm'r.

254. Mar 2, 1796
Pa. Legislature: A bill to enable Samuel SCHERER & Christopher FRUST to erect a ferry over Swettar(?) Creek, near Hummelstown.
Tobias HOLLINGER, Huntingdon Twp, York Co, has taken in a stray red cow.

254. (Con't.)
Whereas the eldest Son & Heir at Law of the Rev. Jacob LESCHEY, late of
York Co, decd, having taken the real estate of said decd at the valuation
thereof, did in pursuance of a decree of Orphans Court of said Co, in
1781 give his obligation to Killilan ZIEGLER & Mary his wife; Henry
ROBINER & Judith his wife; Sarah LESCHEY, Frederick ROEMER & Magdalena
his wife; Elizabeth LESCHEY, Margaret LESCHEY & to Killian ZIEGLER,
Guardian of Catharine & John LESCHEY, children of said intestate; for the
sum of 16 pounds, 9s 4d each, their respective shares after the death of
Susannah, the Widow of said decd; & whereas a claim hath been made to
part of said decd lands, so valued aforesaid--all persons are cautioned
not to take any assignments of said obligations as I am determined not to
pay them. Jacob LESCHEY.
To be sold or let - tract late the property of Andrew TRIMMER, decd, in
Reading Twp, York Co, 1 mile from Berlin, 120 a. Apply to Anthony
DEARDORFF & David TRIMMER, Ex'rs.
Samuel RICHARDS selling tract in Newbury Twp, York Co, on Bennet's Run near
Conowago Creek, 5 miles from Middleton & 12 from York., containing 200
a., late in the tenure of James HANCOCK. Apply to Eli KIRK, York Town or
subscriber at No. 136 South Front St, Philadelphia.

255. Mar 9, 1796
Whereas my wife Mary hath eloped from my bed & board since the 10th day of
Jan inst. with any just cause or provocation, I do forwarn all from
crediting her on my account. John M'INTIRE
Whereas William HEIFFER gave a note to John MONEWELL, persons are hereby
warned that he is determined to not pay same.
Tract to be sold in Strabane Twp, York Co, adj Hunter's Town & lands of
John DICKSON, Esq.; 176 a. Also offers for rent for 3 years, another
tract of land adj the above of 200 a. For terms apply to Wm. SCOTT Esq.,
at Hunter's Town & John DICKSON.
2 Houses & lot for sale in Borough of York. Lot on Water St in said
borough, adj lot of John GUCKES & a 20 ft. alley; on said lot are 2
dwelling houses, late the dwelling place of Luowick HETICK, decd. Apply
to Jacob OPP & Thomas HETICK.
Whereas a certain William HANAGAN, late of the Town of Strawsburg in the Co
of Franklin (Taylor) did obtain by court a credit with me & afterwards
did by virtue of said contract & for his relief obtain from me a Bond for
the security of said HANAGAN's bail, who had forfeited his recogizance to
the Court of the County--& also one other obligation for the balance
that might be still found due on said contract, he has since been
confined in prison at York & is said to be about to apply for the benefit
of the insolvent laws, falsely alledging that he has not received Bonds
on the aforesaid contract. Said bonds should be brought to me &
discharged. Mathew DUNCAN, Strasburgh.

256. Mar 16, 1796
For Sale- Farm in Frederick Co (Md) called The Meadow-Enlarged, on the
Meadow Branch, about 38 miles from Baltimore, 6 from Taney Town, 8 from
Westminster & 26 from Frederick Town, 243 a. 2-story house 36 x 20 ft.,
9 rooms & 6 fireplaaces, barn is framed & weather-boarded, 56 x 30 ft.
Apply to Howard RODGERS, who lives on the pplace. Indisputable title can
be made by Stephen WINCHESTER & William ROBERTS, Junr.

The Pennsylvania Herald & York General Advertiser

256. (Con't.)
For Rent - the best store in York, on the corner of High & Beaver Sts, & the home adj in the tenure of John GREEN. Apply to John CLARK, borough of York.
For Sale or Rent - Well known brick house in Westminster Town (Md) where Jacob SHERMON now lives, with or without 100 a. of land adj. 2-story house with 5 rooms on a floor, Kitchen, Dairy & Smoke House, large yard with sheds for 20 teams, large barn with threshing floor & stables. Has been occupied for 20 years as a Tavern stand. 28 miles from Baltimore, & nearly central between the Towns of Taney, Reisters & Little's. Also for sale one other Plantation about 20(?) miles from the former, 150 a., log dwelling house, barn & stables. Likewise 144 a. of woodland lying on the waters of big Pipe Creek. Apply to Jacob SHERMON living in Westminster Town, Frederick Co, Md.
Stephen WINCHESTER, selling Plantation on which he now lives of 300 a., 2-story frame house 32 x 14 ft., two rooms on a floor & brick smoke house & dairy, corn-house, grainery, barn & stables f80 x 22 ft. Adjacent to the town of Westminster (Md), 28 miles from Baltimore.
Plantation & tract in Paradise Twp, York Co, for sale. Part of the land adj the Great Road from Borough of York to M'ALLISTER's Town. 290 a., log house, double barn & stabling. Will be put up at Public Sale at the late dwelling house of Peter WOLFE, decd by George BARD, Adam WOLFF & Henry WOLFF, Ex'rs.
For Sale - plantation & tract of 270 a. in Cumberland Twp, York Co, adj lands of David DUNWOODY, John SWENEY & lands formerly belonging to Col. Hans HAMILTON, late the property of James M'CLURE, decd. Apply to Samuel EDIE, Esq., near the premises or to John EDIE in York Town.
To be sold - plantation & tract in Paradise Twp, York Co, 9 miles from Borough of York, late the property of Peter DICKS, decd., 157 a., good stone dwelling house, log barn, stone spring house with excellent spring of water. House stands on beautiful eminance commanding a prospect of the Spring Forge. Apply Tempest TUCKER & Christian HERSHEY, Ex'rs.

257. Mar 23, 1796
The fire company in this Borough are desired to attend at the house of Philip GOSSLER in order to appoint officers.
Ran away from Col. Josiah CLAPHAM's Iron Works in Loudon Co, Va, a Negro Man named Joseph; of yellow complexion, 5 ft 4 in high, lusty & well made, about 35 years of age. I expect he will endeavour to get to Pa, as he made an attempt to get there last Aug & was brought from Washington Co gaol in Md, he at that time passed by the name of Tom. Bring to Edmund IDNINGS, living near said Iron Works.
Ran away from Archibald MURTARD, in Hopewell Twp, Co of Cumberland, an Indented Servant Boy named Wm. WATSON, about 15 years of age, fair complexion with short hair. He got hurt in his left arm when he was young, which he cannot lift to his head without pain. $20 reward if taken in Pa.
For sale in Huntington Twp, York Co, Plantation of John WIERMAN, Senr. of 220 a., with orchard of 170 apple trees &c. Also an improvement & tract in Menallen Twp, York Co, property of John WIERMAN, 213 a.
For Sale- dwelling house in Shepherds Town, Berkley Co, Va., 23 x 26 ft. with good cellar & kitchen with running water at the kitchen door, smoke house & good garden. Tanyard adj same with good bark-house 45 x 23 ft. with 10 vats, & Currying Shop. Also Distillery & malt house with stills & utensils. Apply to John BROWN on the premises.

The Pennsylvania Herald & York General Advertiser

257. (Con't.)
Robert WILSON occupies the Tavery kept by Robert DUNN, the sign of the Waggon on the North side of High St., Borough of York.
The Public are hereby informed, that Negro Clem & Negro Chery, formerly of the State of Md are now living at Frederick EIGHELBERGER's, 1 mile from Borough of York. Any persons have any claim to said Negroes are requested to come forward.

258. Mar 30, 1796
John HERSH gave a bond unto Peter BRUGH & he is determined not to pay.
James BRINKERHOFF, of Mountpleasant Twp, determined to leave this State by 1 May next, expects all he hath accounts against unsettled to come forward & settle.
To be sold by virtue of an order of the Orphans Court of York Co, in the Twp of Berwick (Abbots Town) 1 house & lot in said Town, adj lots of Conrad DOLL & Sebastian HEIFFER. Also a lot of 5 a. adj Abbots Town on the West & bounded by lands of Peter ICKES, Henry LEHMER, late the estate of Michael HARDING, decd. Terms made known by Jane HARDING, Adm'x.
To be let, a farm within 1 1/2 miles of York Borough, lately owned by Dr. JAMESON. Apply to Ralph BOWIE, borough of York.

259. April 6, 1796
Eli LEWIS, together with Joseph EDMUNDSON, executed a judgment Bond payable to a certain Jacob FURRY (?), Borough of York, being in part of the consideration money of a plantaton purchased from said Jacob in Newbury Twp, Co of York. Said Bond was declined in the hands of Eli LEWIS & not really delivered to said Jacob, by reason that the title to the Land could not be made.
All persons indebted to Jacob HORST, formerly of Newbury twp, Co of York, decd. are required to settle. John HORST & George SCHROLE, Ex'rs.

260. April 13, 1796
Notice given to delinquent Collectors of the County levy of 1795 to attend at said office to settle & pay off their duplicates. Jos. WELSBHANS(?), Henry WELSH & Thomas BLACK, Commissioners.

261. April 20, 1796
Conrad LAUB, Collector of the Revenue for York Co, informs that those who follow the trade or business of Auctioneer or Vendue-Crier within the county must apply to his office for license.

262. April 27, 1796
George SCHNELBLCHER, Dover Twp, York Co, about 7 miles from Borough of York, has taken in an Iron Gray Mare.
Whereas Christian LAUER in March 1792 executed sundry Bonds to a certain George WAGNER of Northumberland Co, 3 of which remain in the hands of said WAGNER; this warns all that LAUER refuses to pay them.
Adam HOOVER occupies the Tavern formerly kept by Peter DANNER in Dover Town, at the Great road from York to Carlisle & about 7 miles from the Borough of York.

263. May 4, 1796
Peter DRITT begs leave to inform that he has opened a Grocery Store at the house of Jacob DRITT in Windsor Twp, York Co.

The Pennsylvania Herald & York General Advertiser

264. May 11, 1796
Partner wanted by the printer of this paper. John WINTER, Rights of Man
Printing Office (Frederick Town).
Whereas John KERBACH gave a note unto a certain Ludwick WAMPLER in Md. in
May last, he warns all persons from taking assignment of said note.

265. May 18, 1796
Tract of land for sale called Belgrade, in Harford Co (Md), near the
temporary line, 35 miles from Baltimore, 10 from the Susquehanah & 25
from York, 1000a., level & fertile. To view apply to Randal HITCHCOCK,
living thereon. For further particulars inquire of Abraham JARRETT,
living in Belleair (Md).
Sheriff's Sales: (1) Estate of Robert IRWIN, improvement & tract in Mountpleasant twp, 120 a., adj lands of John DONNOLLY & David DEMAREE. (2)
Estate of William CARSON, improvement & tract in Monallen Twp,   80 a.,
adj lands of Henry BOWER. (3) Estate of Jacob SHEAFFER, improvement &
tract in Hopewell Twp, 120 a., adj lands of John EPAUGH & Wm. M'CLELLAN.
(4) Estate of Sebastian ERICH, improvement & tract in York Twp, 240 a.,
adj land of Henry SHEAFFER & Henry AULT. (5) Estate of Benjamin M'KANLEY,
improvement & tract in Cumberland Twp, 60 a. of patented land, adj lands
of Hugh FERGIS & a tract held by a Md right called Frenchman's Purchase.
William M'CLELLAN, Sheriff.

266. May 25, 1796
Sheriff's Sale: Estate of Jacob DAY, improvement & tract in Newbury Twp, 80
a., adj. lands of Henry BOWER.
Whereas James MARSHALL, Senr. executed Bonds to a certain Charles
M'ALLISTER, late of the Co of York, in part of the consideration of a
tract of Land he purchased from said M'ALLISTER, it appears there are
certain legacies to be paid by said M'ALLISTER, which is an incumbrance
on said property. This gives notice that said bonds will not be honored.
All persons indebted to the estate of Daniel BEELER, late of Manchester
Twp, decd, are requested to discharge same. Catharine BEELER & John
QUICKEL, Adm'rs.

267. June 1, 1796
Edward HAND, Inspector of the Revenue for the Third Survey, in the District
of Pa., has observed that owners of Stills within his Survey have two
[sic] general omitted or neglected entering their Stills yearly.
Whereas William M'CLELLAN, Esq., Sheriff of York Co, hath advertised for
sale a certain improvement & tract of 60 a. in Cumberland Co, adj lands
of Hugh FERGIS & a tract held by a Md right called Frenchman's Purchase.
Now I, William STEWART, do herby notify that I duly purchased said
premises from the said Benjamin M'KINLEY, in his life time & have paid
full consideration therefore & warn persons against purchasing same.
The public are informed that a Stage & 4 horses will start from Hanover
(M'Allister's) Town on every Monday morning; run by way of York Town,
Lancaster & West Chester, arrive in Philadelphia every Wednesday, return
the same route & arrive in M'Allister's Town on every Saturday. The
price from M'Allister's Town to the city $6. John REILY & George WEED,
York.

The Pennsylvania Herald & York General Advertiser

268. June 8, 1796
Married Wednesday evening last, by the Rev. Robert CATHCART, John MONTGOMERY, Esq., Attorney at Law of Harford Co (Md) to Miss Polly HARRIS, dau of William HARRIS, Esq. of this borough
Died a few days ago, the Rev. Robert M'MURDIE of Marsh Creek, aged above 70 years. He enjoyed an uncommon state of good health during his whole life, even a few moments before his death he was reading in his chair, from which he fell, & expired without a groan. He was a Chaplain during the greater part of the War & marched at the head of the Regiment with his sword always ready for action. He was a loving husband & affectionate parent, a sincere friend & an outgoing neighbor.
Abraham SIMCOX, Town of Lewisberry, York Co, has taken in a stray horse.
David HART, in Hammiltonsban twp, has taken in a stray brown heiffer.
William M'CLELLAN, Senr., Cumberland twp, has taken in a stray bay mare.

269. June 15, 1796
Whereas WIlliam COLVEN of Fawn Twp, obtained a Note of Hand from me; this note was obtained illegally & without any consideration (through fraud of said COLVEN). Thomas ALEXANDER
Christopher FEIRST has taken up in Chanceford twp, a black year-old filly.
Strayed or stolen out of the pasture of John MITCHELL, Manaughan Twp, about 3 miles from Crowl's Tavern, a sorrel horse.
Ran away from Jonas YONER in Abbot's Town, Berwick Twp, apprentice named Peter TOLLET, 30-40 years of age, black short hair. Had on a dark blue Coat & Jacket lined with yellow Flannel, a wool hat, not much wore & pair of striped overalls. He is troubled with the rheumatism.
James BURD, living in Way'sburg, York Co, offers reward for runaway apprentice boy, by trade a shoemaker, named Charles THOMPSON, lately from Ireland, about 16 years of age, 5 ft 4-5 in high, of a dark complexion, round faced & short black curly hair. Had on dark blue Coat with large metal buttons, corduroy jacket, course overalls, linen shirt, pair of new shoes & an old fine hat with a hole burnt in the rim.
Selling tract of patented land in Hamiltonsbann twp, York Co, 211 a., stone house, log barn, orchard of apple & peach trees. Apply to William M'CLELLAN, Senr., Marsh Creek or John EDIE or Wm. M'CLELLAN, York Town.

270. June 22, 1796
Stolen out of pasture of John RITCHIE near Frederick-Town (Md), a black horse, changed by the heat of the sun somewhat to a brown; $50 reward.
All persons indeebted to the estate of George TEST, late of York Borough, are requested to make payment to William WELSH or George WOGAN, Ex'rs.

271. June 29, 1796
A 4-horse stage will set out from Frederick-Town (Md) every Thursday morning at 4 o'clock, arrive in the city of Philadelphia next Tuesday, about the hour of 1 o'clock p.m., will run by way of York Town, Lancaster, Strasburg & West Chester, return the same route & arrive in Frederick-Town every Tuesday evening. Frederick-Town to the city $8. Humble servants, John REILY & George WEED.
Thomas ABBET, living on the premises, selling plantation & tract in Berwick Twp, York Co, adj Abbets Town, 253 1/4 a., log dwelling house with arch Cellars, barn & stables, spring house.
Jacob DRITT informs all who have demands against him to attend house of Baltzer SPANGLER, Innkeeper in Borough of York for settlement.

The Pennsylvania Herald & York General Advertiser

272. July 27, 1796
The Tavernkeepers in York Co, who made application for license, they are now in the hands of John HAY, Esq., Treasurer. [Aug 2 - this & the following notices show up on microfilm as being under the issue of 27 July, but carry dates of August, the pages could have been mixed up on filming.]
Matthias SLOUGH, John DUNWOODY, Hunt DOWNING & William GEER have entered into a contract to carry the Mail from Philadelphia to Fort Pitt, & will run a stage to carry same along the post road; they find the road from York Town to Carlisle in such a situation as renders the passing of a carriage in many places almost impossible from the great number of loose & tumbling stones which are laying in it and the great number of gulleys which are occasioned by the many heavy rains. They ask nothing unreasonable, nor do they speak for themselves only, but the community in general. They request the general supervisors of the road to put said roads in repair. If a reasonable & prompt attention is not paid to this notice, they will avail themselves of the means the laws of the Co have in such case pointed out.
Wm. M'CLELLAN, Sheriff & William PATTERSON to attend at the house of Isaac GRAEFF, Town of Berlin, when & where all persons indebted to Adam BROWN, late of said place, merchant, are requested to discharge their debts.
Was stolen out of the meadow of James M'CANLES, Hopewell Twp, a dark chestnut sorrel stallion. $20 reward for horse & thief.

August 3, 1796 [Front page says Aug 3, but data on following pages seems same as July 27th. No new local data.]
273. August 10, 1796
All persons having any just demands against the estate of Thomas MINSHALL, Esq., late of Middletown, are requested to come forward. William CRABB
James SPEERY of Chanceford twp, York Co, 2 miles from M'Calls Ferry, offers $3 reward for stray steers.

274. August 17, 1796
Jacob SITLER giving cash for good merchantable wheat, delivered at his mill on Muddy Creek in Chanceford Twp.

275. August 24, 1796
John BRIGHTWELL, Israels Creek, 3 miles from Woodsberry & 15 from Frederick (Md) offering $20 reward for his dark bay gelding, which was stolen out of his pasture. ($10 for horse only.)
Sheriff's Sales: (1) Estate of Samuel HADDEN, improvement & tract in Strabann Twp, 270 a., adj lands of William SCOTT, Esq. & Robert WILSON. (2) Estate of James COOPER, improvement & tract in Manallen Twp, 300 a., adj lands of James M'KNIGHT, Robert M'ILHEANY. (3) Estate of John TOULORTON, improvement & tract in Manallan Twp, 100 a, adj lands of Jacob REX & George HARTZELL. (4) Estate of William BENNET, tract of land in Warrington Twp, 20 a., adj lands of Jacob BRENDLEY & Jacob IPE. (5) Estate of Henry BUCHANAN, a certain messhage & lot of ground on the South side of York St, in Gettysburgh, adj lots of John MILLER & Christian POTSER. (6) Estate of James SHELDON, tract of land in Shrewsbury Twp, 50 a. adj lands of Martin KURTZ & Mathew DAY. William M'CLELLAN, Sheriff.

The Pennsylvania Herald & York General Advertiser

276. August 31, 1796
Valentine COLEMAN of Manchester Twp, informs that his wife, Barbara, was married to him yesterday 3 weeks & has left already: He is forwarning all persons from trusting her on his account.
Benjamin MORRIS carries on the Fulling & Dying business as usual at the Mill where he has lived 2 years, near to Barnet ZEIGLER's Esq. He has leased the said Mill for 7 years.
Michael ROSS has laid out at Town called Williams Port in Lycoming Co, on the East Bank of the West Branch of the River Susquehanna. The town has been surveyed & lots, streets, lanes & alleys thereof are conveniently & advantageously proportioned to contribute to the health & beauty of the Town. Lots will be offered at private sale & application can be made to Mr. ROSS at his house adj the said Town.

277. Sept 7, 1796
$30 reward offered by Elihu UNDERWOOD, Junr., for mare stolen out of the pasture of James MARSH in Warrington Twp, York Co. Supposed stolen by a certain Jonathan PACKER, 25 years of age, between 5 & 6 ft. high, black hair, dark vissage, stoop shouldered & lip fallen.

278. Sept 14, 1796
Ezekiel SANKY, Newbury Twp, York Co, has taken up a stray mare.
John OVERHOLSER, Junr. gave a note to Thomas BALDWIN of Manallan Twp, which he is determined not to honor unless compelled thereto by law.
John MORRIS, formerly Clerk of the Board of Commissioners for Co of York, is a candidate for the Commissioners Office.
The Commissioners hereby notify that the General Election will be held at the usual places. Jos. WELSHANS, Henry WELSH & Thos. BLACK, Commrs.
John JONES informs that he carries on his Fulling Business as usual at his mill in York Twp, about 7 miles from Borough of York, near Nicholas SENTZS's Grist Mill. Cloths left with directions at John JONES's, William MARTIN's or at Henry SHAEFFER's Tavern, at the sign of the Bear in York Borough, will be carefully attended to. Also seeks a Journeyman that understands the business perfectly well.
James STEWART, selling the plantation on which he now lives in Mountjoy Twp, York Co, at the lower end of Rock Creek, 125 a., 2-story log dwelling house, log barn.

279. Sept. 21, 1796
Thomas M'CUNE in Mountjoy Twp, York Co, has taken in a stray cow.
Was committed to the custody of Michael GRAYBELL, Gaoler of York Borough, a certain person who calls himself Robert PAVARD, about 18 years old, 5 ft. 6-7 in high, by Trade a Weaver. He says he came from Letterkenny in Ireland about a year ago & landed at New York. Has a down look when spoken to & appears very stupid. Also confined a Negro man who calls himself James, says he belongs to John or Jonathan MORRIS near Norfolk, VA; about 53 years of age, 5 ft 4-5 in high, very large lips.
Joseph LINDSAY offers six pence reward for return of an Indented Apprentice Boy named Joseph BAPD, who ran away from him in Mountpleasant Twp.
Jacob GOERING, named as a candidate for office of a Delegate to Congress, declines.
The commanding officers of companies of York Co, who were on the Western Expedition are desired to meet at the house of Capt. Philip GOSSLER to appoint a committee to draw a petition to the general assembly in order to get a settlement for the arrears of rations due the officers &

soldiers who were on said expedition. Daniel MAY, Col.

280. Sept 28, 1796
Negro James hereby gives Notice to whom it may concern, that he is now
   in the Borough of York, Pa., where he means to continue until he can have
   a trial with respect to his right of freedom.
Militia of York Co are reminded of mustering dates. Alexander RUSSELL,
   Brigade Inspector or York Co.
To be sold at the house of Frederick STOLL, in Town of Oxford, articles in
   the mercantile line.
Ticket recommended to run at the next General Election: Thomas MIFFLIN,
   Governor; Thomas HARTLEY, Congress; William M'PHERSON, John STEWART,
   Philip GARTNER, William MILLER, Alexander TURNER & Thomas CAMPBELL for
   Assembly; John FORSYTH for Commissioner; Jacob UPDEGRAFF for Coroner.
   1st District: John HERBACH, Jacob GARTNER & Michael SPANGLER. 2nd
   District: George LASHELLS, William M'KIFFIN (M'KISSIN?) & David DEMSTER.
   3rd District: Daniel CLAPSADDLE, John BITTINGER & Daniel BARNITZ. 4th
   District: Benjamin PEDAN & Robert GEMMILL. 5th District: Jese UNDERWOOD &
   John M'ILLAN. From a letter signed "A Citizen" the writer would like to
   name Mr. Martin KREBER, of the Borough of York, a descreet active man.

281. Oct 5, 1796
Samuel TIGART cautions persons from taking bonds from a certain Wm. BYERS,
   late of Cumberland Twp, as he is determined to not honor same.
All persons indebted to the estate of William DOUGLASS, decd, late of
   Strabane Twp, are requested to discharge same. Daniel MENTIETH & David
   DEMAREE, Ex'rs.
To be sold by public vendue, plantation in York Township (for which there
   is a clear patent), late the property of the Rev. Luke ROUSE, decd. 120
   a, house & barn. Aoubt 4 miles from York Borough, adj Jacob MOSSER.
   John ROUSE, Ex'r.
John FISHER, Junr. & Co. at their new store, which hath been occupied these
   many years by John FISHER, Senr., Clockmaker in George St, North, 2 doors
   from the Court House, Borough of York, have a handsome assortment of dry
   goods, hardware, cutlery & groceries.

282. [Front page missing, assume from dates on ads that it is the issue of
Oct 12, 1796.]
Whereas my Wife Caty hath left me with my consent because she is addicted
   to liquor & cursing & swearing, I therefore forwarn all persons from
   giving her credit on my account. John BUZER
Plantation & tract of land in Hamiltonsban Twp, York Co, in Carrol's upper
   Tract, to be sold. 100 a. in the Tract & 24 a. in the outside of the
   tract line. Has log house & barn, Spring House & Smith Shop. Within 1
   mile of a good merchant mill & the great road from York to Nicholson's
   Gap goes through the premises. Apply to Elijah HART, David WILSON or
   David BLYTH, near the premises.
Ran away from Samuel RUSSELL, living in Franklin Twp, York Co, an indented
   servant man, about 3 weeks arrived from Ireland, named James M'NULTY;
   about 5 ft 6-7 in high, slim made, about 19 years of age. Had on when he
   went away a grey coloured sailor jacket, striped waistcoat, linen
   trowsers & no shoes.
Stolen from the house of Philip GOSSLER, Innkeeper in Borough of York, a
   watch, maker's name William KIRK, Ballymony.
Stolen on Friday night last from the Waggon of Michael DOSH, on the road

The Pennsylvania Herald & York General Advertiser

from York to Baltimore at Dickson's Tavern near the Md line; a black mare. 3 pounds reward for return of same.

283. Next issue available, Oct 26, 1796
To be let, that noted public stand in Petersburg (alias Little's Town), now in the occupation of John SHORB. House is suitable & commodious with stables & sheds, 2 good pumps. On road from York to Frederick-Town (Md) & the road from Shippensburg & Chambersburg to Baltimore. Apply to James M'SHERRY, living next door to the premises.
To be sold at public vendue a certain log Messahage & lot on the West side of George St, adj lands of John HAY, Esq. Also an equal 6th part or share of a Shad Fishery in the River Susquehannah, on the property of the heirs of George WELSH, decd., it being the estate of Wm. BURGESS, a Lunatic. John SCHALL & Jacob SHEFFER.

284. Nov 2, 1796
Tomorrow is to be an examination of the Pupils of the English School, Visitors are requested at 10 a.m. Joseph M'MURRAY. Night-school will open on Monday the 7th inst. & continue through the Winter.
To be let, noted inn late kept by Col. Archibald STEEL, in Borough of York; house is 3-story of brick & contains 12 rooms; has cellars & a large kitchen with oven in it. Stable is newly built of brick. From the late improved state of the roads from Philadelphia to York & the Federal city the custom has increased. Also store lately occupied by John GREER, well shelved & countered, on the corner of High & Beaver Sts, adj the above, will be let. Apply to John CLARK, York.

285. Nov 9, 1796
Following is a true Statement of the Election for Electors in the County of York: [all 3222, 3223 or 3224] Israel WHELEN, Samuel MILES, Henry WYNKOOP, John ARNDT, Valentine ECKHART, Thomas BULL, Robert COLEMAN, John CARSON, William WILSON, Samuel POSTLETHWAITE, Jacob HAY, Benjamin ELLIOT, Ephraim DOUGLAS, John WOODS & Thomas STOKELY. Thomas M'KEAN 141, Jacob MORGAN 138, James BOYD 138, Jonas HERTZEL 126, Peter MUHLENBERG, 139, Joseph HEISTER 140, William MACLAY 138, James HANNAH 138; John WHITEHILL 140, Abraham SMITH 139, William IRWIN 139, William BROWN 138, John PIPER 138 & James EDGAR 140. It is remarked that the citizens of York Co never were more united at any Election.
To be sold on the premises, a tract in Warrington Twp of 50 a. 2-story log dwelling house 54 ft long & 21 wide, fronting the Newbury road & within 30 ft. of the Great road from York to Carlisle. Also a number of lots fronting the Newbury road; together with 100 a. within 3 miles of the above lands on the round top Mountain. Also selling one complete sett of Hatter tools consisting of a large Dye Kettle, 2 Copper plank Kettles, 1 Boiler & large Irons with assortment of blocks, bowes &c. Credit will be given by James M'MILLAN. He also asks to settle his accounts owed & due.
Ran away from Adam BLAIR of York Town, an Apprentice Lad named William FISHER, a hatter, appears to be 18 or 19 years of age, 5 ft 8-9 in, smooth faced, yellow hair wears it tied, thin visage & bandy legged. Said FISHER has 2 years, 2 months and 20 days to serve.

286. Nov 16, 1796
Sheriff's Sales : (1) Estate of Anthony WEAVER, a certain Messuage & lot of 5 a. in M'Sherry's Town, York Co, adj lots of Jos. SCHULTZ & Nicholas NOEL. (2) Estate of Jean RICHWINE, Messuage & Lot in Abbots Town, York

The Pennsylvania Herald & York General Advertiser

Co, adj lots of Sebastian HEIFFER & a 40 ft. Alley. (3) Estate Right Title & Interest during the natural life of Edward ABBOT of in & to the quit rents of that part of the Town of Berwick (Abbots Town), Co of York, that lie on the South side of the Main St leading from York to Gettysburgh. (4) Estate of Robert ROSEBROUGH, decd., improvement & tract on Yellow Britches Creek, Monaughon Twp, York Co; 150 a., adj lands of Samuel NELSON & John WILLIAMS. (5) Estate of Samuel BLACK, improvement & tract in Fawn Twp, York Co; 200 a., adj lands of John SUTOR & James GRIMES. William M'CLELLAN, Sheriff.

Plantation in Chanceford Twp, York Co, to be rented, well known by name of Hill Head. 200 a. cleared & under fence. Apply to Robert M'CALL, on the premises, 1 mile from M'Call's Ferry on the Susquehannah.

Jonothan [sic] JESSOP offers reward for apprehending Barzillai GARDNER, an apprentice lad bound to the Clock & Watch making business, who absconded; has 2 years, 5 months & 24 days to serve. About 5 ft 8-9 in, well made, fair hair, walks stiff, it is supposed he will go towards North Carolina.

Adam MOURER offers reward for return of sorrel stallion stolen from his pasture at Daniel BARNITZ's Mill, 3 miles from Hanover (M'Allister's) Town in Manheim Twp, York Co.

Samuel WILLS of Morris Co, NJ, offers $60 reward for the return of his Jet Black Covering Horse, stolen out of his stable.

David KIRKPATRICK of Bernards Twp, Somerset Co, NJ, offers reward of $80 for the return of his sorrel mare.

287. Nov 23, 1796
Tanyard to be let or sold. George LASHALLS to let lot in Hunter's Town, on great road from York to Chambersburg, between 6 & 7 a., on which are 2-story dwelling house, with cellar under same, good stables, garden, apple orchard &c. Also on same Tanyard with Fats, Bark House, Currying Shop &c. Apply to David CASSAT, Esq. in York or Cornelious COSINE on the premises.

James COOPER, Monallan Twp on Conowago, has taken in a stray bull calf.

Michael HEVIC, Reading Twp, York Co, offers 6 cents reward for runaway apprentice boy named Peter WILLIAMS.

To be sold - plantation & tract in Mountpleasant Twp., York Co, late the property of Michael CLAPSADLE, decd.; 150 a., adj lands of Henry KUHN, Andrew M'ILVANE & Edward MARSDEN; has 2 dwelling houses, double barn. Apply Adam CRASSER, Junr. Ex'r.

Strayed from Frederick DIEHL, 4 head of cattle, which were in pasture in the South Mountains. Claim reward of $3 near M'Allister's Town.

Michael GRAYBLE, Gaoler of York, gives notice that he has committed in his custody two Negro Men, one of whom calls himself Henry JOHNSTON or Shadrack WILKINSON, had on long blue coat, corduroy breeches, striped linen jacket, old shoes & stockings; about 21 years of age, 5 ft 8-9 in high, says he belongs to Wm. EDWARDS of Westmoreland Co, Va. Also, one who calls himself Orange COLEMAN or William WIGGINS, about 22 years of age, 5 ft 8-9 in high, says he belongs to Joseph PRICE in said Westmoreland Co, his Master he says lives near Namony Ferry, between Potowmac & Rappahannoc Rivers.

John GRACE has rented that well-knwon ferry on the Susquehannah called Wright's, on the York Co side & also runs the Tavern.

Wheras some designing or evil minded persons have endeavored to propagate a story inimical to the character of James COOPER (Monallen Twp) & have stept behind the curtain not daring to shew themselves; I desire that they would stand forth & attack me face to face, otherwise I shall

The Pennsylvania Herald & York General Advertiser

forever deem them Rascals, Lyars & no Gentlemen.

288. Nov 30, 1796
Henry KING, late of Borough of York, saddler, informs that he has rented Jacob SITLER's Mills on Muddy Creek, on the Peach Bottom road from York Town, where he purposes carrying on the Millering business, where he also keeps a Public House of Entertainment. Said KING purposes to sell at his late Dwelling House in the Borough of York household goods & grains, &c.

289. Dec 7, 1796
James GIBSON, Hopewell Twp, York, has taken in a stray steer.

290. Dec 14, 1796
John SAMPLE, living in Fawn Twp, York Co, bought a horse from a man in March last, whose name he does not recollect--paid him 1/2 in hand, the other half he gave his Note. Would said person come forward.
All persons indebted to the estate of John ANDERSON, decd, late of Hopewell Twp, are requested to discharge same. Andrew ANDERSON.
John LEAS renting or selling a tanyard, shop, bark house & dwelling house. 14-15 a. Also has taken in a stray bull. (Tyrone Twp)

291. Dec 21, 1796
All persons indebted to estate of Wm. SMITH, late of Gettysburg, decd., are requested to make payment to Robert GRAHAM & Robert WILSON, Ex'rs. or to John SCOTT in Gettysburg.
Public Sale at the house of Jacob OPP, Innkeeper, Borough of York where the following tracts will be disposed of: (1) tract called the Diamond, lying in Fawn Twp, 102 a. (2) tract called Long Meadows lying in Hopewell Twp, 65 a. (3) Farm near Peach Bottom Ferry, 61 a., adj lands of Cunningham SAMPLE. Apply to Ralph BOWIE, who is authorized to sell same.
The editor being informed, that pains has been taken to persuade a number of his Subscribers that he means to stop publishing the York Herald in a short time in order (he supposes) to induce them to become subscribers to another English Paper which is to be published in this place; he assures them that there is not a greater falshood contained in the whole first Volume of Stedman's History of the American War. As yet he has had anything of the kind in contemplation.

Dec 28, 1796 [Issue available; no new local data.]
292. Jan 4, 1797
Died on Wednesday night, the 24th inst. at Presqu'Isle, his Excellency Anthony WAYNE, commander in chief of the Federal Army.
$50 reward offered by Godfrey LAINHOFF, In Plumb St, between 2nd & 3rd Sts, No. 38, Philadelphia, for runaway indented Dutch Servant Man named John Philip SPIES, about 21 years of age, 5 ft 10 in high, speaks no English; dark complexioned Fellow, has dark brown short hair & on his head a very remarkable spot about the bigness of a Dollar, quite bald of hair.

293. Jan 11, 1797
Laurence MONTTORT, Strabane Twp, York Co, has taken in 5 stray sheep.
Stolen from George CLARKE's farm near Green-Castle, 2 bright bay horses.

294. Jan 18, 1797
All persons are hereby desired not to give credit to or trust my Wife Eve TIPPLE. Nicholas TIPPLE.

The Pennsylvania Herald & York General Advertiser

Alexander TURNER informs that he has enlarged his Nailing Manufactury & is determined to carry it on by workmen regularly bred to that business.
The inhabitants of the upper end of York Co (West of the Line formerly proposed as the Division Line) are requested to meet at the house of John MURPHY in Mountpleasant Twp, to carry into effect measures as may be thought necessary to the Division of said County.
Thomas D. JAMESON, Physician, Surgeon & Man-Midwife informs the public that he has removed his Shop to the House formerly occupied by Lewis MICHAEL, in the center square, Borough of York, where he has a large assortment of genuine Drugs & Medicines.

295. Jan 25, 1797
All persons indebted to the estate of James DILL, late of Monaughan Twp, Co of York, decd, are requested to make payment. John DILL, Adm'r.
For sale - well-known place at the mouth of Yellow Breeches Creek in Cumberland Co, now in the possession of Henry FORRER; 53 a.; water rate already dug, & Iron works, timber &c. ready for erecting a Saw Mill. Also 2-story log house, 4 rooms of a floor, kitchen, stabling &c.

296. Feb 1, 1797
Pa. Legislature, House of Representatives: Committee appointed on that part of the Governor's address which relates to the French Emigrants residing in this State, viz. That they have learned that there are yet remaining here about 89 French emigrants, consisting of aged & infirm men, destitute women & helpless children, in a situation that loudly calls for the exercise of public benevolence. Resolved: Godfrey HAGA, Samuel Powell GRIFFITHS, Joseph LOWNES, Robert RALSTON & Joseph SANSOM to be by them applied to the relief of certain distressed French emigrants. Also petition from Peter WIKOFF, Co of Philadelphia, referring to a former petition & praying compensation for 652 a. & 127 perches of land, and for which he paid the greatest part of the purchase money & office fees, which land is in the state of New York. Also report on petition of Paul FRASER, of Rye Twp, Cumberland Co was read & a committee appointed to bring in a bill to enable Paul FRASER to erect a Dam on Shearman's creek, opposite his own land in Rye Twp. of sufficient height to supply his Mill with water.
This morning (Jan 27, 1797) fire broke out in the lower part of the Dwelling House of Andrew BROWN, Printer of this City. (Philadelphia) Mr. BROWN, his apprentices & other domestics of the Family escaped with their Lives by rushing thro' the flames or jumping from windows. Mr. BROWN is very much burnt & is dangerously ill. A maid servant is also so burnt that it is thought she cannot recover. Two of the apprentices were much bruised by their fall from the windows. Mrs. BROWN & her 3 children, a son & 2 daughters, fell Victims to the flames & suffocation.
The beautiful horse Badger for sale. He was bred by Nicholas Day M'COMAS of Harford Co, Md. Can be seen at any time at John M'INTIRE's stable, Borough of York.
Subscribers to the York Co Library who have not paid, come forward & do so. By order of the Directors, John FORSYTH, Treasurer.
At a meeting held at the house of John MURPHY regarding the Division of York Co, it was agreed to postpone this business until 6 Feb inst. By order of the meeting, William WALKER, Chairman.

The Pennsylvania Herald & York General Advertiser

297. Feb 8, 1797
HARRIS & DONALDSON, inform that they removed to the House of John CLARK, Esq. on the S. West Corner of High & Beaver Sts, lately occupieed by John GREER, where they have opened a very general & well chosen assortment of merchandise.

298. Feb 15, 1797
To be sold at Public Vendue on the Premises, about a mile from Borough of York, late the property of John SPANGLER, decd, viz. Horses, Horned-Cattle, Sheep, Swine, Waggons, Ploughs, Wheat, Rye &c. Margaret SPANGLER, George BARD & Jacob SPANGLER, Ex'rs.
Sheriff's Sales: (1) Estate of Samuel HADDEN, improvement & tract in Strabane Twp, York Co, 280 a., adj lands of William SCOTT & John DICKSON, Esqs. (2) Estate of William BURGESS, 2 Messuages & 1 lot on the West side of George St, Borough of York, adj lands of John HAY, Esq. (3) Estate of Archibald STEEL, lot in Borough of York, fronting on Duke St, bounded on the East by an Alley & on the South by Nathaniel LIGHTNER's Lot, 57 ft 6 in in front & 200 ft deep, it being known in the General Plan of York by No. 18. (4) Estate of Johannes WILLIAMS, Messuage & lot on the North side of York St, Town of Berwick, adj Lots of Frederick BAUGHER & Edward ABBOT; also one other lot in Berwick Twp, 5 a, adj lands of Jacob SOWER & Jonas YONER. (5) Estate of John KNIGHT, improvement & tract in Berwick Twp., York Co, 114 a., adj lands of Samuel BOWER, John HARTMAN & James KITCHEN. Seized & taken to be sold by William M'CLELLAN, Sheriff.

299. Feb 22, 1797
To be sold agreeable to will of Peter HENRY, decd, late of Managhan Twp, York Co, on the premises, plantation whereon the said decd did live; 250 a. adj lands of Daniel JONES, James ANDERSON, Jacob WAGONER &c. Stone House, double log barn, 2 large Orchards. Likewise another tract of 130 a., adj above & lands of David AYRS, Andrew SANDS &c. This tract has log house & double barn. Also to be sold at same time a lot in Town of Lisburn, Cumberland Co, 1/4 a. Daniel HENRY & John GOSWALER, Ex'rs.
For sale-plantation formerly property of Archibald DOUGLASS, in Cumberland Twp, York Co, adj lands of Thomas DOUGLASS, James DOUGLASS &c., 154 a. 2-story log house with 4 rooms on lower & kitchen adj, log barn with stabling. Apply Thomas DOUGLASS, Junr.
To be sold at public sale, the late dwelling Plantation of Richard M'ALISTER, Esq. decd; adj Hanover Town in York Co., in lots of from 5 to 10 and 20 a. or any quantity to suit purchasers. Likewise, a large 2-story Brick House, being the late dwelling house of said decd, standing on a corner lot at the centre Square of Hanover Town. Archibald M'ALISTER, Jesse M'ALISTER & Jacob RUDISELL, Ex'rs.
For Sale - plantation whereon George HAYS now lives, in Strabane Twp, York Co, 100 a., adj lands of Wm. THOMPSON, Wm. FLEMING &c. Has 2-story dwelling house, large double barn with stabling & smith shop & grinding mill. Also one other tract, the property of Nathan PATTERSON, adj the above, 103 a., 111 perches. Has dwelling house & orchard of 150 apple trees. Apply to George HAYS.
To be sold at Public Vendue - Plantation & tract in Cumberland Twp, York Co, 200 a., adj lands of Samuel COBEAN, Charles FLETCHER &c.; it being part of a larger tract late the property of William M'CLELLAN, decd. Inquire of David MOORE or David EDIE, near the premises or to William M'CLELLAN, York Town.

The Pennsylvania Herald & York General Advertiser

Sheriff's Sale: Borough of York large assortment of Dry Goods, being seized & taken in Execution as the property of John WILLIAMS.

300. Mar 8, 1797
The editor informs his readers that the reason of his not publishing a Paper as usual last week, was owing to being disappointed in procuring paper; for the purpose of obtaining which he used every exertion.
To be rented to the highest bidder, all that Plantation late the property of George WHITE, decd, in Paradise Twp, York Co. John FORSYTH & Hannah WHITE, Ex'rs.

301. Mar 15, 1797
Speech by John ADAMS, newly elected President of the United States, printed & no room given to new local information.

302. Mar 22, 1797
Pa. Legislature, House of Representatives: Petition read from Francis & Robert BAILEY, praying the payment of a balance due them for printing the Journals of the last House. A petition from a number of the inhabitants of Cos of Berks, Northampton & Northumberland, praying that Dewald FRASH may be reimbursed monies expended by him in opening a road from house towards Allemeengle.
Peter DINKLE renting that well-known house at present occupied by Samuel ROBERT's Esq. Also well-known Tavern formerly occupied by Robert WILSON. Also Plantation where John SHOEMAKER, decd, formerly resided on, about 4 miles from Borough of York. Also another Plantation, 3 miles below Mr. EHREHART's on the little run at the road side.
To be sold at Public Vendue at the dwelling house of Frederick STUMP in Hellam Twp, York Co, the following goods viz. Fortepianno, beds, horses, cows, sheep & hogs, grain, wagon, ploughs, harrows, &c.
John SHULTZBACH of Hellam Twp cautions that he through imposition & under a mistake, signed a certain instrument of writing 10 May 1794 "that he would allow the other Heirs of his late Father Philip SHULTZBACH, decd. for what lands it was supposed he held, more than he had a right for:" Whereas in truth & in fact he had a right by the valuation made; & the decree of the Orphans Court of York Co, 6 June 1793, to all lands of said decd., valued by the Jury & therefore will not pay any more than the shares so decreed by the Court.
For Sale - Plantation & tract of 270 a., in Cumberland Twp, York Co, adj lands of David DUNWOODY, John SWENEY & lands formerly belonging to Col. Hans HAMILTON, late the property of James M'CLURE, decd. Apply to Samuel EDIE, Esq. near the premises or to John EDIE in York Town.

303. Mar 29, 1797
Robert BROWN selling 125 a. in Hammiltonsbann Twp, York Co, on the road from Baltimore to Greencastle, within 3 miles of Emmitsburgh (Md) & 1 mile from Col. William REED's Merchant & Saw Mills.
For sale - farm of 280 a., 15 miles from the Borough of York, has dwelling house, barn & orchard. The Frame & Mill-Wright work for a saw mill & one pair of stones, nearly completed. Also nearly 1000 a., 30 miles South of Fort Pitt. Patented 9 years ago. Also to be sold or let, 2-story dwelling house & 2 lots adj, near 3/4 a., in Butt's Town, adj York Borough. Apply to George Lewis LEFFLER, Esq. Borough of York.
For sale - about 2000 a. in Md, Washington Co, on Potomack River & little Conogocheague. Also for sale Mill Seat, where he is now erecting a Grist

The Pennsylvania Herald & York General Advertiser

Mill on Rock Creek, within 1 mile of the Federal City & about the same from George Town. Apply to Samuel BAYLY, who lives adj the Washington Lands & will show it. William BAYLY, George Town.
The horse Tally-Ho will cover mares this season at the stable of James WRIGHT in the Town of Columbia (Wright's Ferry).
Robbery!! Was stolen out of Peter COX's trunks $750 in silver & goods. A reward of $200 is offered for property & theif. Said Robbery was committed at the Sign of the Turk's Head, York Borough.
Wanted- labourers, woodcutters & grubbers, Daniel TURNER, Mifflin Co., Spring Creek Forge.

304. April 5, 1797
Abraham FALCONAR of Baltimore offers $30 reward for a bay gelding that strayed from his farm. If he is taken up in the neighborhood of Col. Conrad SHERMAN, he will pay the reward.

305. April 12, 1797
PA Legislature, House of Representatives: Resolved that a committee be appointed to enquire what quantity of land to the property of persons claiming under PA was settled by the Connecticut claimants previous to the decree of Trenton & to ascertain value of said land & that the committee be authorized to receive proposals from such claimants under PA, as are willing to sell their right to same.
List of Laws enacted during the session of the Legislature of PA: An act for the relief of Henry PENFINGER. An act to enable John MILLER to erect a mill-dam across Swatara-creek, abutting on his own land, about 4 miles below Jone's-town, co of Dauphin. Act to authorize Paul FRAZER to erect a dam across Shearman's creek. An act for the relief of Robert SAMPLE. An act to afford relief to certain distressed French emigrants. An act to authorize Robert DEAN & Joseph SMITH to erect a wing-dam on the south side of the Franks-town branch of the Juniata, Huntington Co. An act to enable the Adm'rs of estate of James PATTERSON, decd, (Franklin Co) to convey tract of land to George CRIDER. An act to provide for educating John KONKAPOT, Junr., a youth of Stockbridge tribe of Oneida Indians & for the relief of John KONKAPOT, Senr. An act to authorize Thomas PROCTOR to commence a suit against this commonwealth, upon certain claims which he has against same. An act to empower Jonathan JARRET, of the co of Montgomery, to sell lands therein specified.
Five Negroes for sale by Samuel HAYS, Strabane Twp, York Co. A young man, 21 years of age, stout active lad, brought up to the farming business; Also a middle aged active woman, understands her business in the house or field. Also a young Wench, 24 years of age, a slave for life, both for farming or housework, particularly spinning. She has 2 very promising children, a boy & girl. All Negroes are legally recorded. They are not for sale for any fault regarding their work; but he intends to disengage himself from the trouble of farming & has no other use for them.
To be sold - large 2-story brick house, 38 ft fronting on George St & 67 1/2 ft fronting on Philadelphia St; occupied by James LOVE as a store. Likewise a house, part frame & part brick, fronting about 30 ft on George St., now in tenure of Solomon SMUCK. Terms made known by John LOVE.

306. April 19, 1797
Thomas ADAMS & Henry SCHREACH selling 200 dozen of American Sickles & 200 dozen of English Scythes, prepared by the above for the season, at Isaiah HARR's Scythe & Sickle Manufactory in York Twp. Also sold at Stores of

The Pennsylvania Herald & York General Advertiser

Messers. HARRIS & DONALDSON, EICHELBERGER, ROTHROCK &c.
Members of fire companies in Borough York are requested to meet. John
MORRIS, Jacob UPDEGRAFF & John DOLL, Secretaries.

307. April 26, 1797
Elizabeth M'MURRAY opening a sewing & reading school for girls in the House
formerly occupied by John FONK in George St, opposite the Rev. Jacob
GOODING.
Whereas on Saturday the 22nd inst., as Robert KERR & a certain Adam COOKIS
were going to a Magistrate to complete the writings of a small tract of
land, which KERR had articled to make over by a deed to said COOKIS; but
on account of some trifling disputes he had by the way, the said COOKIS
got possession of the deed & did feloniously carry it off with design, it
is supposed, to alter it to his own advantage.

308. May 3, 1797
PATTERSON & THOMPSON inform the public that they have set up the Wheel-
Wrighting, Chair-making, settee making & painting business in
Gettysburgh, York Co.
Andrew DUNCAN, Hopewell Twp, York, has taken in a stray cow.
At meeting held in York for the purpose of electing a Town Corporation, the
following were chosen: Burgesses: Philip GOSSLER & Jacob BARNITZ.
Assistants: Christoph LAUMAN, Joseph WELSHANS, Jacob HAY, Jacob GARTNER,
Jacob UPP & John EDIE. High Constable: Christopher STOEHR. Town Clerk:
John DOLL, Junr.
Pursuant to will of John HOUGH, Senr., decd., to be sold the Plantation on
which he lately dwelt, 700 a., in Loudon Co (Va), near the Fairfax
Meeting House, 40 miles from Alexandria & 35 from the Federal City. Has
elegant brick dwelling house, merchant & saw mills, barn &c. Also one
house & lot in town of Leesburg in said co, being known by No. 63. Also
tract In Shannandoah Co, 73 a. One other tract in Hampshire Co, 200 a.
William HOUGH, Samuel HOUGH & Mahlon HOUGH, Ex'rs.
Dr. John MORRIS, Borough of York, thanks friends & customers for favors
received during the 15 years of his residence at this place. He
continues to practice physic & surgery & uses this to announce that he
has found a sure & expeditious remedy for that dreadful Malady called the
Cancer. Already, by the blessing of God, he has cured a number of that
disease & others now under his care are on their way to a speedy
recovery. Testimonies: Baltzer LAWER of Dauphin Co, Lebanon Twp.;
Catharine BAKER of York Co, Manchester Twp., John GRUP, Lutheran
Minister, York Co, Dover Twp; Adam SMITH, York Co, Codorus Twp; William
STOBER, Baltimore Co (Md); Thomas FLINT, Eastern Shore of Md.
Eyewitnesses: John ROTHROCK, John HALLER, Jacob SHILER (?), Matthias
DETTER, Frederick HORN & Peter KUHL.

309. May 10, 1797
All persons indebted to the estate of Thomas WEEMS, late of Mountjoy Twp,
decd, are requested to pay up. Henry BLACK (Rock Creek) & Jonathan
NEELY, Ex'rs.
James M'CARDELL selling 2000 a. on Glade Creek, Greenbryer Co, 25 miles
from Greenbryer Court House & within 20 miles of the Ohio River. Also
for sale 100 a. on little Miami, 10 miles from the River Ohio, not far
from several new invented Towns. Apply to M'CARDELL in Hagerstown (Md.)

The Pennsylvania Herald & York General Advertiser

310. May 17, 1797
Alexander SCOTT, selling at private sale, 1 a. in the Village of Strasburg, Franklin Co, on which are erected a tanyard, currying shop, bark house &c. with large square log dwelling house, not yet finished. Apply to Joseph KERR or George HAMEL of Strasburg to view premises, or to Jacob GRAEF, Esq. or Mr. SCOTT at Lancaster.
On the 4th inst. was found between Anderson's Ferry & Kline's Tavern, in Hellam Twp, York Co, a surtoot & silk handkerchief, with a number of pattrons on paper for jackets, broadcoath, &c. & an English testament with small account book. Owner may apply to Henry WOLF, 1/4 mile from John SHULTZ's Tavern in Hellam Twp.

311. May 24, 1797
William ROSS, living in Warrington Twp, York Co, offering 6 cents reward for return of runaway apprentice boy named Isaac MORGEN, about 16 years of age, of a clumsey make & very much knock-need, fair complexion & can act the scoundrel with a tolerable good countenance.
Strayed from Joseph JONES at Mount Rock Tavern, 7 miles from Carlisle, on his way from York to Bedford - a strawberry roan horse.

312. May 31, 1797
Ran away from the subscriber, living on Elkridge in Annerundel Co, Md, a Negro Man named George, who calls himself George NELSON: About 25 years of age, 5 ft 8-9 in high, yellow complexion, pitted with the small pox. Broad, well made fellow, holds his head pretty high & rather back when he walks & straddles in walking, speaks slow with some hesitation. He has been hired at the brick yards in Baltimore & went away from thence. $30 reward if found; $50 if brought home. Greenberry RIDGELY.
Exhibition at the ball room in the house formerly occupied by Col. Archibald STEEL. Mr. SALENKA has the honor of informing that he will commence exhibiting the wonderful exploits of the Learned Dog. Tickets may be had at Capt. GOSSLER's Tavern.

313. June 7, 1797
James HORNER, Mountpleasant Twp, York Co, has taken in a stray colt.
Whereas the subscriber is legally impowered by Letter of Attorney, duly authenticated under hand & seal of Andrew LANTZ, late of Windsor Twp, Co of York, to demand & receive whatever due owing to said LANTZ--all persons requested to make immediate payment. Philip DECKER, York.
William NES informs that he has removed to his House on the S. West corner of High & Water STs, formerly occupied by Messrs. HARRISA & DONALDSON, where he has opened a very General assortment of merchandise.

314. June 14, 1797
John EICHELBERGER informs friends & public that he has removed his store to the house on the corner of High & Water Sts, formerly occupied by Mr. William NES. Has dry goods, groceries, hardware, &c.

315. June 21, 1797
Robert M'CALL has now provided himself with compleat Ferry boats, 1 47 ft long for waggons & 1 26 ft long for the use of carrying horses. This Ferry is 65 miles from Philadelphia, 46 from Baltimore, 15 from Lancaster, 25 from York & 42 from the head waters of Christeen.
Is hereby given that at June Term 1797 a Petition was presented to the Court of Common Pleas, York Town, at the inita--e of James SHORT, praying

The Pennsylvania Herald & York General Advertiser

the court to supply a lost Deed made by a certain Andrew HICKENLUBER to Hugh MORRISON, James MORRISON & John SAMPLE, ex'rs. of Hans MORRISON, decd. for 600 -- a. of land in Menallen Twp, Co of York. All who have any objection to make to the object of said petition are desired to attend at the Court House. John EDIE, Clerk.

Ran away from John CRAINE, near Middleburg, Loudon Co, Va, two negroes, one a man called Adam, about 30 years of age, 5 ft 9-10 in high, stout bodies with small thighs & legs, but large feet & hands. Took with him his fiddle, which he plays on with the bow in his left hand, as he is left handed. The other is called Mima, who Adam took with him as his wife. She is about 24 years old, 5 ft 2 in high, very stout made & of a darker colour.

316. June 28, 1797
Yesterday York Town & the neighborhood adjacent experienced the most tremendous Storm of Hail, that has been known by the eldest livers in the place. The wind was at the South South East & all glass windows facing that direction were almost totally destroyed.

All persons indebted to estate of John LONG, late of Manheim twp, York Co, decd, are requested to make payment. Conrad LONG & James BOLTON, Ex'rs.

317. July 12, 1797 [Next issue available.]
George HAY, at the south side of High St, 2 doors west from the Market house, Borough of York, has just received an assortment of Ironmongery, cutlery, Groceries &c. Also Brushes, Violins, Flutes & Fifes.

John HALL, Secretary of the Land Office in case of Nicholas BETTINGER vs. Samuel CUNINGHAM, orders notice published to heirs of Samuel CUNINGHAM, decd., to attend & shew cause why a Patent should not issue to Nicholas BETTINGER for land in question.

Last Wednesday night was a season of terror to inhabitants of this place. Between the hours of 12 & 1, a fire broke out in the back buildings of John HAY, Esq., adj his dwelling house. Fire communicated to the house & the German Presbyterian Church, both of which in a few minutes all in flames. The fire threw up living coals, many of which in their descent fell upon houses & stables in different parts of the Town. From 15 to 20 houses, among which was the Court house & Market house, were on fire during the night; all however except the two first were by the vigilance of the citizens preserved. Citizens took stations on the roofs of the neighbouring houses, where they remained for hours together amidst the heat & smoke wetting the roofs & extinguishing the fire which was every moment kindling around them. About 6 this morning the danger was overcome. The loss of Mr. HAY is considerable; besides his buildings, a large quantity of Grain & part of his furniture was consumed, but his papers & most valuable effects were saved. The Church Organ, Bells & Records were entirely destroyed.

Thomas HARTLEY returns his most sincere thanks to his fellow citizens for their great & spirited exertions in preserving his house & property from destruction by the terrifying & dangerous fire on Wednesday night last.

Is hereby given that the Subscriber's Auditors in a domestic attachment brought by John LEE against Neil M'FADDEN, to meet at house of George HAY, Innkeeper. John FORSYTH, Jacob SPANGLER & George HAY, Auditors.

All indebted to estate of Jonothan MARSH, Warrington Twp, Co of York, to meet at house of James M'MILLAN, Warrington Twp, to make payment to Ebenezer BELL.

The Pennsylvania Herald & York General Advertiser

July 19, 1797 [Page 3 missing, no new local news.]
318. July 26, 1797
George LUDMAN, Borough of Carlisle, offers $10 reward for a mare that strayed, deliver to Abraham LOUGHRIDGE, Carlisle.
Jacob SITLER selling house & lot on the north side of High St, Borough of York, adj lots of Christian SINN & George Lewis LEFFLER, Esq.
For sale by James SHORT, all his goods now on hand (all dry goods) & 3 tracts of land in York Co, 2 in Washington on the river Ohio & one in Westmoreland in Harrison Co, VA, 1200 a.; together with smaller tracts of 700 a. in Northumberland Co, on Sinni-mahoning, one of the West branches of Susquehannah, a house & lot in York Town. He also calls on those indebted to him to come forward & settle accounts & has placed them in the hands of William ROSS, Esq., Attorney for recovery.
In reference to an Act entitled 'an Act to provide for the settlement of the Estates of decd. officers & Soldiers who served in the Pa Line during the late War.' Notice is given to John M'CANDLESS, adm'r. of the estate of Thomas MORTIMORE, decd--Thomas CAMPBELL, Esq. adm'r. of the estate of John MILLER, decd., Thomas M'ILVAINE, decd, William FAUGLIY(?), decd. James M'ELBAY, decd., Joseph TAYLOR, decd., & Patrick MAGAW, decd.--Wm. M'CLELLAN, Esq. Adm'r. of the estate of Henry MAXWELL, decd.--George KRAFT, adm'r. of estate of John KRAFT, decd.--Abraham MOSSER adm'r. of estate of Philip COWIZER, decd--Godlieb ZIEGEL, adm'r. of estate of Patrick GLACKEN, decd--William BURGESS, adm'r. of estate of Robert M'GEE, decd, all late soldiers of the Pa. line. That they & every of them are herby required & cited to be & appear before me at the Register's Office at York (without delay) & settle their accounts of their said Intestates Estates & pay balances remaining in their hands. NOTICE is also hereby given to James M'CANDLES & Robert MARTIN, sureties for the above named John M'CANDLESS, adm'r. as aforesaid. John FORSYTH, Esq. & Patrick SULLIVAN, sureties for the above named Thomas CAMPBELL, Esq. adm'r. as aforesaid.--Philip GOSSLER, Samuel RIDDLE & James EDIE, sureties for the above named William M'CLELLAN, Esq., adm'r. as aforesaid. John LEIBESPERGER & Daniel LEIBESPERGER, sureties for the above named George KRAFT, adm'r. as aforesaid. Jacob GOOD & Christian HARNISH, sureties for the above named Abraham MOSSER, adm'r. as aforesaid. Frederick YOU-E & Abraham MOFFER, sureties for the above named Godlieb ZIEGEL, adm'r. as aforesaid--Nicholas BENEDICT & Matthew CHAPMAN, sureties for the above named William BURGESS, adm'r. of the estate of Robert M'GEE, decd., aforesaid. That on neglect or the adm'rs. above named, settling their accounts & paying over the balances, copies will be made out & transmitted to the Attorney General in order to be put in suit. NOTICE is also given to all such other adm'rs. who are not above named & who took out Letters of Administration on Estates of Officers or Soldiers of the late Pa. line in this Co. Signed Jacob BARNITZ, Register.

319. Aug 2, 1797
Dr. James JAMESON practices physic, surgery & midwifery; also wholesale & retail druggist in the town of Hanover, York Co, in the house formerly occupied by Lewis MICHAEL.
Whereas a petition was presented to the Court of Common Pleas of York Co by Henry YOUNG, praying the Court to supply the loss of 2 deeds, one from Richard M'ALLISTER, Esq. to John REISINGER & Henry SHULTZ & the other from said John REISINGER & Wife to said Henry SHULTZ for a house & lot in town of Hanover, known on general plan as No. 138--All persons converned to attend at next Court of Common Pleas. John EDIE, Proth.

The Pennsylvania Herald & York General Advertiser

$40 Reward - for return of Apprentice Lad named Anthony BRAND,, who ran away from Michael MORTHLAND(?) of Warrington Twp, York Co. He is 18 or 19 years of age, 5 ft 10-11 in high, slender made, dark short hair, thin visage, smooth face, brown eyes, with down roguish look. He is a blacksmith by trade & is supposed will pass as a journeyman as he is a cunning active fellow & works well as said business. Perhaps he will change his name to SPENCER, as that was his mother's maiden name.

Aug 9, 1797 [Issue available, no new local data.]
320. Aug 16, 1797
Public notice is given to all persons not to take assignment on 2 notes given by John RANJONS to a certain Casper KREGOR, as they were unlawfully obtained.
A stage will start from the House of William FERREE in Lancaster on every Monday at 4 a.m., arrive in York at the House of Baltzer SPANGLER at 12, set out at 1 & arrive at Baltimore on Tuesday evening; the same stage will start from the House of Abraham KAUFFMAN, in Gay St, Baltimore on Wednesday at 10 & arrive at York on Thursday evening, so that passengers may proceed on to Lancaster or Philadelphia the next day. William M'CLELLAN & Samuel SPANGLER.
Sheriff's Sale: (1) Estate of Charles Wm. PORTER, improvement & tract in Chanceford twp, 100 a., adj lands of William FULLERTON & James PEADEN.
(2) Estate of Thomas ARMOR, decd, improvement & lot in Germany Twp, 101 1/2 a., adj lands of Martin KITZMILLER, George STEVENSON & Diggs Choice.
(3) Estate of Frederick EGHOLTZ & Henry SCHENK, surviving Trustees with Ludwig WIER, decd., land in Dover Twp, 36 a., adj lands of John RUDISELL & Jacob MILLER.
All persons indebted to estate of William THOMPSON, late of Strabane Twp, decd., are desired to make payment. George HAYS & William THOMPSON, Exrs.
John NILSON, Newberry twp, York Co, has taken in a small black mare.

321. Aug 25, 1797
Alexander TURNER, John RIPPEY & James SPREAT have been appointed Commissioners to contract with masons, carpenters, &c for building a Meeting house for Chanceford Congregation.
Peter BOSS has for sale or rent that store, dwelling-house & half lot of ground wherein he now dwells, on the West side of George St, Borough of York; adj lots of Jacob FUNK & Jacob SHAFER.
Notice hereby given by the Register's Office, York Co. of all Legatees, heirs, creditors & others to whom it may concern, that the following administration & guardian accounts have been filed for the Probate of Wills & granting Letters of Administration in & for Co of York.
The account of Anthony ERHART, adm'r. of the estate of Cornelius HIGGINS, late of Menallen Twp, decd.
The accounts of Jemama THORLEY & James LIGGET, adm'rs. of estate of William THORLEY, late of Newbury twp, decd.
The second account of John KOCH & Peter MEYER, ex'rs. of will of George KOCH, late of Borough of York, decd.
The account of Andrew CREMER, adm'r. of estate of Magdalene SULTZBACH, a minor, late of Hellam Twp, decd.
The 3d account of Joseph GLANCY, adm'r. of estate of John ALBERT, late of Newbury twp, decd.
Account of Jacob BUSS & Baltzer YOUNG, ex'rs. of will of Peter BUSS, late of Paradise twp, decd.
Account of Catharine BEHLER & John QUICKELL, adm'rs. of estate of Daniel

BEHLER, late of Manchester twp., decd.
Account of Anna KINDIG & George HEYD, adm'rs of estate of Jacob KINDIG, late of Manchestesr twp, decd.
Account of Mary ANDERSON & Andrew ANDERSON, adm'rs. of estate of John ANDERSON, late of Hopewell twp, decd.
Account of Philip SHAFFER, adm'r. of estate of Catharine SHAFFER, late of Shrewsbury twp, decd.
Account of Jacob LIEBHART, adm'r. (debonis non) of the estate of Catharine LIEBHART, late of Hellam twp, decd.
Account of Henry TYSON & John HERBACH, Esq., ex'rs. of will of Samuel MOSSER, late of York twp, decd.
Account of Dietrich BRUBACHER & John BRILLHART, adm'rs. of estate of Jacob MEYER, late of York twp, decd.
Account of Adam FALLER, Guardian of estate of Michael, Mary, Elizabeth, & Christian LABOOB, Minor Orphan children of Michael LABOOB, decd.
Further account of Tempest TUCKER & Christian HERSHEY, ex'rs. of will of Peter DICKS, late of Paradise twp, decd.
Account of Daniel & Peter KEPLINGER, ex'rs. of will of Peter KEPLINGER, late of Manheim twp, decd.
Account of William WELSH & George WOGAN, ex'rs. of will of George TEST, late of the Borough of York, decd.
Further account of George KUNTZ(?), adm'r. of estate of Conrad SHREIBER, late of Germany twp., decd.
Further account of George KUNTZ & John RIEGEL, ex'rs. of will of John RIEGEL, late of Germany twp, decd.
Account of Philip & Peter MOHR, ex'rs. of will of Nicholas MOHR, late of Manchester twp., decd.
Account of Wm. LANIUS, acting ex'r. of will of John HECKENDORN, late of Borough of York, decd.
Account of John DUNCAN, adm'r. of estate of William JOHNSTON, late of Chanceford Twp., decd.
Account of Henry RIEMAN, adm'r. of estate of Peter KLEINFALTER, late of Shrewsbury twp, decd.
Account of Robert BIGHAM, acting ex'r. of will of Thomas ARMOR the elder, late of the Borough of York, decd.
Account of Jacob FIESER, adm'r. of estate of Anna Maria FIESER, late of Germany twp, widow, decd.
Pursuant to the will of Thomas TAYLOR, Senr., late of Loudoun Co, (Va) decd, to be sold at public vendue at Catharine KIMBOLL's Tavern in Frederick Town, Md, the plantation on which he formerly dwelt; 448 a. in Frederick Co, Md., 5 miles from Frederick Town & 42 from the Federal City. Two other pieces of land adj aforesaid tract; 1 of 63 a. & the other of 56 1/2 a. Also another tract called Pile Hall (?), 188 a., with improvements, about 8 miles from Frederick Town. Also 2 other tracts of land in Loudoun Co, Va, about 16 miles from Frederick Town, one of 100 a. lying on the Katockton Creek, the other adj thereto of 150 a. Thomas TAYLOR & Benjamin H. CANBY, Ex'rs.

322. Aug 30, 1797
Whereas my Wife hath eloped from my bed & board without any provocation; I warn all persons not to harbour or credit her on my account. George BUTLER, Negro.
Thomas DALRUMPLE & Thomas SMILEY offer $6 reward for the return of an Iron Gray Mare, broke out of the stable of Thomas SMILEY, Innkeeper of the Borough of Carlisle.

The Pennsylvania Herald & York General Advertiser

323. Sept 6, 1797
For Sale - merchant mill on Rock Creek, 6 miles from Gettysburg, 9 from Petersburg, 8 from Tawney Town (Md) & 50 from Baltimore; 60 a. Apply to Robert BLACK, living on the premises.
Selling small plantation, late the property of James SIMPSON, decd., in Franklin Twp, York Co, adj lands of James BLACK & Thomas EWING, Esq; 50 a. on which are house & barn. Joseph MORRISON & Marmaduke WILSON, Ex'rs.
Jacob WINTERODE has lately opened a Public House of Entertainment in Petersburg (Little's Town) at the Sign of the Red Lyon, formerly occupied by Andrew SHRIVER.
William ELLIOT selling grist mill & 570 a. in Path Valley, Franklin Co, 3 miles from Fannetsburg & 14 from Chambersburgh. Has log dwelling house, double barn, distillery & grist mill, with 2 pair of stones. Apply to Richard CHILDERSTONE, Esq., near.
Ran away from subscriber, living on the Frederick Town road, about 2 miles from Baltimore, an Indented Servant man named Michael DOYLE, about 5 ft 6 in high, stout made, his ancles very much swelled, a carpenter by trade. It is supposed he went off in company with one John CORIGAN, who is about 6 ft high & has rather an awkward appearance & very much stoop shouldered when walking. Robert TAYLOR.
$20 reward for return of Indented Irish servant man named John CORIGAN, about 6 ft high, etc. [see above]. Wm. P. MATHEWS, Baltimore.

324. Sept 13, 1797
Philadelphia: The Yellow Fever is yet confined principally to the southern parts of the city. A few cases have taken place in the Northern Liberties. Funerals have taken place in all the burial grounds in the city & liberties from Monday noon to Tuesday noon, 12 adults & 3 children; from Tuesday to Wednesday, 5 adults & 4 children; from Wednesday to Thursday, 9 adults & 4 children. Drs. COX, DOBELL, PLEASANTS, CHURCH & LEIB are appointed to seek & administer relief to such persons as want assistance.
Stephen M'KINLEY offering reward for return of black stud horse stolen out of his pasture in Chanceford Twp, York Co. ($10 only for horse alone.)
York & Baltimore Mail-Stage starts from the house of Philip GOSSLER in York Town, every Thursday norning at 5, taking its tout through Hanover (M'Allister's town) & arrive in Baltimore on Friday at 9, at house of David FULTON, (Old Congress Hall), the same stage will start from Baltimore at 2 the same day, arriver at Rister's town (Md) at 6 the same evening & start from there Saturday morning at 5, arrive at M'Allister's Town at 2 the same day & arrive at York the same evening.
Benjamin NORRIS informs the public that he carries on the fulling & dying business as usual at the Mill where he has lived 2 years past, near to Barnet ZEIGLER's, Esq. decd.
John HERSHE & Jared J. LONG, appointed Commissioners to contract with workmen to rebuild the Bridge across Little Conewago Creek, on road from Oxford to Wm. LONG's Mill & from thence to Carlisle, call meeting at John HERSHE's Tavern in Oxford to plan building.

325. Sept 20, 1797
Sheriff's Sales: (1) Estate of David DEMPSTER, improvement & tract in Cumberland twp, 100 a., adj lands of Samuel PATTERSON & George KERR. Also undivided moiety or equal half part of a messuage & lot in Gettysburg, adj lots of John EWING & Frederick RUNDLE.

The Pennsylvania Herald & York General Advertiser

Estate of James DILL, decd, improvement & tract in Monanghan twp, 150 a.; adj lands of John DILL, Michael EGE & heirs of John COROTHEN.
Estate of Abraham UNDERWOOD, messuage & lot of 5 a. in Warrington Twp., adj lands of Wm. NELSON & Peter ARNOLD.
Six cents reward offered by Catharine BOYD for runaway Apprentice Girl named Elizabeth BRAND, who left her home in Warrington twp, York Co. 12 - 13 years of age, 44 ft high, dark hair, slender made. Any person harbouring said Girl, may depend on being put to trouble.
For Sale - square log house 26 ft by 30, 2-story high, in Thompsen-town, Mifflin Co, & a lot 1/4 a., being a corner lot where a story has been kept for several years. Apply to S. DAVIS, on the premises.

326. [Front page missing, from ads presumed date Sept 27, 1797.]
Recommended ticket to be run at the next General Election: Senator - John STEWART. Assembly - Philip GARTNER, William MILLER, William M'PHERSON, Alexander TURNER, Thomas CAMPBELL, Jacob HOSTETER. Commissioner - David EDIE. Signed: Henry TYSON, Jacob GARTNER, Michael SPANGLER & Jacob UPDEGRAFF (1st District); John WAMPLER, Daniel CLAPSADLE & Adam AULT (3d District); Jno. CAMPBELL, senr., Joseph MITCHEL (4th District); William GRIFFITH & Frederick HARMAN (5th District). Delegates from the 2d District after assisting in settling the above Ticket, withdrew without signing.
George P. ZEIGLER & George JULIUS, Ex'rs. of the estate of Jacob CRONBAUGH, decd., request those owing to make payment.
The partnership of THOMPSON & PATTERSON is dissolved. All indebted to them are requested to make immediate payment.
Alexander IRVINE of Gettysburg is requested to those who may be indebted to him to make immediate payment. This is necessary to enable him to meet with satisfaction to himself & his own private engagements.
To be sold at Public Sale noted Tavern known by the name of Butcher FREDERICK's, in the town of Oxford, York Co, with 10 of the town lots adj, on which are erected barn, stables, sheds, &c.; also 60 a. adj said Town. House is large with 2 pumps at the door. John HERSH.
Fred. STUMP informs that he has bought Wright's Noted Ferry (Lancaster shore) & large brick Ferry house lately occupied by Capt. Jacob STAKE. He has a long experience in the business in the time he occupied Anderson's Ferry.
Whereas William M'CLELLAN, Sheriff of York Co, hath advertised 'As the estate of Abraham UNDERWOOD, a lot of 5 a. adj lands of William NELSON, Peter ARNOLD &c.' to be sold; & whereas the title for the same is vested in the subscriber, all persons are cautioned against buying same.

327. [Front page missing, assumed from dates of ads issue is Oct 4, 1797.]
To be sold at the plantation late of Eli KIRK, decd., Manchester Twp, livestock, waggon, plows, harrows, grain, &c. William WELCH, adm'r.
John SCOTT seeks journeyman fuller, 1 with family preferred. Mazara Mills.

328. Oct 11, 1797
Martin SLINKER has taken in a stray steer, Windsor Twp, York Co.
Jesse SPANGLER offers 6 cents reward for the return of his runaway Apprentice Lad named Abraham SITLER(?), (by trade a Hatter), about 5 ft 4 in high.
Philadelphia: During the last 24 hours there have been buried in the City & Suburbs & at the Hospital 25 persons, 8 of whom (as near as we can determine) died of the yellow fever.

93

The Pennsylvania Herald & York General Advertiser

329. Oct 18, 1797
James ALLEN has taken up a stray mare, Fawn Twp.
George KUNTZ, hatter, informs that he carries on the hatting business in
   Beaver St, next door to Abraham DANNER, Tobacconist, Borough of York.
For Sale - small farm near Peach Bottom Ferry, 61 a., adj lands of
   Cunningham SAMPLE &c. Apply to Ralph BOWIE.

330. Oct 25, 1797
Michael GRAYBLE, Gaoler, York, informs that he has taken into custody a
   certain Mulatto Man who calls himself Thomas DUNCAN, about 26 years old,
   5 ft 5-6 in high, well made, very straight hair, which he wears loose.
   Says he belongs to Dr. Richard MURRAY of Md. Also was committed a
   Mulatto Man who calls himself Harry JONES, about 31 years old, 5 ft 8 in
   high, thick bushy wool or hair--says he served his time with William KING
   of Georgetown Md.
At the last Sept term, the Court did appoint Jacob HAY, Esq., Peter KURTZ &
   Charles DEEL to liquidate, audit & settle the accounts of John GEINER(?)
   late of Shrewsbury twp, York Co.
John STROMAN, George HAY & Godfrey LENHART, all candidates for Sheriff.
Ran away from the subscriber, Negro Cuff, about 27 years old, 5 ft 9-10 in
   high, tolerable black, thin visage, his right foot is remarkable, the
   toes of which are very crooked & lean much towards his left foot. He was
   seen in company with Negro Jacob, who also absconded from me & was taken
   in the neighborhood of Tawney Town, on their way to Lancaster or
   Philadelphia.   John ORME, Montgomery Co, Md.
John GRACE informs that he has lately removed from Wright's Ferry
   (Susquehannah) to Borough of York, to that well known stand formerly the
   sign of the Waggon, but now the sign of the Fifteen Stars, next door to
   Peter DINKLE & opposite Solomon MYER's Printing Office; where he provides
   good bedding, liquors &c. for travellers.

331. Nov 1, 1797
Highest price given for good rye at William HARRIS's Distillery, half a
   mile from Borough of York, and at HARRIS & DONALDSON's Store in York.
All persons indebted to the estate of Emanuel HERMAN, late of Manchester
   twp, York Co, decd, are required to pay up. Catharine HERMAN & Michael
   SCHMYSER, Adm'rs.
Escaped over the wall of the Gaol in Borough of York, David MAXWELL,
   apprentice to the Milling Business, about 18 years of age, 5 ft 9 in
   high, of fair complexion & light coloured hair. $20 reward offerd by
   William GOOCH.
George SPANGLER announces as a candidate for sheriff.

332. Nov 8, 1797
2,300 a. for sale in state of Kentucky, patented in 3 tracts, near a
   northern branch of Green river & not more than 20 milesfrom Ohio & 8 or
   10 from town of Vienna. Enquire of William BARBER, Esq. York.
Strayed from the mill of Jacob SITLER in Chanceford twp, York Co, a young
   cow with calf.
Lost yesterday evening in Borough of York a red Morocco pocket book
   containing various notes & a letter directed to Capt. Andrew NEILSON,
   Tavernkeeper at the Sign of the Iniskelln(?) cattle, Phila., favored by
   Mr. LINN. Reward of $20 will be paid to any who delivers said pocket-
   book & contents above described to Capt. P. GOSSLER.
Last notice of A. MAGINLEY to those indebted to him to pay up.

The Pennsylvania Herald & York General Advertiser

All persons indebted to estate of John SPANGLER, late of York Twp, decd. to make payment. George BARD, Jacob SPANGLER & Margaret SPANGLER, Ex'rs.
Jacob UPDEGRAFF informs that he public that he intends to open a Conveyancing & Scrivener's Office in his house, where he now lives in High St, Borough of York, above the Court House.

333. Nov 15, 1797
Married Saturday Evening, last, William HAMILTON, Printer to Miss Juliana HUBLEY, d/o John HUBLEY, Esq. of Lancaster.
Conewago Canal to be opened & boats will pass through the Locks on Wednesday the 22d day of this inst (Nov.)
Jacob STAKE, who for the last 3 years kept the Ferry & Tavern in Columbia on the great road from Lancaster to York, informs the public thata he has taken the old Ferry on the opposite side of the River in York Co, lately kept by John GRACE.

334. Nov 22, 1797
To be sold at public vendue in the Borough of York, 2 tracts of 170 1/2 a. & 34 perches in Hopewell twp, adj lands of Peter BECK, Samuel YOUNG, George GROFF (GROSS?) & Christian SAUTER, attached at the suit of George STAEBLER as the property of John KESNER. Jacob HAY, Peter KURTZ & Charles DEEL, Auditors.
[Letter filmed on top of newspaper, which obliterates the additional data for this date.]

335. Dec 6, 1797 [Next available issue.]
Notice is given to all who left Deeds & Mortgages in my Office to be recorded that the same are recorded & are requested to take them away. Jacob BARNITZ, Recorder.
I James AIKENS do hereby acknowledge that I have without reason exposed the character of Henry ARMSTRONG, of the Borough of York, & acknowledge the same to be wrong. Witnessed by Michael GRAYBLE.
The subscribers, living in Berkley Co, Va, offer for sale 430 a., part of the plantation on which they now live. Price $24 per a., half cash down. WILLIS & BEALL.
Martin KREBER announces that he is a candidate for sheriff.
Died on Monday last, & will be interred at 3 this afternoon in the Presbyterian Churchyard of York, Mr. James SHORT, merchant, aged 42 years. A man of great uprightness & integrity.
Married in Newbury twp on the 10th day of November last, Jacob KAUFMAN to Miss Jane HART.
Married on the 12th Thomas METZLAR to Miss Margaret REIFF.
Married on the 16th Abraham DERUSH to Miss Pamela ROBINSON & Samuel HERMAN to Miss SHERMAN.
On the 28th Andrew BLYMEYER to Miss Peggy ENSMINGER & Edward JONES of Newbury twp to Miss Anna BOYD of Warrington.

336. Dec 13, 1797
Christian CASHMAN, Mountpleasant T., has taken in a stray steer.
Whereas James ROBINSON about 7 or 8 years ago executed a Bond to a certain Wm. NELSON, he is determined to dispute the payment of same.
All those indebted to Lewis MICHAEL of Hanover are to pay up.
For Sale - the following tracts in county of Somerset (Pa): (1) 20,172 a., called Stephen's Green, within 2 miles of Black's Tavern on the South side of the middle Glade rd. (2) 140 a. adj tract #1. (3) 268 a. on the

The Pennsylvania Herald & York General Advertiser

South side of the Allegheny branch of stony-creek, in Quithahoning twp. (4) 309 a. in Elklick twp, adj Samuel FINLEY's claim & the little meadow Mountain. (5) 181 a., called Schryock's choice, about 3 miles n.east of Black's Tavern. (6) 345 a., on the North-fork of Turkey-foot, in Turket [sic]-foot twp. Patents on the titles of these lands are indisputable. Most were warranted previous to the Revolution. Apply to George BURKET, Innkeeper in the town of Somerset or to Samuel RIDDLE in Chambersburg. Also for sale a small tract in Franklin Co, about 4 miles from town of Chambersburg. Apply S. RIDDLE or George HETECH, Esq. at his office in Chambersburg.

Died on Sunday morning last, Mrs. Jean GRAYBLE, wife to Michael GRAYBLE of this Borough, a woman examplary for her charitable disposition. Remains interred yesterday in the Presbyterian burying ground York.

$20 reward offered for return of Negro man Jack, ran away from Peter ICKES, Abbott's-town, York Co. Near 40 years old, pretty black, 5 ft 8 in high, stout & well made, has a hollow nose with the end turned up. He can read English, speaks it well, can speak some German. Formerly belonged to William COCHRAN, Esq. of this Co. and is a compleat farmer. He is very fond of strong drink.

Dec 20, 1797 [Copy is illegible.]
337. Dec 27, 1797
Pa. Legislature, House of Representatives: Petitions read from C. W. PEALE, paying patronage to his newly invented wooden bridge; from inhabitants of Washington co, praying the removal of David ACHESON from his seat on account of his alienage; from James READ praying for an increase of his fees of office; from a number of inhabitants of Lycoming, stating certain objections to the election of Jacob SHOEMAKER & praying that Hugh WHITE may have his seat; from a number of the inhabitants of Montgomery against the election of Nathaniel BOLEAU.

Nicholas GELWICKS announced as a candidate for sheriff.

To be sold at public vendue, all the remaining stock of goods, late of James SHORT, Merchant, Borough of York, decd. John EDIE, Conrad LAUB, Wm. DAVISON, Ex'rs.

Notice is given to all those who are desirous of forming a Troop of Light Horse in the 8th Regiment of York Co Militia, commanded by Col. CAMPBELL, to meet at the house of William BUTT, innkeeper to choose officers.

338. Jan 3, 1798
Pa. Legislature: Petition of J. GIBSON, praying permission to erect a dam across the river Yonghiagenny reported in favour of the petitioner.

Alexander COBEAN, running for sheriff.

Reward for runaway Negro Woman named CASH, about 23 years of age, about 5 ft, of a dark complexion, somewhat out-month'd, has a large lump on the back of her neck & is supposed to be with child. She had on & took with her a new calico gown, a red stuff petticoat, velvet shoes, new stockings & a new wool hat. Return to her master, Cunningham SAMPLE, Fawn twp., York Co.

To be sold - plantation & tract, late the property of Jacob SHREIBER, decd, in Newbury twp, York Co, adj lands of James SMITH, Esq., John HART & Eli LEWIS, 118 a. Has log dwelling house & barn, spring house & orchard. Mill is erected on adj tract. Apply to John EMIG & Michael SCHREIBER, Ex'rs.

All persons having demands against the estate of John BIGHAM, late of York Co, decd, are desired to bring them to the house of John SCOTT, Innkeeper

The Pennsylvania Herald & York General Advertiser

in Gettysburg. Alexander IRVING, Alexander COBEAN & Walter SMITH, Ex'rs.
On 5 April 1796, Jacob GIBSON executed to John TAYLOR of Fawn Twp, York Co,
2 bills of hand & he cautions persons from taking them.
Cheap & Elegant Family Bible. Proposals by William HAMILTON of Lancaster.
Daniel MAY has resigned his office of Justice of the Peace for twps of
Paradise & Dover.
Ran away from Robert FINNEY (of Northumberland Co) at Mr. Ezekiel WEBB's
Tavern in Kennel twp, Chester Co, 3d inst., 2 indented Irish Servant men;
one named Charles M'GINTY, about 22 years of age, 5 ft 7 in high, short
black hair, dark complexion & stout made. Had on a high crown'd wool
hat, blue coat & jacket, old thickset breeches, gray stockings & good
shoes. The other named Thomas TAYLOR, 5 ft 6 in high, dark sandy hair &
stout made. Had on wool hat, old green sailors jacket, corduroy breeches,
gray stockings & good shoes.

339. Jan 10, 1798
Pa. Legislature, House of Representatives: Petition from Benjamin ELLIOT,
praying a law may be passed to compensate him for services rendered.
Petitions were presented signed by upwards of 1800 of citizens of York
Co, praying a division of Co. Bill introduced to increase the fees of
James READ, inspector of flour. Resolutions presented relative to the
seat of David ACHESON.
On the 12th milestone on the Bristol road, on Tuesday last, 2 young men,
twin brothers (sons of Mr. GILBERT) were employed in walling a well and
one was killed by accident.
William WELSH has clover seed for sale on the west side of the bridge,
Borough of York.
$30 reward offered by Peter SCHMYSER for the return of a runaway Mulatto
man names QUILL, 21 years old, 5 ft 9 in high, stout & well built,
somewhat knock-knee'd; has a large scar upon his head, occasioned by
falling into the fire when a child, in consequence of which he wears a
handkerchief about his head, from which he seldom lifts his hat.

340. Jan 17, 1798
Harrisburg, a jury of inquest was summoned in consequence of a female
infant being found dead in a house in this town. A certain Sally TAYLOR,
a single woman, having been too often in conjunction with the opposite
sex, & not wishing her offspring defamed with illegitimacy, took the
terrible resolution to smother her child & denying she ever had any; but
by the timely search of a number of the neighbors, the innocent victim
was found secreted between the bed & bolster! One would think that her
co partner in guilt, whoever he is, just possess very uncomfortable
moments on reflecting his being the cause of so much cruelty.
Harrisburg, Was brought to town & safely imprisoned, John HAUER, Charles
M'MANUS & Francis COX, for the wilful murder of Francis SHITZ. Francis
SHITZ, with his brother Peter SHITZ, had been at a neighboring vendue on
Thursday last, & returning in the evening as supposed somewhat fatigued,
as the former had laid himself on a bench near the stove to rest, while
the latter retired to bed in adjoining apartment. Before long a female
of the house discovered a light in the kitchen & opening the door was
frightened at the apperance of several men & endeavored to waken Francis,
when one of the assassins presented a pistol to his head, which he
discharged & killed him on the spot. Two others proceeded to the bedroom
of the brother, P. SHITZ with axes & at the first stroke which one made,
his axe caught the cord of the curtain, which stopped the force of the

blow: he was, however, very much cut on the shoulder, at which he leapt from his bed & had the presence to seize a chair with which he knocked them both down, but in leaving the room he received a deep wound on his posterior, which did not prevent him from locking the door & escaping out a window, retreating to the barn, where he armed himself with a pitchfork. He then repaired to Shaffer's town (2 miles away) where he spread the alarm & by the vigilance of the inhabitants the above mentioned were taken. This young man, who thus defended himself, is only 17 years of age. The motive which led to the above is thought to have originated with John HAUER, brother-in-law to the deceased, who expected to fall heir to a considerable estate had he accomplished his wicked purpose.

By order of Orphans Court, Co of York, to be sold on the premises a certain tract of 210 a., in Berwick twp, in said Co, adj lands of Joseph HERRIN, Joseph DITTO, Peter MARSHALL &c., being part of the real estate of James M'TAGERT, decd.

341. Jan 24, 1798
Whereas my wife Mary BARNERD, having for sundry times misconducted herself to the dishonor of my bed, by making choice of other men in preference to me, & daily contracting debts which I am unable to pay, I have determined to have no further connection with her, nor pay her debts. James BARNERD. (Baltimore)

The petition of George KLOFSFER of Hellam twp was presented, praying the Court to supply a lost Bill of Sale made by a certain Jacob BRENNERMAN to Henry KEESER & by him assigned to Matthew KLOFSFER (father to the petitioner) for 96 a. & 35 perches of land in Hellam twp, adj lands of Stephen REIB, Henry SHULTZ, Christian LEHMAN, George MANTLE &c. John EDIE, Proty. for York Co.

Ran away from the subscriber, living on Long-Green, Baltimore Co, Md, a Negro Man named Leonard, but changed his name & calls himself Clem, about 25 year of age, 5 ft 7-8 in high, remarkably black, large eyes, flat nose, very thick lips, big mouth, chews tobacco & is fond of liquors, round shouldered, stoops with his neck a little forward, small leg & thigh & very large feet. Also Negro Jerry, who ran away at the same time, the property of Joseph WHEELER of Harford Co (Md), about 23 years of age, 5 ft 5-6 in high, very black. Said Negroes has resided nearly 2 years in the neighborhood of York town, Pa, & probably have a pass, as they had themselves advertised & have since passed for freemen. Philip CHAMBERLAIN & Joseph WHEELER. Reward will be paid by Robert WILSON, York Town.

Joseph SMITH has taken in a stray heiffer, Chanceford twp, York Co.

342. Jan 31, 1798
An attempt was made a few nights past to set fire to the house of Mr. N. ROGERS of Baltimore, who was in bed & smelt something burning, the fire waas discovered downstairs & supressed; & it was found that a bundle of newspapers had been fired in the closet. On Thursday the 11th inst., an attempt was made to burn the house of Edward NORWOOD, near Elk Ridge Landing Ferry (Md) by one of his Negro women. She was brought before G. G. PRESBURY, Esq. of Baltimore & acknowledged she had placed fire under 4 different beds of the house by advice, as she said, of a female slave of Samuel NORWOOD. Both were committed to prison.

Pa. Legislature: Bill reported enabling the Commissioners of Huntingdon co to compensate Benjamin ELLIOT for services.

The Pennsylvania Herald & York General Advertiser

To be sold - on the premises, a plantation late the property of Eli KIRK,
   decd, 122 a.; dwelling house & barn. Also 28 a. of woodland 4 miles from
   Borough of York & 6 from above plantation. Terms to be made known by
   William WELCH, Adm'r.
Daniel CLAPSADLE informs that he has opened a Public House of Entertainment
   in that large 2-story brick house late of Richard M'ALLISTER, Esq., decd,
   on the corner of the center square of Frederick St, town of Hanover. He
   also carries on the Hatting Business as usual.
John BIXLER announces as a candidate for sheriff.

343. Feb 7, 1798
Married at Hanover the 30th ult. by the Rev. Mr. MELTZHEIMER; William D.
   LEPPER, Editor & Printer of the Hanover German Gazette to Miss Esther
   OYSTER, d/o Daniel OYSTER, near Hanover.
For sale - dwelling house & tanyard erected on 1 1/2 lot on the main st,
   Williamsport, Md; the dwelling house of stone, 2 stories high, with other
   necessary buildings. Apply to James STERITT, on the premises.
Samuel BREADY executed a Note of Hand to a certain John POTTS of the Town
   of Lewisbetty & cautions that he is determined not to honor same.

344. Feb 14, 1798
Dr. John SPANGLER informs the inhabitants of Borough & Co of York that he
   has taken up his residence in the house lately occupied by Dr. James
   HALL, where he offers his services.
Adam SEESENUP gave from under his hand an Obligation to Samuel HOLTON of
   Chanceford twp, York Co, all persons are warned not to take same.
Ran away from the subscriber living on the great falls of Gunpowder near
   Cromwell's bridge, 25th Dec last, a negro lad named Bob, 18 years old, 5
   ft 5 in high, well made, is very black & pitted with the small pox. John
   T. RISTEAR.
Stolen from James MURPHY, Chester Co, Newgarden twp, a bay mare.

345. Feb 21, 1798
To be sold - tract in Green twp, about 6 miles from Chambersburg, 900 a.
   upon which is erected a saw mill with other improvements, late the
   property of William LOGAN & by him assigned to the subscribers, Samuel
   PURVIANCE & Samuel RIDDLE.
To be sold at Public Sale - tract of 55 a. in Dover twp, York Co, on
   Conewago creek, on which is erected grist, saw & oil mills, 2 stills,
   stone house & barn. Also to be sold livestock, waggon, plough & barrow.
   Thomas PAUP.
Register's Office, York Co. To all Legatees, heirs, creditors &c. to whom
   it may concern, that the following Administrative accounts have been
   filed in this office for Probate of Wills & granting Letters of
   Administration. The account of Simon & Michael MINICH, ex'rs of Michael
   MINICH, late of Shrewsbury twp, decd.
Account of Moses JENKINS & William M'PHERSON, ex'rs. of Moses JENKINS,
   late of Franklin twp, decd.
Account of Adam HEINDEL, adm'r. of estate of Philip HEINDEL, late of
   Windsor twp, decd.
Account of Jacob & Henry MATTER, ex'rs. of George MATTER, late of Manheim
   twp., decd.
Account of William SCOTT, Esq., ex'r. of William KENNEDY, late of the
   Borough of York, decd.
Account of Robert GRAHAM & Robert WILSON, ex'rs. of William SMITH, late of

The Pennsylvania Herald & York General Advertiser

Cumberland twp, decd.
Account of Margaret STAUFFER, John GOCHENAUR & John HURST, ext'rs. of Peter STAUFFER, late of Newbury twp, decd.
Account of Joseph GARRETSON & Samuel GARRETSON, ex'rs. of John GARRETSON, late of Newbury twp, decd.
Account of Thomas ALLEN, adm'r. of John ALLEN, late of Fawn Twp, decd.
Further account of Catharine GINRICH & John BAER, adm'rs. of Benjamin GINRICH, late of Codorus twp., decd.
5th Account of Anthony YINGER, adm'r. of George YINGER, late of Newbury twp, decd.
Account of John RICHART & Ludwig BOPP, ex'rs. of John FISHER, late of Shrewsbury twp, decd.
Account of Edward JONES, adm'r. of Naphtali JONES, late of Newbury twp, decd.
Further account of Elizabeth EBERT, Andrew RUTTER & Martin EBERT, adm'rs. of Michael EBERT, late of Manchester twp, decd.
Account of Daniel HENRY & John GOSSWEILER, adm'rs. with the will annexed, of Peter HENRY, late of Monaghan twp, decd.
Account of John NICHOLS & William WELCH, ex'rs. of Mary BROWN, late of Manchester twp, decd.
Account of Christian RUPP & Godlieb RUPP, ex'rs. of Baltzer RUPP(?), late of Hellam twp, decd.
Account of George P. ZEIGLER, Esq. & George JULIUS ex'rs. of Jacob CRONBACH, late of Dover twp, decd.
Account of George P. ZEIGLER, Esq. & Peter OPP, ex'rs. of Jacob OPP, late of Dover twp, decd.
Account of Catherine KAUTER, ex'rx. of Barnet KAUTER, late of Manchester twp, decd. Jacob BARNITZ, Register.
Sheriff's Sales: (1) Estate of James COOPER, improvement & tract in Franklin twp, York co, 250 a., adj lands of Andrew NOAL & --- STRAWSPAUGH. (2) Estate of James MAXWELL, tract in Chanceford twp, 34 a., adj lands of Thomas GROVE & William WILSON. (3) Estate of Adam SMITH, messuage & lot in town of Lewisberry, 44 perches, adj lots of John KAUFMAN & Ludwig SHINGLE. (4) Estate of William KLINE, improvement & tract in Newbury twp, 50 a., adj lands of Daniel HOFF & George BYERS. (5) Estate of William NELSON, improvement & tract in Chanceford twp, 207 a., adj lands of George M'CULLOUGH & Joseph AMER. Alsos one other tract of 34 a., adj lands of Joseph AMER.
Ran away from the subscriber in Baltimore Co, in the forks of Long-Green, a likely Negro man, about 5 ft 6 in high, 25 years of age, of yellowish complexion, has his hair combed back & tied behind. His clothes when he went awar were very mean & dirty, as he had been run away several weeks & made his escape from his overseer as he was bringing him home. He has a pass, which is forged; named Jim but will probably change it as he called himself John STONE before. Aquila HALL.
Alexander UNDERWOOD returns his sincere thanks to friends & the public for their votes t the former election for sheriff's office & professes himself a candidate again.
To be sold - that elegant, substantial & well built 3-story brick house & lot thereunto belonging on the North side of High St, Borough of York, near the centre square. House is 30 ft in front, with large brick kitchen & piazza & joins a 20 ft alley with barn & stable. Apply to Jacob HAY, Esq. near the premises. James HALL.

The Pennsylvania Herald & York General Advertiser

346. Feb 28, 1798
Birmingham, on the River Juniata, co of Huntingdon, near the centre of Pa, is laid out for a Manufacturing Town & is situated on the North bank of the River at the head of the Navigation, about 20 miles above the town of Huntingdon, within 1 mile of the Lead Mine & 3 from Huntingdon Furnace. Merchant Grist & Saw mills are now compleat & to be erected a Forge, Rolling & Sliting mill. Between the upper & lower works there is a mine of coal. The town is laid out by actual surveys. Town lots as well as the 100 out lots will be sold by tickets. Town lots $10 each; out lots $30 each. Purchase tickets from John CLARK, Esq., York Town; Joseph CADWALLADER, now at the Birmingham Works & with printer hereof. John CADWALLADER.
Sheriff's Sale: estate of John RENEY, improvement & tract in Hopewell twp, 20 a., adj lands of David KENNEDY & William LIGGET.
George WORLEY informs his customers that 1 mile from Borough of York he carries on the sickle making business. Persons can apply at Daniel REGAN's, at the sign of the sickle in York Borough.

347. March 7, 1798
All persons having demands against the Estate of Christian CLOSS, late of Reading twp, York co, decd., are requested to present accounts at the house of Gabriel SMITH, Esq., Berlin. John CLOSS, Abraham CLOSS & Wendel OYER, adm'rs.
To be rented in Green-Castle, house where Robert M'CULLOH formerly kept a tavern, adj the diamond of said town. Likewise a convenient still house & lot. Apply Robert M'CULLOR.
2 tracts for sale - in Chanceford twp, York co. One contains 250 a. with log dwelling house & double barn; lying on the great road leading from York to Peach bottom Ferry, within 4 miles of M'Call's Ferry & within 6 of Peach Bottom, adj lands of Wm. MORRISON, Tavernkeeper. The other of 150 a., log house & barn with other out-houses. Lying on the great road from York to Peach-Bottom, 4 miles from M'Call's Ferry. Apply to James HILL, Chanceford Twp.
For Rent - Merchant grist & saw Mill in Monaghan twp, York Co, belonging to the estate of Joseph BRADLEY, decd. Apply to John DEARDORFF or Edward OHAIL, Adm'rs.
Public Sale by virtue of the Orphans Court Co of York, plantation & tract in Warrington Twp, on each side of the road from York to Carlisle, about 1 mile from Conewago Creek; adj lands of John NESBIT, Alexr. ROSS & Mathias HOLLOPETER; 360 a.; two messuages, barn. Being the real estate of William M'MULLIN, decd. Terms made known by Robert M'MULLIN, Adm'r. All persons having demands against estate of said decd, are requested to leave their accounts with Samuel NELSON, Monaughan twp.

348. March 21, 1798 [Next available issue.]
Was left in the street, Borough of York, by a Negro in making his escape from the Constable, a bundle containing the following articles, viz: 1 cotton coat, new handkerchief, 1 coarse sheet, 3 old shirts, razor, stockings &c. Apply to John SWENEY in Gettysburg.
Roger KIRK offers $50 reward for bay gelding stolen out of his stable in Nottingham twp, Chester co.
Sheriff's Sale: Estate of John TOULERTON, improvement & tract in Monallan twp, York Co, 100 a. adj lands of Peter SLAYBAUGH, William SLAYBAUGH & Jacob REX.

The Pennsylvania Herald & York General Advertiser

David HARRIS & Co., having in contemplation to remove their store from this place in a short time are under the necessity of requesting all those who are indebted to them to make payment. (Huntington, York Co)
On Friday last, Peter DRITT, son of Capt. Jacob DRITT of this Co, attempting to cross the Susquehanna near his father's house in a canoe, was drowned in the attempt. His parents & friends were spectators of his struggles against the storm.

349. March 28, 1798
For Sale - 2 story dwelling house & 2 lots convenient to Borough of York. Apply to John EDIE in York or John HALLER in Bott's Town.
Charles J. J. POCHON, physician, surgeon & man midwife, late of the Royal Military Hospital of Arras & of Liste in Flanders, but last in the Island of St. Domingo, offers his professional services.
To be sold or rented - tract in Warrington twp, 106 a. adj lands of Jacob BRUGH, Robert NELSON & Conewago creek; 2 dwelling houses & Barn. Also tract of woodland in Dover twp, adj Conewago creek, opposite the former, of 59 3/4 a. Sale made in pursuance of will of David EVANS, decd. Thomas EVANS & Martin RAFFINSBERGER, Ex'rs.
For Sale - tract in Fawn twp, York Co, 250 a., about 4 miles from Peach Bottom Ferry & formerly belonged to William ROWAN, now in possession of Patrick SMITH, to whom it was rented for 1 year. Apply to Thomas GREEVES, No. 73 Walnut St, or to Isaac W. MORRIS at the Brewery in Dock St, Philadelphia.
Whereas I & my wife Mary cannot agree, I have thought it proper to leave her; & caution all persons from trusting her on my account. James CARNEY

350. April 5, 1798
Harrisburgh: At court of Oyer & Terminer for co of Dauphin, Sarah TAYLOR was convicted in the death of a bastard child & sentenced to one years imprisonment. Elizabeth BOMBERGER, convicted of the like crime received same sentence. Susannah KEATON, convicted of larceny, was sentenced to pay a fine of $6 & undergo 1 year's imprisonment. Cornelius STEGOR, convicted of passing counterfeit bank notes was sentenced to 15 year's imprisonment & to pay a fine of $500. The trial of John HAUER & the others charged with the murder of Francis SHITZ was postponed.
As some false imputations have been circulated through your Town under my name, for the malicious purpose of injuring the character of my friend Dr. POCHON, I hasten to destroy these false reports injurious to his character & mine. Lewis BACONAIR, Carlisle.
List of Laws passed in the 8th General Assembly, Commonwealth of Pa: Act for the relief of David JONES. Act to authorize Edmund MILNE to bring a suit against the Commonwealth. Act to empower Walter CLARK, William GREY & William WILTON to sell & con--- certain lot of ground in town of Lew--- in Northumberland Co. Act for the relief of John GLEN.
For Sale - tract of patented land in Chanceford twp, 127 1/2 a., log dwelling house. Apply to John LUSK or Gawin SCOTT, near the premises or Conrad LAUB, John FORSYTH or John EDIE in York.
For Sale or Rent - elegant & well finished 3-story brick house & half lot of ground on the north side of High St, a few doors below the court house, Borough of York; lately occupied & still the property of Dr. James HALL.
Public Sale by virtue of an order of Orphan's Court of York Co, plantation & tract of 90 a. in Newbury twp, adj lands of George M. KERN, Abraham SHELLY &c., late the estate of Napthali JONES, decd. Edward JONES, Adm'r

The Pennsylvania Herald & York General Advertiser

Whereas Napthali JONES, late of Newbury twp, decd. gave (as I understood) an Obligation for the sum of ten pounds to a certain Christian BAUMGARTNER of said twp, all persons are warned not to take said bond. Edward JONES, Adm'r. of said decd.
To be sold, plantation in Monallen twp, York Co, on head waters of great Conowago, 450 a., adj lands of William BOYD, Frederick WARRAN &c. 2 large square log dwelling houses, barn. Also road waggon with 2 pair of working oxen, cows & calves, desk with drawers &c. John MACLEY
John ELEINFRETER has sold his house & movables with an intention to go to Virginia, & his wife not being willing to with him, he cautions all from crediting her on his account.

351. April 18, 1798
Thomas CONRAD, Hatter, informs his customers that he has just returned from a trip in the western country & has opened his former ship, 6th house west from the Ship Tavern, nearly opposite Jacob GARTNER.
John FORSYTH, D.S. notifies land holders in co of York, that he intends going to the City of Philadelphia immedately after June Court--those who may have warrants or patents to procure from the land office he will undertake to do their business.

352. April 25, 1798
George HAY proposes himself as a candidate for the office of sheriff.
Nathan CROMWELL, living in Baltimore Co within 3 miles of Rister's Town, offers $40 reward for runaway dark complexioned negro man named Ben and nick-named Dunk; 23 years of age, 6 ft 8-9 in high; has a down look when spoken to; speaks quick; has short hands and very short thick fingers. Took with him a small white horse, which when tired he will probably sell and proceed on foot or steal another.
To be sold at public sale, plantation & tract in Chanceford twp, York Co. 158 a. adj lands of Matthew KILGORE, John MERLIN & James SPEAR; has 2 dwelling houses, milkhouse & stable. Terms made known by John DUNCAN, Adm'r of the estate of William GODFREY, decd. John EDIE, Clerk of Orphans Court.
Thomas ADAMS & Philip SCHRACK selling by the gross or dozen, American sickles & English scythes at the stores of Messrs. HARRIS & DONALDSON, EICHELBERGER, ROTHROCK, etc.
Solomon KEMPHART, in Emmitsburg (MD), renting large brick store-house & lot, with good stable.
Whiskey & Geneva, of the best quality, to be sold at William HARRIS's Distillery, half mile from Borough of York; by the barrel or single gallon; & at HARRIS & DONALDSON's store in York.
James STEWART has taken up a stray bull in Mountjoy twp., York Co.

353. May 2,1798
School-master wanted in Abbott's Town. Man well versed in the English Tongue & who can teach reading, writing, arithmetic & book-keeping. Apply to Peter ICKES in Abbott's Town.
John JONES, John STROMAN, Martin KREBER, and Nicholas GELWICKS announce as candidates for sheriff.
For sale at public auction tract of land called Springfield, late residence of Jacob LEMMON, decd, 600 a.; 2-story house, kitchen, spinning house, meat house, hen house &c. good barn with stabling. Also tract of 400 a. within 1 mile of former. Appy to Jacob LEMMON, residing thereon. About 25 miles from Baltimore City, 2 miles from Richard JOHN's black rock

The Pennsylvania Herald & York General Advertiser

25 miles from Baltimore City, 2 miles from Richard JOHN's black rock
mills & 9 from Fowble's tavern. Also selling stock of horses & cattle,
farming utensils & household furniture. Joshua & Jacob LEMON, Ex'rs.

354. May 8, 1798
Patrick M'FARLIN, Sign of the Swan, informs his friends & the public that
he now occupies the tavern lately kept by Mr. GEYER in Dover, at the road
from York to Carlisle & about 7 miles from Borough of York.
John BIXLER announces as a candidate for Sheriff.
James LONG seeks bright bay mare colt that strayed from the commons of
York.

355. May 16, 1798
Conrad LAUB, Collector of the Revenue for York Co, gives notice to
distillers that every still within the county must be entered in writing
at his office.
Opened in the Academy, an English Classical School to make the youth of
both sexes intimately acquainted with the English language; to teach them
to read & cultivate their understanding of same. Plan includes Writing,
Arthimetic, Geography, the use of the Globes, Astronomy & the Elements
of Euclid & Trigonometry. Robert HETERICK & Assistants.
Charles de LORUMIER, teacher of the Frency Grammer, informs that through
encouragement of a number of respectable ladies & gentlemen, he has
opened a School for young ladies at the house of Dr. FAHNESTOCK, where he
teaches Grammer and the theory of Geography.
Samuel THOMAS, Henry WAYMAN & Charles Alex. WARFIELD offer 300 silver
dollars reward for apprehending the 3 following negroes, viz: Frank,
property of Samuel THOMAS. He is about 21 years of age, 5ft 10in high,
very black, stout & well made and has large white eyes. Jem, property of
Henry WAYMAN. Is a likely fellow, about 21 years of age, 5ft 9-10in
high, very black and has a wild look when spoken to. Baruch, property
of Dr. Charles A. WARFIELD. He is about 26 years of age, very black,
slim made, about 6 ft high, has a down look and if alarmed stutters very
much when he attempts to speak.
Sheriff's Sales: (1) Estate of John TOULERTON, improvement and tract in
Menallen twp, 100 a, adj lands of Peter SLAYBAUGH, Wm. SLAYBAUGH & Jacob
REX. (2) Estate of John RANKIN, decd, in hands and possession of
Elizabeth RANKIN, Ex'rx., improvement & tract in Newbury twp, 63 3/4 a,
adj lands of Ann NOBLET & Jacob HART. (3) Estate of Samuel HADDEN,
improvement & tract in Strabane Twp, York Co, 280 a, adj lands of Wm.
SCOTT & John DICKSON, Esqs. William M'CLELLAN, Sheriff.
Gun-smiths wanted, apply to Robert M'CORMICK at the gun manufactory, Globe-
mill Philadelphia.

356. May 23, 1798
Sheriff's Sale: Estate of Joseph LITTLE, messuage & lot on south side of
High St, Gettysburg, York Co, adj lots of John MYER & Jacob WOODSECKER.
Also selling livestock, waggons, beds, household furniture &c.
Lost between Mock's tavern on south-mountain & Antietum (MD), a bundle of
notes with sundry other papers. Joseph SHANNON.
Register's Office, York Co, Notice is given to all Legatees, Heirs,
Creditors &c. that the following Administrative accounts have been filed
in the Register's Office for the Probate of Wills & granting Letters of
Administration in and for Co of York, PA; same will be presented to

The Pennsylvania Herald & York General Advertiser

Orphan's Court to be held at York 26 June next. (1) Account of Abraham LEHMAN, adm'r of estate of Margaret BAYER, late of Manheim twp, widow, decd. (2) Further account of Tempest TUCKER & Christian HERSHY, ex'rs. of Peter DICKS, late of Paradise twp, decd. (3) Account of John CLOSS, A. CLOSS & Wendel GEIGER, adm'rs of Christian CLOSS, late of Reading twp, decd. (4) Account of Robert BIGHAM, acting exc'r of Thomas ARMOR, late of Borough of York, decd. (5) Further account of James TODD & John LOVE, ex'rs. of Joseph TODD, late of Newbury twp, decd. (6) Account of Andrew ALBERT and Jacob ALBERT, ex'rs. of Lorentz ALBERT, late of Huntington twp, decd. (7) Account of Michael WENTZ & Catharine his wife, adm'rs of John AYMES, late of Manchester twp, decd. (8) Account of Eve Margaret BACHMAN and John SUMMER, adm'rs of David BACHMAN, late of Germany twp, decd. (9) Further account of Henry WENTZ and Barnet HOLIZAPPEL, ex'rs. of Philip WENTZ, late of Dover twp, decd. (10) Account of Margaret STAUFFER, John GOCHENAUR & Jno. HURIT, ex'rs of Peter STAUFFER, late of Newbury twp, decd. (11) Further account of Andrew JOHNSTON, Esq. and Jacob GARTNER, adm'rs of William JOHNSTON, late of York twp, decd. (12) Account of Peter MESSERLY and John HUBER, ex'rs of Daniel MESSERLY, late of Dover twp, decd. (13) Account of Henry MESSEMER, ex'r of Yoder MESSEMER, late of Manheim twp, decd. (14) Account of Barbara FLECK and Valentine FLECK, adm'rs of Valentine FLECK, late of Huntington twp, decd. (15) Further account of Henry KRIEGER, esq. acting adm'r of Martin SHETTER, esq., late of Newbury twp, decd. (16) Further account of John BOYER and John JOSEPH, ex'rs of Tobias HETZEL, late of Paradise twp, decd. (17) Account of Frederick EICHOLTZ and John HENEISY, ex'rs of Frederick EICHOLTZ, late of Dover twp, decd. (18) Account of Peter MUNDORFF and Samuel GROSS, ex'rs of George RINGER, late of Manchester twp, decd. (19) Account of George HEAGY and Jacob SLENTZ, ex'rs of John SLENTZ, late of Mountjoy twp, decd. (20) Accounts of Jacob KOLLER and Henry RIEHMAN, adm'rs of Baltzer KOLLAR, late of Shrewsbury twp, decd. (21) Account of John ROUSE, ex'r of Rev. Luke ROUSE, late of Borough of York, decd. (22) Account of Elizabeth MATE and Philip DECKER, adm'rs of Philip MATE, late of Hellam twp, decd. Jacob BARNITZ, Register.
Jenet GRIER looking for 2 milch cows that strayed, Borough of York.

357. May 30, 1798
Notice is given to the creditors of Charles HAMILTON that he has applied to the Court of Co of Berks for benefit of law providing relief for insolvent debtors.

358. June 6, 1798
William C. GOULDSMITH, selling upon liberal credit, mill with 160 a. on a never failing stream, the great falls of Gunpowder, about 17 miles from city of Baltimore & upon the stage road from thence to Yorktown. Inquire of William WEATHERALL at the mill or to the subscriber in Baltimore City.
Dr. Samuel FAHNESTOCK informs that he continues the practice of physic and Surgery as usual at his house in Beaver St, Borough of York.

359. June 13, 1798
$40 reward for bay mare stolen out of the pasture of Peter JONES, Newbury twp, York Co.
Abraham GONCE selling plantation in Cumberland twp, York Co, 191 1/2 a. about 3 miles from Gettysburg and 4 from Hunterstown; adj lands of Wm. GILLELAND, Esq., Robert TATE and John SHAKLEY. Has 2-story log house, stable, timber hewd and shingles made for large double barn, has still

The Pennsylvania Herald & York General Advertiser

house at one of the best mill seats in the co. Apply to GONCE on the premises.
Tobacco Manufactory of George EICHELBERGER & Co., Baltimore, informs that they have erected a Tobacco Manufactory in Water St, opposite Wm. VAN WYCK and Co's vendue store.
Plantation & tract for sale in Monaghan twp, York Co, adj lands of Col. Samuel NELSON, John COCHENAUER and Yellow-breeches creek, opposite Rosebery's mill, 140 a. Has log house & barn. Apply to Elioner ROSEBERRY.
Notice is given to creditors of Adam STITH, that he has applied for the benefit of relief for insolvent debtors.

360. June 20, 1798
Josiah HARMER, Adjutant Gen of the militia of PA has been directed by the Govenor to set a meeting and informs Officers of Brigades of such.
For Sale - 2 houses on one lot of ground in Philadelphia St, borough of York, adj lots of Peter MUNDORFF. Also selling household goods.
Yorktown and Baltimore mail stage, for persons desirous of traveling from Philadelphia by way of Lancaster and York town to city of Baltimore and returning the same rout. Will start from house of William GEER, Lancaster every Tues am at 6 o'clock and arrive in York, at the house of Baltzer SPANGLER at 12 o'clock; from whence it starts at 1 o'clock and arrives at Baltimore the following afternoon. Every Fri morning--10 o'clock the same stage starts from the house of Mr. OTTO at the sign of the Bear, Gay St, Baltimore &c. Samuel SPANGLER.
The Exhibition of the French Students will take place at the Courthouse on Friday evening next. Tickets from Capt. GOSSLER's, Mr. B. SPANGLER's and Mr. OPP's.
Land for sale in Frederick Co, MD by John ROSS KEY; 1700 a. on the waters of great pipe-creek, near Bruce's mill.
Ran away from John ROSS KEY a Negro man, Frederick Co, MD (entry is torn).

361. June 27, 1798
Carlisle: Committed to the Jail of this co on Mon last, a certain Sarah CLARK, on suspicion of being the person who has poisoned the family of John CAROTHERS, Esq. in the lower settlement, of which Mr. CAROTHERS and his wife have died and several of the family now very ill.
Edward HAND of Lancaster, inspector of the Revenue for the 3d survey of the district of Pa, gives notice that any one who wishes to take advantage of the 7 1/2% allowed by an Act of Congress may purchase at one time any quantities of Stamped Vellum Parchment or Paper. Apply at the house of John WREN, south Queen St, Borough of Lancaster.
Conrad LAUB, Collector of Revenue for York Co gives notice of an assortment of Stemped Paper to be purchased at the following places within Co of York, viz. At Hanover, Jacob RUDISELL, Esq.; Gettysburg, Alexander RUSSELL, Esq.; Berlin, Samuel FAHNESTOCK.
The petition of Abraham CUSTARD, late of Westmoreland Co, Pa, setting forth that he is at present confined in the gaol of said co, at the suit of James SCOTT for a debt of 50 pounds; which debt he was unable to pay; pray for the benefit of the law for the relief of insolvent debtors. Hearing to be held. By order of the court, Thomas HAMILTON, Prothonotary, Greensburgh.
Ran away from Borough of York, apprentice boy who calls himself John DONNELLAM; about 5 ft 6 in high, sandy complexion, coarse in his speech, inclined to a stoop in his shoulders, thicker in his legs than the

proportion of his body. Some time ago he was Barber in Alexandria and put in prison for Fellony, as I am lately informed. Apply to Charles M'GAURAN, Mason.
Ran away from John THOMAS, Merryland tract, Frederick co, MD, a Negro man named John. A short, well made fellow, about 21 years of age, very talkative and pert; has a scar on his right breast as large as the palms of two hands. He had on a tolerable good castor hat and a pair of boots.

362. July 5, 1798
The officers of the York Brigade of PA Militia, are fully convinced from the sentiments and dispositions manifested in the measures of the French government, that its views are hostile towards America; and that every amicable accommodation has vanished. Sensible that the situation of our Public affairs is critical, it has become expedient to add to the vigilance and activity of our government. We are prepared to secure our country from violence, injuries and insults attempted or meditated by any foreign power. Signed, by order, and in behalf of the officers. John EDIE, Eli LEWIS and Alex. COBEAN, Committee.
The inhabitants of this Borough, attached to the freedom and independence of their country, have ever celebrated the day so sacred to their rights and liberties; but on the present occasion have viewed it as a grand epoch in the history of mankind. The morning was ushered in by the ringing of bells and firing of cannon--the Light Infantry Co, under Capt. GOSSLER and the Troop of Horse paraded, had dinner & drank toasts. In the afternoon a number of Ladies and Gentlemen assembled in Mr. HAY's woods, adjacent to the Borough and spent the evening in great hilarity and festivity. Many patriotic Toasts were given. The young Ladies of the Borough at high noon dressed in robes of white, presented a Standard to their Brothers and young Lovers in arms. This was a spectacle which drew tears from the eyes of assembled thousands. A Letter from the young Ladies to Mr. John FISHER, Senr. and they presented a Flag to the Company commanded by Richard Cutler CAMPBELL and asked Mr. FISHER also "to paint over the arms of the United States, the Cross of Christ, with this motto, 'In this we will conquer.'"
Whereas a certain Adam HORNER, did leave with Samuel OSBURN, living in Strabane twp, several horses and saddles and bridles as a pledge for a certain sum of money; and as he has not since been heard of, the above articles will be sold at the house of George LASHIELS, Innkeeper.
Ran away from James KELLY, borough of York, a negro man named Bill, about 5 ft 5 in high, thick and strong made, marked with the small-pox and halts a little as he walks, owing to an injury to one of his knees. He is an artful fellow, can speak the German language and is fond of spirituous liquors. It is said that a negro who calls himself Clem is gone with him; he has worked about York for some time past in the character of a freeman, but is the property of a certain Philip CHAMBERLAIN of MD, who has offered $100 for taking him up. It is supposed they will attempt to go on board of a ship at Philadelphia or some other seaport. Clem is about 5 ft 6 in high, is very black, has a flat nose, small legs and large feet.

363. July 11, 1798
Carlisle: Further particulars of Sarah CLARK, whom we mentioned in our last, committed on suspicion for poisoning the family of John CAROTHERS, Esq. of East Pennsborough twp. In her consession before James M'CORMICK, justice of the peace for this co, we were able to collect the following:

The Pennsylvania Herald & York General Advertiser

The said Sarah had no wish to injury any of the family, his daughter Ann CAROTHERS excepted and that she had no particular ill will against her, only that she conceived her to be a rival in the business of love. Sarah purchased last fall from Dr. GUSTINE one ounce of white arsenic and gave it to Ann herself, not wishing to injure any person else. No opportunity offering, she put it in a crock among leaven in the house, and bread being made therfrom, the family taking sick with considerable vomiting, except for Mr. CAROTHERS, who could not vomit, and who died on the 26th Feb. and Mrs. CAROTHERS on the 3d of June and the whole family were much afflicted. Andrew CAROTHERS, son of Mr. C. is expected will not survive. Ann, the object of her revenge, may recover. About 3 or 4 weeks ago she purchased another ounce from Dr. STINNECKIE of yellow arsenic, which she says she put into a crock of butter in Thomas CAROTHERS' spring house.

Also Carlisle: On Sat evening last was apprehended by Robert GRAYSON and committed to gaol a certain James WINAUTS(?), with whom were found 5 counterfeit bank notes, some of which he attempted to pass in town.

July 4th in Hanover was celebrated with unusual hilarity and joy. Mr. CLAPSADDLE prepared an excellent dinner for the troop of Majors H. WELSH & KOHN, Militia officers of the Regiment. After dinner toasts were drunk.

William MILLIGAN has taken in a stray horse, Chanceford twp, York Co.

364. July 18, 1798
Those who incline to enroll themselves in the York Corps of Cavalry may apply to Capt. Wm. M'CLELLAN; those who prefer the Infantry Co, apply to Capt. John EDIE, Capt. GOSSLER's Co being filled.

An election held Sat last in Borough of York for officers in the Volunteer Corps of Cavalry elected the following: William M'CLELLAN, Captain; John FISHER, Junr., 1st Lt; David HARRIS, 2d Lt; David CASSAT, Cornet.

365. July 25, 1798
By virtue of an order of Orphans Court, co of Lancaster, to be sold a lot on the North East corner of King-St, Borough of Lancaster, containing in front on King St, 32 ft, 2 in; and in depth on Prince St, 245 ft to a 14 ft alley; whereon are erected a dwelling house and smith shop. Also a certain 2-story house and lot on King street, adj the above. Late the Estate of Jacob STOFFT of Borough of Lancaster, decd, died intestate. The latter building has been kept for a long time as a tavern by Jacob STOFFT. (STOSST?) Sale will be held at the house of Matthias SLOUGH, Borough of Lancaster. Attendance will be given by Henry PICKERIAN and Conrad SCHWARTZ, Adm'rs. By the Court, Henry HUBLEY, for John HUBLEY, Clerk.

George GROVE of Shrewsbury twp, cautions all persons from taking an assignment on 2 bounds, given to him by Adam SITES.

Lawrence HEINDLE cautions all persons against taking assignment on a judgment bond given by him to a certain Nicholas DIPPLE of Hopewell twp.

366. Aug 1, 1798
John M'GRANAHAN, York, hereby gives notice to all his creditors that he has applied to the Hon. Henry SLAGLE and Jacob RUDISELL, Esqs., associate judges of the Court of Common Pleas, Co of York, that they would grant him the benefit of the law for insolvent debtors.

Reward offered for a black horse, stolen out of the pasture of George MILLER in Tawney Town (MD).

The Pennsylvania Herald & York General Advertiser

Aug 8, 1798 [Issue available; no new local data.]
367. Aug 15, 1798
Sheriff's Sale: Certain 2-story brick messuage and lot on North High St, Borough of York, adj lots of George IRWIN and Peter KURTZ, now in possession of Capt. Philip GOSSLER, tenant. Seized as estate of William BAILY, decd, to be sold by William M'CLELLAN, Sheriff.
Whereas a certain Susannah CANZY, of an indifferent character, swore a bastard child to me, and being forced to undergo the ceremony before Thomas BLACK, Esq., where I immediately left her. I suppose she will be bold enough to call herself Susahhan THOMPSON, but I caution all persons from crediting her in that name or on my account. Levi THOMPSON.
To be sold by Public Vendue at the house of Hugh WILSON, now by Mr. BEATES on Buffaloe Valley, Northumberland Co, Nine Farms in the said Valley; one of about 80 a., the others from 147 to 420 a. each. A choice of water-carriage, either on the Penn's creek or West branch of the Susquehannah. Lands lie near and part adj Penn's Creek, 14 miles from Derr's Town, 19 miles from Sunbury. Thomas HARTLEY means to sell 100 Town-Lots. Col. Frederick EVANS of Middle Creek, Mr. Hugh WILSON at Derr's Town and Mr. William DOUGLASS on the premises are impowered to dispose of the property. The said Thomas HARTLEY has land for sale upon the Bald Eagle; Nittany Valley &c.
To be sold at the Market-house, Borough of York 2 copper stills; seized and taken as the property of Thomas OPO, late Distiller of Dover twp, for duties due. To be sold by Conrad LAUB, Collector of the Revenue.
Eleazar BRANDEN of Huntington twp, York Co, offers reward for runaway Negro Boy named Jim; about 13 or 14 years of age, well grown, pretty black, is active and cunning. He wore when he went away a dirty shirt and trowsers, a half worn wool hat and no shoes.
Sheriff's Sales: (1) Improvement and tract in Chanceford twp, York Co, 200 a. adj lands of Wm. ROSS, Esq., Wm. HENRY & John ROBINSON. Seized as the estate of William COWEN. (2) The life estate of Henry BUCHANAN of in and to a certain improvement and tract in Mount-pleasant twp, 180 a., adj lands of Martin BATTORFF(SS?), Conrad SNYDER. (3) Improvement and tract in Hopewell twp, York co, 100 a., adj lands of Alexander M'KITTRICK and Isaac GRIFFITH, seized and taken as the estate of David OWEN.
The partnership of Thomas ADAMS and Philip SCHRACK is dissolved by mutual consent. Thomas ADAMS will carry on the scythe and sickle manufactory on as large a scale as usual at the old stand.
The person who changed a Whip at Mr. GOSSLER's tavern, Borough of York, is requested to return the same.

368. Aug 22, 1798
In pursuance of will of Mary M'DONALD, decd, to be sold at her late dwelling in Hopewell twp, York Co, a certain plantation called Fair Meadow, 363 a., about 35 miles from Baltimore. Has dwelling house, orchard and excellent springs of water. Formerly the farm on which Richard M'DONALD, decd, lived. Also another tract adj above, 131 a., patented land, on which there is a dwelling house. Apply to Robert M'DONALD, living thereon. John MANIFOLD, acting Ex'r.
Sheriff's Sales: (1) Estate of the Rev. Daniel JONES, improvement and tract in Monaghan twp, York co, 410 a.; adj lands of Daniel HENRY and heirs of Wm. MITCHELL, Esq. (2) Estate of Samuel SHAW, improvement and tract in Fawn twp, 96 a.; adj lands of Jacob GIBSON, Esq. and Benjamin CUNNINGHAM. (3) Estate of John MILLER, improvement and tract in Monaghan twp, 73 a.; adj lands of Francis COULSON and Christian CORNER. (4) Estate of Adam

The Pennsylvania Herald & York General Advertiser

SMITH, improvement and tract in Dover twp, 250 a., adj lands of George SCHNELBECKER and George SHELTER. Also 1 a. of meadow ground in town of Lewisberry, in Newbury twp. Also 6 lots of ground in the town of Lewisberry, known in the general plan of said town by numbres 65, 66, 67, 90, 101 and 103. (5) Estate of Casper SMITH, lot on the north side of front st, town of Lewisberry, Newbury twp, known as No. 13, adj lots of John FILKER &c. (6) Estate of Frederick SHETLER, tract in Windsor twp, 15 a; adj lands of Barnet FREY and Conrad KIGER. (7) Estate of Peter SCHENBERGER, improvement and tract in Windsor twp, 40 a; adj lands of Samuel SMITH and Adam FLENCHBAUGH.

Nicholas GELWICKS offers himself as a candidate for sheriff.

369. Aug 29, 1798
Capt. Alexander MURRAY of Philadelphia is appointed to the command of the Montezuma sloop of war, of 22 guns, now lying at Baltimore ready for sea. [Pages 2 and 3 of issue not available.]

370. Sept 5, 1798
Thomas BLACK, John FORSYTH and David EDIE, Commissioners give election notice.

John SWEENY gives notice that he has applied for the benefit of the act of insolvency of debtors.

For Sale - at Jacob STONER's mill in Manchester twp, York co, 3 miles from Borough of York, a great variety of livestock, a waggon, household and kitchen utensils too tedious to mention. Heirs of Isaac STONER, decd.

For sale by James RAMSEY of Peach Bottom, having more negro slaves than he has necessity for, selling negro man about 44 years of age, stout, healthy fellow and an excellent workman at farming. Also his wife, about 38 years of age, an excellent cook. He would wish to sell them together, or at least not many miles apart. They will be disposed of for cash or bartered for a quantity of good rye Liquor.

To be sold by order of Orphans' Court of York Co, a certain frame Messuage and lot adj a lot of Benjamin BLUEBAUGH, known on plan of said Town (?) by No. 96, late the estate of Abraham SPONSELLER, decd. Terms made known by Wm. BEECHER, adm'r. By order of the Court, John EDIE, Clerk. [Name of town not given, but probably York Town.]

William HARVEY, Gunpowder Forest, near the Quaker Meeting-house, Baltimore Co, State of MD, offers reward for runaway negro man named Saul, about 32 years of age, 5 ft 10-11 in high, jet black complection, smiling countenance, good suit of wool, which he generally wore platted at each side of his head and quetted behind. Is a square well made fellow, rather knock kneeed and remarkable large feet. He is a remarkable sober, quiet, orderly fellow.

Sheriff's Sale: Public sale at the house of Jacob UPDEGRAFF, Borough of York, a large and general assortment of cutlery and hardware, beds and bedsteads, tables, chairs, drawers, cupboards, stoves, one milch cow &c. Taken as property of Jacob UPDEGRAFF.

Ranaway from the subscriber (for horse stealing and house breaking), living near Ridgely's furnace, a mulatto man named York, but it is likely he will change his name. About 30 years of age, 4 ft 9-10 in high, stout, well made fellow, has a remarkable full face and eyes. Vincent TALBOTT, Baltimore Co, MD.

Register's Office notice to all Legattes, Heirs, Creditors &c. that the following Administrative accounts have been filed for the Probate of Wills and granting Letters of Administrations for co of York for Orphans

The Pennsylvania Herald & York General Advertiser

Court to be held 2d day of Oct next: (1) Account of Elizabeth MATE and Philip DECKER, adm'rs. of estate of Philip MATE, late of Hellam twp, decd. (2) 3d account of Conrad SHERERTZ and Philip W. WERKING, ex'rs. of will of Ludwich SHERERTZ, late of Manheim twp, decd. (3) Account of Robert WORK, adm'r of estate of Jane SPENCE, late of Cumberland twp, spinster, decd. (4) Account of George MUHLHEIM and Martin MILLER, ex'rs of will of George MUHLHEIM, late of Manheim twp, decd. (5) Account of Jacob BECK and Ludwich BOBB, ex'rs of Jacob BECK, late of Shrewsbury twp, decd. (6) Account of Jacob MARCH, adm'r of estate of Catharine MARCH, late of Paradise twp, decd. (7) Further account of Thomas M'CLELLAN and Robert CUNNINGHAM, ex'rs of Thomas DOUGLASS, late of Cumberland Co, decd. (8) Account of James SAYERS, adm'r of estate of Wm. ASHTON, Junr., late of Newbury twp, decd. (9) Account of Cornelius GARRETSON, acting ex'r of will of Joshua JOHN, late of Newbury twp, decd. (10) 3d account of John COOPER and David COOPER, adm'rs of estate of Archibald COOPER, late of Fawn twp, decd. (11) Account of Conrad LONG and James BOLTON, ex'rs of of will of John LONG, late of Manheim twp, decd. (12) Further account of George OBERDORFF and Adam PAULUS, ex'rs of will of Henry WOLFF, late of Windsor twp, decd. (13) Account of Adam PAULUS and George OBERDORFF, adm'rs of estate of Anna Mary WOLFF, late of Windsor Twp, decd. (14) Account of Adam HENDRIX and Rachel his wife, ex'rs of will of Nicholas YOST, Junr., late of Shrewsberry twp, decd. (15) Account of Jacob EICHELBERGER and Adam FURNEY, ex'rs of will of Benjamin SELTZ, late of Heidelberg twp, decd. (16) Account of Christian LEHMAN and Stephen RICH, ex'rs of will of Christian LEHMAN, late of Hellam twp, decd. (17) Further account of John DUNCAN, adm'r of estate of William JOHNSTON, late of Chanceford twp, decd. (18) Further account of Adam KREBER and Jacob BARNITZ, ex'rs of will of Reinhart BOTT, late of Manchester twp, decd. (19) Account of George STREIN and John GINDER, adm'rs of estate of George STREIN, late of Newbury twp, decd. (20) Account of John LEAS and Andrew SPANGLER, ex'rs. of will of Christopher HOFFMAN, late of Manallan Twp, decd. (21) Account of Anthony DEARDORFF and David TRIMMER, ex'rs of will of Andrew TRIMMER, late of Reading twp, decd. (22) Account of Catharine MILLER and Michael MILLER, ex'rs of will of Tobias MILLER, late of Shrewsbury twp, decd. (23) Account of Jacob LAUER, Guardian of Elizabeth GAUSS, minor orphan child of George GAUSS, decd. (24) Account of Eve WEICKERT and Nicholas AULENBACH, adm'rs of estate of John WEICKERT, late of Mountpleasant twp, decd. (25) Further account of William WELCH, adm'r of Eli KIRK, late of Borough of York, decd. (26) Account of Rachel EWING and Ninian CHAMBERLAIN, adm'rs of estate of Samuel EWING, late of Mountpleasant twp, decd. (27) Account of Catharine HERMAN and Michael SCHMYSER, Esq., admr's of estate of Emanuel HERMAN, late of Manchester Twp, decd.

371. Sept 12, 1798
Charles W. HARTLEY, being informed that his necessary absence for some time past in MD, has occasioned a report of his removing into that state to reside, declares that he has established his residence in this Borough where he intends to pursue his professional business. York Town.

Reward offered by George KRANTZ, Borough of York, for runaway apprentice lad, bound to the house carpenter business, named Joseph MILLER, about 19 years of age, 5ft 9-10 in high; slim made, with large eyes.

The Pennsylvania Herald & York General Advertiser

Sheriff's Sales: (1) Estate of William ADAMS, improvement and tract in Chanceford twp, York co, 525 a., adj lands of Allen SCOTT and John HEAKE. (2) Estate of John LEONARD, Senr., improvement and lot in Mountpleasant twp, 10 a., adj lands of Baltzer YOUNG and heirs of Casper GITTING.
Timothy PLAIN and Godfrey LENHART announce as candidates for sheriff.
Philip GARTNER, Robert IRWIN, Brice POOL, Barnabas CLEMENTS and William MARTIN announce running for Electors.
John BIXLER gives notice that he has applied for insolvent debtor act.
John DUNCAN, adm'r of estate of William JOHNSON, late of Chanceford twp, decd, requests settlement of decd's accounts.

372. Sept 19, 1798
John OYSTER gives notice that he has applied to insolvency debtors act.
On attachment issued by court of Common Pleas, York Co, at the suit of Michael FULWILLER against Henry FIRSLER. Court has appointed Conrad LAUB, Thomas BLACK and John STOUFFER to audit the accounts and adjust the demands of all the defendant's creditors. The said auditors will meet at the house of William BUTT, in Warrington twp.
Died in Philadelphia, Mon 10th inst, Mr. Benjamin Franklin BACHE, Editor of the Aurora. A notice from Mrs. BACHE announces that he has fallen a victim to the Plague that ravages that city.
Died in Philadelphia, Dr. Alexander Scott KERR, 1st physician to the Dispensary.

373. Sept 26, 1798
The fever that rages in the city of Philadelphia, now also rages at Portland, Maine; Portsmouth, New Ham.; Boston, Mass.; Newport, R.Isl; New London, Connect.; New York and New Roshelle, NY.
Died at Philadelphia, the 14th inst. of the prevailing fever, Mr. John FENNO, Editor of the Gazette of the United States. The paper will in future be conducted by Mr. John Ward FENNO. Also died at Philadelphia: Isaac PRICE, Watchmaker, in Market St, one of the Committee of Health; Jacob HILTZHEIMER, member of the state Legislature.
Died at New York: Thomas GREENLEAF, Editor & Proprietor of the Argus.
On an attachment issued from George Lewis LEFFLER, Justice of the Peace for York Co, at the suit of Henry BENTZ against Arthur M'CANN, the justice did nominate Jacob SPANGLER, P.M. and David CREMER to audit the accounts.
Joseph M'MURRAY has removed his School from the Academy to the house where he lives in George St, opposite Mr. GOERING's.
To be sold, plantation and tract in Cumberland twp, York co, 200 a., adj lands of Samuel COBEAN, Charles FLETCHER &c., being part of a larger tract, late property of Wm. M'CLELLAN, decd. Apply to David MOORE or David EDIE, near the premises or Wm. M'CLELLAN, Yorktown.

374. Oct 3, 1798
York. Died the 2d of Oct inst., after a long and painful illness, Mrs. Catherine HARTLEY, consort of the Hon. Thomas HARTLEY, Esq., member of Congress. She was a loving wife, tender parent and indulgent mistress, a sincere friend and benefactress of the poor. Her remains will be intered this afternoon at the Episcopal Church of St. John's, York Borough.
Alex. TURNER endorses Samuel HARPER for Commissioner of the 4th District.
Philip GOSSLER and William WELCH endorse James M'CANDLESS and Maj. Joseph MITCHELL for the 4th District deputies.
Germantown: BICKHAM & REASE have removed their goods from Philadelphia to Germantown, 8 miles from the City, where they have for sale a general

The Pennsylvania Herald & York General Advertiser

assortment of dry goods. Letters addressed to them at Philadelphia will be duly received.
Selling plantation or tract in Strabane twp, 1 mile from Gettysburg, 150 a., with log house and barn. Samuel Minor REED.
John LUSK, Chanceford twp, York Co, selling 2 yoke of oxen and a threshing machine.
Indian King Tavern: Adam DESHLER informs that he has taken that public house and old established stand of Peter DINKEL's, adj his store, near the Court House in High St.
Richard KNIGHT warns all from taking assignment on a note from a certain Caleb BEALS.
Whereas my wife Jennet SHEKLEY has eloped from my bed and board without any cause or provocation, I caution persons from crediting her on my account. William SHEKLEY.
Joshua RUSSELL of Franklin twp has taken up a stray calf.

375. Oct 10, 1798
Notice is hereby given to weavers that James GRAY carries on Reed-making & mending at the house of Barnabas M'SHERRY in Hamiltonbann twp, York co.
Adam GEMPSHORN and Peter STORM of Hanover, some time in the fall of 1796, executed 9 bonds payable to Philip DEWALT, the will not honor said bonds.
Sale at the house of William M'CREARY in Cumberland twp, York co, near Marsh creek, tract of land of 75 a., house and barn, all new. Also selling livestock and household furniture.
William REISER has taken in a stray mare (Newbury twp).

376. Oct 17, 1798
Election returns for York Co: Congress: Thomas HARTLEY 3857, Henry SLAGLE, 659. Assembly: Thomas CAMPBELL 4645, Alexander TURNER 4635, William M'PHERSON 4420, James KELLY 4359, Jacob HOSTETTER 4312, Philip ALBRIGHT 3714. Sheriff: Nicholas GELWICKS 2037, Alexander COBEAN 1027, George HAY 1033, Alexander UNDERWOOD 850, George SPANGLER 749, Martin KREBER 574, John JONES 420, John STROMAN 317. Commissioner: James M'CANDLESS 425.
Taken up on suspicion of being stolen, a dark bay mare. The supposed theif who had her in possession calls himself Elisha TAYLOR, but was committed by the name of Levi ADAMS. Apply to James WALTON, Fawn twp.
John JONES carries on the Fulling business as usual at his mill in York twp, 7 miles from Borough of York, at the place he formerly dwelt. Cloths left with directions at John JONES' or Mr. LOTMAN's tavern in York Borough will be attended to.

377. Oct 24, 1798
Robert HETERICK announces that during the winter he will teach a class of young gentlemen the Principles of Universal Grammar.
For sale or will be exchanged for property near York town, 10,000 a. of land in Kenhawa co, VA, adj waters of Elk and Burch rivers. Inquire of Charles SHOEMAKER in York Town.
Committed to the custody of Michael GRAYBILL, Gaoler of York, a negro man who calls himself Alexander LITTLE, about 27 years old, 4 ft 10-11 in high, has an open pleasant countenance, says he came from the upper part of Washington Co, MD, and says he belonged to David FITZGERALD, decd. At the same time was committed a negro man who calls himself Jack SIMMONDS, says he is about 50 years of age, 5 ft 9 in high, stout made, with a deep dimple on his chin and a very pleasant countenance. Had a pass signed by Jonathan SIMMONDS of Berkeley Co, VA.

The Pennsylvania Herald & York General Advertiser

Robert JONES, Manchester twp, half a mile from Borough of York, has taken up a stray mare.

378. Oct 31, 1798
Persons indebted to estate of Abraham SPONSELLER are requested to make payments. William (?), Adm'r.
On the petition of Alexander HENDERSON, for the benefit of the insolvent debtors law, petitioner heard and discharged on bail. Written notices to be served on all his creditors except William GAMBLE. David RE?, Prothy. Washington Co Court of Common Pleas.
The public are hereby informed that the remains of Mr. Peter DRITT, who was lost in the river Susquehannah in March last, will be interred on the 10 November next, near the dwelling house of Capt. Jacot DRITT.

Nov 7, 1798 [Issue available, but parts missing. No new local data.]
379. Nov 14, 1798
John EDIE, Borough of York, offering reward for runaway negro girl named Priscilla, about 30 years of age, yellow colored, has a bait in her walk occasioned by the loss of all her toes off the right foot. She is supposed to have gone off in the company of a negro man named Clem, who passes for her husband, and for whom a reward of $100 is offered by his master, living in MD.
David MOORE, William M'CLELLAN and David EDIE, Ex'rs of estate of Wm. M'CLELLAN, decd, to attend at house of Capt. James ROWAN in Cumberland twp.
Whereas my Wife Hannah for sometime past hath behaved in a very disgraceful and unbecoming manner--the public are cautioned not to trust her any thing on my account. William MARSHALL.

380. Nov 21, 1798
John DORON gives notice to his creditors that he has applied to the Court of Common Pleas, co of Cumberland, for benefits of debtors insolvency act.

381. Nov 28, 1798
Thomas BRANDON, Huntingdon twp, York co, has taken up a stray mare.
Public Notice: At a meeting of the Board of Commissioners appointed under act of Congress "Act to provide for the valuation of Lands and Dwelling Houses & the enumeration of Slaves within the U.S." at the Borough of Reading, Co of Berks, the Co of York was divided into 2 assesment districts, the 1st of which being composed of the Borough of York and the twps of York, Hellam, Windsor, Chanceford, Fawn, Hopewell, Shrewsbury, Cordous, Manheim, Heidelberg, Berwick, Paradise, Dover, Newbury and Manchester; the 2d district of the twps of Strabine, Mount Pleasant, Germany, Mountjoy, Cumberland, Hamiltonbann, Franklin, Menallen, Tyrone, Huntington, Monaughan, Warrington and Reading; and the following persons nominated Principal and assistant Assessors, viz: 1st District: Godfrey LENHART, Esq., Principal Assessor. Assistants: Philip GOSSLER, George BARD, Christian STONER, Henry TYSON, William MORRISON, Jr., Joseph MITCHELL, Andrew WARRICK, Adam HENDRICKS, Philip BIEGLER, Adam HUPPERT, George NACE, Peter STORM, Frederick BAGER, Kistan ZIEGLER, John HENISEY, Robert HAMERSLY, Jr. and Andrew RUTTER. 2nd District: Principal Assessor Alexander COBEAN. Assistants: Richard BROWN, Alexander LACKEY, Jacob WINTHROTH, Samuel LYNN, James GETTY, Benjamin REED, Samuel COBEAN, Henry SCHMYSER, John KING, George ROBINETTE, Isaac

The Pennsylvania Herald & York General Advertiser

DEARDORFF, Jesse UNDERWOOD and James CHAMBERLAIN. The above from the 1st district are to meet at the house of Capt. Philip GOSLER, Innkeeper in the Borough of York; from the 2nd district to meet at the house of James SCOTT, Innkeeper in the town of Gettysburg. Michael SCHMYSER, Commissioner, 6th District, PA.
Selling plantation and tract of 163 a. in Huntington twp, York co, adj lands of John COLLINS, Vincent PILKERTON &c., late the property of Joseph DODDS, Senr., decd. Has dwelling house & barn. Andrew THOMPSON and John M'GREW, Ex'rs.
Benjamin BOWMAN of Berkeley co, VA offers reward for runaway negro man named Ben, about 5 ft 9-10 in high, has a bold look, a high forehead and keeps his wool always well drest back.
Sheriff's Sales: (1) At the house of Capt. Peter ICKES, in Abbot's town, York Co, livestock, waggons, gears, ploughs and harrows, household goods &c. Seized as the property of William HEISSER, Peter KITT and Thomas ABBOTT. (2) At the house of John BRUGH in Franklin two, York co, livestock, waggons and gears, ploughs, beds, tables & chairs; also wheat, rye, corn, hay, seized in execution as the property of Samuel MARSHALL and John LIVELSBERGER.
Michael MUMPER, Monaghan twp, York Co, has taken up a stray horse.
All indebeted to the estate of William M'CLELLAN, decd, to attend at the house of Capt. James KOWAN, Cumberland twp. David MOORE, William M'CLELLAN and David EDIE, Ex'rs.

382. Dec 5, 1798
Charles SHOEMAKER has just received and is now opening for sale, in the house lately occupied by Doctor James HALL, an assortment of goods.
Died on the evening of the 4th inst. at his residence on Bohemia Manor, Cecil co, MD, Col. Edward OLDHAM, a distinguished officer of the revolutionary war. His passing is lamented by his truly amiable wife and family.
Register's Office Notice given to all Legates, Heirs, Creditors that the following Administration accounts have been filed for the Probate of Wills and granting Letters of Administration, York CO, PA and that the same will be presented to the Orphans' Court at the session Jan 1 next. (1) Account of Joseph MORRISON and Marmaduke WILSON, ex'rs. of will of James SIMPSON, late of Franklin twp, decd. (2) Account of Robert BROWN, adm'r of estate of William BROWN, late of Hamiltonbann twp, decd. (3) Further account of Samuel HARNISH and Peter ENRKHART, adm'rs of estate of John HOSHAAR, late of Manheim twp, decd. (4) Account of Henry LEHMER ex'r of will of Catharine SARBACH, late of Berwick twp, widow, decd. (5) Account of John GOCHNAWER, John HURST and Margaret STAUFFER, ex'rs of Peter STAUFFER, late of Newbury twp, decd. (6) Account of Mary Elizabeth KEFFER (KESSER?) and John KUHN, ex'rs. of Matthais KEFFER, decd. (7) Further account of Henry MARTTER, adm'r of estate of Michael FUNCK, late of Manheim twp, decd. (8) Further account of Edward JONES, adm'r of estate of Naphtali JONES, late of Newbury twp, decd. (9) Account of John HERSHY and Michael GROSS, ex'rs. of John HERSHY late of Manheim twp, decd. (10) Account of William BEECHER, adm'r of estate of Abraham SPONSELLER, late of Cumberland twp, decd. (11) Account of Esther THOMPSON and Samuel COBEAN, surviving ex'rs of will of John THOMPSON, late of Hamiltonbann twp, decd. (12) Account of James WALKER, adm'r of estate of John HARWIN, late of Cumberland twp, decd. (13) Account of James WALKER, Guardian of William STEWART, a minor orphan son of John STEWART, decd. (14) Account of Margaret MENCHGE and Solomon MENCHGE,

adm'rs of estate of John MENCHGE, late of Germany twp, decd. (15)
Account of Killian ZEIGLER, Esq., adm'r of estate of Elizabeth WOLLOT,
late of Paridise twp, decd. (16) Account of Andrew SENST and Peter
SENST, ex'rs of Philip SENST, late of Codorus tpw, decd. (17) Account
of Matthais EICHHOLTZ, ex'r of Catharine SCHNELBECHER, late of Manchester
twp, widow, decd. (18) Account of Anthony DEARDORFF and David TRIMMER,
ex'rs of will of Andrew TRIMMER, late of Reading twp, decd.
To be sold at the house of William STURGEON in Mount-pleasant twp, York co,
sundry Chattels, rights and credits, the property of Jacob KEENEY, late
of Oxford. John KING, Alexander LECKEY and George LASHELLS, Auditors.

383. Dec 12, 1798
Thomas SELBY selling Mill on Middle creek, York Co, distant about 9 miles
from Taneytown (MD), 8 from Gettysburgh, 6 from Millerstown and 2 from
Emmitsburgh (MD), with saw mill and 98 a. of land. The mill house is
strong, built of stone and about 50 ft long and 40 wide; 3 stories high.
On premises frame dwelling house with 2 rooms, a still house &c. Terms
may be known by applying to Brice SELBY at Montgomery Court-house, MD or
to Thomas SELBY living on the premises.
Jacob HAY, Daniel SPANGLER and David HARRIS, Auditors, appointed in a suit
of Jacob BAILY against a certain Jacob ETTER to meet at the house of
Jacob UPP, Inkkeeper.
Take Notice: That the partnership between Samuel JAGO and John John W.
KITTERA, Esq. in Codorus Forge, is from this day dissolved (Dec 7, '98).
John FORSYTH, David EDIE and James M'CANLES, Commissioners of Taxes for
York Co, taking applications for building the Conowago Bridge , on the
Post Road between York and Carlisle. Also, a silver watch was delivered
to said Commissioners by Alexander WALLACE, said to be the property of a
certain I. GREEN, now in York Gaol, convicted for Larceny, will be
exposed to sale towards discharging costs of prosecution.
Plantation to be sold, on which the subscriber now lives, about 1200 a., in
Harford Co, MD, on the waters and near Deer-creek, about 30 miles from
the flourishing city of Baltimore; 15 from Havre de grace and within 10
miles of Navigation. Convenient to 3 sawmills, one of which adj the land
and the other 2 not more than 1 1/2 miles from it. Also for sale,
plantation of about 833 a. on Broad Creek, about 4 miles from former,
consisting of 2 small farms with tenantable buildings. Also to be rented
a number of good farms, property of the heirs of Ignatius WHEELER, Esq.,
decd. Apply to Joseph WHEELER at his plantation.
To whom it may concern, about 12 years ago, Elizabeth FORSYTH put into my
hands 40 pounds as Trustee to be paid to her daughter Mary, when she
should attain the years of 21. Any person duly authorized by the said
daughter, calling upon me & giving approved security shall receive same.
Jacob DRITT, York Co.

384. Dec 19, 1798
The person who borrowed a Fowling Piece belonging to John EDIE will oblige
him by returning it immediately.
Robert BLAINE, Chanceford twp, York co, has taken up a stray mare.
All persons indebted to the estate of John M'FARLAND, decd, formerly of
Strabane twp, York co, are requested to call on the ex'rs. William
HAMILTON and William BOGLE.
John SELL gives notice that he has applied to the court for the benefit of
the insolvency act.
By order of Orphans' Court of York co, to be sold at the premises planta-

The Pennsylvania Herald & York General Advertiser

tion and tract of land in Franklin twp, co of York, 150 a.; late the
estate of John EBY, decd. John EDIE, Clerk of the Court.
Sheriff's Sales: (1) Estate of Henry GREG--, messuage and lot in Abbott's
Town, adj lots of Frederick BAUGHER and widow JOHNSON. Also a 5 a. lot
adj lots of Robert DOYLE and Peter ICKES. Also 1 other 5 a. lot in twp
aforesaid, adj lots of Jacob NOEL and Jacob LINGEFELTER. (2) Estate of
Martin PUTTORSS, improvement and tract in Mountpleasant twp, 251 a., adj
lands of Peter VANDIKE, widow PUFFENBERER &c. (3) Estate of John BIXLER,
stone messuage and parcel of ground, part of lot No. 60 on the east side
of George St, Borough of York, adj lots of George KOCH, decd and Gotlieb
ZEIGLE. (4) Estate of James WILSON, improvement and tract in Hopewell
twp, 70 a., adj lands of James KELLY and Joseph THOMPSON.

385. Dec 26, 1798
Samuel FAHNESTOCK gives notice that he means to remove from the co of York
and requests debts be discharged.

There are no issues of this newspaper available for 1799. In 1800 the name
was changed to the YORK RECORDER.

York Recorder

386. Jan 29, 1800
Thomas BIGHAM of Hamiltonsban Twp. has taken up a stray steer.
Selling plantation of Joseph BRADLEY, late of Monaghan Twp., decd; has
grist and saw mill for rent; 2 dwellings and barns. John DEARDORFF and
Edward OHAIL, Adm'rs.
Sale of plantation of Daniel BUELER, decd, of Manchester Twp; has tract of
150 a. Capt. John QUICKEL, Adm'r. John EDIE, Clerk of Orphans' Court.
Store to let now occupied by Messrs. HARRIS & DONALDSON and house adj, in
which Mr. HARRIS lives. John CLARK
Felix DE ST HILAIRE is opening a dancing school in York.
Daniel DEEL(?) and Henry RHEIMAN, Adm'rs. of estate of Thomas EHRHART, late
of Shrewsbury Twp.
Michael GRAYBELL, gaoler of York, has in custody a mulatto man who calls
himself Zacharia ROBINSON; acknowledges that he is a slave and belongs to
John SNOWDEN of MD; 5 ft 10-11 in high; 24 years of age; he worked with
Mr. DESHLER in York Borough.
Amos HUSSEY selling plantation in Warrington Twp., York Co., 240 a. Beaver
Creek runs through land on which is erected a saw mill; also log house
and barn.
Reward offered for John KENNEDY, deserted from Recruiting Party station at
York Town. Born in Chester Co, 5 ft 5 in high, 25 years of age, fair
complexion, long fair hair, grey-blue eyes. He is a shoemaker. Andrew
JOHNSON, Capt., 10th Reg't, US Infantry.
Dr. KENNEDY of York giving smallpox innoculations.
James LONG & Son selling pine boards.
Selling or renting land in Ross's Town, York Co, on the Post Road from York
to Carlisle and the road from Middletown to Baltimore; 50 a., 2-story log
dwelling house. Also 70 a. contiguous to above; also 100 a. lying on &
including the top of the round top mountain within 3 miles of former.
Also has lot in Miller's Town on the Juniata River. Also 2 lots in
Ross's Town, Warrington Twp., 2 houses and 2 lots in Ross's Town, 66 a.
in Monaghan Twp. adj lands of William WIREMAN; tract in Warrington Twp of
200 a. in tenure of Thomas GRAY; 3/11 of 120 a. in said twp. in tenure of

Samuel COOK, sadler; and 3/11 of 80 a. in same twp. in tenure of Casper BURBROWER, clock maker. Thomas BLOCK, William ROSS and Edward O'HAIL, Auditors.
Joseph EDMUNDSON cautions persons that he has the plantation above in tenure of Thomas GRAY and that he holds the title from the land office.
Gen. Thomas MIFFLIN died Monday last (Lancaster) in the 57th year of his age; served in the American Revolution, was 12 years Governor of PA; buried at the German Lutheran Church.
John NORRIS of Frederick Co, MD, offers reward for runaway negro man named Joe; 5 ft 7 in high, is nearsighted; formerly lived with Capt. GOSSLER in York and had a wife when there.
Jacob SHERB selling 2-story house on Baltimore St. in Hanover; includes warehouse 43x14 ft; double barn 50x20 ft; occupied by a store many years. Also 2 lots adj said town, 5 a. each, 1 fronts on Baltimore St., the other on York St. Also lot 1/2 mile from town of 16 acres.
William WILLIS, selling plantation in Newbury Twp, York Co, 120 a. stone dwelling house, barn, mill 1 1/2 miles from house. Apply to John WILLIS living on same, or subscriber in York Town.
George WOLFORD of Mt. Pleasant Twp, seeking indentured servant boy named James DURHAM, 5 ft 7 in, has left the 1st joint off his left thumb & took a violin with him.
General meeting at York Court House; signed John EDIE & Jacob GARTNER.
Trustees of York Co Academy to attend meeting; signed James SMITH, Pref. pro tem.

387. Feb 5, 1800
George LASHELLS, Straban Twp, candidate for sheriff.

388. Feb 12, 1800
John HAMILTON of Brook Co, VA, did authorize Alexander COOPER of York Co, PA to settle 2 notes in the hands of William PORTER & George EWING; said bond was fraudalently obtained.
Thomas HARTLEY, Esq. selling house in which he formerly resided on High Street, York. Also small white tenement adj house to the east. Shown by Nicholas GELWICKS or John FORSYTH, Esq.
John Ross KEY selling 1800 a. between Pipe Creek & Monocacy in Frederick Co, MD.
William MITCHELL, late of Monaghan twp, decd, James S. MITCHELL & John McCLELLAN, Adm'rs.
Leonard WIDDER hath obtained from Martin RUDY & Christian LONG 3 bonds; said WIDDER has not fulfilled his contract & they intend not to pay.
John ZELLER seeks runaway apprentice lad, Andrew THOMPSON, who was bound to learn the saddler's trade. He wears his own hair, which is pretty black & full of nitts and lice; about 18 years old, 5 ft 5 in high. Deliver him to Windsor twp, York Co. One Cent Reward.
Sheriff's Sales: (1) John RICHTER's estate, 1 house & lot southwest side of High Street in town of Dover, adj lots of John WAGGONER. (2) Jacob BODENHEIMNER's estate, 1 house & lot on north side of High Street in town of Berlin; adj lots of George CONIX. (3) John LIVELBERGER's(?) estate, land in Franklin twp., 180 a., adj lands of Christian KEHRBACK, Jonas BYER &c. (4) John MURPHY's estate tract in Mountpleasant twp, 270 a., adj lands of Samuel SMITH, William BAILEY &c. (5) Peter MUSGENUNG's estate 75 a. in Huntington twp, adj lands of James LOVE, Nicholas MILLER &c. (6) Estate of heirs of James M'TAGGERT, decd, tract in Berwick twp, 164 a., adj lands of Robert LORIMER. (7) Estate of James BLACK, track in

Franklin twp, 230 a. adj lands of heirs of Josiah M'QUINN, Henry HOSACK, James RUSSELL &c. (8) Estate of heirs of Josiah M'QUINN, tract in Franklin twp., 170 a. , adj lands of Andrew GELWICKS, James BLACK & others. (9) Estate of Jacob SITLER tract in Chanceford twp., 100 a. with Merchant Mill, Grist mill, saw mill, boring mill, distillery & smithshop; adjoins lands of James GORDAN, John FINLEY & others. Nicholas GELWICKS, Sheriff.

389. Feb 19, 1800
Peter GRUPE of Huntington Twp. has taken up a stray bull.
Martin KREBER selling clover seed.
Jackson NEELY, dec'd., his 196 a. plantation in Tyrone Twp. for sale; house & double barn. Thomas NEELY & Abraham FICKES, Administrators.
Daniel ROHRER to sell or rent 2-story frame house on the south side of the main street in Oxford; 36 ft front, back bldg. annexed. Has been a tavern for a considerable time.
House of David SIMPSON, dec'd., for sale in Strabane Twp., Adams Co., & livestock, farm implements, household goods, etc. John & Robert SIMPSON, Administrators. Also farm of dec'd. of 340 a. Apply to George LASHELLS near premises or David CASSAT in York.
James SMITH, Pref. pro tem of Academy of York Co., calling meeting.
Public Sale by John HENDERSON & George KERN, Assignees. Property of James COOPER of York Co. for benefit of his creditors, including: a conveyance from Nathaniel MORRISON for 1/2 legacy bequeathed to him by his father, Hance MORRISON. A Bond of performance upon Joseph HENDRICKSON for the conveyance of a tract of 50 a. in Black River Neck, Md. known as "John's Habitation." A Bond on Maj. BAILEY for 3000 acres in Ohio Co., VA. 2 notes on Thomas STAINER now in the hands of James RIDDLE, Esq. A note on John BROWN of Va. for crop Tobacco, now in the hands of William GRAYDON, Esq. of Harrisburg. A note against Jacob KARNS & judgement obtained before David BALTY in hands of James ORBISON, Esq. A note upon James WRIGHT assigned by John TOULERTON. John WEAR to a bond debt, in hands of William GLINLAND, Esq. Bond on Joseph BERINGER. Obligation on John WILSON. Judgement against Peter BOND, merchant, in Annapolis, Anne Arundel Co., MD. Account against Henry BOHANAN. 500 a. known by the name of Seven Islands of Noinchuckey in the Western Territory, patent held by James ARMSTRONG of Arlington, VA. Account against George DUFFIELD, decd., filed before Justice KING.
Sheriff's Sales: (1) Estate of John EHRHART, house & lot on north side of Philadelphia St. in borough of York, adj lots of Timothy KIRK & the Quaker Meeting house. (2) Estate of John REANY? tract in Chanceford Twp, 46 a. adj lands of John GOMMEL, James DOUGLAS & others. (3) Estate of Adam SMITH, tract in Dover Twp., 240 a., adj lands of George SCANETHECKER, Peter ICHOLTZ & others. Nicholas GELWICKS, Sheriff.

390. March 5, 1800
Joseph CORNELLIUS, late of Adams Co., decd, his mills & farm near Gettysburg to be let. John CLARK, Administrator.
Andrew FINLEY, renting well-known Tavern & plantation in Chanceford Twp., known as "The Brouge," with good house to live in.
Sales of plantation of William GRIFFETH, decd. in Warrington Twp., York Co., 100 a., adj lands of Abraham GRIFFETH, Joseph TAYLOR. Dwelling house, one end of stone, the other of log,; framed double barn almost new. Terms will be made known by Jacob & James M'MILLAN, Adm'rs. Charles W. HARTLEY, Clerk of the Court.

York Recorder

The partnership of David HARRIS and Joseph DONALDSON is dissolved by mutual consent.
Robert HORNER is a candidate for sheriff of Adams County.
Jonathan JESSOP asks the person who borrowed Ferguson's Astronomy from him to return it.
Stray heiffer came to plantation of Joshua LOW in Shrewsbury Twp.
Michael SLAGLE is a candidate for sheriff of Adams County.
Sale of plantation of John ZIEGLER, decd, 154 a. in Huntington twp., Adams Co. Large double barn, understory stone & upper part log. Henry ZEIGLER & George ROBINETTE, Extrs.
State of Receipts & Expenditures &c. for preceding year, Commissioners of Taxes, York County.
Cash Received per the Treasurer from collectors: Jacob LINGENFELTER, Berwick twp.; Edward Ward HALL, Cumberland; William MORRISON, Chanceford; Christian HETRICK, Codorus; Philip J. HOFFMAN, Dover; Humphrey ANDREWS, Fawn; Charles GOOD, Franklin; Frederick BACHMAN, Germany; Robert RHEA, Hamiltonbann; Stephen REEB, Hellam; Joseph SMITH, Hopewell; George HERMAN, Huntingdon; George STEIN, Heidelblerg; Robert ALEXANDER, Menallen; Andrew JOHNSTON, Mountpleasant; Samuel HUNTER, Mountjoy; Valentine WENTZ, Manheim; Daniel GRIEST, Monahan; Valentine EMIGH, Manchester; Cornelius GARRETSON, Newbury; Anthony BEVENSHER, Paradise; Christian BUSHEY, Reading; Peter WILLIAMSON, Strabane?; John OPP, Shrewsbury; William MEALS?, Tyrone; Frederick RUFF, Warrington; Samuel KRITER, Windsor; Elias MEYERS, York Twp., Frederick HORN, York Borough.
Cash Paid: Nicholas GELWICKS, Esq., Sheriff, his fees at sundry times; John MURPHY for building bridge over Conowago-creek; Obediah OSBURN & John OVERDEER for building a bridge; William SMITH, Esq., his fees; Rudolf SPANGLER for stones delivered to bridge; George HAY, Jury expenses on the trial of Catharine BEHLER & James SCOTT; George HAY for work at the gaol; George KERBACH as witnesses; George P. ZEIGLER, Esq., fees; Martin WEISER for wood to goal & office; Michael KELLER as witness on action of larceny; Michael GRAYBILL, goaler; William NORRIS, Court-cryer; William ROSS, Esq., deputy Attorney-General; Jacob BARNITZ & Andrew JOHNSTON, Esqr's., Burgesses; John EDIE, Esq., prothonotary & printing; Joseph BURD, Esq. Prothonotary Supreme Court; John SWENEY, constable; James MURRY for gaol work & as witness; James HAYS, witness; Peter HECK, James AGNEW, George KNOPP, John ROSS, Jacob WERTZ, Adam LEVINGSTON, John M'CLURE, George OYSTER, & Abraham BERGAW for damages sustained by a road running through their lands. George Lewis LEFFLER, Esq., for fees; Jacob UPDEGRASS, Esq. as Coroner; Thomas HARTLEY, Esq., deputy Attorney-General; John BURG, goaler of Lancaster Co.; Frederick HORN for glaising; John STONER for plant to bridges; Jacob HAY, Esq., for sundries to the goal; James CROSS, Esq., fees; Thomas BLACK, Esq., General Election Agent. As Witnesses: John DITTO, Peter KIST, William DOUGLAS. David CALLIT?, Esq., Attorney; George KUNTZ, witness; Alexander TURNER, Esq., towards building 2 wooden bridges; Jacob BARNITZ, Esq., Register; William BLAIN, witness; Michael ALTIC, sundry services; John EICHELBERGER, Jury expenses on James SCOTT's trial; Peter SMALL for making election boxes; David M'KIOLEY?, witness; John FORSYTH, Esq., David EDIE, Esq., James M'CAPLES, Esq., Commissioners. Jacob SPANGLER, Clerk to Commissioners. Conrad SHUPE?, witness; James DUNCAN?, witness; Alexander KESSELL, Esq., & others, judges, clerks, etc. General Election district; Anthony HINKLE, Jacob ELBE, James M'CANLES?. William M'CLELLAN?, late sheriff. John STEWART, Esq., judge. John SMITH, as clerk; Samuel MEYERS as witness; Andrew DU---?, J---;Tobias K---, Lewis WAMPLER?, James ARMSTRONG, Charles

William PORTER, as witnesses. John MAY? as -----, George SPRINGER, etc. about 4 more names (can't read). David EDIE, James M'CANLES, & Daniel SPANGLER. Commissioners.
Following accounts have been filed in Register's Office for the Probate of Wills & granting letters of Administration, York Co.: Account of Samuel M'ILHINEY, Ex'r of Esther M'ILHINEY, late of Mountjoy twp., widow, decd. Account of Adam WINTRODS, Jr., of estate of Jacob WINTRODS, late of Germany twp., decd. Account of Luudwich WAGNER & George ----?WEIN, Adm'rs. of the estate of Michael KEATENIAN?, late of Mountpleasant twp., decd. Account of Michael SEIFERT & Christian BRENEMAN, adm'rs. of Julina? BRENEMAN, late of the Borough of York, decd. Account of Jacob GILBERT, adm'r. of the estate of Christian FRONKS?, late of Franklin twp., decd. Account of Kohn KELLY, ex'r. of Patrick M'GEE, late of Chanceford twp., decd. Account of Jacob & James M'MILAN, adm'rs. of estate of William GRIFFITH, late of Warrington twp., decd. Account of Solomon TATE, adm'r. of estate of Jacob TATE, late of Newbury twp., decd. Third account of John DUNCAN, adm'r. of estate of William JOHNSTON, late of Chanceford twp., decd. Fourth account of Philip Werts WERKING, ex'r. of Ludwich SHERRITZ, late of Manheim twp., decd. Account of Ludwich SHRIVER & John M'CREARY, ex'rs. of Philip SLENTA?, decd., who was guardian of the estate of Mary Elizabeth WAGONER, a minor orphan child of Frederick WAGONER, late of Borough of York, decd. Account of Henry BENTZ, guardian of estate of Anna Mary DEH, Michael DEH, Philip DEH, & Daniel DEH, minor orphan children of John Nicholas DEH, late of Manchester Twp., decd. Account of William M'CLELLAN, David EDIE & David MOORE, ex'rs. of William M'CLELLAN, late of Cumberland twp., decd. Account of John & David M'CREARY, adm'rs. of estate of Thomas M'CREARY, late of Mountpleasant twp., decd. Further account of George Philip ZEIGLER, Esq. & George JULIUS, ex'rs. of Jacob CRODBACH?, late of Dover twp., decd. Further account of Peter BOTT & George Philip ZIEGLER, Esq., ex'rs. of Jonas BOTT, late of Manchester twp., decd. Account of George Philip ZEIGLER, guardian of John CRONBACH & Henry CRONBACH, 2 minor sons of Jacob CRONBACH, late of Dover twp., decd. Further account of Jeremia THORLEY, adm'rs. of William THORLEY, late of Newbury twp., decd. Account of Frederick BREAMER, exc'r. of Anita Mary HELTZGLI?, late of Paradise twp., widow, decd. Account of Mary BENIZEL? & Benjamin BOWER, adm'rs. of estate of Felix BENIZEL, late of Warrington twp., decd. Account of Andrew THOMPSON, Esq. & John M'GREW, ex'rs. of Joseph DODDS, late of Huntington twp., decd. Account of William ANDERSON, adm. of estate of William MENTEL? late of Fawn twp., decd. Account of Henry KREIGER & John KAUFNOR?, adm'rs. of estate of John BARE, late of Newburg twp., decd. Account of Archibald & Jesse M'ALLISTER & James RUDISELL, ex'rs. of Richard M'ALLISTER, late of Heidelberg twp., decd.

391. March 19, 1800
Thomas ABBETT is a candidate for sheriff of Adams County.
John ASMORE, living on Brad Creek, Harford Co., MD, offers for rent a grist mill with two pairs of stones; also a saw mill rebuilt last season. Selling 200 a. on said creek. Also 200 a. or 150 a. on said creek, 1 mile from above, both tracts within 35 miles of Baltimore and 11 of water carriage on the Susquehannah. Also 200 a. on the great road from York to Havredegrass, 6 miles from water carriage & 35 from Baltimore.
James BLACK has plantation to let at intersection of 2 roads from York to Chambersburgh & from Baltimore to Shippensburgh. Public house of entertainment long kept on premises. Samuel COBEAN, William GILELAND,

& Alexander RUSSEL, Trustees.
Joseph DONALDSON has begun business in old stand late occupied by HARRIS
& DONALDSON, on south-west corner of High & Beaver Sts., selling dry
goods, hardware & groceries.
David M'CONAUGHT, Jr. is a candidate for sheriff of Adams County.
Capt. Andrew JOHNSON has at his house a sale of store goods, brick house in
Market St., Borough of York, adj house of Maj. John CLARK, 14 ft 9 in
front. Also house & lot in Water St.; 1/4 of a house & 1/2 lot of
ground on Beaver St., Borough of York; 2 lots on west side of Beaver St.
Philip GOSSLER, John EDIE, John SINGER & Thomas HOCKLEY, Trustees.
George & Daniel LEAS have 150 dozen of English scythes & American sickles
prepared at Mr. Isaiah HARR's Scythe & Sickle Manufactory in York. Can
be bought at stores of Messrs. Joseph DONALDSON, James LONG & Son.,
Thomas TAYLOR, John ROTHROCK, all in Borough of York.
Robert M'CONAUGBY, decd., John M'CONAUGBY & Robert HAYES, Adm'rs.
Thomas TAYLOR warns persons bond executed by him to Jane SHORT.
Joseph WORLEY, owner of the noted horse Badger, will let him out. Will be
at the stable of Mr. Robert LONG in Huntington twp. Badger was bred by
Mr. Nicholas Day M'COMAS of Harford Co., MD.
Applying for insolvency action: Ludwick WALTMAN, David MANSON, George
SIDLE, Frederick HEIBNER & Jacob BUTT.

392. March 26, 1800
John DICKSON, candidate for sheriff of Adams County.
John MURPHY announces that the ad for sale of his land inserted by mistake
at last court. N. GELWICKS, Sheriff
Commissioners taking bids for building a Court house & Goal in Adams
County. William M'CLELLAN, Henry HOKE & William HAMILTON, Comm.
The Post Office is removed to the north side of High St., next door to
George Lewis LEFFLER, Esq. & Mr. Christian SINN.

393. April 2, 1800
Frederick RUMMEL, Innkeeper of the Borough of York, sale at his house of
tract in Franklin twp., 170 a. adj tracts of Andrew GELWICKS, James
BLACK & others; seized & taken in exchange as the estate of heirs of
Josiah M'QUINN to be sold by Nicholas GELWICKS, Sheriff.
Thomas STUBBS of Middle-town, Dauphin Co., has manufactured Blister Steel
for 8 years past, his product is stamped with T. STUBBS.
The Gettysburg Gazette & Weekly Advertiser will be printed once a week,
article by Joseph C. CHARLES.
Sheriff's Sales: (1) As the estate of John PENROSE a tract in Huntington
twp., 116 a. adj. lands of William WIREMAN, Joseph CLARK. (2) As the
estate of Peter N?, house & 1/2 lot on east side of George St., Borough
of York, adj. lots of Andrew NEWMAN & George L? (3) As estate of John
EPLEY tract in Newbury twp., 150 a., adj. lands of John STAIN, Abraham
HILL & others. (4) As the estate of Adam SEISENOB? improvement & tract
in Chanceford twp., 204 a. adj. lands of George LEIBESTEIN?, Robert SMITH
& others. (5) As the remainder of the estate of heirs of James
M'FAGGERT, decd., improvement & tract in Berwick twp., 200 a., adj. lands
of Robert LORIMER. (6) As estate of Joseph EDMONDSON, 2-story house & 2
a. in Lewistown, Newbury twp., adj. lands of John FELKER, Lewis SHINDLER
& George ENSMINGER.

394. April 9, 1800
Lt. Col. John EDIE, Captain of 5th Regiment of York County Militia,

announces that the next 2 Saturdays are days appointed by law for them to exercise companies.

1st Lt. John FISHER, announces the York Troop of Horse are required to parade on Saturday at the Court-house, fully equipped, for training of Militia.

Henry FREY has applied for insolvency debtors act.

Jacob TATE, late of Newbury Twp., decd, Solomon TATE, Adm'r.

John WOLF, decd, sale of his 2 dwelling houses & lots contiguous on the north side of High-Street, westward from the bridge, in Borough of York, adj improvements of Adam KREBER. Abraham DANNER & John WELCH, Admrs.

Commissioners of Taxes for York Co. certify that the following sums were paid to the Treasurer for 1799 by the following persons: Paid John HAY, Esq., Treasurer by John FORSYTH, late Commissioner, recovered same from Catharine BEHLER; same recovered from James SCOTT, lately convicted; per Daniel SPANGLER, Commissioner, received arrears of taxes from sundry persons; same per John FORSYTH, Esq., late Commissioner recovered from Francis WEIGLE for his maintenance in York Gaol. David EDIE, James M'CANLES?, & Daniel SPANGLER, Commissioners.

395. April 16, 1800

Capt. Philip GOSSLER requests members of York Light Infantry to meet Saturday next in full uniform.

John KERR, confined for debt in the goal, petitions Court of Common Pleas at Pittsburgh.

Jacob & Henry LIEBHART selling tract of unimproved land in Hellam twp., York Co., 8 miles from Borough of York, adj. lands of Conrad BROBACHER, Ulrich WEAVER; 28 a.

Sheriff's Sales: (1) Seized & taken in Execution as the estate of the Conowago Canal Company, tract in Newbury Twp., York Co., 200 a., adj. lands of Michael SHELLY, Michael KEPLER; whereon is erected & completed a canal & south of said is a Ferry known by the name of "Rankin's ferry," on the River Susquehannah. (2) Improvement & tract in Manheim Twp., 160 a., adj. lands of Henry MORTER, John WAMPLER; seized as estate of William MICHAEL.

396. April 23, 1800

Col. Philip ALLBRIGHT, late of York Twp., sale at his mill 1 mile from Borough of York of Rye, Indian corn, two waggons, one cow, an 8-day clock, 3 good beds, iron pots, hemp & tow, linen, etc. George ALLBRIGHT & George SMALL, Adm'rs.

John ARMSTRONG, land-surveyor, will open a school in the house formerly occupied by Mr. James WORLEY, sadler, on north side of High St., nearly opposite Mr. Charles SHOEMAKER.

Daniel PERKINS, chair-maker of Borough of York, to settle accounts. Also selling back lot & 2 lots on north side of High St., #387 & #388 on town plan.

Sheriff's Sale: Estate of Jacob SHELTER of improved tract in Windsor Twp., 300 a., adj. lands of Jacob LANDERS & Frederick YOUNG, subscriber conceives himself greatly injured in the proceedings against him & is determined to dispute the sale thereof.

Nathan SMITH, selling tract on which he now lives, 230 a. in Harford County, MD; adjacent to John COX's & Thomas UNDERHILL's mills; within small distance of 2 Presbyterians, one Ana-Baptist, one Quaker & one Methodist meeting; within one day's drive of Baltimore. Lies on Deer

Creek.
[Top missing] For sale 1 brick house in Market in said Borough? adjoins house of Maj. John CLARK, 24'9" front, furnished, stable included. Also a house & lot in Water St. Also 1/4 of a house & 1/2 lot on south side of Beaver St. Philip GOSSLER, John EDIE, John SINGER & Thomas HOCKLEY, Trustees.

397. April 29, 1800
John BOOTH of Booth's Mills, Antiteim, Washington Co., offers reward for runaway negro man named George, 26 years of age, 6 ft tall, well made fellow, upper part of one ear is bit off by fighting, etc.

398. May 7, 1800
Jacob CREMAN, 1st Sgt., announces that the men commanding the Volunteer Corps under Capt. GOSSLER are to meet at the Courthouse.
Alexander DOBBIN is selling sundry lots adj Gettysburg, Adams Co, and in the direction of the street leading to Baltimore.
John EICHELBERGER has removed from his old stand to the house next door to John FORSYTH, Esq. and Mr. Peter DINKLE, nearly opposite the new German Presbyterian Church, where he has opened a house of entertainment at the sign of the York Country Waggon.
Ignatius LEITNER now lives next door to Jacob SHAFFER's Store, opposite Abraham MILLER's Tavern, Borough of York; will draw deeds, mortgages, wills, etc. He continues to keep work in his former branches as milling Rifles, Gunmounting, etc.
James MURRAY, cutler in Water St., Borough of York, opposite Dr. Thomas JAMESON; grinds razors, sizzors, knives, etc.
Jacob SALA book-binder is at the store next to Mr. Conrad LEATHERMAN's Store, west side of Beaver St., Borough of York.

399. May 14, 1800
Joseph MOORE, involvent debtor, Thomas HAMILTON, Protonothary.
Solomon MYER has been appointed Brigade Inspector for York Co.

400. May 21, 1800
Philip ALLBRIGHT, decd, of York Co, George ALLBRIGHT & George SMALL, Adm'rs.
John GREER has taken John BAYLY into partnership in his store on High St., near the Markethouse.
Conrad LAUB, Collector of Revenue for York & Adams Counties, selling at auction a copper still, almost new. Seized as property of John OYSTER for duties due the United States.
William LEECH of Warrington married to Miss Jane GARRETSON of Manchester at the Friends Meeting house in Borough of York Wednesday last.
James LONG & Son, selling white & yellow pine boards & shingles.
Jesse WICHESON married to Miss Phoebe JONES in Newbury Twp., at the Meeting House Wednesday last.
Sheriff's Sales: (1) As estate of Adam SEIFEND, improvement & tract in Chanceford Twp, 204 a., adj. lands of George LEIBENSTEIN & Robert SMITH. (2) Estate of William MICHAEL, improvement & tract in Manheim Twp., 160 a., adj. lands of Henry MORTER & John WAMPLER. (3) Estate of heirs of Henry ALLBRIGHT, decd, improvement and 215 a. in Windsor Twp., adj lands of Michael KAUFFELT? & Henry TYSON. (4) Estate of James LOVE, improvement & tract of 106 a. in Huntington & Tyrone Twps., adj. lands of John DUFFIELD? & Willim DELAP, Esq. (5) Estate of Daniel MELONE, a

certain Messuage & Lot on south side of High Street in Town of Berlin, adjoins lots of John FOX & David MEYERS. (6) Estate of Joseph EDMUNDSON, 2-story house & 2 acres in Lewis-town, Newbury Twp., adjoins lots of John FEIKER, Lewis SHINDLER & George ENSMINGER. (7) Estate of Abraham DEHUFF, lot in Borough of York, adj. lots of John MORRIS & the Methodist burying ground. All seized & taken in Execution to be sold by Nicholas GELWICKS, Sheriff. Also for sale by Sheriff GELWICKS: Improvement & 50 a. in Monallen Twp., adj. lands of Joseph HEWIT & John SWARTZ; estate of Richard MARSHALL.

401. May 28, 1800
Conrad LAUB, Collector of Revenues for York & Adams Counties gives public notice to distillers of duties owed.

402. June 4, 1800
Capt. P. GOSSLER, has at his house a new & most elegant collection of wax work; Moulthrop & Street. Exhibit will move to Lancaster next.
Peter KLINGMAN, insolvent debtor.
Adam PLUM, of Monallen Twp., Adams County, passed 10 obligations to John FERGUSON, cautions public not to take said bonds.
Daniel RIDER, insolvent debtor.
Register's Office, York County: Account of Jacob KOLLER, admr. of estate of Magdalene MILLER, late of Codorus Twp., widow dec'd. Account of Maria KAUFFMAN & Michael SEITZ, admrs. of estate of Henry KAUFFMAN, late of York Twp., dec'd. Account of Joseph MEYER, acting ext. of will of Michael MEYER, late of Mountpleasant Twp., dec'd. Third account of Valentine WINTERMEYER, ext. of will of Anthony WINTERMEYER, late of Dover Twp., dec'd. Account of James GIBFORT? admr. of estate of Samuel MARTIN, late of Chanceford Twp., dec'd. Further account of Henry BEHR & Michael GROFF, exrs. of will of Joseph HERSHY, late of Paradise Twp., dec'd. Account of Philip GARDNER, admr. of estate of Appolonia MANN (late Appolonla MATE?) late of Hellam Twp., dec'd. Account of Susanna STREIN & Jacob GILBERT, admrs. of estate of Johan Adam STREIN, late of Menallen Twp., dec'd. Account of Susanna YODDER, Abraham LICHTENWALLTER & Jacob DIEHL, exrs. of will of Martin YODDER, late of Mountjoy Twp., dec'd. Account of William VALE & Joshua VALE, exrs. of will of Robert VALE, late of Warrington Twp., dec'd. Further account of Jemima THOMPSON (late Jemima THORLEY) one of the admrs. of William THORLEY, late of Newbury Twp., dec'd. Further account of Michael SEIFERT & Christian BRENEMAN, admrs. of estate of Joshua BRENEMAN, late of Borough of York, dec'd. Acount of Peter DIEHL & Nicholas DIEHL, exrs. of will of Nicholas DIEHL, late of York Twp., dec'd. Account of George BARD & Adam BAHN, exrs. of will of Henry KAUN, late of Hellam Twp., dec'd. Jacob BARNITZ, Register,

403. Jun 11 1800
Whereas an attachment issued out of the Court of Common Pleas of York Co at the suit of Charles W. PORTER, against Robert ORR, in pursuance whereof, notice is given that the subscribers, auditors in the said attachment will meet at the house of John EICHELBERGER, Innkeeper, Borough of York, to examine claims and acounts against William ORR. John FORSYTH, Godfrey LENHART, Martin KREBER, Auditors.
John B. JONES, Monaghan twp, to let situation for a saw mill, grist mill, forge or furnace.
James FALLOW wishes to dispose of small tract, 26-30 a. on branch of Muddy creek. If not sold at private sale it will be exposed to public sale at the Brogue Tavern.
Persons having demands against estate of Joseph LIGGOT, late of Windsor twp, York co, decd, are requested to bring them to the subscriber. Philip TAYLOR, admr.
Wm. ALEXANDER, wants to purchase two young negro men. A carter and some forgemen are wanted at the Cordorus Forge.

404. Jun 18 1800
The York Cavalry are requested to meet. I. LEITNER, 1st Sergt.
Whereas my sister Sarah LIPERT, who first married to Adam GARRET and after his decease, married to Sebastian STEINMEYER, and left her ususl home about 15 yrs ago, since which time nothing could be heard of her. I think it my duty if she is yet alive to inform her of the affliction of the death of her father, and in the mean time of the legacy of about 200 pounds which is left her by her father, which she can receive from her brother Adam LIPERT, living in New Virginia between Martinsburgh, the Warm Springs, and Potomack River.
In the Common Pleas of York Co. David M'ELWEE vs John FERGUSON/Domestic Attachment. John DICKSON, Richard BROWN, Samuel RUSSEL, Auditors.
Notice to the enrolled inhabitants of the first, second and fourth companies of militia, commanded by Captains BRENEISEN, HAY and BARNITZ, of the Borough of York, in the 113th Regt, commanded by Lieut. Col. EDIE, and those of the other Regts, commanded by Lieut. Cols. MAY, KELLY and HENDRICKS, in the 1st Brigade of York and Adams Counties Militia, who have not elected their Company Officers... Salomon MYER, Brigade Inspector.

405. Jun 25 1800
Appointments by the Governor:
Justices of the Peace for this county: John HIPPLE, Henry REAMAN, John LIEBHART, James PATTERSON, Jacob HECKERT, John WEYER, John DREXLER, Henry MILLER.
U. S. Marshals sales of tract called Conodoguinnet Tract, East Pennsburgh twp, Cumberland co, 532 a.; also tract called Locust Valley, adj the above, 317 a.; also tract called Oak Bank, 270 a. - taken as the property of Oliver POLLOCK, Esq.
John BOWER, living in Huntington twp, Adams Co, offers reward for stolen mare.
James SCOTT, Gettysburgh, Adams Co, has taken up a stray mare.

YORK RECORDER

406. Jul 2 1800
Died Mon night last at the house of Capt. GOSSLER, in this Borough, Lieut. John A. DOUGLASS, late of the 10th U.S. Regt., in the bloom of youth. A few days before the army was disbanded, he was taken ill of a fever. Distant from his relations he was denied the consolation of their presence.
Thomas LEE, Lieut. in the Army of the U.S., Hanover, offers reward for deserters: Michael LINDEN, who deserted at or near York town, inlisted soldier, born in Ireland, 40 yrs of age, 5 ft 10 inches, dark complexion, grey eyes, brown hair; his eyes are not made of the best mettle, particularly the left. Also James ROBB, deserted from confinement, having deserted before from the artillery, born in Ireland, aged 27 yrs, 5 ft 9 inches, dark complexion, brown eyes, and dark hair.
Sale by order of the Orphans' Court, tract of 11 a., adj lands of Michael KEENS, Dennis M'FADDEN and Edward JONES, estate of James MURPHEY, who lately died intestate. Terms made known by Peter MYER, the admr. C. W. HARTLEY, Clerk.

407. Jul 9 1800
I forwarn persons from taking assignment on a note executed by me to Cornelius GARRETSON, for 8 pounds, as I intend to dispute the payment thereof until I am better secured in the title to the property purchased of him. Samuel MILLER.
Person indebted to the estate of Aaron VERNON, late of Newbury twp, decd, are requested to come and discharge the same. John HART, and Samuel MILLER, exrs.

408. Jul 16 1800
The following are collecting Direct Tax (assessed upon Dwelling houses, lands and slaves by act of Congress, 1798) which has not yet been paid: Manchester twp, house of Frederick Hubly; York twp, house of George BEARD; Heidelberg and pt of Manheim, house of Jacob EICHELBERGER, Hanover; Manheim twp at the house of Priscilla DILL, and house of Michael EICHELBERGER; Berwick twp, house of John HERSH in Oxford, and house of Peter ICKES in Abbott's Town; Paradise twp, house of Henry KING and house of John LOUCK; Dover twp, house of Patrick M'FARLAND; Cordorus twp, house of Adam ZEIGLER and house of Christian HETTRICK; Newbury twp, house of Eli LEWIS and house of Christopher WILSON and house of John GINDER; Hellam twp, house of Peter KLINE; Windsor twp, house of Henry TYSON, and house of James CROSBY; Shrewsbury twp, house of Conrad HORT and house of Peter KLINEFELTER; Chanceford twp, house of John CAMPBELL (Brogue), and house of Charles Wm. PORTER; Fawn & Chanceford twps at Jacob SITLER's Mill and house of Robert RAMSAY for inhabitants of Hopewell, house of George BAXTER; and later residue for Chanceford, Fawn and Hopewell twps, at the house of Maj. Alexander TURNER. John EDIE, Collector of the 1st Collection District, composed of part of the counties of York and Adams.

409. Jul 23 1800
Address given by Capt. GOSSLER to his volunteer corps of Infantry, lately commanded by him. Following his address the company then proceeded to an election for Captain, when William ROSS, Lieut. of said company was duly elected. His vacancy was filled by the election of John HAY.

YORK RECORDER

Michael GRAYBELL, goaler, York, has committed a negro man who calls himself Nathan THOMAS, 5 ft 10-11 inches, about 31 yrs of age.

410. Jul 30 1800
Sheriff's sales: estate of James STEEL, 1 undivided third part of 60 a. in Hopewell, adj lands of Andrew FINLEY, Andrew DUNCAN; estate of Daniel MAY, adj lands of Jacob HUBER, Peter MESSERLY, William LENHART; estate of James LOVE, 206 a., in Huntington and Tyrone twp, adj lands of John DUFFIELD, William DELAP; estate of Joseph EDMUNDSON, 300 a., in Newbury twp, adj lands of Daniel PUGH, Daniel M'HENRY; tract of 70 a., in Newbury twp, adj lands of Samuel GROVE, Thomas LEECH. Nicholas GELWICKS, Sheriff; also 178 a. in Hamiltonsbann twp, on the South mountains, adj lands of Thomas LATTA, William WAUGH, estate of John DADDY and Christina his wife.

411. Aug 6 1800
John JACOBS and John BRISCOE, Carrol's Manor, Frederick co, Md., offer reward for negroes: PETER, 5 ft 7-8 inches, 26 yrs of age; SAM, 15 7-8 inches, about 31 yrs of age.
James SMITH to sell house and lot in Gettysburgh, 80 ft from Diamond or Public Square, occupied as a Tavern for a number of yrs.

412. Aug 13 1800
The York Troop of Cavalry are to meet. John FISHER, Capt.
Plantation for sale in Cumberland twp, 2 1/2 miles from Gettysburg, 191 a.; also personal property of Robert M'CONAUGHY, late of Menallen twp, decd, consisting of horses, oxen, cows, sheep and hogs, pair of stills with all the apparatus complete, plows and harrow, furniture, hay in stacks, and other. John M'CONAUGHY, and Robert HAYES, admrs.

413. Aug 21 1800
Peter PLAYFAIR, Good-Hope twp, candidate for sheriff.
Plantation for sale in Chanceford twp, York Co, known as the Meadow Place, 325 a., adj Rev James CLARKSON's land and others, 2 1/2 miles of the Brogue. John CAMPBELL, Senr.
David PARKER has petitioned for relief from debts.

414. Aug 27 1800
The Commissioners of Taxes in and for the County of York will attend at their office to receive proposals for building and erecting a stone bridge over Little Codorus Creek on road from Borough of York to Wright's Ferry. David EDIE, James M'CANLESS, Daniel SPANGLER, Commissioners.
Sheriff's sale at house of John DEMUTH, at the Conewago Canal, Newbury twp, 89 a., in Newbury twp, adj lands of William BAITMAN, David ZUGH, estate of Jacob WESTHAESSER.
William WEBB, West Chester, offers reward for mare stolen from pasture in Newbury twp, York Co.
Sale at house of William MORRISON, Senr, decd, Chanceford twp, York co, of horses, cows, sheep and hogs, good pair of drawing oxen, waggon, ploughs, harrows, farming utensils, furniture, number of negroes. William MORRISON, admr.
Peter SKEKELY and John SNYDER have petitioned for relief from debts.

YORK RECORDER

415. Sep 3 1800
Sale by order of the Orphans' Court of Northumberland co, at the house of Joseph PEGG, on the premises, 11 miles above Sunbury, 1 mile from the north branch of the Susquehannah, plantation in Catawessa twp, 314 a., late the property of Col. Philip ALBRIGHT of York Co, decd. George ALBRIGHT and George SMALL, York, admrs.
Sheriff's sales: estate of Robert ROSEBOROUGH, 50 in Managhan tjwp adj lands of Samuel NELSON and Yellow Breeches Creek; estate of John OBERDIER, 100 a., in Dover twp, adj lands of Philip BEERBROWER, Jacob ZINN; estate of Dr. James JAMESON, house and lot in Hanover on west side off Baltimore st, adj lots of William KITT, George SHRY and a twenty feet alley; estate of Jacob EICHELBERGER, undivided half part of a house and half lot on north side of Market st, Borough of York adj lots of Joseph WESLHHANS and heirs of Jacob KERN, decd; estate of Lewis DECKER, 235 a., in Codorus twp, adj lands of Benjamin BRENNEMAN, John EHRHART; John KNIGHT, 12(?) a. in Berwick twp, Adams Co, adj lands of Samuel BOWSER and John GROSKAST; estate of James LOVE, 206 a., Huntington and Tyrone twp, adj lands of John DUFFIELD, William DELAP, Esq.
The following administration accounts have been filed in the Register's Office: Account of George HAMMOND and Thomas HAMMOND, exrs of James HAMMOND, late of Tyrone twp, decd.
Acount of Elizabeth HENDERSON, admr of estate of James M'TAGERT, late of Berwick twp, decd.
Account of George Michl. and Michael DIETRICH, admrs of estate of George BRAUCHER, late of Tyrone twp, decd.
Account of Peter MEYER, admr of James MURPHY, late of Newbury twp, decd.
Account of Christian STONER and Henry STRICKLER, admrs of estate of Abraham STONER, late of Hellam twp, decd.
Account of Margaret RAMSAY and Robert RAMSAY, admrs of estate of John RAMSAY, late of Fawn twp, decd.
Account of John WINAND, exr of Nicholas BLASSER, late of York twp, decd.
Account of Leah CONDRY, admrx of estate of William WELCH, late of Newbury twp, decd.
Account of John MILLER and Samuel FLICKLINGER, admrs of the estate of John NIDICH, late of Heidelberg twp, decd.
The further account of William PORTER and William COCHRAN, exrs of William SCOTT, late of Hamiltonsbann twp, decd.
Account of Andrew KLEINDINST, surviving exr of David KLEINDINST, late of Codorus twp, decd.
Account of Daniel BEAR and Henry BOYER, guardians of the estates of John HOSHAAR, Elizabeth HOSHAAR, Anna HOSHAAR, and Barbara HOSHAAR, minor orphan children of John HOSHAAR, late of Manheim twp, decd.
Account of Deborah LATTA, Thomas LATTA and Isaac ARMSTRONG admrs of estate of Thomas LATTA, late of Cumberland twp, decd.
Accounty of James M'ALLISTER, admr of the estate of James EVANS, late of Hopewell twp, decd.
Account of Abraham THORLEY, admr of the estate of Mary ASHTON, late of Newbury twp, widow, decd.
Account of George ALBRIGHT and George SMALL, admrs of the estate of Philip ALBRIGHT, late of York twp, decd.
Account of John KUHN and Henry FINCK, exrs of Peter WILL, late of Heidelberg twp, decd.

Account of Andrew CREMER, admr of estate of John CREMER and Margaret CREMER, both late of Warrington twp, decd.
The further account of Catharine HERMAN and Michael SMYSOR, admrs of the estate of Emanuel HERMAN, late of Manchester twp, decd.
Account of Benjamin WALKER and Philip HOBBACH, exrs of Dietrich HOBBACH, late of Warrington twp, decd.
Account of Lilly FRANK, admrs of estate of Doctor Ludwick FRANK, late of Hanover, decd.
Account of George LINCK and Adam HERTZEL, admrs of the estate of Michael LINCK, late of Reading twp, decd.
Account of Thomas EVANS and Martin RAFFENBERGER(?) exrs of David EVANS, late of Warrington twp, decd.
Account of Yost HERBACH, esq. and Peter GOOD, exrs of Anna KINDIG, late of Manchester twp, widow, decd. Jacob BARNITZ, Register.
Joshua MORRISON, Dover twp, has taken up a stray heiffer.

416. Sep 10 1800
Meeting of the Federal Republicans at the house of Capt. GESSLER. Jacob GARTNER in the Chair. The following committee was appointed: Jacob GARTNER, William WELSH, David CASSAT, Abraham MILLER, John HAHN, John GREER, Gotlieb ZEIGLE, Joseph DONALDSON, Daniel SPANGLER, Nathan WORLEY, Martin KREBER, Frederick YOUCE, John COLLINS, Henry KING, William BARBER, George SMALL, Andrew CREMER, Andrew NEWMAN, Jacob LETHER, Jonathan JESSOP, Philip GOSSLER, Michael KLINEFELTER, Philip HECKART, George Lewis LESSLER and John FORSYTH, to correspond with the Federal Electors of Adams Co.
Thomas HARTLEY delines further public service, as a member of Congress.
Sheriff's sale of tract in Germany twp, Adams co, 67 a., adj lands of George UNGER, Philip BARDT, estate of George FRITZLEIN, decd; also tract in Mountjoy twp, Adams co, 190 a., adj lands of John BOWER, Yost RAFFLE(?), estate of Samuel BIGHAM.
Sheriff's sales: estate of Jacob NEASS, tract in Shrewsbury twp, 180 a., adj lands of John OLP, Thomas EHRHART, decd; estate of Benjamin TAYLOR, undivided 6th part of 300 a., in Shrewsbury twp, adj lands of John SCITZ, Thomas DYETH; estate of John TAYLOR, tract in Shrewsbury twp, 232 a. adj lands of Philip SHAFFER, Baltzer KOLLER, Felix HILDEBRAND; estate of Robert ROSEBOROUGH, 50 a. in Managhan twp, adj lands of Samuel NELSON and Yellow Breeches Creek.

417. Sep 17 1800 - Fuller wanted at a new mill erected in Baltimore Co, about 10(?) miles from Baltimore, near middle Turnpike road. Thomas OWINGS.

418. Sep 24 1800
To be sold - two adj tracts of land in Centre Co, on Buffaloe Run, 4 miles from Centre Furnace, 4 miles from Benner's Forge and Rolling Mill. Apply to Jonathan HENDERSON in Huntingdon, or Thomas THOMPSON in Warrior mark Valley, near the land.
At a court of Common Pleas at Washington Co, on petition of George M'COOK for the relief of insolvent debtors on motion of James ASHBOOK, notice of given to petitioner's creditors as reside on this side of the Allegheny Mountain. John GILMORE, for David REDICK, Prothy.

YORK RECORDER

419. Oct 1 1800
The company of Capt. John BRENISEN to meet at the Court house, Borough of York.
James HOUSTON, living near Wrights Ferry, York Co, has taken up a stray horse.

420. Oct 8 1800
Meeting of the trustees of Academy of York Co. John EDIE, Pres. pro tem.
To be sold - plantation in Warrington twp, near Joseph KRALL's Mill, on Bermudian creek. James MARSH.
Peter FAHNESTOCK has petitioned for relief of debts.

421. Oct 15 1800 - All commissioned officers of the 113th Regt of Penn Militia are to convene in the Borough of York. Conrad LAUB, Major Commandant, 113th Regt.

422. Oct 22 1800
Died Fri evening last, Mrs. Anna BOWIE, wife of Ralph BOWIE, Esq. of this Borough.
Election results: John STEWART, Congress; William REED, Senator; Assembly: Jacob HOSTETTER, Frederick EICHELBERGER, William ANDERSON and Michael KIMMEL; Commissioner: Anthony HINKLE.
Adams Co: Assembly: Thomas THORNBURG, Henry SLAGLE; Sheriffs: George LASHELLS, Robert HORNER; Coroner: James COBEAN; Commissioners: David EDIE, Robert M'ILHINNY, Jacob GREENAMEYER.
Officers who belonged to Col. MAY's Regt on the Western Expedition in the year of 1794 are to meet at the house of Capt. GOSSLER, in the Borough of York to have all their accounts for retained rations settled as there is a prospect at present to get payment for the same. D. MAY, Lt. Col.
James LONG & son, have on hands a large quantity of white & yellow pine boards and pine shingles.

423. Oct 29 1800
Premature loss of Mr. MILLER who died here a few days ago of the tetanus or locked jaw.
Sale of cows and heiffers at Abraham MILLER's Tavern in York. John SHALL, Butcher.
Sheriff's sales: estate of Daniel MAY, Dover twp, 140 a., adj lands of Abraham MESSERLY, Jacob HOOVER, 147 a. mountain land in Dover twp, adj lands of Jacob HOFFMAN; estate of John GRACELY, tract in Dover twp, 20 a. adj lands of Michael SMITH, Daniel RAUHOUSER, Michael WILHELM; estate of Samuel BIGHAM, Mountjoy twp, 120 a. adj lands of Yost RIFFLE, John BOWER; estate of Michael FULLWEILER, Warrington twp, 152(?) a., adj lands of Anthony KNISELY, senr, Abraham KNISELY, Abraham BEALS; estate of James LOVE, 206 a. in Huntington and Tyrone twp, adj lands of John DUFFIELD, William DELAP, Esq.; estate of Charles SHOEMAKER, York twp with a merchant's mill, large stone barn, adj lands Michael HENGST, Anthony RITZ, George BARNITZ - also house and lot on south side of High st, Butts-town, adj lots of John WEYER, Esq.

YORK RECORDER

424. Nov 4 1800
Sheriff's sale at the house of James GETTY, Inkeeper, Gettysburgh, 2 story log dwelling house and lot in said town, Baltimore st, occupied as a tavern and now in the tenure of David SHEETS, property of James SMITH.
Sheriff's sales: estate of John RUMMEL, later of the Borough of York, decd, on south side of High st, in borough of York, adj lots of John KERN; estate of John FERGUSON, 13 a., with 8-9 tan vats sunk as a tanyard, in Menallen twp, Adams co, on great road from York to Shipensburgh, adj lands of Francis KNAUSE, Adam BLOOM, Anthony WAGNER; estate of Jacob COMFORT, tract of 79 a., in --- twp, 6 miles from Borough of York, on great road from York to Wright's Ferry, adj lands of Andrew COMFORT, Henry CONN; estate of Baltzer FAUST, 6 lots in New Shrewsbury, 17 miles from borough of York, 2 miles from the Blue Ball; estate of Joseph EDMUNDSON, 300 a. in Newbury twp, adj lands of Daniel PUGH, Daniel M'HENRY.
To be sold, at the late dwelling house of Frederick HUBLEY, Inkeeper, of Manchester twp, decd, furniture [described], draught horses, Indian corn, oats and other. Magdalena HUBLEY and Daniel SPANGLER, exrs.

425. Nov 12 1800
Sale of plantation in Strabane twp, Adams Co, 3 miles from the seat of Justice, 200 a. Robert CAMPBELL.
Laurence HECKES, Exr, desired those indebted to estate of George HECKES, late of Huntington twp, decd, to settle their accounts.

426. Nov 19 1800 - Alexander M'GREGOR and Frederick FISSEL have petitioned for relief from debts.

427. Nov 26 1800
Married Wed last at the Friends Meeting at Pipe-creek, Josiah UPDEGRAFF of this Borough, to Miss Hannah FORKER of Frederick co, Md.
On Sun last at Abbett's Town, Dr. John PENTZ, of this Borough, to Miss Sally HOKE, dau of Peter HOKE of Manchester twp.
Jesse CORNELIUS, Chanceford twp, intends to make resurveys, divide lands, run roads. Leave orders at the Brogue or Blue ball Tavern.
Public sale at the dwelling house of Christopher VOGELSONG in Ross's Town, Warrington twp, York Co, of 200 a. in said twp, now in possession of Thomas GRAY; also one eleventh part of plantation of 100 a.; also claim of lease of lands in Gavock Ireland; also 3 elevenths of plantation in said twp, 430(?) a., property of Thomas EDMUNDSON. Thomas BLACK, William ROSS and Edward O'HALE, auditors under a domestic attachment.
Attachment issued at the suit of Frederick HOOBER against Adam FICKES. Creditors are desired to attend meeting of auditors, Godfrey LENHART, George HAY and Martin KREBER.

428. Dec 3 1800
Died on morning of 31st ult after a short illness, Michael GRAYBELL, keeper of the public gaol of York Co. He has been keeper of the gaol for upwards of 30 yrs. His remains were interred in the Presby burying ground.
Died in Phila, John NICHOLSON, Esq., late Comptroller General of the State of Penn.
The following accounts have been filed in the Register's Office:

YORK RECORDER

Account of Adam SHENBERGER and Matthias BAKER, admrs of estate of Michal DOSH, late of Windsor twp, decd.
Account of Isaac HIMES, admr of estate of Abraham LEAS, late of Reading twp, decd.
Account of Benjamin WALKER and Philip HOBBACH, exrs of Dietrich HOBBACH, later of Warrington twp, decd.
Account of John HERMAN and Thomas LEECH exrs of Isaac TATE, late of Strabann twp, decd.
Further account of Solomon TATE, surviving admr of estate of Jacob TATE, late of Newbury twp, decd.
Account of Henry BLACK and James BLACK, exrs of Robert BLACK, late of Mountjoy twp, decd.
Account of William CLARK, adm of estate of Thomas CLARK, late of Monahan twp, decd.
Account of Robert M'CALL, adm of estate of John M'CALL, late of Chanceford twp, decd.
Further account of Mary Elizabeth KEFFER and John KUHN, exrs of Matthias KEFFER, late of Berwick twp, decd.
Account of Henry EPPLY, exr of Barnet SMITH, late of Botts town, decd.
Account of Elizabeth BYER and Abraham MILLER, admrs of estate of Charles BYER, late of Hopewell twp, decd.
The first and second account of Michael MILLER, exr of Jacob KIMMERLY, late of Windsor twp.
Account of Robert SCOTT guardian of the minor children of William SCOTT, late of Hamiltonsbann twp, decd.
Thomas PETERS has petitioned for relief of debts.
Jacob SAPRE has petitioned for relief from debts.

429. Dec 10 1800
Married Sun last by Rev J. GOERING, George UPP, to Miss Catharine STOEHR, dau of Stophel STOEHR, all of this Borough.
Sale of farm, part of the Silver Springs Estate, in Cumberland Co, adj great road from Phila to Pittsburgh, 240-300 a. David BRIGGS, East Pennsborough twp.
Sale of tract of patented land adj town of Bedford, 350 a.; apply to Samuel DAVIDSON, near the premises.
Daniel STILER, Chanceford twp, cautions persons from taking assignment of 2 notes given to Samuel KEAVANS, then of Lancaster Co, but now of the City of Baltimore.
Leonard EICHELBERGER, Monaghan twp, has taken up a mare which was trespassing in the inclosure of Michael MUMPER by Mary ZIGLER and put into the care of the subscriber.

430. Dec 17 1800 - Lands for sale in Donegal twp, Lancaster Co, 135 a.; will be shewn by Thomas BAYLY, at the mill, near Anderson's Ferry. Thomas BAYLY, John BAYLY.

431. Dec 24 1800
York - The ingenious Timothy KIRK, of this place, inventor of the late improved and admired paper moulds, has contrived and got in operation a machine for shelling corn.

YORK RECORDER

Plantation for sale in Manchester twp, York Co, 5 miles from Borough of York, 232 a. Andrew RUTTER and John MEAS, admrs, near the premises.
For rent - house of John EICHELBERGER, Inkeeper, Borough of York, plantation in Paradise twp, York Co whereon William WHITE now lives, 12 miles from said Borough. Please call on Jacob MARCH who lives adj the premises. Hannah WHITE and John FORSYTH, exrs, York Borough.

432. Dec 31 1800
Obituary to Thomas HARTLEY, Esq., who died at Yorktown, Pa, morning of Dec 21st 1800, aged 52 yrs, 3 mos, 14 days.
By virtue of an attachment issued by William ROSS, Esq, one of the Justices of the Peace for York Co, against John SPROUL, late of Fawn twp, the creditors of said Sproul are requested to attend at the dwelling house of John PHILIPS in said twp. John PHILLIPS
David VINEGAR, Donegal twp, Lancaster Co, at Vinegar's Ferry, has taken up a stray horse.

THE ADAMS CENTINEL (predecessor to the Gettysburg Star)

433. Nov 19 1800 (No. 2, Vol. 1.)
Moses M'CLEAN, Deputy Surveyor, Carroll's Delight, complains of being prevented in executing warrants after the appointment of Samuel SLOAN; gives his political philosophy.

434. Nov 26 1800 - Distillers, of Adams County, take notice that all those who are in arrears for duties due to the U.S. must immediately pay, either to Walter SMITH, Esq. in Gettysburg, or to the subscriber in the borough of York. - Conrad LAUB, Collector of the Revenue of York and Adams Counties.

THE SHIPPENSBURGH MESSENGER

435. Jun 28 1797 (Wednesday - Vol 1, No. 6)   Printed by Henry & Benjamin GRIMLER.
W. & R. DICKSON have removed their office to the house lately occupied by MOORE and KIRKPATRICK, north of the Court-house, Queen St, Lancaster, where they continue to carry on the Printing Business.
Fresh Goods - at the store lately occupied by Samuel GREY, Shippensburgh. Hugh C. SMITH.
John SCOTT, Shipensburgh, duly commissioned a notary public in the county of Cumberland. Draws and attests letters of attorney, apprentices indentures, bills of sale and mortgages, draws and takes proof of accompts to be sent abroad.
William THOMSON, living on Conodogwinet creek, four miles from Newville, Cumberland co, offers reward for two slaves, named Tom and Hannah HALL. Tom is about 5 ft 9 inches, 36 yrs old, and Hannah is a mulatto, about 35 yrs of age, 5 ft 8 inches high.
Shippensburgh Light Infantry Company to meet on Tues. Thomas MARTIN, Capt.

THE SHIPPENSBURGH MESSENGER

Samuel FINLEY, Springfield, at the head of Big Spring, offers reward for missing horse; he had on, when he went away, a choke joke. Deliver to Mr. M'CRACKEN's.
George RESLY, 4 1/2 miles from Hagerstown, offers reward for negro man, CHARLES, 20-21 yrs of age, 6 ft 1-2 inches.

THE FRANKLIN REPOSITORY

437. Thurs Nov 20th 1800, No. 31 of Vol. V The Grammer School in the Chambersburg Academy which has been for a few months suspended, will be opened under the direction of the Rev. Denny, on 17th inst. Samuel Riddle, Sec'ry, Chambersburg.
Caleb Pence, living on the premises of Frederick Byer, Antrim twp, has taken up a stray horse.
Michael Trout, Chambersburg, offers reward for indented German boy named Paul Shisler, about 20 yrs of age, about 5 ft 6 inches, black complexion, black straight hair, round full face with black eyes; had on brown sailor jacket and blue cloth overalls; took with him two pair of tow trowsers, 2 new tow shirts, new shoes and a half worn castor hat.
Persons indebted to the estate of John Morris, late of Montgomery twp, Frankl co, decd, are requested to pay their accounts. Jacob Ditwiler, Margaret Morris, exrs, who will attend at the house of Wm. M'Clelland, Exq. in Montgomery twp to persons having dealings with said estate.
Schoolmaster wanted, capable of teaching an English school. Joseph Culbertson, Culbertson's Row.
Joseph Finley has petitioned for relief from debts.
Tracts of land for sale, one in Montgomery twp, Franklin co, 3 miles of Mercersburg, 420 a., the other in Great Cove, 7 miles from M'Connellsburg, 270 a. John Taggart, living on the first mentioned tract.
Henry Birely has removed from where he formerly lived, to York st, next door to the Prothonotary's office, where he has for sale soal and upper leather, harness, calf skins and boot legs.
Hugh Campbell, Chambersburg, offers reward for indented apprentice to the hatting business, named John Morrison, 19-20 yrs old, 5 ft 8-9 inches, slender made, sandy complexion.
1-2 active boys wanted, 12-14 yrs of age, as apprentices to the tayloring business. Charles Hawkins, Chambersburg.
Sale of 2-story stone house and stone kitchen, on corner of the Diamond in Chambersburg. Apply to Joseph Shannon on the premises. Thomas Shannon, Chambersburg.
John Early, 1 miles of Chambersburg, has taken into custody a boy about 11 yrs of age, dark complexion, of small size; says his name is Cornelius M'Donnal.
This day the office of The Franklin Repository will be removed to York St, 2 doors from the Prothonotary's Office.
Plantation to be sold on Muddy Run, Antrim twp, Franklin co, late the property of Conrod Fisher, of the same place, decd. Peter Withmor, John Stetler, exrs.
German newspaper to be published on Sat 29th inst, entitled, The German Farmers Register. Subscriptions will be received by George M'Clellan,

THE FRANKLIN REPOSITORY

esq., Strasburg, John Shryock, Chambersburg, and Maj. George Clark, Greencastle, Franklin co. and by the printers in Greensburg, Westmoreland co. Snowden & M'Corkle.

APPENDIX A: Letters remaining at the Post Office (Carlisle Gazette)

[These lists were published in alphabetcial order by first letter of last name only; they have been rearranged in strict alphabetical order.]

Letters in the Post-office, Carlisle, May 1796 - if not taken away in three months from this date, will be returned to the General Post-office: William ABERCROMBIE; James ADAMS; Edward ARMSTRONG; John ARNELL; Joshua ASH; Matthew ATKINSON; Jane BARNHILL; Thomas BEATTY; Andrew BLAIR; John BOLTON; Margaret BOYLE; Widow BRADLEY; Joshua BRANDON; Elizabeth BROWN; James BRUCE; George BUCK; John CADWALLADER; Charles CAMBLE; Armstong CAROTHERS; Andrew CLENDENNING; Mrs. CONNELLY; Charles COPELY; Abraham CRAIG; Samuel CRAWFORD; John CULBERTSON; George DAVIDSON; William DAVIDSON; John DONNAL; Alexander DRUMMOND; Thomas EKHART; Robert FORGY; Alexander W. FOSTER; Thomas FULTON; Robert GOMLEY; John GORELY, sen.; James GRAHAM; John GRAHAM; Andrew GRAMBLE; Guion GREER; Hugh HAMILTON; William HARPER; Robert HASLET; Andrew HENDERSON; James HENDERSON; Jonathan HENDERSON; John HENNON; Thomas HILLHOUSE; Stephen HOLMES; Andrew HUSTON; William JAMISON; John JOHNSTON; Rev. Daniel JONES; Thomas JORDAN, hatter; James KEAN; Thomas KELLY; Thomas KENNEDY; William KENNEDY; Mark KERR; William KERR; William KERR, Kishacoquilis; David KESSLER; Robert LEMAN; James LOUGHREA; James M'CASLEN (M'CAFLEN?); Isabella M'CAUNE; David M'CLINTOCK; John M'COLLOUGH; Alexander M'CONNEL; Daniel M'CONNELL; John M'COY; John M'DOWEL; Col. William M'FARLANE; John M'GIL; John M'KEAN; Revd. Mr. M'KENNEY; Michael M'MULLAN; Dunning M'NAIR; Patrick M'NAUGHLON; John M'WILLIAMS; Jonathan MARTIN; Michael MARTIN; Philip MILLER; Robert MILLER; William MILLER, taylor; John MILLIGAN; Mary MITCHEL; Michael MONKAN; James MOOR; John MOOR; John MORRISON; Andrew MUNROE; Martha MUTILMORE(?); Thomas ORR; Henry PASKLE; James PAXTON; William PAXTON; William PETRIKIN; William PORTERFIELD; Thomas REDDING; David REED; Thomas ROBINSON; Arthur ROGERS; Thomas RUSSELL; Capt. James SERVICE; John SKINNER; Robert SKINNER; Robert SMITH, Alexandria; Col. William STERRETT; James STEWART; James STUART; Thomas STUART; John SUTTON; William TATE; George THOMPSON; John THOMPSON; Robert THOMPSON; David WALKER; John WALLIS; Thomas WATSON; Henry WEAVER; John WEBLEER; George WEER; David WHITE; Lewis WHITE; John WILSON; Anthony WOODRUFF; John WOODS; Samuel WOODS; James YOUNG; William YOUNG.

Letters remaining at P.O. Carlisle, August 1796: Hugh ALDERDICE; James ALEXANDER; John ALEXANDER; George ALLEN; Abraham ANDERSON; Alexander ANDERSON; James ANDERSON; John ANDERSON; Mrs. Jean ANDERSON; William ANDERSON; Benjamin ATCHESON; John BARBER; William BARR; William BEAN; William BEATTY; William BEATTY, schoolmaster; Nathaniel BECK; Robert BECK; William BELL, Path Valley; William BELL, Tuscarora; David BLACKIE; John BOLTOP; James BONER; Thomas BORLAND, Carlisle; James BRANDON; Daniel BROLLEY; David BROLLEY; Alexander BROWN; Allen BROWN; Elenor BROWN; William BROWN; Frederick BROWNING; Mr. CAIN; Charles CAMPBLE; James CAMPBLE, near Carlisle; James CAMPBLE, Path Valley; John CAROTHERS, Esq.; Patrick CASSADY; Samuel CAUGHEY; John CHAPLAIN; Donald CLARKE; John CLARKE, miller; William C. COAN; Richard COCHRAN; William COCHRAN; Isaac CONNELLY; John COOKE; Daniel C. COOPER; Spencer COOPER; William COPELY; John COSSACK; Alexander CRAWFORD; James CRAWFORD; John CRAWFORD; Joseph CRAWFORD; David CREE; Willam CROSSAN; William CROW; James DAVIDSON; Samuel DENMAN; William DEYUELL; John DOYLE; Thomas DUNN; Andrew EBERHEART; William EDGAR; Robert ELLIOTT; James

137

APPENDIX A: Letters remaining at the Post Office (Carlisle Gazette)

FAIRMAN; William FAIRMAN; William FERGUSON; Benjamin FITH(?); James FLEMING, Burnt Cabbins; John FLENNIKEN, Esq.; Robert FORGEY; James GARRETTE; Henry GASS; Thomas GIBSON; Robert GORDON; John GRAHAM; Patrick GRAHAM; Thomas GRAHAM; John GRAY, care James LAMBERTON; John GRAY, care Robert BARKLEY; John GREENWOOD; Galon GREER; Thomas GREER; William GREER; Robert HAMILTON; James HARDIE; Thomas HARRIS; Daniel HENDERSON; Robert HENDERSON; Steel HENDERSON; William HENDERSON; John HENRY; William HENRY; Robert HERVEY; William HILL, B. Tavern; Isaac HODGE; Jonathan HOGGE, Esq.; Joseph HOLLAND; Joseph HOLLAND; James HUDDLESON; Andrew HUSTON; Andrew JOHNSTONE; James JOHNSTONE; John JOHNSTONE; Miss Nancy JOHNSTONE; Thomas JOHNSTONE; Thomas JOHNSTONE, Lewistown; Robert JONES; Miss Jean KEAN; John KELLEY; Thomas KENNEDY; Thomas KERR; Miss Hannah KING; James KIRKPATRICK; William KIRKPATRICK; Samuel KYLE, Esq.; James LAMBERTIN; David LAUGHLIN; Abraham LEECH; William LIVINGSTON; William LUDLOW; Patrick M'ALISTER; Elizabeth M'CABE; William M'CANDALISH; George M'CLELLAND; Robert M'CLURE; William M'COMMON; Neil M'COY; Samuel M'CREA; William M'CREA; Robert M'CREARY; Nancy M'DANEL; William M'DONNELL; John M'DONNELL, Walnut Bottom; Samuel M'DOWEL; John M'ELROY; James M'ELWAIN; Hugh M'FADIAN; Anthony M'GAHAN; William M'GAHAN; John M'GAW; James M'GUMRY; Charles M'INTYRE; David M'KEE; David M'KEE; John M'KEE; John M'KENE; John M'KENNAN; Thomas M'KREARY; John M'NIGHT; James M'QUAID; Archibald M'SWOARS; William MAFFET; John MALOY; James MARKEY; Robert MARSHALL; Jonathan MARTIN; Robert MARTIN; James MATEER; Peter MICHAEL; Robert MILBY; Matthew MILLER; Messrs. MILLIKEN and MEUIL(?); Robert MISKELLEY; John MITCHELL; Samuel MITCHELL; Michael MONAHAN; David MONERIEL; James MOORE; Thomas MORELAND; John MORROW; William MORROW; Edward MORTON; Joseph MULLAND; Andrew MUNROW; George NELSON; James NICKOLSON; Edward O'DONNEL; John OWENS; John POULTNEY; Widow POWER, Shearmans valley; James PURDY; John PURDY; James RAINER; James RAY; William REED; James REED, Student; William RIDDLE; Samuel ROSS; Edward RUTLER; Andrew SCOTT; Francis SEMPLE; Isaac SIFFORD; James SMILEY; James SMITH; Adam SNIDER; David SNIDER; William SPRATT; John SPROATS(?); Joseph STEEL; Alexander STEVENSON; Nathaniel STEVENSON; Samuel STEVENSON; Archibald STILE; William STILE; Robert STUART; William STUART; Hugh SWEENEY; Joseph SWITLAND(?); John TAWNEYHILL; William TAWNEYHILL; William TAYLOR; James TERREY; James THOMPSON; Joseph THORN; John TINNER; David TOMB(?); J. VINEGAR; Ludwick WALDEN; Robert WALES; Andrew WALKER; William WALKER; Squire WALKER, Mifflin; Hugh WALLACE; John WALLACE, Carlisle; Archibald WATTSON; Thomas WATTSON; David WHITE; John WHITE; Joseph WHITE; Captain Hugh WILEY; Mrs. WILEY; Hugh WILLIAMSON; James WILSON; Thomas WILSON; William WILSON; Samuel WOODS, junior; Robert WORK; John WRAY; Thomas WRIGHT; Thomas YOUNG - Thomas ALEXANDER, Postmaster, Carlisle

Letters at the Post Office, Carlisle, May 1787: John ADAMS; Thomas ADAMS; Joseph AKULF; Robert ALCORN; Jamesx ALEXANDER; John ALEXANDER; William ALEXANDER; James ANDERSON; John ANDERSON; William ANDERSON; Thomas ARMOR; John ARNELL; John ATWISE; Henry BARNS; Thomas BASKINS; David BEARD; John BEATTY; Adam BECKER; John BEGLEY; Mathew BETTY; Archibald BLACK; William BLACK; Robert BLAINE; Daniel BLAIR; Joseph BLAKELY; Samuel BLYTH; Mr. BOTTAHO; David BOWER; William BOYD; James BRADLEY; Elizabeth BRENNAN; Daniel BROLEY; Elenor BROWN; George BROWN; John BROWN; Mathew BROWN; Robert BROWN; William BROWN; William BROWN, esq.; Robert BRUICE; Nancy BUCHANAN; Robert BUTTNUT; Gen. John CADWALLADER; Alexander CALBONA; Sarah CALWELL; William

Letters remaining at the Carlisle Post Office

CAMELON; Charles CAMPLE; Daniel CAMPLE; Moses CANAN; Col. CANON; John CANON; Col. John CARATHERS; George CHAMBERS; Joseph CHARLES; Andrew CLARK; George CLARK; William CLIDE; Vincent COCKEN; John COLLENS; James COLLINS; John COLLINS; John COLWELL; Haugh CONNELY; Isaac CONNELY; John CONNELY; Stephen CORNELIUS; John COVENHAVEN; Abraham CRAIG; George CRATTON; Jane CRAUFORD; James CRAWFORD; Patrick CREIGHTON; Robert CRISWELL; Robert CROOKS; William CROUMLEIGH; Feremiah DALY; Thomas DAVIS; Samuel DEMAN; Daniel DENNY; Jane DENNY; Henry DIXON; Robert DOWNEY; Alexander DRUMON; William DUFFLE; John DUNBAR; Andrew DUNN; James ELLIOT; Thomas EVANS; Jacob FARNEY; Thomas FERGISON; John FLENNER; William FOLTON; Robert FORGEY; Robert FORSYTH; James FOSTER; Simon FRESER; GABRIEL & STEELY; Andrew GALBRAITH; Duncan GALBRAITH; James GALBRAITH; Robert GALBRAITH; Richard GALLAGHER; James GARRET; Robert GERTESS; Samuel GETTY; William GETTY; Bryce GILMORE; John GILMORE; GIVIN and HENDERSON; Elizabeth GLENN; William GODFREY; Robert GORDON; Edward GORREL; Samuel GOUDY; John GREENWOOD; Edward GUY; Alon HALKS; Andrew HALKS; John HALSTED; Hugh HAMILTON; Thomas HAMILTON; James HARDIE; John HARPER; Titus HARRY; John HASSON; Jonathan HASSON; Patrick HASSON; George HATFIELD; Joseph HEGARTY; Widow HEMPHILL; James HENDERSON; William HENETY; John HENNESY; John HENRY; John HESSIN; William HOFFMAN; Klet HOGG; John HOLLINGSHEAD; Joseph HOLMES; Thomas HOR; Andrew HUNTER; John HUNTER; Robert HUNTER; Andrew HUSTON; Philip HUSTON; Alexander IRVIN; Christopher IRVIN; William IRVIN; Mary IRWIN; Robert IRWIN; Daniel IUNERAY, junior; Capt. JOHNSTON; John JOHNSTON; JOHNSTON & ALEXANDER; William JUNKIN; Robert KERR; Samuel KERR, STEEL and KIRK; David KESSLER; Henry KEYLE; John KING; Thomas KRE; Henry KYELS; Thomas LASH and Co.; Robert LAURENCE; Abraham LEECH; Robert LEYBURN; Robert LINCH; Andrew LINDSEY; Mary LINN; William LOGAN; Mathew LOUDON; John LOVE; Robert LOWERY; Andrew M'ALISTER; Tole M'CALLISTER's executors; William M'CANDLISH; John M'CAUGHAN; Hugh M'CLARN; John M'CLEAN; Joseph M'CLELLAND; William M'CLENACHAN; James M'CLENACHIN; Hugh M'COLLOGH; Hugh M'CORMIC; Robert M'CULLOGH; John M'DEAL; James M'DERMIT; James M'DONNEL; John M'ELROY; John M'FARLAN; George M'FERREGE; James M'GOVERN; Charles M'INTYRE; William M'KEE; Alexander M'KEEHAN, junior; Charles M'LAUGHLIN; James M'LAUGHLIN; John M'NEAL; John M'NEIGHTEN; Alexander M'NUTT; James M'SCHADDIN; James MACKEY; Patrick MAGARY; Benjamin MAIRS; James MAIZE; William MARTIN; Peter MENTH; Charles MILLER; George MITCHEL; William MOBEN; Michael MONAGHAN; Jane MONTGOMERY; James MOORE; John MOORE; Joseph MOORE; William MOORE; David MORELL; Evan MORGAN; Mary MORGAN; John MORPLY; Hugh MORRISON; William MORROW; James MURPHEY; John MUSSER; Thomas MYERS; John NELSON; Lawrence NIBELT(?); George NIMON; Alexander NIVER; Thomas NORTON; William O'DEAR; Henry O'NEIL; Hugh O'NEIL; Archey ODAIR; James OHARA; James ORR; Letice(?) ORR; William PARK; John PARSLEY; James PATTON; James PAXTON; John Cole PENNOCK; William PERRIKIN; George PERRY; James PHILIPS; Isaac PLUNKET; Margaret POKE; John PURDY; Patrick QUIN; Mathew RABB; Andrew REED; James REED; John REED; John REIN; Miss RICHEY; John RIDDLES; John ROBINSON; Samuel ROSS; Robert ROWLAND; James RUTLEDGE; Joseph SCOTT; John SCOTT(?); James SCROGGS; John SEMPLE; James SHALES; William SIMP; Nathaniel SIMPSON; James SLOWNE; James SMILEY; James SMITH; John SMITH; Richard SMITH; Robert SMYTH; George SNIDER; Michael SPANGENBURG; John SPROLE; STEADMAN & SMITH; John STEEL, miller; James STERLING; William STERRET; John STEVENSON; David STEWART; Isabella STEWART; Joseph STEYMAN; Robert STORY; William STUART; Ann SWANZE; Charles SWENEY; James TAYLOR; John TAYLOR; Robert TAYLOR; Robert THOMPSON; Joseph THORN; Daniel TURNER; Jane WADDEL; Hugh WALLACE; Nicholas

APPENDIX A: Letters remaining at the Post Office (Carlisle Gazette)

WALSH; Jacob WALTIBERGER; Ludwig WALTMAN; James WATTS; John WATTS; David
WHITE; Robert WHITEHILL; Robert WHITEHILL, jun.; James WIDNEY, junr.; John
WILKIN; William WILL; Edward WILSON; James WOODBURN; Amos WOODRUFF; William
WOODS; Alexander YOUNG

Letter remaining at Post Office, Aug 1797: James ALEXANDER, care John
WATSON; Cairns ALLEN, Cumberland co; Cornelius ANDERSON, care of Robert
SMITH; James ANDERSON, Toscarora; Mr. ANDERSON, care of John HUNTER; Samuel
ANDERSON; ARTHURS & MOORE, Alexanderia, Huntingdon; David AYERS; William
BARBER and Jacob MILLER, care of Michael EGE; William BARR, care of William
BROWN, Mifflin; John BARTON, Mifflinburgh; Joseph BEARD, care of Stephen
DUNCAN; Richard BEARD, care of James LAMBERTON; John BEATTY, care of William
BEATTY; William BEATTY, care of Robert LEYBURN; Alexander BIGGS, Carlisle;
Alexander BLACK, Franklin co; John BODEN, care of John CULBERTSON, esq.;
John BOLTON, Bigspring; George BOYD, Mifflin town; Daniel BRADLEY; Jane
BRANDON, York co; Daniel BROLLEY, care of Esquire QUIGLEY; Hamilton BROWN,
Shearman's valley; Hugh BROWN, care of Robert LEYBURN; Alexander CAMERON,
Mifflin co; Phineas CARL; John CARSON, Bigspring; William CASCADDEN(?);
Patrick CASSADY, Frankstown; Richard COCHRAN, care of James LAMBERTON;
William COCHRAN, care of James LAMBERTON; William COCHRAN, care of James
RAMSEY, esq. Mifflin; Richard COLEGAT, Newville; Paul COLLINS, Mifflinburgh;
Charles CONNNING?), Yellow breeches; Philip CONTZE, Dills; Mary COOK, care
of John HUNTER; John COWDEN, Cumberland co; Israel CRIDER(?), Huntingdon;
George CROCKET, care Michael EGE; James CROCKET, care of David M'GOWAN;
James CROCKET, care of Michael EGE; William CROSBY, Dickinson twp; John
CULBERTSON, fuller, esq.; William CURSEADDIN(?), care of Hugh M'CUMMINS;
Joseph DIVIN, Pennsvalley; Henry DIXON, Juniata; Patrick DIXON, care of
George RUPPLEY; John DOUGHERTY, taylor, Lewistown; Alexander DRUMMON,
Shavers creek; James DUNLAP, Student; James DUNLAP, taylor, Lewistown;
Andrew DUNN, care of J; Samuel EAKIN, care of Daniel DUNLAP; James ELDER,
Paty valley; William ESPY, care of William WALLACE; William FARIS(?); Thomas
FARRAN, Warrington twp; James FEA, Cumberland co; James FERGUSON, care of
James HARRIS; William FERGUSON, Newville; James FISHER, Eastpensbro'; Samuel
FISHER, Shearman's valley; Robert FORSSYTH Lewistown; James FRENCH, Juniata;
James FULTON, care of Robert LEYBURN; James FULTON, mason, care of David
M'MUTRY, Huntingdon; James GARRETT, care of John HUNTER,; Joseph GEHR;
Samuel GEHR, Lisburn; William GERRET, care of John HUNTER; Robert
GILFILEN(?), care of James LAMBERTON; David GILLELAND, care of C. QUIGLEY,
Esq.; Bryce GILMORE, care of Robert LUSK; Samuel GILMORE; James GLENDINING,
care of Robert LEYBURN; John GORDLEY, care of James PATTERSON; Edward GOUDY,
Huntingdon; John GRAHAM, Shearman's valley; Thomas GRAHAM, care of Mr.
MONTGOMERY; William GRAHAM, near Carlisle; Sarah GREEN, Mifflin co; Patrick
GREER, care of Robert LUSK; Samuel GREER, Carlisle; George HACKETE;
Archibald HAMILTON, care of John HUNTER; Gloud HAMILTON, care of John
HUNTER; Hugh HAMILTON, Shearman's valley; John HAMILTON, Pike creek; Andrew
HENDERSON, prothonotary, Huntingdon; Thomas HENDERSON, Carlisle; John
HENDRY; William HENRY, care of Robert LEYBURN; James HILL, Carlisle; George
HOGG, care of John OFFICER; Mary HOLMES, Carlisle; Thomas HOLMES, Rye twp;
Adam HOUKE; James HUNTER, Bigspring; John HUNTER, Pike creek; Robert HUNTER,
Mifflin; William HUNTER, Bigspring; James INGRAM, care of Judge BROWN; James
IRVINE, Lewistown, care of Col. James M'FARLAND; Alpleus JOHNSON, Carlisle;
Rev. JOHNSTON, Hundingdon co; William JOHNSTON, Lewistown; John JOHNSTON,

Letters remaining at the Carlisle Post Office

Tuscarora; John KAMP; Ricahrd KANE, Huntingdon; Jane KELLY, care of James LAMBERTON; Joseph KENNEDY, near Carlisle; William KERR, Mifflin; Nicholas KESEKER, Yellow breeches; Henry KILER, care of James DAVIS; John KNOX, Carlisle; Joseph KYLE, Mifflin; John LARD, Carlisle; Robert LAWRENCE, Huntingdon; John LEE(?); Thomas LEE; Henry LIKELY(?), care of James THOMPSON; Thomas LINTON, Greenwood twp; Thomas LOUGHHEAD, care of Andrew PARKER; John LOVER, care of John POLLOCK; Matthew M'Cullough, care of Robert LUKS; James M'CAUGHON, care of Robert LEYBURN; Margaret M'CORMICK, care of Robert NECA(?); Edward M'CORTY, Lewistown; Charles M'COY, Sh. valley; Jane M'COY, Mifflin co; Joseph M'COY, Tuscarora; William M'COY, care of Joseph M'COY; William M'CREA, care of Joseph PEARCE; William M'CULLOUGH, Huntingdon; Barney M'DONALD, care of Philip STRONCE; William M'DONALD, Walnut bottom; John M'DOWEL, Shippensburgh; Samuel M'DOWEL, Bigspring; Alexander M'ELROY, care of John HUNTER; James M'FARLAND; George M'FETRICH, near Carlisle; John M'HENRY, care of Henry DIXON, Mifflin co; David M'KEE, care of John HUNTER; Robert M'KEE, Silver Spring; John M'KENNAN, care of Robert LEYBURN; Michael M'LAMON, Newville; John M'LANDSBURGE, care of William M'CRACKEN; Thomas M'LEARY, care of Abraham LOUGHRIDGE; Neal M'MANIGAL, Mifflin co; Arthur M'NAUGHTON, Greenwood twp; William M'PHERSON, care of John WRAY; John MAGILL, Mifflin co; Hugh MALHEIM(?), care of D. STUART, Huntingdon; William MARTIN, Shearman's valley; John MATSON, Walnut bottom road; patrick MELAY, Huntingdon co; John MILLER, Juniata twp; Master William MILLER; C. MILTY, Pack, Newville; Robert MISKELLY, care of Epharim STEELE; George MOOR, Mifflin co; George MULHOLM, Lewistown; Crowel NEWVILLE; Luther NEWVILLE; William OFFICER, near Carlisle; Peter PAWL, Thompson's town; William PIPER, near Carlisle; William PORTER, near Dills; Thomas PROVIANCE, Huntingdon co; James PURDAY, Mifflin co; Charles RAINEY, Southampton twp; James RAINEY, Shearman's valley; David RALSTON, care of Samuel WEAKLEY; William REA, Mifflin co; John READ, Newton twp; James REED, Carlisle; Andrew REID, Mifflin co; John ROBERTS, Huntingdon co; William ROBERTSON, Mifflin co; James ROBINSON, Standingdone; William RODMAN, Bigspring; James ROGERS, Cumberland co; William SELFRED, Lewistown; James SHARON, Shearmans valley; Elizabeth SHAW, Newville; William SHAW, care of William LYONS, Esq.; Daniel SHIELDS, care of William BROWN, Esq., Mifflin; John SIMMISON, care of John ANDERSON; Jane SMITH at Col. BLAINS; John SMITH, Carlisle; Robert SMITH, shoemaker, Carlisle; William SMITH, care of John HARPER; Daniel STEEL, Mifflin co.; William STEVENSON, Bigg-spring; Isaballa STUART, Shearmans valley; James SUMMERS, Lewistown; George Michael SWARTZ, Cumberland co; Charles SWEENY, care of Abraham LOUGHRIDGE; Andrew TAYLOR, Bigg-spring; Samuel TEAZ; James THOMPSON, Andersons mill; James THOMPSON, Shearmans valley; Robert THOMPSON, care of Robert LAYBURN; John TINKLER, Carlisle; David TOMB, care of John CREIGH; John TOMB, care of John CREIGH; John WACHOP, Shearmans valley; Daniel WILLIAMS, York co; Isac WILLIAMS, Carlisle; George WILLIAMSON, near Carlisle; John WILLIAMSON, near Carlisle; Thomas WILLIAMSON, near Carlisle; Elie WILSON, care of William MOORE; James WILSON, care of Robert LUSK; James WOODBURN, Newville; William WOOLS; Joseph YOUNG, Carlisle; William YOUNG, Pennsvalley

Letters remaining at P.O., Carlisle, Dec 20th 1797: James ADAMS; John ADAMS; David ALBERTSON; James ALEXANDER; James ALEXANDER; Mary ALLEN; William ALLISON; William ALLISON; Abraham ANDERSON; Abraham ANDERSON; James ANDERSON; John ANDERSON; William ANDERSON; Gabral ARMSTRONG; John ARMSTRONG;

APPENDIX A: Letters remaining at the Post Office (Carlisle Gazette)

John ATWELL; John BARBER; John BARCKLEY; John BARR; Robert BARR; William BARR; John BEARD; Joseph BEARD; William BEATY; Joseph BIVEN; James BLACK; John BLACK; Charles BLEAKLY; Joseph BLEAKNEY; John BODDEN; Daniel BRADLEY; Patrick BRADLEY; James BRADSHAW; Charles BRODLEY; James BROWN; John BROWN; Michael BROWNLEE; Robert BURNS; Joseph CALDWELL; John CAMPBLE; Alexander CARNAHAN; William Alexander CARR; Revd. Robert CATHCART; Thomas CECIL; John CHISTER(?); Andrew CHRICHTON; Robert CHRISTY; Robert CHRISWELL, Senr.; William Henry COAN; William COCHRAN; Nathaniel COMAN; John CONNER; James COUGHRAN; Patrick COULTER; William COX; John CRAFORD; Abraham CRAIG; Patrick CULBART; John CUNNINGHAM; Robert CUNNINGHAM; William CUSEADDIN; John CUSICK; Robert DARAGH; John DAVIS; Robert DELRUMPLE; William DEVIN; George DICKEY; Andrew DONAL; Alexander DONALDSON; James DUNCAN; Ander DUNN; Samuel EAKIN; Widow EDGAR; John EDWARDS; Frances ELLIOT; James ELLIOTT; Alexander EMITT; Miss Margaret ESKIN; William ESKIN; James EWING; William FARRIER; James FEAR; John FEE; Thomas FERGUSON; Hugh FLECHER; Henry FLEMING; John FORGY; James FOSTER; John FRENCH; Thomas FULTON; William FULTON; James GAILY; Frances GALLACHER; Richard GALLACHER; Aaron GAMBLE; James GARDNER; John GIBSON; George GILLEES; Daniel GILLESPY; John GILLILAN; James GILMORE; John GILMORE; William GLENN; Robert GORDON; Edward GOUDY; John GRAHAM; James GRAY; Thomas GRAY; Alexander GREDDON; Samuel GREER; Philip GROVE; Melcher HAFFER; Maitilin HALLMAN; Goud HAMILTON; John HAMILTON; William HANREGAN; Thomas HARBISON; James HARGAN; William HARKIN; William HARKIN; Amos HARPER; John HARPER; Thomas HARRIS; Daniel HASTY; Samuel HAWTHORN; John HOGAN; Samuel HOGG; Joseph HOLMES; Thomas HOLMES; James HOOD; William HUMPHRIES; James HUNTER; John HUNTER; James IRVIN; Christopher IRVINE; Robert JACKSON; William JACKSON; Jarman JACOBS; Revd. John JAMISON; William JAMISON; Eliza JODON; James JOHNSON; Messrs. JOHNSON and ALEXANDER; Revd. Daniel JONES; David KANNIDY; Thomas KANNIDY; Andrew KARR; Aaron KEE; William KELLY; Rekah KELSO; James KENNY; David KESSLER; James KIRKPATRICK; George KITCH; George KUICKEL; William LADLER; John LAMB; Captain Andrew LEE; Thomas LINTON; John LORD; Thomas LOUGHEAD; William LYON; Samuel M'ALHINNY; John M'CAHAN; John M'CALLASTER; John M'CAUGHAN; Peter M'CAUGHLIN; James M'CLANNACHAN; Hugh M'CLARING; William M'CLASKY; George M'CLELLAND; Robert M'CLELLAND; Mannassus M'CLOUGLIN; James M'CLURE; John M'CLURE; Robert M'CONAGHY; Alexander M'CONNAL; Daniel M'CONNEL; Margret M'CORMACK; William M'CORMACK; William M'COY; William M'CREA; Francis M'CULLAGH; George M'CULLAGH; George M'CULLOCH; William M'CULLOCH; Francis M'CULLOUGH; Henry M'CULLY; Thomas M'CULLY; William M'DONNELL; John M'ELHINNEY; John M'FARLAND; William M'FARLAND; Alexander M'GAHEY; James M'GAHEY; Peter M'GINN; Thomas M'GLOUCHLIN; Matthew M'GOLRICK; Matthew M'GOLRICK; James M'GOUVAN; Daniel M'GUIRE; John M'HENRY; Daniel M'INTIRE; James M'INTIRE; Thomas M'INTIRE; Robert M'KEE; William M'KEE; Henry M'LAUGHLIN; Peter M'LOUGHLIN; John M'LURE; Robert M'MILLEN; Daniel M'MONEGAL; Patrick M'MULLON; Charles M'MYRE; James M'NEAL; John M'NUTT; James MACHON; Charles MARCH; Charles MARTIN; Mr. MARTIN; Mr. MELBOY; Alexander MILLER; Robert MILLER; Richard MILLS; James MITCHEL; James MONTGOMERY; James MONTGOMERY; John MONTGOMERY; John MOORE; Samuel MOORE; Peter MORGROT; William or Noble MORRISON; Abraham MORROW; Thomas MULLOY; James MURDOCK; Robert MURDOCK; James MURPHY; Abraham NEIDIG; John Lennon NEIGH; George NELSON; William NICKSON; Anne NIXON; Thomas NORTON; James O'HARRA; Levy OWENS; James PARKER; Samuel PARKHILL; James PARKINSON; Mr. PATTERSON; Peter PAUL; Samuel PAXTON; Robert PETERSON; james PETTIGREW; Nancy POLLOCK; Francis PORTER; James PORTER; Mary PORTER; Robert

Letters remaining at the Carlisle Post Office

PORTER; William PORTER; William POWELL; Charles RAINEY; James RAINEY; Sarah RANDELL; Benjamin RANKIN; David RANKIN; William RANKIN; William REA; James READ; Thomas READING; James REDMENT; James REDWOOD; Andrew REID; William REILEY; Widow RICHEY; James ROBERSON; John ROBESON; John ROBESON; Samuel ROBINSON; Elizabeth ROBISON; William ROBISON; Barnard ROGAN; James ROGERS; William ROGERS; Conra ROTH; Stuart ROWAN; Robert SETON; Ann SHANNON; Lenard SHANNON; Martha SHANNON; Elizabeth SHEARMAN; John SHERIFF; Elizabeth SIMSON; Charles SMITH; James SMITH; John SMITH; Robert SMITH; Thomas SMITH; Hugh SPEER; Samuel SPROUL; Andrew SPROWL; Samuel STANSMY; Samuel STEEL; William STEEL; Robert STEEN; Isabella STEWART; Jeoackim STORM; John STREAN; Benjamin TAYLOR; Joseph TAYLOR; Robert TAYLOR; George THOMAS; John THOMAS; John THOMPSON; Thomas THOMPSON; Walter THOMPSON; Catharine TODD; Alexander TOMSON; Isaiah VANHORN; John WACHOP; William WALKER; John WALLACE; Patrick WARD; Andrew WARSON; Alexander WATSON; Olivia WATSON; William WHITE; James WILKEN; John WILKINS; James WILLIAMSON; John WILSON; Samuel WILSON; Thomas WILSON; Alexander YOUNG; William YOUNG; Henry ZIEGLER - William LEVIS, P.M.

Letters remaining at Post Office, Shippensburg, March 1799: Mary ADAMS, York co, care of Samuel ADAMS, Carrol's Tract; Charles ANDERSON; John BARKLY, for the Post Office; John BARR, care of capt. Robert PEEBLES; Thomas BOARLAND, care of John KILE, Esq. Paty Valley; William BOYD, Gap; Joseph BRADY, student; Samuel BRISON; William BURNSIDE, care of Stephen M'GURK; Andrew BYERLY; John CALDWELL; Samuel CALDWELL, merchant, Roxberry; Arthur CLELAND, Brush Valley; Matthias CLINE; Solomon CLOYDE, care of Samuel QUIGLEY; John CLYDE, care of Samuel QUIGLY; Patrick COLLINS, Fannetsburgh; William CRAWFORD; Patrick DELANEY, care of Patrick COCHRAN; Elizabeth DEMPSEY, care of Frederick SHIPLEY; Mary DOYLE; Elizabeth DREEGAN, care of Samuel QUIGLEY; Alexander DUMARS, care of the Post office; William GAW, Lurgan twp; Thomas GEATS, Mason; John GIVIN; Elizabeth GREEN, care of William BELL; Thomas GREEN, care of Capt RIPPEY; Henry and Benjamin GRIMLER; James HAGERTY, Mason, care of Thomas or Mark M'FEE; William HARVEY, care of Daniel DUNCAN; William HARVEY, Path Valley, care of Daniel DUNCAN; Hugh HAZLETON, Milford; Hugh HAZLETON, care of John M'ILROY, Walnut Bottom; Molly HAZLETON, care of William GLADSON; Samuel D. HEAP; Jacob HEILLER, 9 miles from Shippensburg, care of Mr. RAHM; Margaret HENDERSON; Robert HEYLANDS, care of Matthew ADAMS; Andrew HUSTON, tavern keeper; James HUSTON, care of Hugh SMITH, merchant; Alexander JOHNSON; Alexander KARR, care of I. KIB, Esq, Fannetsburgh; Ann KENNEDY, care of capt. Thomas GREER; Samuel KIRK, care of George M'CANLIS; Henry F. KURTZ; Isaac LAW; Henry LECKEY, Tuskarora Valley; John LEE, Dickinson twp; Thomas LEE, Dickinson twp; Jas. LYNCH, care of James BATEY (or BAREY); Elizabeth M'CLAY; David M'CLOY, near Shippensburg; John M'CULLOUGH, Newton twp, care of Robert LEECH, Newville; Andrew M'CULLY, Chambersburgh; Margaret M'DONNELL; Samuel M'FARLIN, care of Richard RODGERS; Robert M'GINNESS, care of James BATESON; William M'ILHENEY, care of Samuel PURVIANCE, Chambersburgh; Patrick M'KEEVER, care of Matthew ADAMS; Samuel M'MATH, care of John HEAP, Esq., Shippensburgh; James MAUGHAN, care of Mr. SHEPLY, P.M.; Andrew MICKEY, near Shippensburgh; Hoseas MILLER; Richard MILVEN, Fayette co; Noah or William MOFFIT; William MOOREHEAD, care of Hugh SMITH; Sarah MULHOLLAND, care of James BUCHANAN; George MULL, shoemaker; Elizabeth NOBLE, care Andrew CULBERTSON; Thomas OFFICER, near Newville; James PEOPLES, care of capt. Robert PEOPLES; Enoch PRICE; Samuel PRICE, Esq.; James QUIGLEY, care of Samuel QUIGLEY; Edward REYLY, care of George

APPENDIX A: Letters remaining at the Post Office (Carlisle Gazette)

M'CANLIS; Samuel ROSS, care of James HUSTON, Mercersburgh; Matthew SCOTT, care of Mr. BALDRIDGE, Westmoreland co; Joseph SHOWALTER, Newville; Elizabeth SMITH, 4 miles from Shippensburg; James SMITH, care of Patrick CAMPBLE, Chambersburgh; William SMITH, care of Mr. BARR, merchant; John SNODY, care of Mr. RAHM; Alexander SPEER, care of William BARR; David SPRINGLE, care of James LOWERY, Esq.; Benjamin STERRIT, Strasburgh; David STEWART, care of Mr. M'CANDLASS; Samuel TEAS, care of William LEEPER; James THOMPSON, Shearman's Valley, care of William M'CUNE, Esq.; John THOMPSON living at Arnold DUNCAN's; John THOMPSON, Huntingdon co, care of Squire HEAP; Charles TROY; William WOODBURN, care of Frederick SHEPLEY

Letters remaining at Post Office, Shippensburgh, Sep 1799: James AGNEW, merchant, M'Connel's town; John BARLOW, near Shippensburgh; Capt. James BROWN, Bigspring; David BROWN, care of Mr. RAHM, Shippensburgh; General Thomas BUCHANAN, near Shippensburgh; Jacob CASSEL, merchant, Strasburg; John CUNNINGHAM, near Shippensburg; Peter DEAL, near Shippensburg; James GRAY, near Pittsburgh; Samuel HAMILL, near Shippensburgh; William HUNTER, near Shippensburgh; Samuel IRVIN, care of John Woods, Esq.; David IRVIN, near Shippensburgh; Joseph KREE, Strasburgh; George LUCAS, Strasburgh; Miss M'CLINTOCK, Shippensburgh; William M'CRACKEN, near Shippensburgh; John M'CULLOUGH, near Shippensburgh; Samuel MEANS, Shippensburgh; William MEANS, tanner, Shippensburgh; Miss Peggy MORRISON, Shippensburgh; Patty MOULDER, Shippsneburgh; Howard OGLE, care of James CISNA, Shippensburgh; Robert PORTER, care of Mr. COCHRAN; Charles RAINEY, Winchester; John RANEY, Winchester; James READ, Winchester; Sarah ROSS, near Winchester; William ROWEN, Cumberland Co; Rachel SCROGS, Shippensburgh; Jacob SKILES, Cumberland co.; Philip SLUSHER, Cumberland co.; Messrs WILBY, M'LANE and Co., Strasburgh - William Bell, Post Master

Letters remaining at Post Office, Shippensburgh, Dec 1799: Thomas ARMSTRONG, care of Thomas ORR, near Shippensburgh; Mrs. AULBRIGHT, Shippensburgh; Christopher BARTON, Shippensburgh; William BONNILL, sadler, Strasburg; Joseph BREADY, Shippensburgh; Sarah CLARKSON, near Nicholson's Mill; Robert COFFEY, care Patrick COCHRAN, Shippensburgh; John COOPER, care of John HERRON, Shippensburgh; John COPLEY, Shippensburgh; Henry DAVIS, Strasburgh; James DICKEY, sen. Francklin co, Shippensburgh; Sarah DUGAL, Streasburgh; John DUNBAR, Newville, near Shippensburgh; George FRY, near Shippensburgh; Ebenezer FRY, Shippensburgh; James HAMILTON, care Mr. RAHM, Shippensburgh; James HARTFORD, Shippensburgh; Charles HAWKINS, care Mr. COCHRAN, Shippensburgh; Joseph HENDERSON, care Hugh SMITH, Shippensburgh; Robert HENDERSON, care Hugh SMITH, Shippensburgh; Cornelius HIGERTY, Shippensburgh; William HILANDS, near Shippensburgh; Henry HILL, care Sam. QUIGLY, Shippensburgh; Jonathan HOGE, Shippensburgh; Christian HOOVER, Shippensburgh; Richard JAMES, care Mr. COCHRAN, Shippensburgh; Christian KEEFER, Strasburgh; James KILSO, Shippensburgh; John LYNCH, care of Mr. Thomas GATES, Shippensburgh; Cornelius M'CLAIN, Shippensburgh; David M'CLEALAND, Cumberland; John M'CLURE, Shippensburgh; Thomas MARTIN, Shippensburgh; James MAUGHIN, care Mr. SHIPLEY, Shippensburgh; John MEENS, Shippensburgh; Miss Betsy MOORE, near Shippensburgh; Peggy MORRISON, Shippensburgh; James PEOPLES, Shippensburgh; Margaret PEOPLES, Shippensburgh; Samuel PERRY, Shippensburgh; Robert PORTER, Shippensburgh; David QUICKLY, care Mr. M'CRACKEN, Big spring; Richey RODGERS, care Mr.

Letters remaining at the Shippensburg Post Office

RIPPEY, Shippensburgh; Frederick SHEPLEY, Shepherdstown; George SMITH, care Messrs. BARR & M'KNIGHT; Adam WEIR, care Mr. DUNCAN, Shippensburgh; Mrs. Jane WOODS, Shippensburgh. - William Bell, Post Master.

Letters remaining at Post Office Shippensburgh, March 26 1800: Mathew ADAMS, care of Mr. RAHM, Shippensburgh; Margret ALLEN, care of Ellenor ALLEN, Strasburgh; Frances ANDERSON, care of Wm. BELL, Strasburgh; Mr. BARE; John BOELL(?); William BUTTS, care of Mr. RAHM; William CARSIDON; James CLARK, Franklin co; Joseph DUNCAN; James DUNCAN, care of Capt. Robert CULBERTSON; William GIBSON, care of Robert PORTER; James HAMILL; Samuel HANNA, near Shippensburgh; William HIGHLANDS, care of Captain RIPPEY; Capt. James JAMISON, Burnt Cabbins; Jacob KELLER; Isabel KENNEDY, care of Wm. SCOTT near Shippensburgh; Margret KINSLE(?); Samuel LONG, care of widow SHUTLEY; Michael LONGENECKER, near Shippensburgh; Hugh LOWIMER, care of Robert GEORGEHILL; Joseph LOWRY, care of Wm. BELL; Michael M'CREA, care of Charles READ; Robert M'GINNESS, care of Matthew ADAMS; Roger M'KINNEY, care of James BATESON, store-keeper; James M'PIKE, care of Patrick M'LAUGHLIN; Archibald MAHON; John MARSHALL, Walnut-Bottom road; Thomas MOORE; Robert PEEBLES, near Shippensburgh; John RAUM; Charles READ, care of Capt. Thomas GREEN; Simon RICE; William ROBINSON, care of George M'CANDLESS; Alexander SCOTT, near Shippensburgh; Peter SKILES; Casper SLOAN, Newville; Thomas STUTE, care of Post-master; Edward WARK, Esq., Shippensburgh; Samuel WEAKLEY, Walnut Bottom; John WILSON, near Shippensburgh; Adam WOLF

Jun 18 1800
Letters remaining at Post Office, Jun 1800, Shippensburgh: William BAWROTT, Shippensburgh; Arthur DONNELY, care of John M'KUNN, miller, near Shippensburgh; Joseph DUNCAN, merchant, Shippensburgh; Stephen HARLIN, near Shippensburgh; William HUNTER, chair maker; Daniel M'DONALD, near Newville; Robert M'GAHY, care of George KIRK, America; Alexander MAGEE, Shippensburgh; Frederick SHEPSLEY, Shippensburgh; Jacob TOMBAUCH, in Shippensburgh; John WADE, powder maker; John WRIGHT, Jun., tanner

APPENDIX B: Letters remaining at the Post Office (York Advertiser)

List of Letters remaining in the Post Office at York Town, Jan 1, 1796, which if not redeemed before the 1st day of April next, will be returned to the General Post Office as Dead Letters: David AGNEW, Marsh Creek; William BIGHAM, York Co; Jas. BIRD, Shoemaker; Rev. Jno. BLACK, Marsh Creek; H. H. BRACKENRIDGE, York; James & Samuel CALDWELL, York Co; James CARROLL c/o Alexr. LACKEY, York Co; John CHAMBERS, Mountpleasant T.; Esther CLARK c/o David AGNEW, Marsh Creek; Robert CUNNINGHAM c/o John BRIEN, Spring Forge; Joseph DAVIS, Conowago; Robert DAVIS c/o Andrew DINSMORE, near Peach Bottom Ferry; Esther DOOL c/o Joseph REED, Chanceford Twp; George GAYTEE, Little York; John GORDON, Hopewell Twp. c/o James SHORT, merchant; Thomas GORDON c/o James GORDON, near Peach Bottom; William GRAY c/o Wm. LONG, York Co; Robert HOMES, York Co; Robert HUGHS c/o Mr. UPDEGRAFF, hatter, York; Charles HUMES c/o James SHORT; John JEFFERIES, York Co; Hugh KING & Francis PLUNKET, York Co; John KIRKWOOD, Chanceford Twp; Alexander LACKEY, York Co; James LONG, Chanceford Twp; James M'GATTICK, York Co c/o Jacob UPP; Jno. M'JUNKINS c/o Wm. MITCHELL, Esq. Monaughan T.; Wm. M'CANDLEY, Chanceford; John M'DONALD, Shrewsbury Twp; William M'KINNEY c/o Joseph REED, Esq. Chanceford Twp; Charles M'NONAGLE, Fawn T.; Edward MACKEL, York Co; James MARSHALL, Carrols Delight c/o John GREER; Robert MARSHALL, York Co; Robert MARTIN, Chanceford T; Bernard MILLER, Berlin, York Co; John MILLER, painter York; Robert MOORE, Mountjoy Twp, York Co; John MULLEN, shoemaker c/o Thos. THORNBURG, Warrington; Christian NESTLERATH, York Co; Wm. OWENS, Chanceford Twp; Wm. PORTER, Monaughan Twp; Andrew PROUDFOOT, Hopewell T. c/o Jas. SHORT; John RICHEY, York; Rev. John SLEMMONS, York Co; David STEWART c/o Robert STEWART, Marsh CReek; John STEWART, Chanceford Twp; Peter TINKLE, merchant, York Borough; Anne TRIMBLE, York Co; John VALE, York Co; Dr. VANIIARLING, Strabane Twp; Sarah WAGGONER, York; Benj. WALKER; John or Charles WALLACE, America; Thomas WARD, York Co; Robert WARK, Pa; James WHITE, York; --- WILSON c/o Dr. Franklin --- (?); Warrington T; Dimoke WINDUS, York. Jacob SPANGLER, P. M.

List of Letters remaining in the Post Office at York Town 1 April 1796: David AGNEW, Marsh Creek; John AMES, near York c/o Robert WILSON; John BLACK, Marsh Creek; Jacob BODENHAMER, York Co; William BOYD, Fawn Twp.; Henry & Robert BROWN, Marsh Creek; James CARLIN, Md; Miss Esther CLARK, Marsh Creek; Henry CLAYTON, near York; Thomas DAVIS, Newbury Twp; Thomaas DEMISTER c/o Dr. D. DEMSTER, Gettysburgh; Baltzer DIETRICH; Caty DIVER, Marsh Creek; Rev. Alexander DOBBINS, Marsh Creek; James DOUGHERTY, Chanceford Twp; Elizabeth ELLISLY(?) c/o Col. STEEL; Robert ELLIST, Spring Forge; John FINLEY, Fawn Twp; William HAIL c/o Charles Wm. PORTER, Chanceford Twp; John LINTON, Marsh Creek; Allaw M'BEATH c/o Rev. SAMPLE; Andrew M'KAIN; William M'SHERRY, Marsh Creek; Col. John MILLER; George MITCHELL c/o Col. Michael SCHMYSER; John MURRAY, taylor; Moses PACKER c/o John COLLINS: Assa PARMELE; Samuel ROSEBURGH, Hopewell Twp c/o Jacob UPP; Alexander RUSSELL, Esq., York Co; Andrew SMITH c/o Andrew BILLMEYER; Peter STEWART c/o Andrew MARTIN, Hopewell; Mr. TWERING, Little York; Michael WANNER, Botts Town. Jacob SPANGLER, P.M.

A List of Letters remaining Post Office at York Town July 1, 1796: Fransmus(?) ALSUP, Miller of the Spring Mines, South Mountain; David AYRES, near Lisburn; Elijah P. BARROWS, Gettysburgh; Jeremiah BARTON, York; Jacob BODENHEIMER, Conowago; Charles BRANNON (hatter), Middle Town; Thomas BREDEN, Gettysburgh; James BUCHANAN c/o Joshua RUSSELL; Samuel CALVIN, near the Frame Meeting House; John CAMPBELL, Chanceford; Alexander COOPER, York; Archibald COULTER, Strabann; Meadow Place; Peggy CSIDSDEL(?), York; John

Letters remaining at the York Post Office

DENNIS c/o Mr. David HARRIS; William DOUGHERTY c/o Mr. BRIEN Spring Forge; Thomas DOWLING, York; Catharine FARMER c/o Mr. OWINGS, near Hanover; Andrew FINLEY, Barrons of York; Michael FISSEL, near York; John GALLAGHER, Marsh Creek; John GRAHAM, Chanceford; Robert GRIER, Hunters Town; Dr. James HAMILTON, near York; Susannah HAMMESON(?), 22 miles from York; William HANNA, Fishing Creek; William HENRY, Little Britain; William JAMMESON c/o Mr. UPP; Thomas KELLY, Chanceford; Hugh KING, Conowago; Samuel KNOX, near Gettysburgh; Maj. Eli LEWIS, Hugh LINN c/o Mr. IRWIN, Gettysburg; James LONG, Chanceford; Alexander M'CAULEY; John M'CORD; William M'EIWEE, Hopewell Twp; James M'GAUGAY, Marsh Creek; Andrew M'ILVANE, Distiller, Berwick Twp; James M'MULLIAN, Fawn twp, near M'Candlesse's Store; Joshua MALLIN c/o Mr. John COLLINS, York; Messrs. Lewis & Wendle MICHAEL, York; Michael MORRISON, Hopewell co. c/o Mr. SHORT; Robert NELSON, Chanceford Twp, York Co; Samuel NELSON, near M'Calls Ferry; Andrew PATTON, Bernn; Hugo PATTERSON, near the Brogue; Jas. PATTERSOSN, near the Brogue Tavern; Benjamin PEDAN, York Co; William PORTER, Monaughan; Gabriel PORTERFIELD, Fawn Twp; Wm. REYNOLDS, Mountpleasant; David RICHEY c/o A. THOMPSON, Esq.; John ROBINSON, Marsh Creek; Thomas SHANNON, Tom's Creek; Peter SMUCK, merchant, York; David STEWART, Marsh Creek; John STEWART, Esq.; Peter STEWART, Hopewell; John STRICKER, York Co; William THOMPSON, Mason, Strabane; Polly TRUMP, widow, Paradise Twp; Jacob UPP, York Town; Molly WALLACE c/o James CHAMBERLAIN, Reading Twp; Nicholas WALTMAN c/o Mr. RAAP; Samuel WILSON c/o Joshua RUSSELL, Marsh Creek; John YOUNG, near Gettysburg c/o Capt. KERR; Robert YOUNG, Mountjoy c/o Capt. KERR, Gettysburg. Jacob SPANGLER, P.M.

List of Letters remaining in the Post Office at York Town, Oct 1, 1796: Archibald AIKIN c/o Thomas PATTERSON, Tom's Creek; George ALLEN, Wrights Ferry; William ALKINS c/o of Rev. CLARKSON; William or Alexander ALLISON, Chanceford Twp; Mrs. ARNOTT c/o the Rev. CLARKSON; Isaac BAITMAN; Elijah P. BARROWS, Gettysburgh; Jacob BODENHAMER; Christopher BOOTH c/o Alexander TURNER; Andrew BOYD c/o Alexander COBEAN; Samuel BOYLE; William BRADLEY, M'Callister's Town; John BRIEN, Spring Forge; John BROWN, Jr. c/o Gawin SCOTT, Chanceford T.; Joseph BROWN, Strabant T.; William BROWN c/o Jas. DUNCAN, Penn's Valley; Elizabeth BRUMFIELD and John MULLAN; John BULL, near York; Henry BURBACH, Minor near Nicholson's Gap, South Mountain; Samuel CALDWELL; Thomas CAMPBELL c/o Jacob DRITT; James CLARK c/o John GREER; Alexander COCHRAN, Dover Twp; Robert COCHRAN c/o Saml. EDIT, Esq.; William COLOQUE c/o David HARRIS, York; James COOPER, Conowago, Monallan Twp; John COOPER, Fawn Twp; William DAUGHERTY c/o John BRIEN; James DAVIDSON, Fawn Twp; Issabella DEAL; Andrew DEAZETT; Thomas DICK, Marsh Creek; Adam DINSMORE; Rev. Alexander DOBBINS, Marsh Creek; Wm. DONNON, near M'Call's Ferry; James DOUGHERTY c/o Samuel M'MULLAN; John DOUGLASS c/o Joseph REED, Chanceford Twp; Alexr. DOWNING, Chanceford; Thomas DUNCAN c/o Alexander TURNER; Solomon DUNGAN, Little's Town; Andrew DYSERT, Marsh Creek; Thos. FEENY c/o John FORSYTH; Jas. FLANAGEN, Chanceford; Edward FRAIZER c/o Wm. SCOTT, Esq.; John FULTON, Monaghan; John GILMORE c/o Jas. and Wm. ROSS, Warrington; Daniel GLASS, Warrinton T.; David GLEAN; Madam GLESENHUYSEN, c/o Frederick STUMP; Robert GORDON; Robt. GRAHAM; Thomas GRAY, Warrinton Twp; Luke GREEN; James GREER, Red Hook Ferry; Samuel HALL, Strabane Twp; Wm. HANNAGEN; Francis HARBISON, Marsh Creek; John HARGIN c/o Alexr. TURNER; Samuel HAYS, Chanceford; John HENDERSON c/o C. Wm. PORTER; Jos. HENDERSON, Hunter's Town; George HINDS, Junr., Carrols Tract; Peter HOKE, Senr.; Samuel HOLTEN, Chanceford; Robt. IRWIN, Mount Pleasant; Jain JOHNSTON c/o Jas. EDGAR; Thos. JOHNSTON; George JOICE, Monallen; David JORDON c/o Wm.

APPENDIX B: Letters remaining at the Post Office (York Advertiser)

EDGAR, Hopewell; Thomas KELLY, M'Allister's Town; John KENEDY; Robt. KIDD, Franklin; Jain KINCAID; Col. John KING; Wm. KNOWLES; Thos. LATTA & Joshua RUSSELL, Marsh Creek; David LEE c/o John CAMPBELL; Jas. LOGUE, Chanceford; Issabella LONG, Chanceford; Wm. LOWDEN; James M'ALLISTER, Hopewell; Thomas M'ALLISTER, Hopewell; John M'ANULLY c/o Wm. BRADLEY, M'Allister's Town; George M'CAUSHLIN c/o John GREER, Merchant; John M'CAY, Fawn; Patrick M'CEAVER c/o A. TURNER; James M'CLAIN, Hatter, Hanover; Polly M'CLEARY, Gettysburgh; John or Thomas M'CLELLAN c/o Rev. A. DOBBINS; Alexander M'CLOSKY, Chanceford; Samuel M'CONAUGHY; John M'CULLOUGH; James or David M'GIBONEY; John M'GINLEY; Charles M'GONEGLE c/o Cunningham SAMPLE; Robert M'KINZEE, Tavern Keeper; Jas. M'KOWAN; Mary M'KOWAN c/o the Rev. DOBBINS; Wm. M'MAULEY, Chanceford; Neal M'MENEMIE; James M'NAUGHT, Marsh Creek; James M'NIGHT, Conowago; Jas. M'NIVAN, Marsh Creek; Charles M'NULTY, Mountjoy; Collin M'NUTT; Adley MATSON; Frederick METZGAR, Hanover; John MILLER c/o A. TURNER; Robert MILLER, Fawn; George MONTGOMERY; Daniel MOONY c/o Daniel GLASS; Dorothea MORTZEN c/o Rev. SCHROEDER, Hanover; Elenor MURPHY; John NEAL, Slate Ridge; John NELSON--Thomas NILSON c/o Andrew FINLEY, Hopewell; John NESBITT, Fawn Twp.; Wm. NEVITT, Warrington; James PATTERSON, Hammiltonsbann; Samuel PATTERSON, schoolmaster, Pine Creek; Samuel PATTERSON; Francis PLUNKERT, Conowago; Mary POLLOCK living with Saml. BOYD near Wright's Ferry; John RAMSEY c/o John GREER, Mercht; Reynolds RAMSEY, Gettysburgh; Ludwig REFENMILLER, Huntington c/o Mr. HARRIS; Bernard REILY c/o Charles W. PORTER; James ROSS c/o John CAMPBELL, Chanceford; Joseph RUSSELL, Marsh Creek; John SHARP, Esq., Dover; James SHIELDS c/o John KOCH, Wheelwright, Beaver St; John SHULTZ, Creitz Creek; Robert SMITH c/o Joshua RUSSELL; William SMITH, Junr., Berwick; Michael SPRENKLE, near Wolf's Tavern; Thomas STEEL, Slate Ridge; James STERRIT, Little Brittain; David STEWART, French Broad c/o Robert STEWART, Marsh Creek; James STEWART, Chanceford; John STEWART, Marsh Creek; Robert STEWART, Marsh Creek; Rowland STEWART, Chanceford; William STURGEON, Conowago; John TAGERT, Fawn; Joseph or Mathew THOMPSON, Conowago, Mountpleasant or Hammiltonsbann; Matthew THOMPSON, Middle Creek; Alexander TURNER, Chanceford; Brees VINCENT (B. SMITH) c/o Mr. BRINDLEY at the Canal; John VINCENT, Hatter; James WALKER, Tyrone; James WALTEN, Mercht; Wm. WATSON, c/o A. TURNER; John WILEY c/o A. TURNER; Daniel WILLIAMS, Senr., Monaughan; Peter WILLIAMSON, Mercht, Conowago; James WILSON, c/o A. TURNER; John WILSON, Rock Creek; John YOUNG, Carpenter, Hanover.

List of Letters remaining in the Post Office at York Town, Jan 1, 1797: John ALEXANDER; George ASPER; Wm. BARNS, Weaver; John BARRINGTON, Printer; James BEAN, Newbury Twp; Martin BINDER, Warrington Twp; John BITTINGER, near Abbot's Town; Wm. BLAIN c/o Robert BLAIN, near the Brogue; Mary BLANDRUM; Andrew BOYD, Marsh Creek; Robert BREWS; Samuel CALDWELL; Catharine CALHOON, Marsh Creek; John CAMPBELL, Chanceford Twp; Robert CATHER, near Gettysburgh; William CAVENAUGH; John CLARK, Farmer, near Hunters Town; Samuel COBEAN, Marsh Creek; James or Samuel COLWELL; Henry CONN, York; James CONN, Blacksmith; John CUMMINGS, near Peach Bottom; Eleanor DAVLIN(?) c/o James YOUNG, York; Michael DENISTON; Andrew DENNINGSTON; Andrew DIZART, March Creek; John DONNELL, Muddy Creek; John DONNELLY; James DORSIE, Chanceford Twp; Margaret DOUGHERTY c/o Capt. DOUGLASS; Patrick DOUGHERTY; William DOUGHERTY, Chanceford Twp; Robert DUNLAP; Christopher ELMBERT; Michael ELMBERT c/o John COLLINS; Thomas EWING, Marsh Creek; Henry FERGUSON; Richard FERGUSON, Carrol's Tract; James FIFE; James FITZIMONS c/o Samuel JAGO; John FITZIMONS c/o George BARD; James FLANAGEN, Chanceford; John FLEMMING c/o David AGNEW; John GALLAGHER;

Letters remaining at the York Post Office

Gawin GELESPY; Philip GERMAN, Merchant; Daniel GILDEA; John GILMORE; Hugh GORMAN c/o Col. WALKER; Samuel GRAHAM; Nancy GRIER; John HARDEN; Doct. Patrick HARRAH; John HENDERSON, Berwick Twp; Frederick HOKE; Alexander IRWIN, Gettysburgh; John JOHN c/o Adam BLAIR; Wm. or Babtist JOHNSTON; David JOURDAN; Jacob JULIUS, Dover Twp; Christian KELLER, Windsor Twp; George KERR; William KERR c/o Isaac DIERDORF; Peter KURTZ, Merchant York; John LILLY; Patrick LINCH, Senr. c/o Rev. PELLANCE; Nathaniel M'CLURE, Fawn Twp; John M'COLOUGH; James M'CUTCHIN; William M'DIVAT; Wm. M'FARLAND; Michael M'GILL, Fawn Twp; John or James M'MULLAN, Fawn Twp; John MAY, Monaughan Twp; Daniel MILL; Robert MILLER, Fawn Twp; Robert MOOR, Mountjoy Twp; Mary MORGAN c/o John VANCE; Adam MORRISON c/o Hugh MORRISON; Michael MORRISON, Hopewell Twp; John MULLAN, Shoemaker; Dorothea MUTZEN, Silver Run c/o Rev. SHROEDER; Thomas ORBISON; Wm. PANKER c/o John JACK; Nathan PATTERSON, Fawn Twp; William PATTERSON, Merchant Berlin; Jacob PAUP c/o Jacob SITLER; Wm. PICKEN, House Carpenter; Richard PLATT, near Wright's Ferry; William PORTER, Monaughan; William ROBINSON; Aron ROSS; Thomas SAUNDERS, near Hunter's Town; Robert SCOTT; William SMITH, Junr., Berwick Twp; Robert SPEERS, Marsh Creek; John STEWART c/o Rev. HENDERSON; William STEWART, Marsh Creek c/o the Rev. DOBBINS; Jacob STRICKLER, Creitz Creek; James TARBOT, House Carpenter; Joseph TAYLOR, Nicholsons Gap; Jas. THOMPSON, Paradise; Matthew THOMPSON; Wm. THOMPSON, Strabane; John TOMENY; Henry TYSON; William WALKUP; David WILEY, Hopewell; John WILEY.

List of Letters remaining in the Post Office at York Town, April 1, 1797: Thomas ADAMS, Cutler; George ASPER; George BARD; Samuel BARNHILL; William BARNS; Rezin CASH; Margaret DAUGHERTY c/o Capt. DOUGLASS; Joseph DELINGER; Nicholas ENDERS, Paradise Twp; Samuel FISHER, Newbury Twp; Benedict FOSTER, Codorus Twp; James GORMLEY; Jacob HAY, Esq.; Valentine HOESLICH; John JOHN, Dover Twp; Thomas KELLY; William KING c/o Abraham FLORY, Hellam Twp; Wm. C'CALVEY, Hopewell Twp; Alexander M'CONNELL, Merchant; Samuel M'CULLOUGH; Thomas M'INTIRE c/o Wm. DOUGHERTY, Chanceford; Thomas M'KEE; Stephen M'KUNE c/o Wm. ROSS, Warrington Twp; Ann M'MULLEN, widow c/o Wm. MITCHELL, Esq.; Samuel NELSON, Monaughan Twp; Martin O'DONNELL; John PARRINGTON; Samuel REAVER at Archibald CAMPBELL's, M'Call's Ferry; Bernard SLOUGH, 6 miles from York; Andrew SMITH, Senr. near York; Benjamin SMYTH c/o Peter BOSS, Merchant; Mrs. Elizabeth SNIDER c/o Jacob UPP; Thomas SPROUL; George SWEENY, Wright's Ferry; John THEAKER, Chanceford Twp; John WILEY c/o Major WILEY, Hopewell; Wm. WILSON, alias Burgess RUSSELL; Wm. WRIGHT, Hatter, York.

List of Letters remaining in the Post Office at York Town, July 1, 1797: Margeret ANDERSON c/o John GREER, Merchant, York Borough; James BAILEY, Mercht., Bailey's Mills c/o ditto; Thomas BROWN c/o George JOYCE, Monallan Twp; Conrad BRUBAKER, ten miles from York; Ebenezer BUCK; Rev. John CAMPBELL, York; John CAMPBELL, Chanceford Twp; Col. Matthew DILL; Andrew DINSMORE, Fawn Twp; Robert DUNKIN, Chanceford Twp; Andrew DUNLAP c/o Charles Wm. PORTER; Adam EWING c/o George IRWIN; John FITZIMONS c/o George BEARD; Aaron FOSTER c/o Jacob UPP; Valentine FOURNEY, Manheim Twp; Jacob HAHN, Merchant, York; Mr. HARTWICK, Musick Master, York; Matthew KILGORE, Chanceford Twp; John LEE, Coppersmith, York; Alexander M'CONNELL, Merchant, M'Connell's Town; James M'GAUGHY c/o John EDIE, Esq; John M'KEAVER; Rose M'NUTT; Robert M'WROTH, York; John MAGOSSIN c/o George LASHELIS; Daniel MILLER; Wm. NEVITT or George ALEXANDER; Solomon NUNEMAKER, Shrewbury Twp; Samuel OSBURN, Strabane Twp; Thomas PHARAH; Elizabeth PORTER, Sulpher Springs; Samuel ROBERTS, Esq.; Charles SHUMAN; Richard SMITH c/o Wm. SMITH,

APPENDIX B: Letters remaining at the Post Office (York Advertiser)

Esq; William SMITH, Berwick Twp; John or Wm. STANLEY; James TEMPLETON, Fawn Twp; Philip WHITERMEYER; Daniel WILLIAMS, Monaghan Twp; James WILSON c/o Michael GRAYBILL; Selah WOODRUFF c/o John MURPHY, Mountpleasant Twp; James WRIGHT, Warrington Twp.

A List of Letters remaining in the Post Office at York Town, Oct 1, 1797: John BAILY; Sarah BALLY, Monaghan Twpp; Michael BEAR, Marsh Creek; Robert BELL c/o Gawin SCOTT; Malcom BOGLE c/o Rev. A. DOBBIN or John FORSYTH; Solomon or Daniel BOVSER(?), Manheim Twp; John BOWLIN or BOWEN; Thomas BRADLEY, Monallen Twp; Christian BRENNEMAN, Codorus Twp; Joseph BROWN c/o Rev. A. DOBBIN; Mary CHAPMAN, near Bollinger's Mill; Rev. Rezin CATH; Robert Johnston CHESTER, Berlin; James CINKAID; James CLARK c/o Messrs. HARRIS & DONALDSON; James COCHRA, Conewago Canal; Daniel COLLINS; Hugh CRISTEN, Marsh Creek; John DAVIDSON, Groom to the Horse Governors; James DERAUGH, Fawn Twp; Dennis DEVENY, Mason, Shrewsbury Twp; William DEVITT; Catharine DONAN, Hopewell Twp; John DONNEL, Fawn Twp; Margaret DOUGHERTY c/o Capt. DOUGLASS; Thomas DUNKIN; Adam EWING c/o Mr. IRWIN; Martha the widow of John FINDLEY c/o Baltzer SPANGLER; William FINDLEY, M'Call's Ferry; James FLANAGEN, Chanceford Twp; John FORSYTH; JOHN FOSTER, Marsh Creek; Sinclair GIBSON; William GIBSON; Daniel GLASS, Warrington Twp; John GORDAN, Hopewell Twp; Thomas GORDAN, Taylor, c/o James GORDAN, Peach Bottom; Hugh GORMAN, Tyrone Twp; Thomas GRAY, Monaghan Twp; Samuel GRAHAM; John GREER, Monallen Twp; Joseph HAMILTON c/o John LAIRD, Brogue Tavern; William HANLIN, Little Brittain; John HENDERSON, Marsh Creek settlement by Dr. Patrick HARRAH; John HENDERSON c/o Charles Wm. PORTER; John HOLMES; John IDLE, Windsor Twp; Jane JOHNSTON c/o Capt. EDGAR; Capt. John JOHNSTON, York Springs; Thomas JOHNSTON and John JOHNSTON, near Peach Bottom Ferry; Thomas JOHNSTON; James JORDAN; Darby KANE; Dr. William KERR; Robert KIDD, Franklin Twp; Wm. KING; Thomas KIRKWOOD; Andrew KREMER, Tanner, York; James LAIRD, Chanceford; Betty LOGAN; Samuel M'CONAUGHY; Polly M'CORLY; Neil M'CORMICK; James M'CULLY; David M'GIBBONY; James M'GIBBONY, Chanceford Twp; Robert M'HENRY c/o George BAXTER; Jane M'KAUGHEN; Catharine M'KENDRIE c/o John FORSYTH; William M'KINNEY c/o Joseph REED, Chanceford Twp; Catharine M'LAUGHLEN c/o John FORSYTH; John MAGOFFIN (MAGOSSI?) c/o George LASHELLS; William MARCHLAND c/o Gawin SCOTT; Benjamin MARSHALL; William MILEHAM, Newbury Twp; James MILLER, Fawn Twp; William MITCHELL, Esq. Monaghan; Robert MOOR, Mountjoy Twp; Wode MORRISON; John MULLEN, Shoemaker; Francis MURRAY c/o Gawin SCOTT; George NAILOR; John NEISBET, Fawn Twp; Robert NELSON; Thomas NELSON c/o Andrew FINDLEY; Nathen PATTERSON, Fawn Twp; John PATTON, Mountpleasant Twp; William PORTER, Monaghan Twp; Thomas PROCTOR; Mrs. Wall REDEN; Wm. ROSS, Esq., Chanceford Twp; Joshua RUSSELL, Marsh Creek; Robert SHANKLIN; Messrs. SITLER & DEHOFF; Alexander SMART; Wm. SMITH, Junr. Berwick Twp; Thomas SMULLEN; James SPEAR; Robert STEWART, Rock Creek; Sharlot STOUGH, Dover Twp; Patt TEGART, Tyrone Twp; John THEAKER, Chanceford Twp; Joseph WATSON and John WATSON, Conewago Canal; David WEILEY; Isaac WILLIAMS, Chanceford Twp c/o Jacob UPP; Samuel WILSON; Wm. WILSON, Chanceford; Daniel WIRE; James YOUR c/o Charles Wm. PORTER.

List of Letters remaining in the Post Office at York Town, Jan 1, 1798: John AGNEW, Senr., Marsh Creek; John ALEXANDER: James ANDERSON; John BOWER; Catharine BOYD, Warrington Twp; Samuel BOYLE, Schoolmaster; Joseph BROWN, Strabane twp; James BUCKHANNEN; Benjamin BUCKWALKER; John BUSH; James & Samuel CALDWELEL; Rev. Thomas CAMEN; Capt. Hugh CAMPBELL; John CAMPBELL, Meadow place, James CONN, Blacksmith; Thomas COURTNEY; James DAVISON, Fawn; Garret DEMAREE, Mountpleasant; Robert DINSMORE; William EDGAR, Hopewell

Letters remaining at the York Post Office

Twp; John, David or William FINLEY; John FITZIMONS; John FULTON, Manallan c/o George IRWIN; Alexr. GILBRAITH, Fawn; William GILBRAITH; Hector GILES; Charles GLENN; David GORDAN; Andrew GORMLEY c/o Andrew DINSMORE; George GREER; Sarabel HALBISON, Butts town; Peter HARKIN c/o James BRINLEY at the Canal; Mary HERRON, Muddy-creek; Robert HOLMES, Taylor; John JOHNSTEN; Saml. KEAVIN, Chanceford; John KELLY, Chanceford; John LAFERTY; Rev. James LAIRD; Isaiah LAMBARN; Conrad LAUB, Esq.; John LEATHER; John LESHIE; Conrad LONGEDORN; James and Thomas M'ALLISTER c/o Alexr. Turner, Esq.; Alexr. M'CLELLAN c/o Thos. GORLEY; William M'COLDEN; Thos. M'COMBS; John M'CORMICK; Hugh M'DILL; Hugh M'FADDEN, Fawn; Daniel M'GLAUGHLIN; James M'KISON; James M'MUNN, Bricklayer; Joseph M'NEELY; Jas. M'NIVAN; James M'NUTT, Windsor; James M'NUTT, Junr.; Capt. Wm. MACKEY; Hyman MARKS, Merchant; Robert MARSHALL, Marsh-creek; Jas. MASSEN; Margaret MEE c/o Jas. PEDAN; Dorothy MILLER, Mountpleasant; Thomas MOFFET, M'Calls Ferry; Laurence MONTSORT; Widow MOOR, Mountjoy twp; Robt. MOOR, Mountjoy; George MYERS, York; Jas. MURPHY; John NELSON c/o A. TURNER; Samuel NELSON; Thomas NELSON c/o Andrew PINDLEY; William NEVITT, Warrington; George OYSTER, Gunsmith; Jos. REBEAU, Distiller; Andrew RICHEY, Fawn; Samuel ROSEBURGH, Hopewell; Wm. ROSS, Esq., Chanceford; Jos. RUSSELL; George SHEFFEL, John SHEPHARD; Jacob SITLER, York; Wm. SMITH, Junr.; John SMOCK; Thomas SMULLEN; Henry SPEAKER c/o Michael SCHMYSER; John SPEER; David SPICKART; John SPROWL; John STEEL; Thomas STEEL; George STICKEL in Ross's town; Robert STUART; Edward TAYLOR, Newbury Twp; Patrick TEGART; John THEAKER, Senr., Chanceford; George TODD; Jacob TRITT: James TURNER c/o Alexr. TURNER, Esq.; Elihu UNDERWOOD, Esq.; John WILEY, Chanceford Twp; Samuel WILSON; John WIREMAN.

A List of Letters remaining in the Post Office, York Town, April 1, 1798: John ANDREW, Clerk, at the spring-forge; John ANDREWS, Chanceford; John BAILEY; William BAILEY; Thomas BALDWIN, Monallan; Benjamin BASSET; Wm. BEACKUMP; Maj. Jno. BONER, Huntingdon; Richard BULL; James CAPOOT; Christopher CARBAUGH; John CELLON, Taylor; Jas. COCHRAN; Mary COLCLASER, living with George LAUX; Wm. CROSS; John DALLYMORE; Mathias DETTOR; Daniel DIEHL; Matthew DILL, Andrew DINSMORE; Robert DINSMORE; Robt. DOUGLASS; Miss Issabella DUNERLY; James FAKENDER; John FALKER, Tanner; James FALLOW; Sinclair GIBSON; Joseph GLANCEY, Newbury; Peter GONTNER, Hatter; James GRANT; Robert HAMILTON; Ludwick HANAWOULD; Samuel HARPER; Wm. HAYS; John HEAGY, Mountjoy; Jacob HERMAN; Wm. HOCY; James HUGHY; Geo. HUTZ; Samuel ICHELBERGER; Joshua ISAAC; Eliaser JOHN; George KANN; Helser KROMER, Codorus; John KUNTZ; Christian LEAVY; Andrew LITTLE, Mountjoy; John LITTLE; James M'ALLISTER; Nancy M'CUSLOW(?); Patrick M'FARLAND; James M'GRIFF; Stephen M'KAIN; Neal M'NULTY; Susanna MILLER; William MOBENY; John NEIL; Jacob NEWCOMER; Samuel NELSON; Mrs. NICHOLSON; Susanna PATTERSON; Francis PETTIT; Henry PLATT; Randle RAMSEY; Andrew RASMUSEN, Genesee river; John ROBERTSON; Samuel ROBESON; Widow ROPE, near Poplar run; Samuel ROSEBURG; William ROSS, Warrington; Mr. SHINDLE; Jacob SMITH; Patrick SMITH; John SPENCE; Thomas STEEL; Robert STEWART; Joseph SUMMERSETT at Mr. JAGO's Forge; John THEAKER; William THOMPSON, Berwick; Thomas THORNBURGH; Martin TSHUTY; Alexander WALLACE; John WHEEMS, Mountjoy; Peter WOLF, Saddler.

List of Letters Remaining at the Post Office at York Town, July 1, 1798: Matthew ADAMS, Chanceford Twp; Thomas ADAMS; James ANDERSON, Fawn twp; George BAXTER; Solomon BEALS, Huntington; William BEATY, near Peach Bottom; Thomas BLAKE, Reading; Christian BRENNEMAN, Codorus c/o John ROTHROCK; Marla BURRES; John CAMPBELL, Meadow Place; Margaret CASSAT; John CLARK,

APPENDIX B: Letters remaining at the Post Office (York Advertiser)

Menallen; Alexander COCHRAN; Daniel COMINGORE; Francis COOPER, Fawn; Thomas COOPER, near Peach Bottom; Robert CUNINGHAM; Robert DUNN; Polly FULTON, Fawn twp; James GIBSON, Hopewell; John GILMORE, Warrington; Thomas GLEN, Fawn; William HENRY or Charles Wm. PORTER, near M'Call's Ferry; Jacob HERMAN; Jonothan HEZLET; David HOOVER, Berwick; Andrew IRWIN, Strabane; John JOHN, Dover; Joseph JOHN; Samuel JOHNSON, Windsor; George KANN, Dover; Matthew KILLGORE; Capt. George LASHELLS; Conrad LAUB, Esq.; Eli LEWIS; Andrew LITTLE; Christian LONG; James LOQUE; Jonathon LUTES; William M'CALLA, Chanceford; William M'CALVEY c/o Rev. CATHCART; Andrew M'ELVAIN, Berwick; Michael M'GILL c/o Jacob GIBSAON, Esq.; Sarah M'MILLAN; William MAY; James MAHARY, Codorus Forge; Rosanna MILLER; William MORROW, Hopewell; Hester NESBIT, Mountpleasant twp; Mr. PETICOLAS, Limner; William PICKAN; Gabrial POTERFIELD c/o Mathew CLARK; James RAMSEY, Peach Bottom; Andw. RASMUSSEN; Samuel ROBERTS; Cunningham SAMPLE, near Peach Bottom; John SAMPLE, do.; John SHITTER; Jacob SITLER; Rev. John SLEMONS; Sally SLEMONS; Philip SMITH; Robert SMITH, Hopewell c/o George BAXTER; James SPEERS, Chanceford; Thomas STEEL; Robert STEWART; Robert TATE; Eliza TUCKER; James WALKER, near Hunterstown; George WEIRS; James WILLETS c/o Joseph GLANCEY; Peter WILLIAMSON, Mountpleasant; Thomas WILSON; Sarah WOODRUFF, Mountpleasant; Jacob WORLEY, Junr.; John YOUNG c/o William ROSS, Warrington.

List of Letters Remaining at athe Post Office at York Town, Oct 1, 1798: Patrick ALLISON; George ASPER; Wm. ATKINS, Chanceford Twp; George BAXTER; Robert BELL; Philip BIGLEY; John BYERS; John CAMPBELL, Meadow Place; James CAPOOT, Taylor; Col. James CHAMBERLAIN; William CUMMINGS, Peach Bottom; Lambert DARLAND; Thomas DINSMORE; William DOUGHERTY; John DOUGLAS; Thomas DUNCAN; Philip EBERMAN, Tinman; James EWING, Esq.; Robert FIFE c/o Adam HENDRIX; the Rev. J. GOERING; Peter GRANT; Peter GRUBB; Susanna HAMBLETON, near the Blue Ball; Charles HANIE, Doct.; Patrick HARRAH; Samuel JAGO, Esq.; Thomas JOHNSTON; William KERR; Matthew KILLGORE; William KIRKPATRICK; John KITZMILLER;Thomas LATTA; Conrad LAUB, Esq; John LEATHERM; Nathaniel LEVY; Mr. LONG; William M'CALLA; James M'CANLESS c/o John GREER; Rowly M'CORLY; Samuel M'GOWAN; Robert M'ILHENY; William M'KINNEY; Anne M'MULLEN; Susannah MILLER; Andrew MOYER; George NAILON; James NELSON; Joseph NELSON c/o Andrew JOHNSTON, Esq.; Thomas NELSON; William NEVITT; William NEWINIAH; John NIELL; Phelim O'RORKE; George PALTSEIR; Mr. PETICOLAS; Alexander RAMSEY; Nathaniel REED; James RINGLAND; John ROGERS; Jacob SADLER; Gawin SCOTT; John SCOTT, Esq.; John SHALES; Edward SHOEMAKER; James SPEER; Samuel SMITH; William SMITH; Robert SQUIBB; John George STERY; Robert STEWART; Philip I. STOUT; Henry SUMMERS; Thomas TAYLOR; Paul THOMPSON; Jacob UPDEGRAFF, John VANDIKE; George WEIRS; David WILSON, Merchant; Thomas or Wm. WILSON, near the Brogue; William WILSON; Barney WINTER; John YOUNG.

APPENDIX C: Letters remaining at the Post Office (York Recorder)

Letters Remaining at the York Post Office, January 1800: Thomas ACKNEY; Joseph ANDERSON, Warrington; Thomas ANDREW c/o Charles William PORTER; Thomas ARMSTRONG, Chanceford Twp; John ASH; John AUSTIN; James BARR c/o Col. BRATTON; Nicholas BEMHART, York; Mr. BERGENHIMER, wheelwright, Berlin; Conrad BEVERSIME (?); Grace BLADING at James KELLY's Esq.; Thomas BORLAND c/o Tempest TUCKER; William BRENAND, Carroll's Tract; Christian BRENNEMAN c/o John ROTHROCK; Alexander BROWN; James BUCKHANNON (?) of Marsh Creek; Philip BYERLY in York gaol; Daniel CADEAYNE, York; Archibald CAMPBELL c/o Charles William PORTER; John CAMPBELL, Gen. Thomas CAMPBELL; Meadow-place; Jean CANADY; David CANDLER; John & William COULTER c/o William MORRISONM; John COZINE, Conewago; George CUMMINGS c/o William NESS; Thomas CUNNINGHAM c/o Andrew DINSMORE; William DELAP or William DUNLAP; Samuel DINSMORE c/o Andrew DINSMORE; Mrs. DITTMAN; Ester DOLL c/o William MC CINNEY, York; John DOUGHERTY c/o Matthew DILL; David DRENNER near Wright's Ferry; John ELCOCK; George FAHNESTOCK, Berlin c/o Jacob HAY, Esq.; Casper FISHER; James FULTON, paper-maker from East Nottingham, now at York;   Isaac GARRETSON, York; Mawrice GRAHAM c/o Rev. CATHCART; Lorentz HEINDEL, Hopewell Twp.; Adam HOOVER of Dover; Frederick HORN of York; Thomas HYNDMAN c/o Joseph REED; James JORDAN of Middle-creek; Mrs. LEE, Hopewell Twp.; John LUSK, Chanceford Twp; William M'ALLEY, Chanceford Twp.; Patrick M'BRIDE; Mary M'KELVY near York; Roley M'ORLEY, Fawn Twp; Barnabas M'SHERRY of Marsh Creek; Samuel MARKLY c/o Philip WALTEMEYER; Simon MINICH near York; Michael MOORE at present at or near Mr. BEARD's tavern, York; John MORRISON of Hellam Twp., Jacob NEWCOMER of Manchester Twp.; Andrew ORRACK; James PEDAN; Ludwick POPE, Shrewsbury Twp.; William PORTER c/o Thomas BLACK, Esq.; Andrew PROUDFOOT, Hopewell Twp; Patrick RUSSEL c/o Henry HULL, Reading Twp; John SAMPLE, Peach-bottom; James SCOTT c/o Michael KLINEFELTER, York; Jean SCOTT c/o Rev. DOBBINS; Robert SCOTT;, Nicholas Gap; Joseph SIDES, Shrewsbury Twp; Rev. SLEMONS near M'Call's Ferry; Anthony SLOAN, Fawn Twp.; Joseph SMITH c/o C. W. PORTER; Richard SMITH, Hopewell Twp.; Samuel SMITH, Chanceford Twp; William SMITH, Schoolmaster c/o A. TURNER, Esq.; John STEWART, near Rock-creek; John STOUFFER; Alexander TURNER, Esq.; Cornelius VANSANT; Henry WAGGONER, Potter, York; John WAGGONER c/o John HERSH, innkeeper; George WEARS; James WILLIAMSON c/o C. W. PORTER; Samuel WILSON, Marsh-creek settlement; William WILSON or Thomas WILSON near the Brogue. James YEWART, Jr. c/o W. C. PORTER; Frederick ZORGER of York.

List of Letters remaining at the Post Office at York April 1, 1800. Where no place of residence is mentioned, York County is intended. William ATKINS, Chanceford Twp; Miss Kitty ANTTONE(?); Stephen BEGLEY; Adam BLOUNT; Benjamin BRINKERHOFF, Strabane Twp; James CAMPBELL c/o James YOUNG; John CAMPBELL, Meadow Place; Casper CARVER; William CHIFAM(?) c/o George SPANGLER, Jr.; Nathaniel CLARK, Jr.; William or Moses CREAGE; David a son of Robert CUNNINGHAM; William CUNNINGHAM c/o C. William PORTER; Eleanor DAVILN (?) c/o James YOUNG; William DOUGLASS, Chanceford Twp; Patrick DRAIN; Catharine DUAN (?); Margaret DUNN; Mary DUGAN; John EGNEW; John ELCOCK, Warrington Twp; Thomas FEILY, Menallan; Henry FINK, Berwicks; Hoppy FITCHERTY; Robert FITE c/o Andrew HENDRIX; Philip FRASKENBERGER, Newbury; John FULTON c/o ----- FAHNESTOCK, Berlin; William GALLAGHER c/o John GREER, merchant; George GRIER c/o Johan RUSSELL; Conrad GUIGER, Windsor; Henry HAMM c/o Adam HENDRIX; Samuel HARPER, Hopewell; Elizabeth HENDRICKS c/o Joseph WORLEY; Peter HOKE near York; Frederick HOOBER, Man ---; John HORN; Rebecca HOSE (HOFE?); Oley HUBER; Christopher IRWIN, Muddy Creek; Dr. Thomas JAMESON; Thomas JOHNSTON; Sarah KENSEY; Hugh KERR; John KLEBET (?); Hugh LAIRD c/o Alexander TURNER; Ann LASSLEY (?), Conewago; William LAWSON,

APPENDIX C: Letters remaining at the Post Office (York Recorder)

Hopewell; John LEITNER, mason; Eli LEWIS; Stephen M'CANN, near Ross's Town; James M'CARTER; John M'CLEERY, Hopewell; John M'CLOSKEY; John M'ELHENY, Hunterstown; Patrick M'KEEVER; Anthony M'LAUGHLIN; James M'LUCAS; Dennis M'PHADEN, Newbury; Patrick M'VENAN; Robert MARSHALL, Franklin; Thomas MILLER; John MOSTMON (?); John OBLENNS (?), Reading Twp; George PACKER, Warrington; John PORTER, Jr., Mau---; Andrew PROUDFOOT, Hopewell; Thomas ROBERTSON; James SCOTT; William SCOTT, Esq., Hunter's Town; Andrew SMITH; Peter SMITH; William SMITH, Esq., Hopewell; Peter SNIDER, Huntington; Christopher STEHR(?); John THOMAS; Robert WALLACE; James WALTON, Fawn; Catherine WILHELM, near Anderson's Ferry; James WRIGHT.

Letters remaining at York P.O., July 1800: John ANDERSON; Martin ARMSTRONG, Chanceford twp; John BALDWIN, Hopewell twp; George BARD, York twp; John BEITZEL, Dover twp; Andrew BROWN, Marsh creek; Charles CAMERON, Maytown; Col. Thomas CAMPBELL; John CAMPBELL; William CHISAM; John COLLINS, Hopewell; Alexander COOPER; Moses DAVIS, Dover twp; John DELANY; Thomas DICK, Marsh Creek; Elizabeth DOBBIN; Mr. DUNNER; George ENSLEY; Gen. James EWING; Jacob FINK; Samuel FISHER; James FULTON, Chanceford; Daniel GLASS, Warrington; Thomas GLENN, Fawn; John GORDON, Hopewell; Thomas GROVE, York Barrons; Edward HART, Huntington twp; George HARTZELL, Menallen twp; Leonard HATTON; John HENDERSON, Windsor twp; John HENDERSON, Windsor twp; Adam HENDRIX; Philip HERING, Dover twp; Jacob HERWICK; Mr. HONSENST; Henry HOUSHOLDER; Thomas HUNT, care of Adam HENDRIX; Michael KIMMEL, 12 miles from York; Henry KUSTER; Mrs. LIVINGSTON; Thomas M'CARLAND, Menallen twp; Thomas M'CASHLEN, Menallan twp; James M'CLEARY, Codorus Forge; Charles M'GONABLE, Fawn twp; James M'KNIGHT, Conewago creek; Thomas MAJOR, near Slate Ridge; Israel MEREDITH, Newbury twp; John MILLER, 4 miles from York; James MILLIKEN, care of John RIPPEY; Alexander MORRISON; Solomon MYERS; Col. Samuel NELSON, Monaghan twp; Widow PATTERSON, near Oxford; James PEDAN, Chanceford twp; James PEDAN, junr., care of Benjamin PEDAN; Henry PETERMAN, Windsor twp; John PORTER, junr, Monaghan twp; James RAMSAY, Peach-bottom Ferry; James ROBINSON, Chanceford twp; William ROSS, care of Jacob UPP; Peggy SCOTT; Gawin SCOTT, Chanceford twp; William SCOTT, Chanceford twp; Gabriel SMITH, merchant, Berlin; George SMITH, Monsieur STAINSLAS, Roman CHAPPELL; Barnet SPANGLER; Robert STEWART, senr.; Christopher STOEHR; Sharlotta STOUCH, Dover twp; Samuel STRAIN, Chanceford twp; John STRECHER, junr., Warrington twp; John TAYLOR, York; Juliana TREET; Alexander TURNER, merchant; George WAGGONER; Mary WAY, at George BARD's; Henry WOLF, 6 miles from York; William YOUNG; Frederick YOUSE - Jacob SPANGLER, P.M.;

Letters at P.O. York, Oct 1800: Robert ALEXANDER; George BARD, near York; Robert BARRUN; George BAXTER; Elijah BERHILL; Arnold BERLIN; William BEVERS, York; Andrew BILMEYER, esq. York; Alexander BLAIR; Alexander BLAIR, otherwise Hugh GLASGOW, esq.; Michael BLESSING, Hellam twp; Christopher BOOTH, Chanceford; Michael BOSSERMAN, Marsh Creek; Samuel BOWMAN; Samuel BOYD, Chanceford twp; Anna BOYERIN, York; William BRUCE, Chanceford; Dr. John BURGOIN; John BURNS, Marsh creek; Mary CALHOON, York; Mrs. Jean CALWELL, care of Robert M'CALL; Daniel CAMERON, care of Charles Wm. PORTER; Alexander CAMOGHAM, Marsh Creek; Archibald CAMPBELL, care of Charles Wm. PORTER; Thomas CAMPBELL, care of John SMALL; John or James CAMPBELL, near the Brogue; John CHALMERS, York Springs; William CHISAM, care of George SPANGLER; Hugh CHRISTIAN, Marsh creek; George CONN, York; Thomas COOK, a black man; James COOPER, near the slate Ridge; William COULTER, Chanceford; William CRAIG; Joseph CUNNINGHAM; Moses DAVIS; Thomas DEVEROLL, shear maker;

154

Letters remaining at the York Post Office

Adam DIEHL, Hopewell twp; William DONNEL; Frederick DOSEH; Patrick DOUGHERTY; John DOUGLAS, care of the Rev CLARKSON; James DRIVER, York; William EDMUNDSON, Warrington; Maria EHRISMAN, near Hubley's tavern; John ELCOOK, Warrington; John ERNST, Manheim twp; James FALLOW, Chanceford; James FERGUSON; Jacob FICKES, Huntington; Andrew FINLEY, Hopewell; John FULLERTON, merchant, Mount Pleasant; James FULTON; Michael FUNK, at Hinkles Mill; Hugh GALLAGHER, Conewago; John GALLOR, shoemaker, York; George GARDNER, near Wright's Ferry; Jacob GARDNER, York; Casper GREGOR, Abbetts-Town; Jean HAMILTON; John HARGIN, Chanceford; Samuel HARPER, Hopewell twp; Joseph HAVIT, Menallen; James HELMS, care of Capt. STAKE; George HENRY, near the Brogue tavern; Thomas HICKWOOD, Chanceford; William HIME; Christopher IRWIN, Muddy creek; Benjamin JENNINGS, Newbury; Thomas JOHNSTON; George JONES, care of William WEAKLY, Round Hill; Henry P. KELLER; John KELLY, care of James KELLY, esq.; Robert KIDD, Franklin twp; Christian KING, near Berlin; Col. John KING; Mary KING, care of Joseph REED, Chanceford; Samuel KING, care of Joseph REED, Chanceford; John KNOX, care of James YOUNG; William LAWSON, care of Joseph REED; Eli LEWIS, Newbury; Joseph LILLY; Robert LINSEY, Chanceford; Jacob LISLER, care of Conrad LAUB; James LOGUE, care of Joseph REED; Edward LOVE; William M'AULEY, Chanceford; James M'CARTNEY; James and William M'CARTNEY; James M'CAWN; Moses M'CLURE; Neal M'CORMICK; John M'COSKER, care of Gotlieb ZEIGLE; James M'ELROY, lately from Phila.; Henry M'GEE; Ketrin M'GLAUGHLIN; Margaret M'GLAUGHLIN, care of Col. M'CLAIN; John M'GUFFIN, care of George LASHELLS; James M'HENRY, Mountjoy; Andrew M'ILVAIN, Distiller; William M'KELVY, Hopewell; James M'NAUGHT, Great Conewago; James M'NAUGHT, Marsh creek; Neal and John M'NULTY, care of Andrew WARRICK, Hopewell; John M'OWEN, care of William ANDERSON; William M'SHERRY, Marsh creek; Joseph MARSH, near Lisben; Robert MARSHALL, Franklin; William MARTIN; James MATEER, Newbury; Hugh McCUTCHEON; Jacob MILLER, York; John MITCHELL, Menaghan; James MITCHELL, Monaghan; William MORRISON, Chanceford; Michael MORRISON, Hopewell; William MURCHLAND, care of Gawin SCOTT; Joseph MURPHY; Joseph MURPHY, Chanceford; James NAILOR; Mathew NELSON, near Turner's mill; John NESBIT, Fawn twp; William OLIVER, Mount hope; Robert ORR, care of William M'AULEY; John PAGOT, York; James PARKS, Berlin; James PIKE, at the Sulpher Springs; Jeremiah RANKIN; Hugh REED, Menallen; Michael RITTER, shoemaker; Joshua RUSSELL; James SCOTT, care of Alexander TURNER; James SHIRKEY, Marsh creek; Mr. SHORT of Alegheny, now at York; John SINCLAIR, Sulpher Springs; Andrew SMITH, Jun.; James SMITH; Joseph SMITH, Chanceford; Margaret SMITH, care of George BAXTER; Patrick SMITH, near Peach bottom; Samuel SMITH, care of Joseph REED; William SMITH; William SMITH, care of Joseph REED; William SNODGRASS, Peach bottom; Peter SPRENKLE at the oil mill; Christopher STAIR, potter, York; Monsieur STANISLOS, at the Roman Chappel; Robert STEWART, care of Joshua RUSSELL; John STEWART, Marsh creek; William STEWART, Schoolmaster; Robert STEWART, schoolmaster, Chanceford; James STREIN, Fawn twp; George THOMPSON, Marsh creek; John THOMPSON, sulpher springs; Robert THOMPSON, York; Alexander TURNER; Philip WALTEMYER; William WEAKLY, near the Round Hill; Jacob WELSH, York; Leonard WESTHAFFER (?), near York; John WHITE, Monallan twp.; Simon WHITMYER; Jesse WICKERSHAM, Newbury; Isabbella WILSON, care of Alexander TURNER; James WILSON, care of Alexander

APPENDIX C: Letters remaining at the Post Office (York Recorder)

TURNER; Andrew WILSON, care of Andrew M'ILVAIN; John WILSON, Dogwood run; Marmaduke WILSON, Marsh creek; Barney WINTER, Monshan; Mary WORLEY, York - Jacob SPANGLER, P.M.

INDEX (to the paragraph number)

--- John 138
--- William 378
ABBET Thomas 271
ABBETT Thomas 391
ABBOT Edward 286, 298
ABBOTT Thomas 381
ABERCROMBIE James 79
ABERCRUMBIE James 61
ABERNATHY Jean 179; John 179
ABRAHAM Benjamin 16
ABRAM Enoch 70
ACHESON David 337, 339
ADAIR James 139
ADAM 315
ADAMS David 176; Dr. 55, 107; John 123; John C. 154; Levi 376; Matthew 139; Rev Dr. 57; Thomas 206, 306, 352, 367; William 176, 371
AGNEW James 390; John 10; Samuel 139
AIKENS James 335
ALBERT Andrew 356; Jacob 356; John 321; Lorentz 356
ALBRIGHT George 415; Philip 376, 415
ALEXANDER Isabella 42; John 14, 139; Robert 390; Thomas 269; William 49, 118, 131, 159, 182, 187, 202, 210, 403
ALLBRIGHT George 396, 400; Henry 400; Philip 396, 400
ALLEN James 253, 329; John 345; Thomas 345
ALLISON Mathew 60, 216; Robert 51
ALTER David 86; Jacob 9, 26, 115, 182, 218
ALTIC Michael 390
AMBLER John 82
AMER Joseph 345
ANDERSON Andrew 290, 321; Benjamin 132; George 60; Graham 138; James 153, 195, 299; John 48, 129, 239, 290, 321; Joseph 55, 160, 206; Mary 321; William 390, 422
ANDREW Ludwick 148
ANDREWS Humphrey 390
ANGNEY Isaac 145, 171
ARMOR Thomas 57, 320, 321, 356; William 79, 91
ARMSTRONG George 169, 206; Henry 335; Isaac 415; James 10, 63, 129, 151, 182, 389, 390; John 97, 158, 396; Joseph 30, 67; Rebecca 97; Robert 1, 13, 222
ARNDT John 285
ARNOLD Peter 325, 326

ARTHUR J. 149; John 3, 12, 16, 59, 63, 145, 155
ASHBOOK James 418
ASHER Anthony 133
ASHTON Mary 415; William 370
ASMORE John 391
ASPEN Philip 123
ATCHISON John 129
AULENBACH Nicholas 370
AULT Adam 326; Henry 265
AYMES John 356
AYRS David 299

BACHE Benjamin Franklin 372; Mrs. 372
BACHMAN David 356; Eve Margaret 356; Frederick 390; George 181
BACONAIR Lewis 350
BACONAIS Mr. 110
BAER John 345
BAGER Frederick 381
BAHN Adam 402
BAILEY Francis 302; Major 389; Robert 302; William 248, 388
BAILY Jacob 383; William 367
BAIRD James 123, 146
BAITMAN William 414
BAKER Catharine 70, 308; Hilary 53; John 118; Matthias 428; Philip 46, 56, 117, 118
BALDWIN Thomas 278
BALSBAUGH George 188
BALTY David 389
BAPD Joseph 279
BARBER John 84, 92; William 332, 416
BARCLAY Robert 26
BARD George 256, 298, 332, 381, 402
BARDT Philip 416
BARE John 390
BARKLEY Robert 204
BARNERD James 340; Mary 340
BARNHIZEL Jacob 53; John 53; Samuel 53
BARNITZ Captain 404; Daniel 280, 286; George 423; Jacob 308, 318, 335, 345, 356, 370, 390, 402, 415
BARR Alexander 126; John 175; Robert 140; William 111, 127
BARRICKSTRESSER Jacob 206
BARTHOLOMAY Peter 138
BARTON William 106
BARUCH 355
BASKINS Mitchell 85; William 169
BASZLER John 51
BATTORFF Martin 367
BATTORSS Martin 367

INDEX (to the paragraph number)

BAUGHER Frederick 298, 384
BAUMGARTNER Christian 350
BAXTER George 408
BAYER Margaret 356
BAYLY John 400, 430; Samuel 303; Thomas 430; William 303
BEAL Thomas 80
BEALE Thomas 93
BEALS Abraham 423; Caleb 374
BEAR Daniel 415
BEARD George 408
BEATES Mr. 367
BEATTY --- 206; James 22
BECK George 181; Jacob 370; John 181; P. 133; Peter 334
BECKSON Jacob 140
BEECHER William 370, 382
BEELER Catharine 266; Daniel 266
BEERBROWER Philip 415
BEHLER Catharine 321; 390, 394; Daniel 321
BEHR Henry 402
BELL David 165; Ebenezer 317; James 126; John 152; W. 133; William 13, 85, 92, 112, 130, 203
BEN 352, 381
BENEDICT Nicholas 318
BENIZEL Felix 390; Mary 390
BENNER 418
BENNET William 275
BENSON Joseph 207
BENTZ Henry 373, 390
BERGAW Abraham 390
BERINGER Joseph 389
BERNHIZLE Martin 56
BERRYHILL Alexander 35
BETTINGER Nicholas 317
BEVENSHER Anthony 390
BEYERLY Michael 114
BICKHAM and REASE 374
BIEGEL John 185
BIEGLER Philip 381
BIEGLEY John 128
BIGHAM John 338; Robert 321, 356; Samuel 416, 423; Thomas 386
BIGLER John 68
BILL 234, 362
BINGHAM William 79, 91
BIRELY Henry 437
BITTINGER John 280
BIXLER John 342, 354, 371, 384
BLACK Henry 309, 428; James 249, 323, 388, 391, 393, 428; John 104, 152, 209; Peter 151; Robert 323, 428; Samuel 286; Thomas 260, 278, 367, 370, 372, 390, 427; William 61, 79
BLACKBURN Samuel 243
BLACKFORD Benjamin 177
BLAIN William 390
BLAINE Alexander 49, 111, 136, 162, 223, 231; Ephraim 9, 41, 44, 89, 92; James 106, 181; Mary 162; Robert 93, 129, 162, 384; William 158
BLAIR Adam 285; Isaiah 48, 92, 101, 217; Runnel 151, 230; William 62, 70, 192, 196, 237
BLASSER Nicholas 415
BLOCK Thomas 386
BLOOM Adam 424
BLOUCHER Matthias 149
BLUEBAUGH Benjamin 370
BLYMEYER Andrew 335
BLYTH David 282
BOAB 70
BOAL David 113
BOAR Nicholas 213
BOARS Nicholas 176
BOB 344
BOBB Ludwich 370
BODEN Hugh 43, 44, 48, 143
BODENHEIMNER Jacob 388
BOFFONETT Charles 188
BOGLE William 384
BOHANAN Henry 389
BOLEAU Nathaniel 337
BOLTON James 316, 370
BOMBERGER Elizabeth 350
BOND Peter 389
BONNER James 152
BOOR William 75
BOOTH John 397
BOPP Ludwig 345
BORDENHEIMER Widow 253
BORE William 247
BOSS Peter 321
BOTT Jonas 390; Peter 390; Reinhart 370
BOVARD Charles 89, 93, 192, 238
BOW Michael 215
BOWER Benjamin 390; Christopher 10; Henry 265, 266; John 252, 405, 416, 423; Samuel 298

BOWIE Anna 422; Ralph 66, 258, 291, 329, 422
BOWMAN Benjamin 381
BOWSER Samuel 415

INDEX (to the paragraph number)

BOYD Anna 335; Catharine 325; James 12, 206, 285; Simon 50, 180; William 225, 350
BOYER Frederick 184; Henry 415; John 356; Mary 184
BOYLE Daniel 20; Edward 157; John 151
BRADLEY Joseph 347, 386; Mr. 185
BRADY Joseph 89
BRAND Anthony 319; Elizabeth 325
BRANDON Eleazar 367; Thomas 381
BRATTEN Edward 104; James 104; John 103, 110, 133
BRATTON John 13
BRAUCHER George 415
BREADY Joseph 139; Samuel 343
BREAMER Frederick 390
BREDEN William 64, 90
BRENDLEY Jacob 275
BRENEISON Captain 404
BRENEMAN Christian 390, 402; Joshua 402; Julina 390
BRENISEN John 419
BRENIZER John 129
BRENNEMAN Benjamin 415
BRENNERMAN Jacob 341
BRIANT John 69
BRIGGS David 18, 155, 429; Eleanor 146; Mr. 44, 137, 165; Mrs. 44; Polly 206
BRIGH David 1
BRIGHTWELL John 275
BRILLHART John 321
BRINDLE George 79
BRINKERHOFF James 258
BRISBIN William 5
BRISCOE John 411
BRITAIN Adam 206
BRITT Daniel 196
BRITTAIN Adam 151
BROBACHER Conrad 395
BRODHEAD Daniel 169
BROOKENS William 111
BROOKINS David 206
BROTHERTON James 139
BROWN --- 149; Adam 253, 272; Andrew 296; James 112, 115, 145, 253, John 35, 40, 84, 125, 151, 257, 389; Joseph 60, 129; Mary 345; Nancy 128; Neal 182; Peggy 207; Richard 381, 404; Robert 303, 382; Samuel 200; William 54, 128, 176, 285, 382
BROWNLEE James 79
BRUBACHER Dietrich 321
BRUGH Jacob 349; John 381; Peter 258
BRYSON Hugh 165; Samuel 143, 198

BUCHANAN Andrew 139; Arthur 181; Henry 275, 367; John 159; Mrs. 75; Nancy 181; Thomas 47, 65, 75, 79, 85, 91, 129, 144; William 159
BUCKEY LYdia 88
BUCKLEY Jeremiah 85
BUCKWORTH Mr. 99
BUELER Daniel 386
BUITZFIELD John 129
BULL Levi 139; Thomas 285
BULLOCK Moses 54, 115
BURBROWER Casper 386
BURCHFEILD Thomas 112
BURCHSTEAD Henry 41, 50, 55
BURD James 269; Joseph 390
BURDOYNE John 48
BURG John 390
BURGESS Nancy 252; William 252, 283, 298, 318
BURKET George 336
BURNS Barney 69; Francis 81; James 10; Thomas 131
BUSHEY Christian 390
BUSS Jacob 321; Peter 321
BUTLER Col. 59; family 54; George 322; Thomas 176
BUTT Jacob 391; William 337, 372
BUZER Caty 282; John 282
BYER Charles 428; Elizabeth 428; Frederick 437; Jonas 388
BYERLY Andrew 158, 166, 207; Ann 75; George 345; Jacob 22, 75; William 281

CADWALLADER John 346; Joseph 346
CAESAR 56, 232
CALHOON Andrew 167; Sally 167
CALLENDER Catherine 16
CALLIT David 390
CALWELL James 135
CAMBELL Rev 37
CAMBRIDGE Archibald 158
CAMELON William 242
CAMPBELL Agness 102; Col. 337; D. 206; David 102, 206; Ebenezer 240; Francis 111; Hugh 437; James 30, 67; John 118, 206, 326, 408, 413; Mary 206; Rev 229; Richard Cutler 362; Robert 176, 229, 425; Thomas 44, 280, 318, 326, 376
CAMRON Daniel 135
CANBY Benjamin H. 321
CANZY Susannah 367
CAPP John 140
CARLAND Daniel 161; Nancy 161
CARNEY James 349; Mary 349

INDEX (to the paragraph number)

CAROTHERS Andrew 363; Ann 363; Armstrong 206; James 85, 91, 141, 156, 196, 203, 246; John 9, 111, 119, 122, 123, 143, 153, 154, 163, 181, 193, 206, 235, 361, 363; Mary 122; Mrs. 363; Rodger 156; Thomas 153, 363
CARPENTER John 26
CARR Jacob 50, 156
CARSON David 53; John 179, 285; William 265
CART George 238; Jacob 116, 156, 179, 180
CASH 338
CASHMAN Christian 336
CASSAT David 287, 364, 389, 416
CATHCART Rev 22; Robert 268
CATO James 3
CATON Ned 35
CAUGHLIN John 94
CAVIT John 34
CERFASS Daniel 198
CESSNA James 56, 96
CHAIN John 192, 237
CHAMBERLAIN James 381; Ninian 370; Philip 341, 362
CHAMBERS Col. 145; Jane 106; Peggy 66; Robert 18, 61, 66, 92, 106, 181; William 15, 59, 66
CHAPMAN Matthew 318
CHARLES 159, 435
CHARLES Joseph C. 24, 393
CHESNER Samuel 247
CHEVENEY Pat 216
CHILDERSTONE Richard 323
CHURCH Dr. 324
CLAPHAM Josiah 257
CLAPSADDLE Daniel 280; Mr. 363
CLAPSADLE Daniel 248, 326, 342; Michael 248, 287
CLARK Barnabas 176; Daniel 234; George 437; John 16, 59, 221, 234, 256, 284, 297, 346, 386, 390, 391, 396; Joseph 393; Sarah 123, 181, 193, 206, 361, 363; Thomas 148, 174, 206, 428; Walter 350; William 206, 428
CLARKE G. 62; George 12, 30, 293
CLARKSON James 413
CLAUDY Martin 50
CLAY Robert 215
CLEM 341, 362, 379
CLEMENTS Barnabas 371
CLENDENING John 206
CLENDENNEN James 181, 226, 234
CLENDINEN John 244

CLOSS A. 356; Abraham 347; Christian 347, 356; John 347, 356
CLOUZER Simon 63
CLUNN Joseph 188
COBEAN Alexander 248, 338, 362, 376, 381; James 422; Samuel 249, 299, 373, 381, 382, 391
COCHENAUER John 359
COCHRAN John 60; Patrick 207; Robert 66, 149; William 336, 415
COLEMAN Barbara 276; Orange 287; Robert 285; Valentine 276; William 153
COLLINS Ann Eve 3; Daniel 3; John 381, 416
COLVEN William 269
COLWELL Robert 55
COMFORT Andrew 424; Jacob 424
COMPTON John 56
CONDRY Leah 415; William 148
Conewago Canal 333
CONIX George 388
CONN Henry 424
CONNEL Mary 142; William 142
CONNELLY Henry 7, 13; John 206
CONOWAY George 91
CONRAD Thomas 351
COOK Samuel 386
COOKIS Adam 307
COOKSON --- 176
COOPER Adam 233; Alexander 388; Archibald 370; Charles 66, 143; David 370; James 253, 275, 287, 345, 389; John 139, 370; William 253
COOVER George 206
COPE Adam 206
COPELY John 61

COPPANHAFFER Benjamin 2
CORIGAN John 323
CORNELIUS Jesse 427
CORNELLIUS Joseph 390
CORNER Christian 368
CORNMAN Felty 47
COROTHEN John 325
COSINE Cornelious 287
COSTINE Jacob 188

COUCHER George 1
COULSON Francis 368
COULTER Richard 16
COVER George 182
COWEN William 367
COWIZER Philip 318

160

INDEX (to the paragraph number)

COX Dr. 324; Francis 125, 126, 340;
    John 396; Peter 303
CRABB William 273
CRAIG Abram 14; John 169
CRAIGHEAD Gilson 9, 95, 188, 240;
    James 108, 132; Nancy 240; Thomas
    46, 129
CRAIN Benjamin 98
CRAINE John 315
CRALL William 203
CRANE Benjamin 247; John 50
CRASSER Adam 287
CRAVER Jacob 9
CRAWFORD Joseph 78, 112, 159; Robert
    78
CREE Robert 56
CREEK Philip 88
CREIGH Elizabeth 208; John 19, 34,
    60, 63, 82, 90, 106, 143, 166, 208
CREIGHEAD Gilson 39
CREMAN Jacob 398
CREMER Andrew 321, 415, 416; David
    373; John 415; Margaret 415
CREVER Jacob 4, 10, 28, 50, 61, 63,
    75, 82, 92, 104, 116, 150, 156,
    183, 206   ; John 46, 56, 57, 63,
    75, 84, 92; Polly 57
CRIDER George 305
CRISWELL Samuel 11, 86, 114, 119
CROCKET Andrew 148; Elizabeth 148;
    George 234; James 7; John 7;
    Margaret 7
CROCKETT Thomas 152
CROGHAN George 68, 169
CRONBACH Henry 390; Jacob 345, 390;
    John 390
CRONBAUGH Jacob 326
CROOK George 234
CROSBY James 408
CROSS James 390
CROUL Samuel 50
CROUSE Simon 61
CROWEL Samuel 12, 62, 105
CROWELL Samuel 65, 133, 155, 221
CUFF 330
CULBERTSON Andrew 111, 134; Joseph
    43, 437; Samuel 43, 165; William
    97, 121, 187
CULL John 61
CUMMINGS James 79
CUMMINS Clarles 234
CUNEY James 180
CUNINGHAM Samuel 317
CUNNINGHAM Benjamin 169, 368; Robert
    370

CUPELS Grizzy 236
CURTAIN Rowland 243
CURTIS Jotham W. 151
CUSKADAN Mary 79
CUSKADEN James 79
CUSTARD Abraham 361
CUSTIS George Washington 129

D'HAPPART Jh. 1 215
DADDY Christina 410; John 410
DAELHOUSEN Henry D. 93
DALRUMPLE Robert 74; Thomas 322
DANNER Abraham 329, 394; Peter 262
DARLINGTON Meredith 206
DAVIDSON Dr. 2, 115, 205; Dr. R. 144,
    148; James 234; John 134; Matthew
    11; Patrick 66, 94, 206; Rev 206;
    Rev Dr. 16, 19, 22, 41, 54, 66,
    142, 143, 165, 211, 222; Robert 46,
    47, 62, 89, 208; Samuel 8, 148, 429
DAVIS A.D. 169; Benjamin 105; James
    10, 105, 110, 148, 150; John 41,
    193; Margaret 193; Mordecai 208;
    Mrs. 48; Polly 46; S. 36, 325
DAVISON William 337
DAVOLT John 49
DAWSON George 168, 232; Mr. 234;
    William 26
DAY Jacob 266; Mathew 275
De LORUMIER Charles 355
De ST. HILAIRE Felix 386
DEAN Robert 305
DEARDORFF Anthony 254, 370, 382;
    Isaac 381; John 347, 386
DECKER Lewis 415; Philip 313, 356,
    370
DEEL Charles 330, 334; Daniel 386
DEH Anna Mary 390; Daniel 390; John
    Nicholas 390; Michael 390; Philip
    390
DEHUFF Abraham 400
DELANCEY John 10, 34
DELAP William 400, 410, 415, 423
DEMAREE David 265, 281
DEMPSTER david 325
DEMSTER David 280
DEMUTH John 414
DENN Mary 52
DENNY Rev. 437; William 11, 109
DERUSH Abraham 335
DESHLER Adam 374; Mr. 386
DETTER Matthias 70, 308
DEVLIN Margaret 32; Roger 32, 206,
    221; Sarah 221
DEWALD John 33
DEWALT Philip 375

161

INDEX (to the paragraph number)

DIBLER Michael 65; Sarah 65
DICKEY John 31
DICKINSON 206
DICKS Peter 256, 321, 356
DICKSON Andrew 181, 182; John 255, 298, 355, 392, 404; R. 435; W. 435
DIEHL Frederick 248, 287; Jacob 402; Nicholas 402; Peter 402
DIERMENT Joseph 135
DIETRICH Michael 415
DIGG (family) 253
DILL James 295, 325; Jean 56; John 39, 43, 295, 325; Matthew 56; Mr. 192; Priscilla 408
DILLER Caspar 46, 56; John 164; Margaret 182
DILLON Patrick 135
DININGER George 185
DINKEL Peter 374
DINKLE Peter 302, 330, 398
DIPPLE Nicholas 365
DITLER Baltzar 115
DITTERLINE William 36
DITTO John 390; Joseph 340
DITWILER Jacob 437
DIVEN James 206
DIXON William 30, 67
DOBBIN Alexander 398
DOBELL Dr. 324
DODDS Joseph 218, 221, 381, 390
DOLL Conrad 258; John 306, 308
DONAGAN Patrick 125, 126
DONALDSON Joseph 390, 391, 416; Mr. 386
DONNELLAM John 361
DONNELLY James 69
DONNOLLY John 265
DONOVAN Daniel 80
DORON John 144, 380
DOSH Michael 282, 428
DOUGHERTY Alexander 85; George 180; Priscilla 139; Richard 242
DOUGLAS Ephraim 285; George 53; Hannah 235; James 389; John 223; William 390
DOUGLASS Archibald 299; James 35, 299; John 235; John A. 406; Thomas 299, 370; William 281, 367
DOWNEY Charles 128, 146; William 139
DOWNING Hunt 29, 272
DOYLE Michael 323; Robert 384
DREVER Jacob 43
DREVISH William 44, 184, 211
DREWISH William 104, 127
DREXLER John 405

DRINKER John 61
DRITT Jacob 263, 271, 348, 378, 383; Peter 263, 348, 378
DU--- Andrew 390
DUBENDORFF Rev 86
DUCKET William 112, 179, 187
DUCKETT William 82
DUFF Barney 6
DUFFEY William 123, 182
DUFFIELD George 389; John 400, 410, 415, 423; Samuel 252
DUFFY Barnabas 232; Michael 215
DUGAN 16
DUM John 180
DUNBAR John 19, 30, 56, 66, 148; Nelly 19; William 16, 186
DUNCAN Alexander 30, 67; Andrew 308, 410; Benjamin 143; Daniel 91; David 198; James & Co. 95; James 30, 35, 55, 127, 144, 158, 162, 217, 223, 232, 390; John 55, 321, 352, 370, 371, 390; Joseph 129   ; Mathew 255; Samuel 140, 208, 232; Sarah 89; Stephen 55, 206; Thomas 30, 47, 138, 152, 176, 206, 247, 330
DUNK 352
DUNLAP Daniel 203; James 91; John 111
DUNN Archibald 60; Robert 248, 257
DUNNING Ezekiel 29, 85, 91
DUNWODIES James 16
DUNWOODY David 248, 250, 256, 302; John 29, 272
DURANT Jane 53
DURHAM James 386
DYETH Thomas 416

EAKIN William 43
EAKINS William 114
EARLY John 437
EATON Joseph 52
EBERT Elizabeth 345; Martin 345; Michael 345
EBY Henry 48; John 384
ECCLEBERGER Henry 206
ECCLES Nathaniel 182
ECKENROTH John 250
ECKHART Valentine 253, 285
EDGAR James 285
EDIE David 299, 326, 370, 373, 379, 381, 383, 390, 394, 414, 422; James 318; John 248, 269, 302, 308, 315, 319, 337, 341, 349, 350, 352, 362, 364, 370, 379, 384, 386, 390, 391, 394, 396, 408, 420; Lieutenant Colonel 404; Samuel 256, 302

162

INDEX (to the paragraph number)

EDMONDSON Joseph 393
EDMUNDSON Joseph 259, 386, 400, 410, 424; Thomas 427
EDWARDS William 287
EGE Major 7; Michael 12, 129, 148, 149, 177, 182, 212, 232, 325
EGHOLTZ Frederick 320
EGNEW William 248
EHREHART Mr. 302
EHRHART John 389, 415; Thomas 386, 416
EICHELBERGER --- 306, 352; Frederick 251, 422; George 359; Jacob 370, 408, 415; John 314, 390, 398, 403, 431; Leonard 429; Michael 408
EICHHOLTZ Matthais 382
EICHOLTZ Frederick 356
EIGHELBERGER Frederick 257
ELBE Jacob 390
ELEINFRETER JOhn 350
ELFRY John 147
ELLIOT Benjamin 43, 285, 339; James 181; John 48, 55, 74, 107, 195; Joseph 32, 63, 68, 79, 121; Mrs. 153; Robert 148; William 323
ELLIOTT Joseph 40
ELLIS 25
EMIG John 338
EMIGH Valentine 390
EMMENGER Andw 247
EMMINGER Andrew 182
EMMIT William 248
ENGLISH David 10, 177; Elenor 10
ENRKHART Peter 382
ENSMINGER George 393, 400; Peggy 335
EPAUGH John 265
EPLEY John 393
EPPLY Henry 428
EPRIGHT Catherine 9; Ludwig 9
ERB? Jacob 248
ERHART Anthony 321
ERICH Sebastian 265
ERNEST Catherine 9; John 9
ERWIN John 196
ESPY George 35, 84, 91; Widow 9
ESSLEMAN David 7
ETTER Jacob 383
EVANS Cadwalader 1; David 349, 415; Frederick 367; James 415; Lieut 219; Robert 41; Thomas 349, 415
EVERS John 192
EWING George 388; John 129, 325; Rachel 370; Samuel 370; Thomas 323; William 129, 206

FAHNESTOCK Dr. 355; Obed 92; Peter 420; Samuel 92, 358, 361, 385
FALCONAR Abraham 304
FALLER Adam 321
FALLOW James 403
FATMAN 68
FAUCET Robert 64
FAUGHLIY William 318
FAUGHT Henry 141
FAUS Jacob 248
FAUST Baltzer 424
FEIKER John 400
FEIRST Christopher 269
FELKER John 393
FENNO John 373; John Ward 373
FERGIS Hugh 265, 267
FERGUSON Col. 206; John 402, 404, 424; William 56
FERREE William 320
FERRIER Capt. 66
FETTER Jacob 169, 227
FICKES Abraham 389; Adam 427
FIESER Anna Maria 321; Jacob 321
FILKER John 368
FILSON Mary 223
FINCK Henry 415
FINDLEY John 209
FINLEY Andrew 390, 410; John 388; Joseph 437; Major 160; Samuel 6, 43, 57, 336, 435
FINNEY Robert 338
FIRSTLER Henry 372
FISHBACH Catharine 123
FISHBURN Peter 118
FISHER Conrod 437; John 281, 345, 362, 364, 394, 412; Leonard 61; Mrs. 61; William 285
FISSEL Frederick 426
FITZGERALD David 377
FITZPATRICK James 65
FLECK Barbara 356; Valentine 356
FLEMING James 33, 143, 158; Rebecca 148; Susanna 47; William 66, 299
FLEMMING James 122; Mrs. 122; William 133
FLENCHBAUGH Adam 368
FLETCHER Charles 299, 373; James 104; James and Co. 104
FLICKINGER Samuel 415
FLINT Thomas 308
FLORA 181
FONK John 307
FORBES Betsey 16; James 217; John 217
FORKER Hannah 427
FORRER Henry 295

INDEX (to the paragraph number)

FORSYTH Elizabeth 383; John 185, 252, 280, 296, 300, 317, 318, 350, 351, 370, 383, 388, 390, 394, 398, 403, 416, 431; Mary 383
FORTNEY Michael 206
FOSLER George 52
FOSTER Jonathan 67, 162; Josiah 176; Mr 104, 106, 141, 153, 207, 208, 223; Thomas 12, 30, 50, 67, 68, 93, 110, 124, 163, 243
FOULK Stephen 242, 243
FOWLER William 176
FOX George 79; John 133, 158, 400; Samuel 79
FRANK 355
FRANK Dr. 107, 156; Lilly 415; Ludwick 415
FRANKLIN Lieut 218
FRASER Paul 296
FRASH Dewald 302
FRAZER Paul 305
FRAZIER Paul 83
FREDERICK Butcher 326
FRESHER George 39, 129, 221
FREY Barnet 368; Henry 394; Jacob 79
FRIDLEY George 115
FRITZ John 9, 192
FRITZLEIN George 416
FRONKS Christian 390
FRUST Christopher 254
FRY John 194, 239
FULLERTON William 320
FULLWEILER Michael 423
FULTON David 324
FULWILLER Michael 372
FUNCK Michael 382
FUNK Jacob 321
FURNEY Adam 370
FURRER Henry 234
FURRY Jacob 259

GALBRAITH Andrew 8, 145; James 8; Mary 8; Robert 8
GALBREATH Andrew 73, 166; Jane 166; Samuel 206; William 6, 9, 115; William N. 127
GALE Lieut. Anthony 199
GALLOWAY Benjamin 174
GALLY Alexander 206
GAMBER Valentine 97
GAMBLE William 378
GANDER Peter 233
GARDNER Barzillai 286; John 206; Philip 402
GARRET Adam 404

GARRETSON Cornelius 370, 390, 407; Jane 400; John 345; Joseph 345; Samuel 345
GARTNER Jacob 280, 308, 326, 351, 356, 386, 416; Philip 280, 326, 371
GARVIN John 206
GAUSS Elizabeth 370; George 370
GAW John 215
GAZZAM Taylor Jones 230
GEDDES James 143; John 65
GEER William 29, 55, 272, 360
GEIGER Wendel 356
GEINER John 330
GELWICKS Andrew 388, 393; N. 392; Nicholas 337, 353, 368, 376, 388, 389, 390, 393, 400, 410
GEMMILL Robert 280
GEMPSHORN Adam 375
GEORGE 39, 54, 312, 397
GEORGE Barney 6; David 6, 91; Martin 131; Robinette 381
GESSLER Captain 416
GETTY James 381, 424
GEYER Mr. 123, 354
GIBB Capt 218
GIBBONS John 211
GIBFORT James 402
GIBSON Francis 47; George 168; J. 338; Jacob 338, 368; James 289; Mrs. 158; Robert 50, 69, 118, 131, 159
GIFFEN James 66
GILBERT Jacob 390, 402; Mr. 339
GILBREATH Hannah 101
GILELAND William 391
GILLELAND William 249, 359
GILLESPIE William 103
GILLIS Thomas 69
GILMORE John 418
GILSON William 244
GINDER John 370, 408
GINE Isaac 26
GINRICH Benjamin 345; Catharine 345
GIRLLING & KIMPTON 21
GIRLLING William 182
GITTING Casper 371
GIVEN James 152; John 125
GIVIN James 26, 106, 193
GLACKEN Patrick 318
GLANCY Joseph 321
GLEN Alexander 159; Jane 111; John 114, 115, 137, 203, 211, 350
GLENN Gabriel 111; John 129, 152, 158
GLINLAND William 389
GLONINGER Philip 140

INDEX (to the paragraph number)

GOCHENAUR John 356
GOCHENAWER John 382
GOCHGNAUR John 345
GODFREY Hannah 229; William 188, 229, 352
GOEBEL Henry 141, 162, 223
GOERING Jacob 279; Mr. 373; Rev J. 429
GOLDING Aquila 215
GOMMEL John 389
GONCE Abraham 359
GONSE George 251
GOOCH William 331
GOOD Charles 390; Jacob 318; Peter 415
GOODING Jacob 307
GOOT Peter 14
GORDAN James 388
GORDON Alexander 2; Mary 2; Miss 93
GOSLER Philip 381
GOSSLER Captain 223, 312, 360, 362, 364, 386, 398, 406, 409, 422; Captain P. 332, 402; Mr. 367; Philip 124, 248, 257, 279, 282, 308, 318, 324, 367, 374, 381, 391, 395, 396, 416
GOSSWEILER John 345
GOSWALER John 299
GOULDSMITH William C. 358
GRACE John 35, 287, 330, 333
GRACELY John 423
GRAEF Jacob 73, 310
GRAEFF Isaac 272
GRAFF John 97
GRAHAM Isaiah 169; James 40, 64, 90; Jared 189, 209; John 10, 27; Robert 291, 345; Thomas 40
GRAY James 375; Samuel 132, 152; Thomas 386, 427
GRAYBELL Michael 249, 279, 386, 409, 428
GRAYBILL Michael 377, 390
GRAYBLE Jean 336; Michael 287, 330, 335, 336
GRAYDON William 389
GRAYSON Mr. 168; Robert 25, 39, 43, 119, 127, 152, 163, 188, 206, 363; William 43
GREASON James 139; William 93
GREEGER John 203
GREEN George 177; I. 383; John 256
GREENAMEYER Jacob 422
GREENLEAF Thomas 373
GREER David 242; Isaac 90; John 248, 284, 297, 400, 416; Polly 211; Samuel 129; Thomas 64, 90

GREEVES Thomas 349
GREG-- Henry 384
GREGARY Richard 188
GREGG Amos 188; Charles 43; John 243; Margary 243
GREGORY Richard 221
GREY Samuel 435; William 350
GRIBBEL Vincent 188
GRIER George 231; Jenet 356
GRIEST Daniel 390
GRIFFEN William 94
GRIFFETH Abraham 390; William 390
GRIFFITH --- 232; Isaac 367; William 326, 390
GRIFFITHS Samuel Powell 296
GRIMES James 286; John 61
GRIMLER Benjamin 435; Henry 435
GRISE John 175
GROFF George 334; Michael 402
GROSKAST John 415
GROSS George 334; John 85; Michael 382; Samuel 356
GROUSE Simon 169
GROVE David 84; George 365; Jacob 41; Philip 233; Samuel 410; Thomas 345
GRUP John 70, 308
GRUPE Peter 389
GUCKES John 255
GUSTINE Dr. 23, 211, 363; James 139; L. 205; Lemuel 106
GUTHRIE James 139

HABLE George 23
HACKER George 47
HACKET George 9, 192
HADDEN Samuel 275, 298, 355
HAGA Godfrey 296
HAGER Jonathan 67
HAHN John 416
HAINES Maximilian 121
HALL Aquila 345; Edward Ward 390; Hannah 76, 435; James 143, 234, 344, 345, 350, 382; John 169, 317; Tom 76, 435
HALLER F. I. 159; Frederick J. 235; John 70, 308, 349
HAMEL George 310
HAMERSLY Robert 381
HAMILTON --- 10; Charles 357; Hans 256, 302; James 63, 73, 76, 106, 129, 136, 158, 186, 189, 205, 221; John 388; Robert 163; Thomas 361, 399; William 96, 333, 338, 384, 392
HAMMOND George 415; James 415; Thomas 415

INDEX (to the paragraph number)

HANAGAN William 255
HANCOCK James 254
HAND Edward 267. 361
HANNA and MARTIN 143
HANNA John 165
HANNAH Isabella 95; James 285
HARDING Jane 258; Michael 258
HARE Jacob 17
HAREHOEFF Jacob 14
HARMAN George 252
HARMER Josiah 360
HARNISH Christian 318; Samuel 382
HARPER John 103, 129, ; Robert 139; Samuel 374
HARR Isaiah 306, 391
HARRIS & DONALDSON 297, 306, 313, 331, 352, 391
HARRIS David 143, 348, 364, 383, 390; James 148; John 148; Mr. 386; Polly 22, 268; William 22, 248, 268, 331, 352
HART David 268; Elijah 282; Jacob 248, 355; Jane 335; John 338, 407; Ruth 248
HARTER Frederick 151
HARTLEY C.W. 406; Catharine 141, 374; Charles W. 206, 371, 390; Major Gen 247; Thomas 141, 206, 280, 317, 367, 374, 375, 388, 390, 416, 432
HARTMAN John 298
HARTZELL George 275
HARVEY William 370
HARWIN John 382
HASLET Samuel 54; William 59
HATELY Henry 68
HATHORN Adam 173
HAUER Elizabeth 126; John 125, 126, 340, 350
HAUGHTON Richard 48
HAUTZ Rev 187
HAWKINS Charles 437
HAWTHORN Robert 206
HAY Captain 404; George 317, 330, 352, 376, 390, 427; Jacob 285, 308, 330, 334, 345, 383, 390; John 272, 283, 298, 317, 394, 409; Mr. 362; Samuel 67
HAYES Robert 412; Samuel 305; William 88
HAYS David 139; George 139, 299, 320; James 390; Joseph 47, 180, 188; Robert 391
HAZLETON Hamilton 115; Hugh 182
HEAGY George 356
HEAKE John 371

HEAP John 19, 58, ; Margaret 19
HEARY John 49
HECK Peter 390
HECKART Philip 416
HECKENDORN John 321
HECKERT Jacob 405
HECKES George 425; Laurence 425
HEFFEINGER Martin 27
HEIBNER Frederick 391
HEICKS Andrew 85, 91
HEIFER Sebastian 286
HEIFFER Sebastian 258; William 255
HEIFGEN Morta 5
HEIGLE William 109, 192
HEINDEL Adam 345; Philip 345
HEINDLE Lawrence 365
HEISSER William 381
HEISTER Joseph 285
HELGLE William 230
HELTZGLI Anita Mary 390
HEMMILE George 73
HEMMING Richard 240
HENDEL Jacob 34, 163, 174, 182, 239
HENDERSON Alexander 378; Andrew 7, 17; Daniel 80; Elizabeth 415; James 93; John 239, 389; Jonathan 418; Matthew 113, 203; William 80, 93
HENDRICKS Adam 381; Lieutenant Colonel 404
HENDRICKSON Joseph 389
HENDRIX Adam 370; Rachel 370
HENEISY John 356
HENESSE Daniel 80
HENGST Michael 423
HENISEY John 381
HENRY Alexander 1; Daniel 299, 345, 368; John 232; John Joseph 232; Peter 299, 345; William 367
HERBACH John 280, 321; Yost 415
HERBST John 216; Rev 57
HERFLEYJohn 215
HERMAN Catharine 331, 370, 415; Emanuel 331, 370, 415; George 390; John 428; Samuel 335
HERR Abraham 136, 192, 206
HERRIN Joseph 340
HERRON Francis 246
HERSH John 258, 324, 326, 408
HERSHE John 324
HERSHEY Christian 256, 321
HERSHY Christian 356; John 382; Joseph 402
HERTZEL Adam 415; Jonas 285
HERWICK Andrew 140
HETECH George 336

INDEX (to the paragraph number)

HETERICK Robert 355, 377
HETICK Ludowick 255; Thomas 255
HETRICK Christian 390
HETTRICK Christian 408
HETZEL Tobias 356
HEVIC Michael 287
HEVICE Michael 249
HEWIT Joseph 400
HEWITT Joseph 177; Thomas 177
HEYD George 321
HICE Henry 126
HICKENLUBER Andrew 315
HICKES Nicholas 206
HICKSON Thomas 47
HIDE Abraham 203; Elizabeth 203
HIEGEL William 86
HIGGINS Cornelius 321; John 169
HILDEBRAND Felix 416
HILL Abraham 393; Henry 236; James 347
HILTZHEIMER Jacob 373
HIMES Isaac 428
HINDS Jacob 61; Joseph 61
HINKLE Anthony 390, 422
HIPPLE John 405
HITCHCOCK Randal 265
HITTER George 152
HOBBACH Dietrich 415, 428; Philip 415, 428
HOCKLEY Thomas 391, 396; William B. 79
HOFF Daniel 345; John 184
HOFFER Isaac 175
HOFFMAN Christopher 370; Jacob 423; Philip J. 390
HOGE David 205; Isabella 165; J 214; James 235; James R. 149, 240; Jonathan 146, 165, 202,213, 231, 235; Thomas 142; widow 113
HOGG John 88
HOGUE Serah 57
HOKE Henry 392; Peter 427; Sally 427
HOLCHAM Hannah 46
HOLIZAPPEL Barnet 356
HOLLING William 220
HOLLINGER Tobias 254
HOLLOPETER Mathias 347
HOLME Andrew 91
HOLMES Andrew 28, 123, 127; Betsey 142; John 66, 127; Mary 62; Nancy 144; Thomas 139, 144; Thompson 64; William G. 24
HOOBER Frederick 427; Jacob 250
HOOVER Adam 262; George 92, 115; Jacob 133, 423

HOPEWELL 205
HOPPER Alexander 36
HORN Frederick 70, 308, 390
HORNER Adam 362; James 313; Robert 390, 422

HORST Jacob 259; John 259
HORT Conrad 408
HOSACK Henry 388
HOSHAAR Anna 415; Barbara 415; Elizabeth 415; John 382, 415
HOSTETTER Jacob 326, 376, 422
HOUBBLE Christian 182
HOUGH John 308; Mahlon 308; Samuel 308; William 308
HOUGHINBERGER Henry 114
HOUSENOT Christian 103
HOUSTON James 419
HOWARD John 228
HU... John 182
HUBER Jacob 410; John 356; Peter 248
HUBLEY Frederick 408, 424; Henry 365; John 96, 333, 365; Juliana 96, 333; Magdalena 424

HUGHES Betsey 222; John 7, 14, 19, 100, 105, 153, 222
HULINGS Marcus 143
HUMEL 188
HUNTER Andrew 216; John 9, 41, 115, 130, 158, 163; Matthew 114; Robert 206; Samuel 390; William 41
HUPPERT Adam 381
HURIT John 356
HURST H. 169; John 345, 382
HUSSEY Amos 386
HUSTON John 6, 226; Robert 113, 139, 203, ; William 43, 48
HUTCHENSON Samuel 248
HUTTON James 206

ICHOLTZ Peter 389
ICKES Peter 258, 336, 352, 381, 384, 408
IDNINGS Edmund 257
IPE Jacob 275
IRVINE Alexander 326; C. 162; Callender 144, 157; David 206; James 206; Samuel 206; William 63, 83, 203
IRVING Alexander 338
IRWIN George 367; James 14, 20, 244; Mathew 211; Robert 265, 371; William 285
ISETT John 106

INDEX (to the paragraph number)

J--- 390
JACK 336
JACKSON Alexander 80, 93; Samuel 73, 80, 93, 206, 237
JACOB 330
JACOB Jarmin 80
JACOBS Jerman 169; John 411
JAGO Samuel 383
JAMES 51, 279, 280
JAMES Thomas 67; William 16, 206
JAMESON David 133; Dr 258; James 43, 319, 415; Thomas 398; Thomas D. 294
JARRET Jonathan 305
JARRETT Abraham 265
JEM 355
JENKINS Moses 345
JERRY 341
JESSOP Jonathan 286, 390, 416
JIM 345, 367
JOE 99, 386
JOHN 181, 361
JOHN Joshua 370; Richard 353
JOHNSON Adam 131; Andrew 386, 391; John 188; Widow 384; William 371
JOHNSTON Alexander 152; Andrew 170, 248, 356, 390; Capt. 187, 188; Francis 169; Henry 287; James 55; John 91, 137; Miss 36; Robert 40, 63, 68, 79; Samuel 222; William 321, 356, 370, 390
JOLLY Samuel 240; William 94
JONATHAN 39
JONES Daniel 299, 368; David 350; Edward 335, 345, 350, 382, 406; Griffith 138; Harry 330; Isaac 16; John 278, 352, 376; John B. 403; Joseph 311; Joseph Z. 167; Naphtali 345, 350, 382; Peter 123, 359; Phoebe 400; Robert 377; Thomas 51
JORDAN John 140, 175, 176, 197, 198, 206, 247
JOSEPH Aaron 86; John 356
JULIUS George 326, 345, 390
JUMPER Abraham 233
JUNKIN Benjamin 59; Elizabeth 209; Joseph 59, 192, 209; Mr. 202

K--- Tobias 390
KAFFMAN Peter 26
KAIRNS John 6; William 6
KARNS Jacob 389
KAUFFELT Michael 400
KAUFFMAN Abraham 320; Henry 402; Maria 402
KAUFMAN Jacob 335; John 345

KAUFNOR John 390
KAUN Henry 402
KAUTER Barnet 345; Catherine 345
KEAN John 138
KEATENIAN Michael 390
KEATON Susannah 350
KEAVANS Samuel 429
KEENEY Jacob 382
KEENS Michael 406
KEESER Henry 341
KEFFER Mary Elizabeth 382, 428; Matthais 382, 428
KEHRBACK Christian 388
KEIGLEY Jacob 123
KELLER Jacob 95; Leonard 206; Michael 390
KELLEY Mrs. 129
KELLY Francis 61, 92; Henry 65; James 362, 376, 384; John 390; Lieutenant Colonel 404; Samuel 65; Thomas 61, 92
KEMPHART Solomon 352
KENDRICK Abraham 79
KENNEDY --- 153; Anna 30; David 346; Dr. 386; Gilbert 59; John 386; Robert 30, 64, 90; Thomas 35, 39, 84, 118, 167; William 345
KENNY Robert 46, 125
KEPLER Michael 395
KEPLINGER Daniel 321; Peter 321
KERBACH George 390; John 264
KERN George 389; George M. 350; Jacob 415; John 424
KERR Alexander Scott 372; George 196, 325; John 395; Joseph 73, 310; Robert 252, 307
KESNER John 334
KESSELL Alexander 390
KESSER Mary Elizabeth 382; Matthais 382
KESSLER David 143
KESSLOR Jacob 133
KEY John Ross 360, 388
KEYSER Jacob 248
KIDD John 85
KIEHL Francis 41, 51
KIGER Conrad 368
KILGORE Matthew 352; William 104
KIMBOLL Catharine 321
KIMMEL Michael 422
KIMMERLY Jacob 428
KINCAID John 39
KINDIG Anna 321, 415; Jacob 321
KING Henry 288, 408, 416; John 381, 382; Justice 389; William 330

INDEX (to the paragraph number)

KINKEAD Deborah 206; John 129, 181, 206
KIPPLER Benjamin 44
KIRK Eli 253, 254, 327, 342, 370; Roger 348; Timothy 389, 431; William 282
KIRKPATRICK David 286; Joseph 113; William 161
KIST Peter 390
KITCH Martin 98
KITCHEN James 298
KITE Martin 247
KITT Peter 381; William 415
KITTERA John W. 235, 383
KITZMILLER Martin 320
KLEINDINST Andrew 415; David 415
KLEINFALTER Peter 321
KLINE George 2, 40, 99, 106, 112, 161, 206; Peter 408; William 345
Kline's Tavern 310
KLINEFELTER Michael 416; Peter 408
KLINGMAN Peter 402
KLIPPINGER Frederick 51
KLOFSFER George 341; Matthew 341
KNAUSE Francis 424
KNIGHT John 298, 415; Joshua 139; Richard 374
KNISELY Abraham 423; Anthony 423; John 60
KNOPP George 390
KNOX Joseph 127; Mr. 235
KOCH George 321, 384; John 321; Major 363
KOLLAR Baltzer 356
KOLLER Baltzer 416; Jacob 356, 402
KONKAPOT John 305
KOPE Adam 208
KOWAN James 381
KRAFT George 318; John 318
KRALL Joseph 420
KRANTZ George 371
KREBER Adam 370, 394; Martin 280, 335, 353, 376, 389, 403, 416, 427
KREGOR Casper 320
KREHL Nicholas 134
KREIGER Henry 390
KRIEGER Henry 356
KRITER Samuel 390
KRITZ Nicholas 192
KRITZER Honicle 93
KROP Samuel 187
KROTZER Mr 209
KUHL Peter 70, 308
KUHN Andrew 105; Henry 287; John 382, 415, 428

KUNTZ George 321, 329, 390; Isaac 187
KURTZ Martin 275; Peter 330, 334, 367
KYFER Barbara 92; George 92

L... George 393
LABOOB Christian 321; Elizabeth 321; Mary 321; Michael 321
LACKEY Alexander 381
LAINHOFF Godfrey 292
LAIRD James 47, 60, 111, 145, 206; Mathew 91; Samuel 16, 63, 73, 88, 106, 162, 221
LAMB James 121; John 206
LAMBERTON James 48, 206, 213
LANDERS Jacob 396
LANE Peter 247
LANG James 139
LANIUS William 321
LANTZ Andrew 313
LAPOLE Charles 30
LASHALLS George 287
LASHELLS George 280, 382, 387, 389, 422
LASHIELS George 362
LATSHAW Joseph 196, 221; Peter 165
LATTA Deborah 415; Thomas 410, 415
LAUB Conrad 248, 261, 337, 350, 355, 361, 367, 372, 400, 401, 421, 434
LAUER Christian 262; Jacob 370
LAUFFMAN Mr. 104; Philip 84, 92, 238
LAUFMAN Philip 39
LAUGHBAUGH Henry 114
LAUGHLIN Alexander 4, 206; Atcheson 223; John 94; Robert 206
LAUMAN Christoph 308
LAUSH Andrew 70
LAW John 43
LAWER Baltzer 70, 308
LAWSHE John 93, 113, 160
LAY Michael 53
LAYBOURNE Lieut 219
LAYBURN Robert 67
LAZELEAN Benjamin 188
LEAB John 82
LEAMOR John 252
LEAR Henry 229
LEAS Abraham 428; Daniel 391; George 391; John 290, 370
LECHLER Henry 70, 115, 216; John 216
LECKEY Alexander 182, 382
LEE James Brown 61; John 317; Richard 17, 185; Thomas 406; Thomas Sim 248
LEECH Robert 43, 93, 188; Thomas 410, 428; William 400
LEEPER James 187

INDEX (to the paragraph number)

LEFEVER Barbara 148; Isaac 110
LEFFLER George Lewis 303, 318, 373, 390, 392
LEHMAN Abraham 356; Christian 341, 370
LEHMER Henry 258, 382
LEIB Dr. 324
LEIBENSTEIN George 400
LEIBESPERGER Daniel 318; John 318
LEIBESTEIN George 393
LEIBHART Catharine 321
LEITNER 1st Sergeant I. 404; Ignatius 398
LEMMON Jacob 250, 353; Joshua 250
LEMON Jacob 353; Joshua 353
LENHART Daniel 9; Godfrey 330, 371, 381, 403, 427; William 410
LEONARD 341
LEONARD John 371; Mr. 84
LEPPER William D. 343
LESCHEY Catharine 254; Elizabeth 254; Jacob 254; John 254; Margaret 254; Sarah 254; Susannah 254
LESSLER George Lewis 416
LETHER Jacob 416
LEVER Isaac 87
LEVINGSTON Adam 390
LEVIS Billy 208; William 48, 126, 181
LEWIS Eli 259, 338, 362, 408; Enoch 145; John 207; Mordecai 79, 91; Reuben 234; William 186
LEYBURN Mrs. James 201; Robert 44
LICHTENWALLTER Abraham 402
LIEBHART Henry 395; Jacob 321, 395; John 405
LIGGET James 95, 321; Patrick 222; William 346
LIGGOT Joseph 403
LIGHTCAP Solomon 101
LIGHTNER Nathaniel 298
LINCK George 415; Michael 415
LINDEN Michael 406
LINDSAY David 151; Joseph 279
LINDSEY David 44, 176; Robert 206
LINGEFELTER Jacob 384
LINGENFELTER Jacob 390
LINN Jane 246; John 88; Mr. 332; Rev. 52; William 236, 246
LINSEY David 1
LIPERT Adam 404; Sarah 404
LITTLE --- 129; Alexander 377; Joseph 356; Peter 253
LIVELBERGER John 388
LIVELSBERGER John 381
LIVENGER Martin 186

LLOYD Richard 188
LOGAN James 141; John 66, 181; Margaret 181; William 345
LOGUE Adam 183; George 1, 32, 44, 48, 106, 143, 148, 162, 206, 214, 220, 221, 245; John 66
LONG Christian 388; Conrad 316, 370; James & Son. 391; James 124, 354, 386, 422; Jared J. 324; John 28, 61, 316, 370; Robert 391; William 324;
LONG, James & Son 400
LONGNECKER Abraham 206
LONGSTAFF Adam 9, 43, 93, 192; Martin 43
LONGWELL & WHITLEY 105
LOOS Abraham 152
LORIMER Robert 388, 393
LOTMAN Mr. 376
LOUCHRY Daniel 66
LOUCK John 408
LOUDEN Archibald 166
LOUDON A. 244; Archibald 13, 39, 75, 46, 206, 234; Christen 234; James 234
LOUGHBRIDGE 159
LOUGHMAN Phillip 43
LOUGHRIDGE Abraham 41, 54, 72, 318; Nancy 54
LOUTHER James 169
LOVE James 305, 388, 400, 410, 415, 423; John 85, 91, 305, 356
LOW Joshua 390
LOWER Elijah 40
LOWNES Joseph 296
LOWRY James 152
LUCAS Robert 249
LUCUS Edmund 77
LUDMAN George 318
LUDRIDGE Edward 77
LUKENBILL Abraham 41, 51
LUSK John 350, 374; Robert 50, 104, 174, 236; William 184
LYDICK Adam 241
LYNCH Patrick 174
LYNN Samuel 381
LYON Alexander 206;   Mr. 5; Samuel 158; William 3, 63, 69, 129, 144, 158, 162, 171
LYTLE John 148

M'ALISTER Archibald 249, 299; Hugh 124, 233; Jesse 249, 299; John 232; Richard 249, 299; William 232
M'ALLISTER Abdiel 249; Archibald 390; Charles 266; Hugh 69; James 415;

INDEX (to the paragraph number)

Jesse 253, 390; Richard 253, 319, 342, 390
M'BETH Alexander 70, 91, 119, 202; Peggy 115
M'BRIDE Alexander 49, 57; Tobitha 49
M'CALL James 40; John 428; Robert 286, 315, 428; William 44
M'CALLAY, James 1
M'CALLEY James 79
M'CALLS John 60
M'CALLY James 113
M'CAN Robert 115
M'CANDLESS James 318, 374, 376; John 318; Mr. 58
M'CANDLISS George 240
M'CANLES James 272, 383, 390
M'CANLESS James 394, 414
M'CANN Arthur 373
M'CAPLES James 390
M'CARDELL James 309
M'CARTHNEY Patrick 47
M'CLACKEN --- 123; Patrick 123
M'CLEAN John 170; Moses 433
M'CLELAND Joseph 180
M'CLELLAN George 437; Thomas 370; William 253, 265, 267, 268, 269, 272, 275, 298, 299, 318, 320, 326, 355, 364, 367, 373, 379, 381, 390, 392
M'CLELLAND William 299, 437
M'CLINTOCK Daniel 172; James 37, 85, 92, 138; Samuel 50
M'CLOSKY Arthur 69
M'CLURE --- 66; Charles 45, 47, 62, 150, 158; James 256, 302; John 390; Robert 47, 59, 60; Samuel 111; Thomas 155, 192; William 47, 56, 60; Wilson 236
M'COMAS Nicholas Day 296, 391
M'CONAUGBY John 391; Robert 391
M'CONAUGHT David 391
M'CONAUGHY John 412; Robert 412
M'CONNEL Henry 131; Rev 209
M'CONNELL William 13
M'COOK George 418
M'CORD William 185, 206
M'CORMICK --- 22; Charles 129; James 51, 53, 126, 145, 152, 162, 231, 363; Robert 355
M'COSKRY Capt. A 74; Dr. 131, 203; Samuel A. 41, 129, 161, 182
M'COUMB Mrs. 95
M'COY Archibald 215; Gilbert 40, 63, 68, 79; John 40, 63, 68, 79, 169,
180; Mary 210; Robert 210; William 148
M'CRACKEN Jane 91; Mr. 435; William 35, 39, 53, 63, 91
M'CREARY David 390; John 390; Thomas 390; William 375
M'CULLAGH Robert 118
M'CULLOH Robert 347
M'CULLOR Robert 347
M'CULLOUGH George 345; John 187
M'CUNE Robert 247; Samuel 248; Thomas 248, 279
M'CURDY David 91; Eleanor 97; John 14, 97, 203, 208
M'DANIEL John 206
M'DANNEL Daniel 245; John 199
M'DANNELL John 115, 140, 205
M'DONALD John 40, 145; Joseph 49; Mary 368; Richard 368; Robert 368
M'DONNAL Cornelius 437
M'DONNALD Joseph 50
M'DOWEL Alexander 43; Samuel 35
M'ELBAY James 318
M'ELHENEY William 188
M'ELWEE David 404
M'EWEN Rossana 88
M'FADDEN Dennis 406; Neil 317
M'FAGGERT James 393
M'FARLAND John 384; Patrick 408; William 129, 139, 144
M'FARLANE Andrew 35; James 149; John 65; Mrs. 75; William 75, 188
M'FARLIN Patrick 123, 354
M'GAGHEY Anthony 234
M'GAURAN Charles 361
M'GAW Col. 66
M'GEE Patrick 390; Robert 318; William 40
M'GINLEY Amos A. 139
M'GINTY Charles 338
M'GLAUGHLIN John 206
M'GOSKRY Samuel 109
M'GRANAHAN John 366
M'GREGOR Alexander 426
M'GREW John 381, 390; William 253
M'HENRY Daniel 410, 424
M'ILHEANY Robert 275
M'ILHINEY Esther 390; Samuel 390
M'ILHINNY Robert 422
M'ILLAN John 280
M'ILVAIN Andrew 248
M'ILVAINE Thomas 318
M'ILVANE Andrew 287
M'INTIRE John 255, 296; Mary 255
M'KANLEY Benjamin 265

INDEX (to the paragraph number)

M'KEAN Thomas 285
M'KEE John 59, 94, 205, 206, 221, 224; Thomas 159
M'KEEHAN Alexander 48, 50, 96; Benjamin 111,   ; David 25; George 109, 148, 206; Jannet 96
M'KENEY David 205
M'KIBBEN Jeremiah 44
McKIBBIN Jeremiah 44
McKIBBON Jeremiah 160; Robert 19
M'KIFFIN William 280
M'KINLEY Henry 92, 120, 133; Stephen 324
M'KINNEY Capt. 179; David 59, 206; John 253; Joseph 32, 145
M'KIOLEY David 390
M'KISSIN William 280
M'KITTRICK Alexander 367
M'KNIGHT David 58, 145; Dr. 127; James 275
M'KOY Archibald 209
M'LAUGHLIN James 169
M'LURE Abdiel 85
M'MANUS Charles 125, 126, 134, 236, 340
M'MEEN John 182; Josias 79; William 79
M'MILAN Jacob 390; James 390
M'MILLAN Jacob 390; James 285, 317, 930
M'MONIGLE William 173
M'MULLAN Hugh 92
M'MULLEN Hugh 85
M'MULLIN Robert 347; William 39, 95, 347
M'MURDIE Robert 268
M'MURPHY Daniel 188
M'MURRAY Elizabeth 307; Joseph 284, 373; Thomas 16, 148; William 16, 148
M'MURTRIE David 7
M'NAIL Daniel 206
M'NAIR Alexander 206, 221, 234
M'NAMARA --- 206
M'NAUGHTON Jesse 163; Patrick 145, 163
M'NEAL Hugh 112
M'NULTY James 282
M'PHERSON William 280, 326, 345, 376
M'QUEAD John 206
M'QUINN Josiah 388, 393
M'SHERRY Barnabas 375; James 283, 340, 415
M'TAGGERT James 388
MACBETH Alexander 44
MACLAY William 285

MACLEY John 350
MACOMB Thomas 64; Thomas I. 90
MAFFET William 169
MAGAURAN Edward 105, 160, 230
MAGAW Colonel 106; Patric 318; Robert 73, 106, 221
MAGEE Alexander 50
MAGINLEY A. 332
MAGUIRE Philip 69
MAHON David 111, 206
MAHONEY Catharine 206
MAIZE William 26
MANIFOLD John 368
MANN Appolonia 402
MANSON David 391
MANTLE George 341
MARCH Catharine 370; Jacob 370, 431
MARSDEN Edward 287
MARSEHALD Lieut. 97
MARSH James 277 420; Jonothan 317
MARSHALL James 248, 266; Joseph 250; Peter 340; Richard 99, 400; Samuel 381; William 379
MARTIN James 143, 206; Paul 60; Robert 318; Samuel 83, 117, 402; Thomas 50, 60, 101, 134, 209, 435; William 231, 278, 371
MARTTER Henry 382
MARYLAND, Baltimore 342; Elk Ridge Landing Ferry 342; Harford Co 341; Williamsport 343
MASON Isaac 86
MATE Appolonla 402; Elizabeth 356, 370; Philip 356, 370
MATEER Polly 234; Samuel 43
MATEET Andrew 182
MATHEWS Mr. 54; W.P. 65; William P. 323
MATTER George 345; Henry 345; Jacob 203, 345
MATTHIAS David 68
MAXWELL David 331; Henry 318; James 52, 345; Jane 52; William 140
MAY Colonel 422; Daniel 279, 338, 410, 423; John 390; Lieutenant Colonel 404; Lieutenant Colonel D. 422
MAYER Solomon 216
McCLELLAN John 388
McCLELLAND Joseph 3
McCORMICK Hugh 22
McCRACKEN 107
MEALS William 390
MEANS James 60
MEAS John 431

INDEX (to the paragraph number)

MEASON Isaac 152
MEEK William 115
MELL Adam 247; Betsey 86; John 247
MELONE Daniel 400
MELTZHEIMER Mr. 343
MENCHGE John 382; Margaret 382; Solomon 382
MENTEITH Alexander 139
MENTEL William 390
MENTIETH Daniel 281
MERLIN John 352
MESSEMER Henry 356; Yoder 356
MESSERLY Abraham 423; Daniel 356; Peter 356, 410
METZLAR Thomas 335
MEYER Jacob 321; Joseph 402; Michael 402; Peter 321, 415
MEYERS David 400; Elias 390; Samuel 390
MICHAEL George 415; Lewis 253, 294, 319, 336; Wendel 63, 84, 99, 104, 111, 115, 129, 137; William 395, 400
MICHAN Thomas 44
MIFFLIN Thomas 280, 386
MILES Samuel 285
MILLER Abraham 398, 416, 423, 428; Catharine 370; David 26, 93; Elizabeth 187; General 253; George 366; Henry 37, 405; Jacob 34, 53, 182, 320; Jeremiah 17, 97, 136, 185, 192; John 43, 145, 151, 185, 193, 203, 244, 275, 305, 318, 368, 415; Joseph 371; Juliana 37; Magdalene 402; Martin 370; Mathew (Matthew) 70, 166, 182, 240, 234; Melchor 136; Meremiah 43; Michael 370, 428; Mr. 423; Nicholas 388; Robert 1, 49, 82, 90, 118, 131, 159, 175, 178, 240; Samuel 407; Tobias 370; William 49, 151, 181, 189, 206, 280, 326
MILLIGAN William 363
MILLS Hannah 16
MILNE Edmund 350
MIMA 315
MINICH Michael 345; Simon 345
MINNICH Simon 51
MINNICK Joseph P. 188; Simon 41
MINSHALL Thomas 273
MIRES John 43
MITCHEL George 206; Joseph 326
MITCHELL David 216; James 63, 206; James S. 388; John 269; Joseph 129, 374, 381; Ross 66, 118, 131, 159; William 139, 368, 388
MIXSELL Jacob 149

MOFFATT John Sidney 192
MOFFIT Hugh 109
MOHR Nicholas 321; Peter 321; Philip 321
MONEWELL John 255
MONEY Patrick 206
MONROE George 206
MONTGOMERY Betsey 16; John 14, 17, 22, 56, 63, 71, 89, 103, 143, 169, 206, 268; Moses 64, 90; Mr. 166; Sally 143; William 59, 186, 206
MONTTORT Laurence 293
MOODY Robert 50
MOOR Henry 85; James 115, 240; John 10
MOORE and KIRKPATRICK 435
MOORE Andrew 145; David 299, 373, 379, 381, 390; Henry 92; James 39, 56, 107; John 27, 107, 129, 206; Joseph 399; Thomas L. 195; William 65, 105, 106, 152, 203, 214, 221, 233
MOREHOUSE Stephen 79
MOREL D. L. 1, 30, 65
MORGAN Jacob 285; John 20
MORGEN Isaac 311
MORLAND James 238
MORREL David L. 206
MORRIS Benjamin 276; Isaac W. 349; John 70, 248, 278, 279, 306, 308, 400, 437; Jonathan 279; Margaret 437
MORRISON Hance 389; Hans 315; Hugh 315; James 206, 315; John 145, 165, 182, 206, 437; Joseph 323, 382; Joshua 415; Margaret 86; Mr. 7; Nathaniel 389; Robert 63, 84, 92; William 347, 381, 390, 414
MORROW Finley 60; George 115
MORTER Henry 395, 400; Ludwick 149
MORTHLAND Michael 319
MORTIMORE Thomas 318
MORTON Edward 140; James 43
MOSES Peter 27
MOSSER Abraham 318; Jacob 281; Samuel 321
MOURER Adam 286
MUHLENBERG Peter 285
MUHLHEIM George 370
MULHOLLAN Roger 140
MUMPER Michael 381, 429
MUNDORFF Peter 356, 360
MURPHEY James 406.
MURPHY James 344, 415; John 294, 296, 388, 390, 392
MURRAY Alexander 369; Andrew 234; James 398; Richard 330; Thomas 92

INDEX (to the paragraph number)

MURRY James 390
MURTARD Archibald 257
MUSGENUNG Peter 388
MYER John 356; Peter 406; Salomon 404; Solomon 330, 399
MYERS David 1

N... Peter 393
NACE George 381
NAILER George 248
NAVE Henry 77
NEAFF Henry 252
NEAL John 206
NEASS Jacob 416
NEELY Jackson 389; James 1, 115; Jonathan 309; Thomas 389
NEILSON Andrew 332
NELSON Andrew 80, 93 ; Catherine 153; George 312; Robert 349; Samuel 286, 347, 359, 415, 416; William 153, 325, 326, 336, 345
NES William 313, 314
NESBIT Dr. 159; John 347; Rev Dr. 16, 220, 235
NEVIN Daniel 61
NEWALL Robert 60
NEWMAN Andrew 393, 416
NICHOLS John 345
NICHOLSON James 7, 188, 206; John 149, 243, 428; Samuel 105
NIDICH John 415
NILSON John 320
NISBET Charles 234
NOACKER Frederick 63
NOAL Andrew 345
NOBLE James 128; John 48, 50, 178, 205
NOBLET Ann 355
NOEL Jacob 384; Nicholas 286
NOGGLE John 253
NOLAND William 16
NORRIS Benjamin 324; John 386; William 390
NORTH Catharine 247; John 197, 247; Joshua 247; Katherine 197; William 197, 206, 247
NORWOOD Edward 342; Samuel 342
NUGENT Peter 133, 159

O'BRIAN John 69
O'BRIEN --- 153
O'DONNELL Edward 51; Margery 51
O'HAIL Edward 386
O'HALE Edward 427
OBERDIER John 415

OBERDORFF George 370
OFFICER John 17, 22, 185, 230; Mrs. 22
OFFLEY Lieut 211
OGDEN Jane 232; Mary 232
OHAIL Edward 347, 386
OLDHAM Edward 382
OLIVER James 145; John 145, 162, 229, 245
OLP John 416
OPO Thomas 367
OPP Jacob 255, 291, 345; John 390; Mr. 360
ORBISON James 389; Thomas 248
ORME John 330
ORR Robert 403; William 403
ORTH Henry 206
OSBURN Obediah 390; Samuel 362
OTTO Mr. 360
OURICH Philip 31
OVER D. 133
OVERDEER John 390
OVERHOLSER John 278
OWEN David 367; Thomas 253
OWINGS Thomas 417
OYER Wendel 347
OYSTER Daniel 343; Esther 343; George 390; John 372, 400

PACKER Jonathan 277
PAINE Thomas 196
PARK William 138
PARKER Andrew 65, 121; David 413; James 196; Rebecca 62; Rebeckah 196; Richard 173; William 40, 238
PARKS --- 44; John 85, 92
PATTAW Peter 143
PATTEN Mrs. 105; Robert 36
PATTERSON & THOMPSON 308
PATTERSON Andrew 170; George 91; Henry 224; James 129, 305, 405; Jered 209; Nathan 299; Robert 91, 234; Samuel 325; William 272
PATTISON Charles 234; George 79, 130, 133, 162, 239
PATTON James 206; John 50, 181; Joseph 206; Robert 81; William 50
PAULEY John 138
PAULUS Adam 370
PAUP Thomas 345
PAVARD Robert 279
PAXTON Agnes 188, 221; Samuel 188, 221
PEADEN James 320; William 185
PEALE C. W. 337; Jacob 226

INDEX (to the paragraph number)

PEDAN Benjamin 280; William 180
PEEBLES Alexander 59; John 7, 13, 47, 53, 63; Robert 20, 47, 73, 118
PEGG Joseph 415
PENCE Caleb 437
PENDERGRASS Philip 97
PENFINGER Henry 305
PENROSE John 393
PENTZ John 427
PERKINS Daniel 396
PERRY Samuel 176
PERSELL Jonathan 188
PETER 411
PETERS Thomas 428
PETERSON Elizabeth 75, 221; Henry 75
PETICOLES Mr. 23
PFOUTZ John 26
PHILIPS John 432
PICKERIAN Henry 365
PIERCE Joseph 145, 206
PILKERTON Vincent 381
PINKERTON William 25
PIPER John 285
PLAIN Timothy 371
PLAYFAIR Peter 413
PLEASANT Dr. 324
PLUM Adam 402
POCHON Charles J. J. 349; Dr. 350
POE James 207
POISTLE Andrew 185; Stophel 185
POLLOCK James 10, 231; Jereat 206; John 179; Margaret 153; Mr. 11; Oliver 9, 44, 153, 162, 178, 186, 221, 252, 405; Polly 178
POOL Brice 371
POPE John 192
POPENMIRE Gabriel 5
PORTER Charles W. 403; Charles William 320, 390, 408; David 59; John 249; Robert 142, 232; Samuel 59, 248; William 388, 415
POSTLETHWAIT James 165; Joseph 27; Mr. 50; Samuel 92
POSTLETHWAITE Samuel 144, 182, 285
POTSER Christian 275
POTTAW Peter 65
POTTER James 207
POTTS John 343; Lieut 222
POWER Alexander 182, 198; James 182; William 26, 182
PRATT George 61
PRESBURY G. G. 342
PRICE Isaac 373; Joseph 287
PRISCILLA 379
PROCTOR Thomas 305

PROUDFIT Robert 139
PUFFENBERER Widow 384
PUGH Daniel 410, 424
PURDY Thomas 47
PURVIANCE Samuel 345
PUTNAM Edwin 64, 90
PUTTORSS Martin 384

QUICKEL John 266, 386
QUICKELL JOhn 321
QUIGLEY & BROWN 200
QUIGLEY John 51; Samuel 118, 229
QUILL 339

RAFFENBERGER Martin 415
RAFFINSBERGER Martin 349
RAFFLE Yost 416
RAINEY William 139
RALSTON David 9, 59, 61, 79; Robert 296
RAMSAY James 235. ; John 415; Margaret 415; Robert 408, 415; Samuel 237
RAMSEY Archibald 108; James 56, 207, 208, 370; John 206; William 221
RANDOLPH Paul 47
RANJONS John 320
RANKIN Elizabeth 355; John 355
RANNALS Samuel 219
RASTER James 149
RASTON David 112
RAUHOUSER Daniel 423
RAUM Jacob 182
RAUSH Martin 65
RE... David 378
READ James 337, 339
READER Joseph 61
REAM Henry 57
REAMAN Henry 405
REANY John 389

REDICK David 418
REEB Stephen 390
REED Benjamin 381; John 207; Samuel 253; Samuel Minor 374; William 40, 44, 48, 143, 303, 422
REEHM Henry 189, 223
REGAN Daniel 346
REIB Stephen 341
REID Frances 17, 162; George 139
REIFF Margaret 335
REILEY Messr. 55
REILY John 104, 267, 271
REINHART Frederick 145

INDEX (to the paragraph number)

REISER William 375
REISINGER John 319
RELING Justus 38
RENEY John 346
RESLEY George 435
REX Jacob 275, 348, 355
REYNOLDS John 234; Samuel 207, 226
RHEA Robert 390
RHEIMAN Henry 386
RHINE John 70, 156, 192; Stephen 9
RHOADES Gaspar 145
RICH Stephen 370
RICHARD 165
RICHARDS Samuel 254
RICHART John 345
RICHTER John 60, 388
RICHWINE Jean 286; Stophel 104
RIDDLE Elizabeth 133; James 133, 248, 389; John 131; Judge 30, 67; Mrs. 131; Polly 196; S. 336; Samuel 318, 336, 345, 437; William 186
RIDER Daniel 402
RIDGE Thomas 206
RIDGELY Greenberry 312; Henry M. 90
RIDGLEY Henry 64
RIEGEL John 321
RIEHMAN Henry 356
RIEMAN Henry 321
RIFFLE Yost 423
RINEHART John 105
RINGER George 356
RIPPETH John 204
RIPPEY John 127, 321
RISTEAR John T. 344
RITCHIE John 270
RITTENHOUSE David 26
RITZ Anthony 423
ROBB David 206; James 222, 406
ROBERTS Brintnell 253; J. 133; Samuel 302; William 256
ROBERTSON John 91
ROBINER Henry 254; Judith 254
ROBINETTE George 390
ROBINS William 107
ROBINSON Agness 115; James 222, 336; John 205, 367; Pamela 335; Richard 5; Samuel 178; William 115, Zacharia 386
RODDY Charles 91
RODGERS Howard 256; Richard 82
ROEMER Frederick 254; Magdalena 254
ROGERS N. 342; Rev Dr. 113, 163; William 39
ROHRER Daniel 389

ROMICH Jacob 248; Rosina 248
RONEY James 180
ROSBERRY 176
ROSBROCK John 70
ROSEBERRY Elioner 359
ROSEBOROUGH Robert 286, 415, 416
ROSS Alexander 347; David 175; Elizabeth 162; James 182,   ; John 390; Michael 18, 276; William 39, 311, 318, 367, 386, 390, 409, 427, 432
ROTHROCK --- 306, 352; John 253, 308, 391
ROUSE John 281, 356; Luke 281, 356
ROWAN David 65, 151; James 379; William 349
ROWNEY James 206
RUDISELL Jacob 249, 253, 299, 361, 366; James 390; John 320
RUDY Barnabas 26; Martin 388
RUFF Frederick 390
RUMMEL Frederick 393; John 424
RUNDLE Frederick 325
RUPP Baltzer 345; Christian 345; Godlieb 345
RUSSEL Alexander 391; Samuel 404; Thomas 178
RUSSELL Alexander 248, 249, 280, 361; James 388; John 104; Joshua 374; Samuel 282; Thomas 207
RUTTER Andrew 345, 381, 431
RYALL Mr. 39

SALA Jacob 398
SALENKA Mr. 312
SALL 35
SAM 411
SAMPLE Cunningham 291, 329, 338; David 155; James 155; John 290, 315; Robert 305
SAMUEL 115
SANDERS Elizabeth 6, 31; Frederick 6; Godfrey 31, 169
SANDERSON Jean 220; John 236, 238; William 53, 85, 127
SANDS Andrew 299
SANKY Ezekiel 278
SANSOM Joseph 296
SAPRE Jacob 428
SARBACH Catharine 382
SASSERMAN Henry 85
SAUL 370
SAUNDERS Elizabeth 220; Godfrey 220
SAUTER Christian 334
SAYERS James 370

176

INDEX (to the paragraph number)

SCANETHECKER George 389
SCHALL John 283
SCHENBERGER Peter 368
SCHERER Samuel 254
SCHMYSER Henry 381; Matias 249; Michael 249, 331, 370, 381; Peter 339
SCHNEIDER George 186
SCHNELBECHER Catharine 382; George 368
SCHNELBLCHER George 262
SCHRACK Philip 352, 367
SCHREACH Henry 306
SCHREIBER Michael 338
SCHROLE George 259
SCHULTZ Joseph 286
SCHWARTZ Conrad 365
SCITZ John 416
SCOBEY James 14, 50, 77, 169
SCOBY James 50, 203
SCOTT Alexander 73, 310; Allen 371; Cunningham 178; Gawin 350; James 13, 176, 361, 381, 390, 394, 405; John 13, 291, 327, 338, 435; Mathew 111, 121; Robert 428; William 255, 275, 298, 345, 355, 415, 428

SCROGGS Alexander 51
SEABRIGHT William 40
SEARFASS Daniel 44
SEARIGHT Gilbert 206
SEARLE D. 183
SEARS John 124
SEELY Christopher 169; Jonas 79; Sylvanus 79
SEESENUP Adam 344
SEIFERT Michael 390, 402
SEISENOB Adam 393
SEITZ Michael 402
SELBY Brice 383; Thomas 383
SELFEMOB Adam 400
SELL John 384
SELTZ Benjamin 370
SEMPLE Catharine 208; David 85; Robert 132; Steel 208
SENST Andrew 382; Peter 382; Philip 382
SENTZ Nicholas 278
SHADE Christian 159, 206
SHAEFFER Henry 24, 278
SHAFER Jacob 321
SHAFFER Catharine 321; Jacob 398; Philip 321, 416
SHAFFNER Martin 44
SHAKLEY John 359
SHALL John 423

SHANNON John 145; Joseph 165, 356, 437; Leonard 206; Thomas 437
SHARP John 59, 188; Lieutenant 187
SHAW Alexander 203; John 134; Peter 50; Samuel 368
SHEAFFER Henry 265; Jacob 265
SHEARMAN 169, 192
SHEETS David 424
SHEFFER Jacob 283
SHEKLEY Jennet 374; William 374
SHELDON James 275
SHELLY Abraham 350; Michael 395
SHELTER George 368; Jacob 396
SHENBERGER Adam 428
SHEPLER Henry 167, 213
SHERB Jacob 386
SHERERTZ Conrad 370; Ludwich 370
SHERMAN Conrad 304; Miss 335
SHERMON Jacob 256
SHERRITZ Ludwich 390
SHETLER Frederick 368
SHETTER Martin 356
SHILER Jacob 308
SHIMP John 233
SHINDLER Lewis 393, 400
SHINGLE Ludwig 345
SHIPPEN Captain 147; Elizabeth 184; John 30, 67, 127, 133, 166; Joseph 184
SHISLER Paul 437
SHITZ Francis 125, 340, 350; Peter 340
SHOEMAKER Capt. 197; Charles 377, 382, 396, 423; Edward 113, 176; Jacob 337; John 302; Lieutenant 93
SHORB John 283
SHORT James 100, 248, 250, 315, 318, 335, 337; Jane 391
SHOUP Henry 65
SHOWALTER J. 133; Joseph 147
SHREIBER Conrad 321; Jacob 338
SHRIVER Andrew 323; Ludwich 390
SHROM Joseph 49, 140, 175, 206
SHRY George 415
SHRYOCK John 437
SHUEMAKER E. 74
SHULER George 46; Jacob 90
SHULTZ Henry 319, 341; John 310; Mr. 114; Nicholas 157
SHULTZBACH John 302; Philip 302
SHUMAN John 26
SHUP Martin 248
SHUPE Conrad 390
SICKQUOINNEYOUHEE 53
SIDLE George 391

INDEX (to the paragraph number)

SIDLIE Godfrey 47
SIMCOX Abraham 268
SIMISON Elizabeth 175; John 56, 61, 175; Samuel 56, 203
SIMMONDS Jack 377; Jonathan 377
SIMPSON David 389; James 323, 382; John 127, 389; Robert 389
SINGER John 391, 396; Nicholas 253
SINN Christian 318, 392
SIPE Peter 103
SIPES Peter 129
SITES Adam 365
SITLER Abraham 328; Jacob 70, 248, 274, 288, 318, 332, 388, 408
SKEKELY Peter 414
SKINNER John 31
SKIPTON John 6
SLAGLE Henry 366, 376, 422; Michael 390
SLAYBAUGH Peter 348, 355; William 348, 355
SLENTA Philip 390
SLENTZ Jacob 356; John 356
SLINKER Martin 328
SLOAN James W. 135; Samuel 433
SLOUGH Matthias 29, 55, 124, 272, 365
SLOVER Betsey 81; Isaac 81
SMALL George 396, 400, 415, 416; Peter 390
SMILEY --- 68; John 129, 138, 169; Thomas 74, 129, 134, 135, 138, 159, 169, 206, 322
SMITH Aaron 135; Abraham 233, 246, 285; Adam 70, 308, 345, 368, 389; Balser 82; Barnet 428; Benjamin 107, 115; Betsey 165; Casper 368; Charles 44; Elizabeth 75, 235; Gabriel 347; Hannah 165; Hopewell 390; Hugh 89, 93, 127; Hugh C. 435; Jacob 233; James 59, 135, 165, 233, 338, 386, 389, 411, 424; James and Co. 135; John 65, 94, 135, 158, 165, 181, 234, 235, 390; Joseph 305, 341; Josiah 244; Michael 423; Nathan 396; Patrick 349; Peter 75; Philip 114; Robert 30, 393, 400; Samuel 368, 388; Walter 338, 434; William 291, 345, 390
SMUCK Solomon 305
SMYSER Michael 145
SMYSOR Michael 415
SNAVELY Jacob 227
SNIDER David 206
SNIVELY Henry 234; Jacob 70
SNODY John 205
SNOWDEN & M'CORKLE 437

SNOWDEN John 386; Nathaniel 91; Rev 16, 178
SNYDER --- 115; Catherine 50; Conrad 367; David 152; John 50, 414; Philip 108
SOMERVILLE David 206, 234; John 234
SORRIL James 188
SOWER Jacob 298
SPANGLER Andrew 370; B. 360; Baltzer 248, 271, 320, 360; Daniel 383, 390, 394, 414, 416, 424; George 331, 376; Jacob 298, 317, 332, 373, 390; Jesse 328; John 298, 332, 344; Margaret 298, 332; Michael 280, 326; Rudolph 390; Samuel 320, 360
SPARKS --- 68
SPEAKLY Jacob 253
SPEAR James 352
SPECK Frederick 182
SPEERY James 273
SPENCE Catharine 249; Jane 370; John 50
SPENCER --- 319; John 209; Michael 319; William 249
SPENDER John 50
SPIES John Philip 292
SPOART Thomas 231
SPONSELLER Abraham 370, 378, 382
SPONSLER Nicholas 162
SPOTSWOOD Catharine 187
SPOTWOOD John 218
SPREAT James 321
SPRECHER George 58
SPRINGER George 390
SPROUL John 432
ST. CLAIR Gen. 170
STACKHOUSE Joseph 188
STAEBLER George 334
STAIN John 393
STAINER Thomas 389
STAKE Jacob 326, 333
STARR James 149; Thomas 28; William 28
STARRITT Robert 157
STAUFFER Margaret 345, 356, 382; Peter 345, 356, 382
STAYMAN John 61
STEEL Archibald 59, 248, 284, 298, 312; Cast 88; David 22; Ephraim 14, 65, 158, 211; James 410; John 50, 61, 80, 83, 92, 120, 234, 240; Joseph 36
STEELE John 77, 94, 97, 141; Joseph 88
STEGOR Cornelius 350
STEIN George 390

178

INDEX (to the paragraph number)

STEINMEYER Sebastian 404
STEPHENS John 9, 41, 92, 192
STEPHENSON George 253; William 253
STERITT James 343
STERREM John 192
STERRET William 93
STERRETT James 152;
    Ralph 7; William 80
STETLER John 437
STEVENS Peter 149
STEVENSON Dr. 26; George 12, 39, 320
STEWART James 112, 278, 352; John 280, 326, 382, 390, 422; William 267, 382
STICHLER Ludwick 86
STICKLER Ludwick 127
STILER Daniel 429
STIMMECKIE Charles 234
STINMETZ John 13
STINNECK Dr. 107
STINNECKE Charles F. 128; Dr. 50
STINNECKIE Dr. 34, 363
STINNECKLE Dr. 23
STITH Adam 359
STOBER William 70, 308
STOCKTON Thomas 139
STOEHR Catharine 429; Christopher 308; Stophel 429
STOFFT Jacob 365
STOKELY Thomas 285
STOLL Frederick 280
STONE John 345
STONER Abraham 415; Christian 381, 415; Isaac 370; Jacob 370; John 390
STONES Andrew 127
STORM Peter 375, 381
STORY John 117
STOSST Jacob 365
STOUFFER John 127, 372
STRAUSS Ephraim 185
STRAWSPAUGH --- 345
STREIN George 370; Johan Adam 402; Susanna 402
STRICKLER Henry 415
STROMAN John 330, 353, 376
STRUM George 207, 208
STRUMBAUCH Philip 141
STUART John 83, 154, 179
STUBBS Thomas 393
STUMP Frederick 302, 326
STUNTZ Peter 70
STURGEON William 248, 382
STURM George 44, 104, 115, 127, 137, 184
SULLIVAN Patrick 318

SULLY Mr. and co. 129
SULTZBACH Magdalene 321
SUMMER John 356
SUMMERFIELD John 249
SUTOR John 286
SWAGER Henry 11
SWARTZ John 400
SWEENY John 370
SWEEZY John 69
SWENEY John 256, 302, 348, 390
SWOPE Kitty 199; Mrs. 205

TAGGART John 437
TALBOTT Vincent 370
TATE Isaac 428; Jacob 390, 394, 428; Robert 359; Solomon 390, 394, 428
TAYLOR Benjamin 416; Elisha 376; John 61, 92, 219, 338, 416; Joseph 318, 390; Philip 403; Robert 92, 323, Sally 340; Sarah 350; Thomas 321, 338, 391; William 248, 250
TEMPLETON John 191
TERREY James 113
TERRY James 74, 176
TEST George 270, 321
THATCH Bob 44
THOMAS George 155, 192; John 361; Nathan 409; Samuel 54, 355
THOMPSON & PATTERSON 326
THOMPSON Alexander 230, 245; Andrew 205, 381, 388, 390; Charles 269; David 187; Edward 63; Elizabeth 215; Esther 382; Gitty 202; James 17; Jean 45; Jemima 402; John 11, 382; Joseph 384; Levi 367; Rev. 45, 202; Samuel 206; Susanna(h) 75, 221, 367; Thomas 418; William 20, 50, 68, 215, 299, 320
THOMSON Andrew 59; James 64, 90; John P. 208; Mrs. 112; Susannah 11; William 11, 76, 110, 435
THORLEY Abraham 415; Jemama 321; Jemima 402; Jeremiah 390; William 321, 390, 402
THORNBURG Thomas 422
THORNBURGH Joseph 63; Thomas 12
TIDWILER Christian 61
TIGART Samuel 281
TIPPLE Eve 294; Nicholas 294
TODD James 356; Joseph 253, 356
TOLLET Peter 269
TOOL John 77
TOULERTON John 348, 355, 389
TOULORTON John 275
TOWERS George 82

179

INDEX (to the paragraph number)

TRIMBLE Thomas 93
TRIMMER Andrew 254, 370, 382; David 254, 370, 382
TROUT Michael 437
TUCKER Tempest 256, 321, 356

TURNBULL William 150
TURNER Alexander 280, 294, 321, 326, 374, 376, 390, 408; Daniel 11, 303; Maj 253; William 2
TWAMLY Josiah 113
TYSON Henry 321, 326, 381, 400, 408

UHLER Teedrick 182; Teeterch 129, 206
UNDERHILL Thomas 396
UNDERWOOD Abraham 325, 326; Alexander 345, 376; Elihu 277; Jesse 280, 381; John 106, 146, 238
UNGER George 416
UPDEGRAFF Jacob 280, 306, 326, 332, 370; Joseph 252; Josiah 427
UPDEGRASS Jacob 390
UPP George 429; Jacob 308, 383
URIE Thomas 121, 164, 165
USHEA John 123
UTTER Samuel 208

VALE Joshua 402; Robert 402; William 402
VAN WYCK William 359
VANCE William 251
VANDIKE Peter 384
VANSKER Martin 84
VARNOR Conrad 247
VERNON Aaron 407
VINEGAR David 432
VOGELSONG Christopher 427

WADE Thomas 68, 79
WAGGONER Jacob 41, 133, 247; John 388
WAGNER Anthony 424; George 262; Ludwich 390
WAGONER Frederick 390; Jacob 299; Mary Elizabeth 390
WALKER Benjamin 415, 428; David 183; James 382; John 53, 107, 145, 182, 192, 202; Joseph 221; Mr. 9, 51; Rachel 206, 221; William 96, 296
WALLACE Alexander 383; Benjamin 185; James 82, 99, 113; Jane 23; John 112; Jonathan 82, 105, 119, Joseph 106; Lieut. B. 185; Mr. 110; Robert 206; widow 149; William 9, 27, 48, 79, 93, 113, 181, 192, 207,
WALTENBERGER Jacob 164

WALTERS Chrisopher 187
WALTMAN Ludwick 391
WALTON Benjamin 188; James 376
WAMPLER John 326, 395, 400; Lewis 390; Ludwick 264
WARFIELD Charles A. 355; Charles Alexander 355
WARRAN Frederick 350
WARRICK Andrew 381
WARTIN Margaret 248
WATSON William 257
WATT David 206
WATTS David 37, 47, 85, 106, 157; Frederick 169
WAUGH John 139; Rev 86, 146, 166, 192, 234; Samuel 95, 235; William 410
WAYMAN Henry 355
WAYNE Anthony 292; Isaac 139
WEAKLEY Edward 206; James 22, 53; Jean 22; Margaret 220; Nat 220; Nathaniel 65, 66, 68, 129, 210; Rebecca 46
WEAKLY Samuel 145
WEAR John 389
WEATHERALL William 358
WEAVER Anthony 286; John 240; Ulrich 395
WEBB Ezekiel 338; William 414
WEED George 267, 271; Mr. 55
WEEMS Thomas 309
WEICKERT Eve 370; John 370
WEIGLE Francis 394
WEIN George --- 390
WEIR Alexander 31
WEISE George 149, 163, 228
WEISER Martin 390
WEISS George 192; Jacob 171; Mrs. 171
WELCH Daniel 111; John 394; William 327, 342, 345, 370, 374, 415
WELSH George 283; Henry 260, 278; Jacob 250; Major H. 363; William 181, 182, 249, 270, 321, 339, 416
WELSHAN Joseph 278
WELSHANS Joseph 260, 308
WELSHHANS Joseph 415
WENTZ Catharine 356; Henry 356; Michael 356; Philip 356; Valentine 390
WENZEL George 206
WERKING Philip 370; Philip Werts 390
WERTZ Jacob 390
WEST Edward 145, 206; William 176
WESTHAESSER Jacob 414

INDEX (to the paragraph number)

WEYER John 405, 423
WHEELER Ignatius 383; Joseph 341, 383
WHELEN Israel 285
WHITE George 300; Hannah 300, 431; Hugh 337; Isabella 113; James 61; William 431
WHITEHILL John 285
WHITMORE Jacob 233
WHITTAKER Samuel 10, 40
WICHESON Jesse 400
WIDDER Leonard 388
WIER Ludwig 320
WIERMAN John 257
WIGGINS William 287
WILAND Christian 92; Christopher 79; Michael 79
WILCOCKS Alexander 79; John 79
WILEY Elizabeth 115; John 149; Thomas 182
WILHELM John 167; Michael 423
WILKINSON Shadrack 287
WILL 54
WILL Peter 415
WILLIAMS Charles 105; Humphrey 149; Isaac 97; Johannes 298; John 286, 299; Peter 287
WILLIAMSON Charles 249; David 242; James C. 152; Peter 390; Samuel 43; Thomas 39, 93
WILLIS & BEALL 335
WILLIS John 386; William 386
WILLS David 59, 205; John 94; Samuel 286
WILLSON William 10, 26
WILSON Christopher 408; David 282; George 113; Henry 139; Hugh 367; James 65, 85, 144, 234, 246, 384; John 59, 389; Joseph 40; Levi 234; Margaret 246; Marmaduke 323, 382; Mathew 9; Nathaniel 63, 72, 202; Rev 160; Robert 248, 257, 275, 291, 302, 341, 345; Thomas 92; William 40, 234, 285, 345, 350
WINAND John 415
WINANT John 206
WINANTS John 206
WINAUTS James 363
WINCHESTER Stephen 256
WINGART --- 192
WINROTH Jacob 381
WINTER John 21, 264
WINTERMEYER Anthony 402; Valentine 402
WINTERODE Jacob 323
WINTRODS Adam 390; Jacob 390

WIREMAN William 386, 393
WISE George 61, 129, 220
WISER Jacob 9, 44, 47, 53, 93
WITHMOR Peter 437
WITMER Balser 62; Jacob 75; Mr. 55
WOGAN George 249, 270, 321
WOLF Daniel 86; Henry 310; John 394
WOLFE Peter 256
WOLFF Adam 256; Anna Mary 370; Henry 256, 370
WOLFORD George 386
WOLLOT Elizabeth 382
WONDERLICH Daniel 98; John 140
WOOD Joseph 171; Richard 137
WOODBURN J. 133
WOODS Jeannet 13; John 82, 206, 285; Nathan 22; Richard 26; Samuel 190; William 153, 190
WOODSECKER Jacob 356
WOODWARD Ellis 175
WOOMELSDORFF Ann Eve 3; Daniel 3
WORK Robert 370
WORLEY George 253, 346; James 248, 396; Joseph 391; Nathan 416
WORMLEY Englehart 206
WORMLY John 206
WORSHAM Joshua 252
WRAY John 60, 106, 113, 116, 167, 207, William 104
WREN John 361
WRIGHT James 303, 389; John 139; Robert 93, 124, 144, 179; William 207
WUIGLEY Henry 95
WUNDERLICH Daniel 8
WYLAND Christian 68
WYNKOOP Henry 285

YARMUTH Valentine 70
YEALY John 206
YEATS George 138; Thomas 138
YINGER Anthony 345; George 345
YODDER Martin 402; Susanna 402
YONER Jonas 269, 298
YOST Nicholas 370
YOU-E Frederick 318
YOUCE Frederick 416
YOUNG Baltzer 321, 371; Frederick 396; Henry 319; Joseph 129, 159, 185, 203; Matthew 143; Samuel 334
YUN? William 232

ZEIGLE Gotlieb 384, 416
ZEIGLER Adam 408; Barnet 276, 324; George P. 326, 345, 390; George Philip 390; Henry 390; Killian 382

INDEX (to the paragraph number)

ZELLER John 388
ZIEGEL Godlieb 318
ZIEGLER George Philip 390; John 390;
  Killian 254; Kistan 381; Marks 34;
  Mary 254
ZIGLER Mary 429
ZINN Jacob 415
ZUGH David 414

Other books by F. Edward Wright:

Abstracts of Bucks County, Pennsylvania Wills, 1685-1785

Abstracts of Cumberland County, Pennsylvania Wills, 1750-1785

Abstracts of Cumberland County, Pennsylvania Wills, 1785-1825

Abstracts of Philadelphia County Wills, 1726-1747

Abstracts of Philadelphia County Wills, 1748-1763

Abstracts of Philadelphia County Wills, 1763-1784

Abstracts of Philadelphia County Wills, 1777-1790

Abstracts of Philadelphia County Wills, 1790-1802

Abstracts of Philadelphia County Wills, 1802-1809

Abstracts of Philadelphia County Wills, 1810-1815

Abstracts of Philadelphia County Wills, 1815-1819

Abstracts of Philadelphia County Wills, 1820-1825

Abstracts of Philadelphia County, Pennsylvania Wills, 1682-1726

Abstracts of South Central Pennsylvania Newspapers, Volume 1, 1785-1790

Abstracts of South Central Pennsylvania Newspapers, Volume 3, 1796-1800

Abstracts of the Newspapers of Georgetown and the Federal City, 1789-99

Abstracts of York County, Pennsylvania Wills, 1749-1819

Bucks County, Pennsylvania Church Records of the 17th and 18th Centuries Volume 2: Quaker Records: Falls and Middletown Monthly Meetings
Anna Miller Watring and F. Edward Wright

Caroline County, Maryland Marriages, Births and Deaths, 1850-1880

Citizens of the Eastern Shore of Maryland, 1659-1750

Cumberland County, Pennsylvania Church Records of the 18th Century

Delaware Newspaper Abstracts, Volume 1: 1786-1795

Early Charles County, Maryland Settlers, 1658-1745
Marlene Strawser Bates and F. Edward Wright

Early Church Records of Alexandria City and Fairfax County, Virginia
F. Edward Wright and Wesley E. Pippenger

Early Church Records of New Castle County, Delaware, Volume 1, 1701-1800

Frederick County Militia in the War of 1812
Sallie A. Mallick and F. Edward Wright

Inhabitants of Baltimore County, 1692-1763

Land Records of Sussex County, Delaware, 1769-1782

Land Records of Sussex County, Delaware, 1782-1789
Elaine Hastings Mason and F. Edward Wright

Marriage Licenses of Washington, District of Columbia, 1811-1830

Marriages and Deaths from the Newspapers of Allegany and Washington Counties, Maryland, 1820-1830

Marriages and Deaths from The York Recorder, 1821-1830

Marriages and Deaths in the Newspapers of Frederick and Montgomery Counties, Maryland, 1820-1830

Marriages and Deaths in the Newspapers of Lancaster County, Pennsylvania, 1821-1830
Marriages and Deaths in the Newspapers of Lancaster County, Pennsylvania, 1831-1840
Marriages and Deaths of Cumberland County, [Pennsylvania], 1821-1830
Maryland Calendar of Wills Volume 9: 1744-1749
Maryland Calendar of Wills Volume 10: 1748-1753
Maryland Calendar of Wills Volume 11: 1753-1760
Maryland Calendar of Wills Volume 12: 1759-1764
Maryland Calendar of Wills Volume 13: 1764-1767
Maryland Calendar of Wills Volume 14: 1767-1772
Maryland Calendar of Wills Volume 15: 1772-1774
Maryland Calendar of Wills Volume 16: 1774-1777
Maryland Eastern Shore Newspaper Abstracts, Volume 1: 1790-1805
Maryland Eastern Shore Newspaper Abstracts, Volume 2: 1806-1812
Maryland Eastern Shore Newspaper Abstracts, Volume 3: 1813-1818
Maryland Eastern Shore Newspaper Abstracts, Volume 4: 1819-1824
Maryland Eastern Shore Newspaper Abstracts, Volume 5: Northern Counties, 1825-1829
F. Edward Wright and Irma Harper
Maryland Eastern Shore Newspaper Abstracts, Volume 6: Southern Counties, 1825-1829
Maryland Eastern Shore Newspaper Abstracts, Volume 7: Northern Counties, 1830-1834
Irma Harper and F. Edward Wright
Maryland Eastern Shore Newspaper Abstracts, Volume 8: Southern Counties, 1830-1834
Maryland Militia in the Revolutionary War
S. Eugene Clements and F. Edward Wright
Newspaper Abstracts of Allegany and Washington Counties, 1811-1815
Newspaper Abstracts of Cecil and Harford Counties, [Maryland], 1822-1830
Newspaper Abstracts of Frederick County, [Maryland], 1816-1819
Newspaper Abstracts of Frederick County, 1811-1815
Sketches of Maryland Eastern Shoremen
Tax List of Chester County, Pennsylvania 1768
Tax List of York County, Pennsylvania 1779
Washington County Church Records of the 18th Century, 1768-1800
Western Maryland Newspaper Abstracts, Volume 1: 1786-1798
Western Maryland Newspaper Abstracts, Volume 2: 1799-1805
Western Maryland Newspaper Abstracts, Volume 3: 1806-1810
Wills of Chester County, Pennsylvania, 1766-1778

www.ingramcontent.com/pod-product-compliance
Lightning Source LLC
Chambersburg PA
CBHW060528100426
42743CB00009B/1457